W9-BXP-843

The
Copyeditor's
Handbook

The Copyeditor's Handbook

A Guide for Book Publishing
and Corporate Communications

❖ ❖ ❖

With Exercises and Answer Keys

Third Edition

AMY EINSOHN

UNIVERSITY OF CALIFORNIA PRESS
Berkeley   Los Angeles   London

University of California Press, one of the most distinguished
university presses in the United States, enriches lives around the
world by advancing scholarship in the humanities, social sciences,
and natural sciences. Its activities are supported by the UC Press
Foundation and by philanthropic contributions from individuals
and institutions. For more information, visit www.ucpress.edu.

University of California Press
Berkeley and Los Angeles, California

University of California Press, Ltd.
London, England

Copyright © 2000, 2006, 2011
by The Regents of the University of California
ISBN 978-0-520-27156-2 (pbk. : alk. paper)

The Library of Congress has cataloged an earlier edition as follows:

Library of Congress Cataloging-in-Publication Data

Einsohn, Amy.
    The copyeditor's handbook : a guide for
book publishing and corporate communications,
with exercises and answer keys / Amy Einsohn. — 2nd ed.
        p.   cm.
    Includes bibliographical references and index.
    1. Copy-reading — Handbooks, manuals, etc.
    2. Journalism, Commercial — Editing — Hand-
books, manuals, etc.   3. Editing — Handbooks,
manuals, etc.   I. Title.

PN4784.C75E37   2006
808'.027–dc22   2005048579

Manufactured in the United States of America

19   18   17   16   15   14   13
10   9   8   7   6   5   4   3

In keeping with a commitment to support environmentally
responsible and sustainable printing practices, UC Press has printed
this book on Rolland Enviro100, a 100% post-consumer fiber
paper that is FSC certified, deinked, processed chlorine-free, and
manufactured with renewable biogas energy. It is acid-free and
EcoLogo certified.

Contents

Preface

This handbook is addressed to new and aspiring copyeditors who will be working on nonfiction books, journal articles, newsletters, and corporate publications. Many of the topics will also be of interest to copyeditors working for newspapers and magazines, although I do not discuss the editorial conventions peculiar to journalism.

One of the first things a new copyeditor learns is that there are two general-purpose style manuals (*The Chicago Manual of Style* and *Words into Type*), two widely used scientific style manuals (*Publication Manual of the American Psychological Association* and *Scientific Style and Format: The CSE Manual*), and a variety of specialized style manuals. (All the manuals are discussed in chapter 3.) This guide is intended as a supplement to, not a substitute for, an editorial style manual.

Given that each of those manuals runs hundreds of pages, you might wonder why a copyeditor would need this handbook in addition. One reason is that although all the manuals are filled with rules, preferences, exceptions, and examples, they assume that their readers already understand what copyeditors do, why the rules matter, and how and when to apply, bend, or break the rules. Second, because the manuals are addressed to both copyeditors and authors, they do not discuss the procedures peculiar to copyediting, nor the kinds of minute-by-minute decisions that copyeditors make.

Here's the example I used in the second edition of this book. In 2005 I was editing a memo intended to help employees manage their e-mail. The manuscript read: "You'll find it easier to locate a particular message if you folderize your emails." "Folderize your emails" piqued my curiosity: Was *folderize* a widely recognized word? If so, was this writer using it correctly? Would the company's employees understand it? Might some, recalling their schoolroom Strunk and White, snicker?[1] What was it that readers were to folderize: their emails (count noun) or their email (mass noun)? Did the company's style guide recommend *email* or *e-mail*?

I was working on a tight deadline, and the schedule called for me to edit roughly 1,500 words an hour. The most practical, most efficient way to handle the sentence was to propose that the writer revise it, and I wrote him a quick note: "*Folderize* too techie for your readers? How about: You'll find it easier to locate a particular message if you save your messages in folders—one for each of your projects or clients."

A week later, after I was off the clock, I sought to satisfy my curiosity. I began with *folderize*: Nothing in any of my print dictionaries, nothing at www.onelook.com, and nothing when I typed "definition:folderize" in the Google search box. At that time Google displayed only 95 hits for the term. Many of these were from blogs and e-bulletinboards, but a handful were from edited publications, for example:

> Sure, you can categorize and folderize all of your links for easy finding, but a really savvy and cool way to access all of the sites you regularly visit is to create what's called a Start page, or in my case, a Super Kickstart page. (Alexandra Krasne, GeekTech column, PC World website, April 27, 2004)

At least one computer-literate employee wondered about the term ("I've also heard 'folderize' at my work, and I'm still trying to figure out exactly what is meant by it! Is that like 'filing'?" at www.ezboard.com, undated),

---

1. After labeling *customize, prioritize,* and *finalize* as "abominations," Strunk and White lay down the law: "Never tack *-ize* onto a noun to create a verb. Usually you will discover that a useful verb already exists. Why say 'moisturize' when there is the simple, unpretentious word *moisten*?" (*Elements of Style,* pp. 50–51). Because, dear sirs, the remedy for dry skin is not to moisten it (make it slightly wet) but to moisturize it (rub in a small amount of an emollient that is to be absorbed). And even if these words were closer in meaning, can writers and speakers ever have too many synonyms?

Fortunately, dozens of verbs made their way into the language before Strunk and White's edict: agonize, alphabetize, apologize, categorize, demonize, deputize, digitize, emphasize, hospitalize, idolize, itemize, lionize, monopolize, patronize, philosophize, satirize, serialize, sermonize, stigmatize, symbolize, terrorize, unionize, vandalize, winterize.

and another used scare quotes ("I need to be able to 'folderize' emails on arrival, so I can keep jobs separate" at www.mobileminds.com, undated). One writer pounced on the term to characterize the speaker: "'It's better to spend one hour getting organized than to spend 10 hours being frustrated,' says the woman who uses verbs like 'folderize'" (www.wright.edu/news_events, November 1998).

A patent application (March 2004) doubled my pleasure by introducing a normalizer to do the folderizing: "a normalizer adaptively tailors and folderizes markup based information content. . . . The user of the electronic device can then further explore the folders of interest as desired."

I concluded that *folderize* was for now the property of the techies. Even among the in crowd, various meanings of *folderize* seemed to radiate from the core notion of sorting digital information into folders. And though I don't blink at *prioritize* or *moisturize,* I was taught to be suspicious of newfangled terms ending in *-ize.*[2] Delicate sensibilities aside, *folderize* seems to fill a semantic need, and I suspect it will move into general circulation someday soon.

My research into *e-mail* was easier: both *e-mail* and *email* are in current use. In conversation, I have heard *e-mail* used as a count noun ("He sent me six e-mails on this topic alone!") and as a mass noun ("We received a lot of e-mail on this topic"), and the examples in *M-W Collegiate* showed both usages.

Of course, working copyeditors usually cannot devote hours to researching a word or two. Instead, as they go about their job of advising authors and mending manuscripts, copyeditors develop judgment about when to leave something alone, when to ask the author to recast, and when to propose a revision. Some problems are easily solved: there is only one correct

---

2. Two usage notes in *Merriam-Webster's Collegiate Dictionary* (11th ed., 2003) attest to the ubiquity of this prejudice in certain circles:

The suffix *-ize* has been productive in English since the time of Thomas Nashe (1567–1601). . . . Nashe noted in 1591 that his *-ize* coinages were being criticized, and to this day new words ending in *-ize* . . . are sure to draw critical fire.

Finalize has been frequently castigated as an unnecessary neologism or as United States government gobbledygook. It appears to have first gained currency in Australia (where it has been acceptable all along) in the early 1920s. . . . Currently, it is most frequently used in government and business dealings; it usually is not found in belles-lettres.

way to spell *accordion*. But many questions do not have a single correct answer, and these require the copyeditor to consult more than one reference book, to identify and weigh conflicting opinions, and to make an informed decision about when to apply, adapt, or ignore various conventions and rules. This guide is intended to help you make just those sorts of informed decisions.

TIPS FOR USING THIS BOOK

1. The sequence of chapters in this book follows the order I use in teaching copyediting courses. We explore the general tasks, procedures, and processes (part 1) before scrutinizing the mechanical conventions (part 2), and then we look at grammar, organization, and other "big picture" topics (part 3). You may, however, prefer to read part 3 before part 2.

2. If you are perplexed by a term, consult the Glossary of Copyediting Terms and the Glossary of Grammar Terms at the back of the book. You could also check the index to see if the term is discussed elsewhere in the book.

3. Most of the recommendations in part 2 follow those stated in *The Chicago Manual of Style,* but widely used alternatives are also discussed. To locate the precise point in one of these style manuals, consult that manual's index.

4. Indisputably incorrect sample sentences are preceded by the symbol ✗. Either an explanation or a corrected version or both follow. Sample sentences that are unsatisfactory but not incorrect are preceded by a label such as *Weak* or *Tangled.*

5. Cross-references within the text are by first-level head and chapter number; all first-level heads are listed in the table of contents. (If you're wondering why the cross-references are not to page numbers, see the discussion of cross-referencing under "Organization" in chapter 15.)

6. The Answer Keys provide hand-marked manuscript and line-by-line explanations for the exercises in part 2. (Don't peek.)

7. Because *The Chicago Manual of Style* is the style manual used by the University of California Press, this book was copyedited to conform to that manual. Eagle-eyed readers, however, will notice a few spots in which the editorial style here diverges from Chicago, especially on some matters of hy-

phenation (see "One Word or Two?" in chapter 5). Kindly construe all errors in the text as opportunities for you to exercise your editorial acumen.

8. For supplementary online tools, visit the *Copyeditor's Handbook* webpage (www.ucpress.edu/go/copyeditors) at the University of California Press website.

9. The following short titles are used for works frequently cited in the text. (For complete bibliographical data, see the Selected Bibliography at the back of the book.)

APA	*Publication Manual of the American Psychological Association*
CSE	*Scientific Style and Format: The CSE Manual for Authors, Editors, and Publishers*
Chicago	*The Chicago Manual of Style*
DEU	*Merriam-Webster's Dictionary of English Usage*
MAU	Wilson Follett, *Modern American Usage: A Guide*
M-W Collegiate	*Merriam-Webster's Collegiate Dictionary*
New Fowler's	R. W. Burchfield, ed., *The New Fowler's Modern English Usage* [Later editions dropped *The New* from the title.]
WIT	*Words into Type*

ACKNOWLEDGMENTS

Since the mid-1980s I have taught copyediting classes to hundreds of students, both in Berkeley, California, and through correspondence study. I want to thank all these students for their inquisitiveness and high spirits as we explored the picayune aspects of the copyeditor's life.

I am also grateful to the two people most responsible for my editorial career: Gracia Alkema, the first managing editor to hire me as a freelancer (at Jossey-Bass in San Francisco), and Marilyn Schwartz, managing editor of the University of California Press, who has always given wise answers to my questions. She also guided this book from acquisition through production with meticulous care and unflagging enthusiasm. Barbara Ras—first at the University of California Press, then at North Point Press, and now at Trinity

University Press—has been extremely helpful and generous. Many other editors at California—Rose Vekony and Mary Lamprech, in particular—and dozens of my colleagues in Editcetera (a Bay Area editors' co-op) have offered valuable professional advice over the years.

Suzanne Knott did a first-rate job on the editorial equivalent of deciphering a lithograph by Escher (copyediting a manuscript about copyediting written by a copyeditor). All the remaining mechanical inconsistencies and errors are mine and represent instances when I failed to heed her advice.

Barbara Jellow designed this book, Anne Canright and Desne Border did the proofreading, Zippie Collins reviewed the Answer Keys, and Elinor Lindheimer wrote the first draft of the index. I thank and salute all of them for their skills and assistance.

The support of long-time friends Carolyn Tipton, Ellen Frankel, Laura Rivkin, and Evan Frances Agnew has made all the difference. Above all, I thank my husband, Chris Raisner, for sweetly nudging me to finish this book.

PART 1

❖ The ABCs of Copyediting

The three chapters in this part introduce the craft of copyediting. Chapter 1 outlines the copyeditor's responsibilities and principal tasks. Chapter 2 shows how copyeditors hand-mark manuscripts and edit on-screen. Chapter 3 describes a variety of reference books and online resources for copyeditors.

❖ 1 ❖

What Copyeditors Do

Copyeditors always serve the needs of three constituencies:

the author(s)—the person (or people) who wrote or compiled the
manuscript
the publisher—the person or company that is paying the cost of
producing the printed material
the readers—the people for whom the material is being produced

All these parties share one basic desire: an error-free publication. To that end,
the copyeditor acts as the author's second pair of eyes, pointing out—and
usually correcting—mechanical errors and inconsistencies; errors or infelicities of grammar, usage, and syntax; and errors or inconsistencies in content.
If you like alliterative mnemonic devices, you can conceive of a copyeditor's
chief concerns as comprising the "4 Cs"—clarity, coherency, consistency, and
correctness—in service of the "Cardinal C": communication.

Certain projects require the copyeditor to serve as more than a second set
of eyes. Heavier intervention may be needed, for example, when the author
does not have native or near-native fluency in English, when the author is a
professional or a technical expert writing for a lay audience, or when the author
has not been careful in preparing the manuscript.

Sometimes, too, copyeditors find themselves juggling the conflicting
needs and desires of their constituencies. For example, the author may feel
that the manuscript requires no more than a quick read-through to correct
a handful of typographical errors, while the publisher, believing that a firmer

hand would benefit the final product, instructs the copyeditor to prune verbose passages. Or a budget-conscious publisher may ask the copyeditor to attend to only the most egregious errors, while the author is hoping for a conscientious sentence-by-sentence polishing of the text.

Copyeditors who work for publishers are usually given general instructions about how light or heavy a hand the text is thought to need. But no one looks over the copyeditor's shoulder, giving detailed advice about how much or how little to do. Publishing professionals use the term *editorial judgment* to denote a copyeditor's intuition and instincts about when to intervene, when to leave well enough alone, and when to ask the author to rework a sentence or a paragraph. In addition to having a good eye and ear for language, copyeditors must develop a sixth sense about how much effort, and what kind of effort, to put into each project that crosses their desk.

In the pre-computer era, copyeditors used pencils or pens and marked their changes and questions on a typewritten manuscript. Today a few copyeditors still work on hard copy, but most sit at a computer and key in their work—a process variously called *on-screen editing, electronic manuscript (EMS) editing,* or *online editing.* Regardless of the medium, though, a copyeditor must read the document letter by letter, word by word, with excruciating care and attentiveness. In many ways, being a copyeditor is like sitting for an English exam that never ends: At every moment, your knowledge of spelling, grammar, punctuation, usage, syntax, and diction is being tested.

You're not expected to be perfect, though. Every copyeditor misses errors here and there. But do respect the four commandments of copyediting:

- Thou shalt not lose or damage part of a manuscript.
- Thou shalt not introduce an error into a text that is correct. (As in other areas of life, in copyediting an act of commission is more serious than an act of omission.)
- Thou shalt not inadvertently change the author's meaning.
- Thou shalt not miss a critical deadline.

PRINCIPAL TASKS

Copyediting is one step in the process by which a manuscript is turned into a final published product (e.g., a book, an annual corporate report, a newsletter, a PDF). Here, we will quickly survey the copyeditor's six principal tasks;

the procedures and conventions for executing these tasks are described in the chapters that follow.

1. MECHANICAL EDITING

The heart of copyediting consists of making a manuscript conform to an *editorial style* (also called *house style*). Editorial style includes

> spelling
> hyphenation
> capitalization
> punctuation
> treatment of numbers and numerals
> treatment of quotations
> use of abbreviations and acronyms
> use of italics and bold type
> treatment of special elements (headings, lists, tables, charts,
>   and graphs)
> format of footnotes or endnotes and other documentation

Mechanical editing comprises all editorial interventions made to ensure conformity to house style. There is nothing mechanical, however, about mechanical editing; it requires a sharp eye, a solid grasp of a wide range of conventions, and good judgment. The mistake most frequently made by novice copyeditors is to rewrite portions of a text (for better or for worse, depending on the copyeditor's writing skills) and to ignore such "minor details" as capitalization, punctuation, and hyphenation. Wrong! Whatever else you are asked to do, you are expected to repair any mechanical inconsistencies in the manuscript.

For an example of the differences purely mechanical editing can make in the look and feel—but not the meaning—of a document, compare these selections from articles that appeared on the same day in the *New York Times* and the *San Francisco Examiner.*

New York Times	*San Francisco Examiner*
February 22, 1987	February 22, 1987
TARGET QADDAFI	**TARGET GADHAFI**
By Seymour M. Hersh	By Seymour M. Hersh
Eighteen American warplanes set out from Lakenheath Air Base in England last April 14 to begin a 14-hour, 5,400-mile round-trip flight to Tripoli, Libya. It is now clear that nine of those Air Force F-111's had an unprecedented peacetime mission. Their targets: Col. Muammar el-Qaddafi and his family. . . .	Eighteen U.S. warplanes set out from Lakenheath Air Base in England last April 14 to begin a 14-hour, 5,400-mile round-trip flight to Tripoli, Libya. It is now clear that nine of those Air Force F-111s had an unprecedented peacetime mission. Their targets: Col. Moammar Gadhafi and his family. . . .
Since early 1981, the Central Intelligence Agency had been encouraging and abetting Libyan exile groups and foreign governments, especially those of Egypt and France, in their efforts to stage a coup d'état. . . . Now the supersonic Air Force F-111's were ordered to accomplish what the C.I.A. could not.	Since early 1981, the CIA had been encouraging and abetting Libyan exile groups and foreign governments, especially those of Egypt and France, in their efforts to stage a coup d'etat. . . . Now the supersonic Air Force F-111s were ordered to accomplish what the CIA could not.

Which is correct? (Or which is "more correct"?): American warplanes or U.S. warplanes? Col. Muammar el-Qaddafi or Col. Moammar Gadhafi? F-111's or F-111s? coup d'état or coup d'etat? C.I.A. or CIA? In each case, it is not a matter of correctness per se but of preference, and the sum total of such preferences constitutes an editorial style. A copyeditor's job is to ensure that the manuscript conforms to the publisher's editorial style; if the publisher does not have a house style, the copyeditor must make sure that the author has been consistent in selecting among acceptable variants.

At book publishing firms, scholarly journals, newspapers, and magazines, a house style is generated by having all copyeditors use the same dictionary and the same style manual (e.g., *The Chicago Manual of Style, Words into Type, The Associated Press Stylebook, Publication Manual of the American Psychological Association*). In contrast, companies that produce documents, reports, brochures, catalogs, or newsletters but do not consider themselves to be bona fide publishers often rely on in-house style guides, on general lists of do's and don'ts, or on the judgments and preferences of copyeditors and editorial coordinators.[1]

---

1. I use the term *editorial coordinator* to denote the person who is supervising an in-house copyeditor or who is assigning work to a freelance copyeditor. In book publishing, this person's

2. CORRELATING PARTS

Unless the manuscript is very short and simple, the copyeditor must devote special attention to correlating the parts of the manuscript. Such tasks include

> verifying any cross-references that appear in the text
> checking the numbering of footnotes, endnotes, tables, and illustrations
> specifying the placement of tables and illustrations
> checking the content of the illustrations against the captions and against the text
> reading the list of illustrations against the illustrations and against the captions
> reading the table of contents against the manuscript
> reading the footnotes or endnotes against the bibliography

Some types of texts require special cross-checking. For example, in cookbooks the list of ingredients that precedes a recipe must be read against the recipe: Is every ingredient in the initial list used in the recipe? Does every ingredient used in the recipe appear in the list of ingredients? Similarly, when copyediting other kinds of how-to texts, one may need to check whether the list of equipment or parts matches the instructions.

3. LANGUAGE EDITING: GRAMMAR, USAGE, AND DICTION

Copyeditors also correct—or ask the author to correct—errors or lapses in grammar, syntax, usage, and diction. Ideally, copyeditors set right whatever is incorrect, unidiomatic, confusing, ambiguous, or inappropriate without attempting to impose their stylistic preferences or prejudices on the author.

The "rules" for language editing are far more subjective than those for mechanical editing. Most copyeditors come to trust a small set of usage books and then to rely on their own judgment when the books fail to illuminate a particular issue or offer conflicting recommendations. Indeed, the "correct" usage choice may vary from manuscript to manuscript, depending on the

---

title may be *managing editor, chief copyeditor, production editor,* or *project editor.* In other industries, the title begins with a modifier like *communications, pubs* (short for "publications"), or *documentation* and concludes with one of the following nouns: *manager, editor, specialist.*

publisher's house style, the conventions in the author's field, and the expectations of the intended audience.

A small example: Most copyeditors who work for academic presses and scholarly journals are taught to treat *data* as a plural noun: "The data for 1999 are not available." But copyeditors in corporate communications departments are often expected to treat *data* as a singular noun: "The data for 1999 is not available."[2] Moreover, a corporate copyeditor is likely to accept *1999* as an adjective and to favor contractions: "The 1999 data isn't available."

A second example: Between the 1960s and the late 1980s, many prominent usage experts denounced *hopefully* as a sentence adverb, and copyeditors were instructed to revise "Hopefully, the crisis will end soon" to read "It is to be hoped that the crisis will end soon." Almost all members of the anti-*hopefully* faction have since recanted, though some people, unaware that the battle has ended, continue what they believe to be the good fight.[3]

The history of the *hopefully* controversy serves as a reminder that there are fads and fashions, crotchets and crazes, in that cultural creation known as grammar. For copyeditors who work on corporate publications, a solid grasp of current fashion is usually sufficient. But an understanding of current conventions alone will not do for copyeditors who work on manuscripts written by scholars, professional writers, and other creative and literary authors. To succeed on these types of projects, the copyeditor needs to learn something about the history of usage controversies:

> [A copyeditor] should know the old and outmoded usages as well as those that are current, for not all authors have current ideas—some, indeed, seem bent upon perpetuating the most unreasonable regulations that were obsolescent fifty years ago. Yet too great stress upon rules—upon "correctness"—is per-

2. The origin of the controversy lies in the etymology of *data*, which is the plural form of *datum* in Latin but functions differently in English: "*data* occurs in two constructions: as a plural noun (like *earnings*), taking a plural verb and certain plural modifiers (such as *these, many, a few of*) but not cardinal numbers, and serving as a referent for plural pronouns (such as *they, them*); and as an abstract mass noun (like *information*), taking a singular verb and singular modifiers (such as *this, much, little*), and being referred to by a singular pronoun (*it*). Both of these constructions are standard" (*DEU*, s.v. "data").

3. For a history of the debate and its resolution in the United States, see *DEU*, s.v. "hopefully"; on the controversy in the United Kingdom, see *New Fowler's*, s.v. "sentence adverb." Surprisingly, the 2009 edition of *The Associated Press Stylebook* labels *hopefully* "wrong" when the desired meaning is "it is hoped."

ilous. If the worst disease in copyediting is arrogance [toward authors], the second worst is rigidity.[4]

In all these matters, then, copyeditors must strive to strike a balance between being overly permissive and overly pedantic. Copyeditors are expected to correct (or ask the author to correct) locutions that are likely to confuse, distract, or disturb readers, but copyeditors are not hired for the purpose of imposing their own taste and sense of style on the author. Thus when reading a manuscript, the copyeditor must ask, "Is this sentence acceptable as the author has written it?" The issue is *not* "If I were the writer, would I have written it some other way?"

4. CONTENT EDITING

Copyeditors are expected to call to the author's attention any internal inconsistencies or discrepancies in content as well as any structural and organizational problems. On some projects you may be asked to fix these kinds of problems by doing heavy editing or rewriting. More often, though, you will be instructed to point out the difficulty and ask the author to resolve it.

Copyeditors are not responsible for the factual correctness of a manuscript, but you are expected to offer a polite query about factual statements that you know to be incorrect.

Manuscript: The documents arrived on February 29, 1985.
Copyeditor's query: Please check date—1985 not a leap year.

Manuscript: Along the Kentucky-Alabama border . . .
Copyeditor's query: Please fix—Kentucky and Alabama are not contiguous.

Manuscript: During the Vietnam War, the most divisive in American history, . . .
Copyeditor's query: Accurate to imply that Vietnam was more divisive than the Civil War?

4. William Bridgwater, "Copyediting," in *Editors on Editing: An Inside View of What Editors Really Do,* rev. ed., edited by Gerald Gross (New York: Harper & Row, 1985), p. 87.

If you have some knowledge of the subject matter, you may be able to catch an error that would go unquestioned by a copyeditor who is unfamiliar with the subject. Such catches will be greatly appreciated by the author, but only if you can identify the errors without posing dozens of extraneous questions about items that are correct.

Another misdeed you must guard against is inadvertently changing the author's meaning while you are repairing a grammatical error or tidying up a verbose passage. And it is never acceptable to alter the author's meaning simply because you disagree with the author or believe that the author could not have meant what he or she said. Whenever the content is unclear or confusing, the copyeditor's recourse is to point out the difficulty and ask the author to resolve it.

Most publishers also expect their copyeditors to help authors avoid sexism and other forms of biased language. In addition, copyeditors call the author's attention to any material (text or illustrations) that might form the basis for a lawsuit alleging libel, invasion of privacy, or obscenity.

5. PERMISSIONS

If the manuscript contains lengthy quotations from a published work that is still under copyright, the copyeditor is expected to remind the author to obtain permission to reprint the quotations. Permission is also needed to reprint tables, charts, graphs, and illustrations that have appeared in print. Copyright law and permissions rules also apply to works that appear on the Internet. Special rules pertain to the reproduction of unpublished materials (e.g., diaries, letters).

6. TYPECODING

Copyeditors may be asked to typecode the manuscript, that is, to identify those portions of the manuscript that are not regular running text. These pieces of text, called *elements,* include part and chapter numbers, titles, and subtitles; headings and subheadings; lists, extracts, and displayed equations; table numbers, titles, source lines, and footnotes; and figure numbers and figure captions.

Copyeditors working on hard copy are usually asked to pencil in the typecodes in the left margin of the manuscript. Copyeditors working on-screen may be asked to insert or verify typecodes that identify special elements.

WHAT COPYEDITORS DO NOT DO

Given that there is no consensus about how to spell *copyediting*,[5] it is not surprising that the meaning of the term is somewhat unsettled. In the world beyond book and journal publishing, *copyediting* is sometimes loosely applied to cover a range of editorial tasks. For clarity's sake, the following distinctions are worth preserving:

Copyeditors are not proofreaders. Although many copyeditors are good proofreaders, and all copyeditors are expected to catch typographical errors, copyediting and proofreading are two different functions. Copyeditors work on an author's manuscript and are concerned with imposing mechanical consistency; correcting infelicities of grammar, usage, and diction; and querying internal inconsistencies of fact or tone. Proofreaders, in contrast, are charged with correcting errors introduced during the typesetting, formatting, or file conversion of the final document and with identifying any serious errors that were not caught during copyediting.[6]

Copyeditors are not rewriters, ghost writers, or substantive editors. Although copyeditors are expected to make simple revisions to smooth awkward passages, copyeditors do not have license to rewrite a text line by line. Making such wholesale revisions to the text is called *substantive editing* or *content editing.*

Copyeditors are not developmental editors. Copyeditors are expected to query structural and organizational problems, but they are not expected to fix these problems. Reorganizing or restructuring a manuscript is called *developmental editing.*

Copyeditors are not publication designers. Copyeditors are expected to point out any item in the manuscript that may cause difficulties during production, for example, a table that seems too wide to fit on a typeset page. But copyeditors are not responsible for making decisions about the physical appearance of the publication. All physical specifications—typefaces, page

---

5. The closed forms (*copyedit, copyeditor, copyediting*) are recommended in *Chicago* 16 and are routinely used in book publishing, but newspapers are apt to employ *copy editors* who *copy edit. WIT* prefers *copy editor* (recognizing *copyeditor* as a variant) and *copy-edit. M-W Collegiate* shows *copy editor* and *copyedit.*

6. Some publishers skip the word-by-word proofreading stage when a manuscript has been typeset directly from copyedited files. The author is usually sent a set of proofs and encouraged to proofread them carefully, but at the publishing firm the proofs are simply spot-checked for gross formatting errors.

TABLE 1. Levels of Copyediting

	Light Copyediting	Medium Copyediting	Heavy Copyediting
Mechanical editing	Ensure consistency in all mechanical matters—spelling, capitalization, punctuation, hyphenation, abbreviations, format of lists, etc. Optional guideline: Allow deviations from house style if the author consistently uses acceptable variants.		
Correlating parts	Check contents page against chapters; check numbering of footnotes or endnotes, tables, and figures. Check alphabetization of bibliography or reference list; read footnote, endnote, or in-text citations against bibliography or reference list.		
Language editing	Correct all indisputable errors in grammar, syntax, and usage, but ignore any locution that is not an outright error.	Correct all errors in grammar, syntax, and usage. Point out or revise any infelicities.	Correct all errors and infelicities in grammar, syntax, and usage.
	Point out paragraphs that seem egregiously wordy or convoluted, but do not revise. Ignore minor patches of wordiness, imprecise wording, and jargon.	Point out any patches that seem wordy or convoluted, and supply suggested revisions.	Rewrite any wordy or convoluted patch.
	Ask for clarification of terms likely to be new to readers.	Ask for or supply definitions of terms likely to be new to readers.	Ask for or supply definitions of terms likely to be new to readers.
Content editing	Query factual inconsistencies and any statements that seem incorrect.	Query any facts that seem incorrect. Use desktop reference books to verify content. Query faulty organization and gaps in logic.	Verify and revise any facts that are incorrect. Query or fix faulty organization and gaps in logic.
Permissions	Note any text, tables, or illustrations that may require permission to reprint.		
Typecoding	Typecode all elements.		

layout, the formatting of tables, the typographical treatment of titles and head-ings, and so on—-are set by the publication's designer or by someone wear-ing the designer's (not the copyeditor's) hat.

LEVELS OF COPYEDITING

If time and money were not an issue, copyeditors could linger over each sen-tence and paragraph in a manuscript until they were wholly satisfied with its clarity, coherency, consistency, and correctness—even with its beauty and elegance. But since time and money are always an issue, many book and cor-porate publishers use the terms *light, medium,* or *heavy* to let copyeditors know how to focus and prioritize their efforts.

A publisher's decision about the level of copyediting to request for a given project is based on

> the quality of the author's writing
> the intended audience
> the schedule and budget for editing and publication
> the author's reputation, attitude toward editing, and work schedule
> the size of the final print run
> the importance of the publication to the publisher

In the best of all possible worlds, decisions about the level of copyediting would be based solely on an assessment of the quality of the writing and the needs of the intended audience. But in many cases, financial considerations and deadline pressures win out: "This manuscript is poorly written, but our budget allows for only light copyediting" or "This manuscript would benefit from a heavier hand, but the author has many pressing commitments and won't have time to read through a heavily edited manuscript, so let's go for light editing."

There are no universal definitions for light, medium, and heavy copy-editing, but you won't be too far off target if you follow the guidelines pre-sented in table 1. You could even show these guidelines to your editorial coordinator and ask which statements best match his or her expectations for your work.

In addition, before beginning to copyedit, you should ask the following kinds of questions:

Audience
- Who is the primary audience for this text?
- How much are readers expected to know about the subject?
- How will readers "use" the publication? Will it be pleasure reading or professional reading? Is it a reference guide or a skim-once-and-throw-away document? Will most readers read the piece straight through, from start to finish, or will they consult sections of it from time to time?

Text
- How long is the text?
- What physical form is the text in?
    For hard-copy editing: Is the text double-spaced? (Single-spaced text is difficult to copyedit unless only a sprinkling of commas is required.) How many words are on a page? How legible is the font? Are all four margins at least one inch?
    For on-screen editing: What word processing program did the author use? Has the publisher converted the author's files into another program or format?
- How will the copyedited manuscript be processed?
    For hard-copy editing: Will the entire document be rekeyed, or will someone be inputting only the changes? (If the latter, the copyeditor must use a brightly colored pencil or pen for marking, so that the inputter can easily spot all the changes.)
    For on-screen editing: Is the copyeditor to supply redlined files (i.e., files that show insertions and deletions) or clean files (i.e., files that contain only the copyedited text)? Is the copyeditor expected to code elements or special characters (e.g., letters that carry diacritic marks, foreign alphabets)?
- Does the manuscript contain material other than straight running text (e.g., tables, footnotes or endnotes, bibliography, photos, graphs)? How much of each kind?
- Are there legible photocopies of all art?

Type of editing
- What level of copyediting is being requested: light, medium, or heavy?

- Is that request based on scheduling or budget constraints?
- Has the person making the request read the entire manuscript or skimmed only parts of it?
- How many hours or dollars have been budgeted for the copyediting?
- Is the copyeditor expected to substantially cut the text?
- Is the copyeditor expected to check the math in the tables? to verify bibliographical citations?
- Are there any important design constraints or preferences: limits on the amount of art, size of tables, number of heading levels? use of special characters (foreign alphabets, math symbols, musical notation)? footnotes or endnotes?

Editorial style

- What is the preferred style manual? the preferred dictionary?
- Is there an in-house style guide, tipsheet, or checklist of editorial preferences? (A sample checklist is presented on pages 421–29.)
- Are there earlier editions or comparable texts that should be consulted? Is this piece part of a series?

Author

- Who is the author? Is the author a novice or a veteran writer?
- Has the author seen a sample edit?
- Has the author been told what kind of (or level of) editing to expect?

Administrative details

- To whom should the copyeditor direct questions that arise during editing?
- What is the deadline for completion of the editing? How firm is it?

THE EDITORIAL PROCESS

Once you have a sense of the assignment, the next step is to inventory the materials you have been given and ascertain that the materials are complete. Make a list of items that seem to be missing, and track them down immediately.

If you are copyediting on hard copy, make sure you have

all the pages (numbered in sequence)
copies of any tables, charts, or illustrations

captions for the illustrations
text for any footnotes or endnotes
the bibliography or reference list (for an article or book that includes
    references)
any supplementary materials (e.g., appendixes or glossaries)

If you will be editing on-screen, make a working copy of all the computer files and keep the original files in a separate folder. Open each of your working files and scroll through its contents. Check to see that the files are compatible with your equipment,[7] and be sure you have all the files for the document. Each type of nontext element (e.g., tables, captions for illustrations, endnotes) should be in its own file. On-screen copyeditors are often given a printout of the document; check to see that this printout is complete. If the author, rather than the publisher, printed the hard copy, you must verify that the hard copy and the files are identical. For a quick spot-check on long projects:

- Open each file and look at the opening paragraphs. Read the first line of each paragraph against the hard copy; they should match exactly.
- Repeat this comparison for the last paragraphs in each file.

If you find any discrepancies, immediately report them to your editorial coordinator.

Ideally, the publisher's schedule allows enough time for a preliminary skimming of the entire text and two complete editorial read-throughs (*passes*) of the text. Two passes seems to be the universal magic number: No copyeditor is good enough to catch everything in one pass, and few editorial budgets are generous enough to permit three passes (unless the text is only a few pages long).

The preliminary skim is a quick read-through of the manuscript to size up the content, organization, and quality of the writing; to note elements that

---

7. Copyeditors who work in-house and those who work as independent contractors (freelancers) for publishers will receive compatible files from the publisher. Freelance copyeditors who work directly with authors should discuss file formats and compatibility with prospective clients. These freelancers will also want to examine sample files to evaluate the author's word processing skills. (Yes, there still exist authors who create a paragraph indent by hitting the space bar five times.)

may require special attention (e.g., footnotes, tables, appendixes, glossary); and to identify any weak sections of the manuscript that will require extra time.

The next step is to grab a pencil or a mouse and plunge in for your first pass. On the first pass through the text, most copyeditors read very, very slowly. Let me say that again, because it is crucial to your success as a copyeditor: You must train yourself to read v-e-r-y, v-e-r-y slowly—slowly enough to scrutinize each comma ("OK, comma, what are you doing here? Do you really belong here? Why?"), to interrogate each pronoun ("Hey, pronoun, where's your antecedent? Do you two agree in gender and number?"), to cross-examine each homophone ("You there, 'affect'! Shouldn't you be 'effect'?"), and to ponder each compound adjective, adverb, and noun ("Does our dictionary show 'cross section' or 'cross-section'?"). Moreover, you must read slowly enough to catch missing words (a dropped "the" or "a"), missing pieces of punctuation ("We need a hyphen here"), ambiguities in syntax, and gaps in logic.

On your first editorial pass through the manuscript, then, you will want to read as slowly as you can. To slow yourself down, read aloud or subvocalize. An added advantage of reading aloud (or muttering) is that your ear will pick up some discrepancies that your eye will ignore. On this pass, you should look up *anything* that you are unsure of. With your dictionary, style manual, usage guide, thesaurus, and other reference books at your side, this is the time to read up on troublesome mechanical issues, brush up on tricky grammar and usage controversies, and verify your suspicions about factual inaccuracies or inconsistencies in the manuscript. If you have any large, global questions—questions that pertain to the manuscript as a whole—make your best effort to get the answers, from your editorial coordinator or from the author, before you begin your second pass.

The second pass through the text is usually a much quicker read for the purpose of incorporating the answers to any global questions that arose on the first pass, catching the mechanical errors you missed on the first pass, and fixing any errors you inadvertently introduced on your first pass. For a book-length manuscript, try to schedule the second pass so that you can read the entire work in a few days, without interruptions; you are more likely to catch inconsistencies if large chunks of the manuscript are residing in your short-term memory. If the text contains tables or charts, you will need to make a special pass to be sure that all items in the batch are consistent in style and format.

(Some experienced copyeditors reverse this procedure, doing a quick first pass and a slow second pass. During the first pass, they fix all the obvious mechanical errors; the second pass is for less routine matters, issues that they feel can be better addressed after they have read the entire manuscript. Some on-screen copyeditors also make a quick first pass, during which the redlining or mark-revisions feature is turned off and only nondiscretionary changes are made; they then turn on the redlining for the second, in-depth pass. I don't recommend this approach to novice copyeditors, however, for two reasons. First, because few mechanical issues are truly routine for beginning copyeditors, the "quick first pass" is unlikely to be quick. Second, this system deprives copyeditors of the opportunity to catch any errors they have inadvertently introduced, because the in-depth copyediting is done during the second, and final, pass.)

The copyedited manuscript is always sent to the author for review. Some authors make relatively few changes during this review; others may spend considerable time revising, rewriting, and reorganizing. Publishers encourage authors to make changes at this stage rather than later in the process, when alterations can be expensive and time consuming.

The author then returns the manuscript to the publisher for *cleanup*— one final pass made by the copyeditor or the editorial coordinator.[8] If the author has ignored any of the copyeditor's queries or restored (*stetted*) or added text containing an error, the troublesome passages are resolved in consultation with the author before the manuscript is released for production.

During cleanup, the editor scans every page looking for marks by the author and for the author's responses to queries. For a paper-and-pencil copyedit, the cleanup editor sometimes literally cleans messy pages, using an eraser or white-out, or even retypes hard-to-read paragraphs or pages.

Occasionally, cleanup requires the wisdom of Solomon and the diplomacy of Dag Hammarskjöld. These problem cleanups arise when a copyeditor has been overly zealous or has failed to explain persuasively why certain proposed

---

8. Some publishers reserve cleanup for a senior editor; others expect the copyeditor to do the cleanup because the copyeditor is the person most familiar with the manuscript. Should an author seem extremely dissatisfied with the copyediting, the cleanup may be handed over to another editor, both to spare the copyeditor's feelings and because a fresh pair of eyes may be more objective in resolving the disputes between the copyeditor's suggestions and the author's preferences. Having someone other than the copyeditor do the cleanup may also be preferable when the editorial coordinator wants to get a better sense of the project or evaluate the quality of the copyeditor's work.

changes are preferable, or when an author is quite attached to unconventional locutions or mannerisms. The cleanup editor cannot override the author, and the cleanup editor cannot ask the author to re-review every rejected change. Instead, the cleanup editor needs to rethink each disputed issue and decide whether the point is worth revisiting with the author: Is one of the 4 Cs (clarity, coherency, consistency, and correctness) at stake? Or is the matter one of conflicting preferences about some small point that will not affect readers one way or another?

In other words, cleanup editors have to select their "battles" very carefully. If the cleanup editor is convinced that the author is inviting peril by rejecting a particular piece of copyediting, the proper course is to rephrase (rather than simply repeat) the concern and, if possible, propose one or two additional alternative remedies. In disputes concerning less important issues, however, the cleanup editor should respect the author's preferences and not raise the matter again. After all, it's the author's name, not the editor's, that appears on the cover.

EDITORIAL TRIAGE

Sometimes a copyeditor is asked to meet what everyone involved in the project knows is an unreasonable deadline for even a light copyedit. In such cases, the copyeditor's first step is to ask the editorial coordinator to help set priorities: Which editorial tasks are most important for this particular project, and which niceties must fall by the wayside?

The list of priorities depends on the project, of course; but for most projects, a minimal task list would include attending to those errors that would be most embarrassing to the publisher and those that would be most confusing to readers. Thus the copyeditor would

> correct spelling errors, serious grammatical errors (e.g., faulty
>   subject-verb agreement), and egregious punctuation errors
> query factual inconsistencies
> make sure all abbreviations and acronyms are defined
> list pages containing material for which permission to reprint
>   is required
> carefully read the title page, copyright page, and contents page
> check the numbering of footnotes, tables, and figures

In other words, mechanical inconsistencies or discrepancies that do not inter-fere with communication (e.g., capitalization, hyphenation, use of italics, for-mat of lists) would be ignored, as would be almost all matters of diction, syntax, usage, and content. The copyeditor would, however, keep track of the permissions needed (to save the author and publisher from being named in a lawsuit) and would check the contents page and numbering of elements (to save readers the frustration of missing or out-of-sequence items).

If the schedule is a bit more generous, the following items may be added to the task list:

Break up overly long sentences and overly long paragraphs.
Revise overuse of the passive.
Prune repetitions and redundancies.

When straining to meet a tight schedule, you may also have to choose between doing two quick passes or doing one slower pass and either forgo-ing the second pass entirely or doing a selective second pass. During a selec-tive second pass, you could either read only the most important sections of the manuscript or revisit only those paragraphs that you found most trou-bling on your first pass. (To help you locate these spots, on your first pass you can either keep a list, lightly mark an X in the left margin of a hard-copy document, or place a hidden comment in an on-screen document.) The choice between one pass or two will depend on the type of material, the priorities list, and your own work style.

This kind of triage is painful: It goes against a copyeditor's nature and train-ing to leave poorly punctuated, convoluted sentences and paragraphs whose logic is inside-out or upside-down. But when time is short, it is more impor-tant to have read every page than to have labored over the first half of a proj-ect and barely glanced at the rest.

Triage for business documents.   An entirely different list of triage priorities is offered by Gary Blake, co-author of *The Elements of Business Writing* and *The Elements of Technical Writing.* Arguing that errors in spelling, gram-mar, and punctuation will not "send customers out the door"—unless the misspelled word is the customer's name—Blake places all these mechanical issues at the bottom of his ten-point priority list for business writing. At the top of the list, instead, are those issues that defeat the twin purposes of a busi-ness document: to inform and persuade readers and to convey the sponsoring organization's authoritativeness and expertise. For Blake the top-priority items are fixing errors in organization, rewording sentences that are inappropriate in tone, and clarifying language that is overly vague.[9]

Triage for technical documents.   In *Technical Editing: The Practical Guide for Editors and Writers,* Judith Tarutz advises technical copyeditors to ask the following kinds of questions when creating a list of priorities for triage: What matters to the readers? What kinds of errors will readers notice and care about? How important is the document to the readers? What kinds of errors are easy to fix within the time constraints? In practice, then, Tarutz says, "Sometimes you'll fix something that's not very important but is so easy to fix that it would be silly not to. And sometimes you need to ignore something that bothers you but it's OK with the customers, it's expensive to change, and it's not important to change. (Just because it bothers you does not make it wrong)" (p. 167).

ESTIMATES

Because so many people are involved in publishing a piece of printed material, every member of the team must be able to make reliable estimates of completion dates for each task. Copyeditors are typically asked for two estimates: How many hours will the project take? On what date will the copyediting be completed?

The following rules should help you improve your accuracy in making estimates and help you set reasonable deadlines for yourself.

Rule 1. Do not make an estimate or confirm anyone else's estimate of how long a copyediting project will take until you have seen the manuscript. Sometimes a copyeditor is asked to make an estimate after being given a quick description of a manuscript. Unless you have worked with the "describer" before and have great confidence in his or her ability to evaluate a manuscript, your best response is a polite, "I'm sorry but I can't give you a useful estimate until I've seen the manuscript." Once you have the manuscript in

---

9. In the middle of Blake's list—after revising vague wording and ahead of correcting punctuation errors—are attending to the overuse of the passive voice, fixing overly long sentences and paragraphs, rewriting "weasel" words and hedging phrases, cutting redundancies, and selecting the correct member of a confusible pair of words; see Blake, "It Is Recommended That You Write Clearly," *Wall Street Journal,* April 3, 1995, p. A14.

TABLE 2. Typical Pace for Copyediting Hard Copy, Two Passes
(pages per hour)

	Standard Text	Difficult Text
Light copyedit	6–9	4–6
Medium copyedit	4–7	2–4
Heavy copyedit	2–3	1–2

Standard text: Carefully prepared double-spaced hard copy, 250–325 words on a page. Text is not technical and has few or no tables, figures, footnotes, endnotes, or reference citations. Manuscript has no bibliography or a short, well-prepared bibliography.

Difficult text: Manuscript contains many typographical errors, count exceeds 325 words a page, or the font is difficult to read. Text is technical or has many tables, figures, footnotes, or endnotes. Reference citations are carelessly prepared, inconsistent, or incomplete.

hand, you can skim it, select a representative chunk, do a sample edit (say, ten pages), and time yourself. In general, the more material you sample, the more accurate your estimate will be. Remember that your estimate has to allow you enough time for two passes through the manuscript, although the second pass goes a lot faster than the first.

Rule 2. Adjust your base estimate to allow extra time for patches of difficult copy. For hard-copy editing: The heart of an estimate is based on a pages-per-hour rate. But pages that have 450 words take longer than pages that have 300 words. And if the manuscript is printed in a difficult-to-read font, you will find your pages-per-hour rate declining over the course of the day as your eyes tire. How much of a difference can such factors make? Table 2 shows estimates of how many pages an hour an experienced copyeditor would need to complete two passes on a hard-copy manuscript; novice copyeditors will (and should) work at a slower pace. For on-screen editing: Allow extra time for difficult copy (e.g., technical text, tables, eccentrically styled footnotes or endnotes and bibliographies) and for poorly prepared files (e.g., idiosyncratic spacing, extraneous formatting codes, improperly formatted extracts).

Rule 3. As appropriate, allow time for nonediting chores, such as photocopying hard copy, converting or copying files, and writing memos. For some projects, these tasks will take no more than an hour or two. But other projects may require five or more hours of administrative or housekeeping duties.

Rule 4. Unless you are extremely experienced in making estimates, always add a fudge factor to your best guess. Suppose your sampling of a 150-page manuscript suggests that you can complete 5 pages an hour. Use 30 hours, then, as the base for your estimate. Now add in a fudge factor—from 10 to 20 percent, depending on how confident you feel about your base estimate and how long the project is: The less confident you feel, the larger the fudge factor; the shorter the project, the larger the fudge factor. For a 30-hour base estimate, a 10 percent fudge factor would be 3 hours; a 20 percent fudge factor would be 6 hours. Present your estimate as a range, say, 33 to 37 hours, or 36 to 40 hours.

Rule 5. Be realistic about how many hours a day you can copyedit and still do a good job. Most editors find that they cannot copyedit manuscripts for more than five or six hours a day except in times of utmost emergency. Be sure your work schedule includes time for breaks: at least fifteen to twenty minutes every two hours.

Rule 6. Err on the side of overestimating the amount of time you need. Because copyediting comes early in the production cycle, a missed deadline can throw off the entire schedule. Don't checkmate yourself by setting too tight a schedule.

ONE PARAGRAPH, THREE WAYS

To conclude this overview of the copyediting process, let's look at a short example that illustrates both the levels-of-editing concept and the nature of editorial awareness and editorial reasoning. The sample manuscript reads:[10]

> Murphy's Law assures us that no amount of proofreading will uncover all the errors in a work about to be published. The question is, how many re-readings are reasonable? In my personal experience I have found that two readings of galleys and two of page proofs will catch 99 percent of the errors. Unfortunately the remaining 1 percent are often the mistakes that not only cause embarrassment but trouble. For example, the wrong numbers for ordering merchandise or misspelled names.

---

10. This example is based on a passage in Arthur Plotnik's *The Elements of Editing: A Modern Guide for Editors and Journalists* (New York: Macmillan, 1982), p. 7. For the purpose of this example, errors were introduced and other changes were made to the published text.

Assume that the editorial coordinator has requested a light copyedit. If you want to use the sample to test yourself, pick up a pencil and copyedit the passage. Focus on mechanical issues and make only those changes in wording that are necessary for the sake of correctness and clarity. For this exercise, the house style manual is *Chicago,* and *M-W Collegiate* is the preferred dictionary.

Let's follow Kate as she copyedits this passage. After skimming the entire manuscript, she carefully reads the first sentence:

Murphy's Law assures us that no amount of proofreading will
uncover all the errors in a work about to be published.

Kate is unfamiliar with the term "Murphy's Law," so she looks it up in the dictionary and ascertains that the usage is appropriate and that the spelling and capitalization are correct. She detects no mechanical errors in this sentence and makes no changes to it.

Kate moves on to the second sentence:

The question is, how many re-readings are reasonable?

Uncertain about how to treat a question ("how many re-readings are reasonable?") embedded in a sentence, she picks up *Chicago,* turns to the index, and looks under "question marks," where the subentry "within sentences, 6.67–68" leads her to a discussion and examples that match the syntax of the sentence in the manuscript. Relevant examples also appear in 6.70. She decides to apply the following conventions:

1. The embedded question should be preceded by a comma.
2. The first word of the embedded question is capitalized only when the question is long or has internal punctuation. A short, informal embedded question begins with a lowercase letter.
3. The question should not be in quotation marks because it is not a piece of dialogue.
4. The question should end with a question mark because it is a direct question.

Since the author has followed all these conventions, Kate changes nothing.

She next wonders whether to keep or delete the hyphen in "re-readings." She knows that for words beginning with prefixes, both *Chicago* and *M-W*

Collegiate usually prefer the closed forms: *redo, prenatal, postwar,* and so on. But *Chicago* recommends using a hyphen if the absence of one might cause confusion or misreading: *re-cover* (as opposed to *recover*), *co-op,* and *pro-choice.* So the question is, will "rereadings" be confusing? She thinks not and decides to delete the hyphen.

Kate now scrutinizes the third sentence:

> In my personal experience I have found that two readings of galleys and two of page proofs will catch 99 percent of the errors.

She changes "personal" to "professional"—because "personal experience" is a bit redundant (an individual's experience is, by definition, "personal") and, more importantly, because the power of the author's observation comes from his professional expertise, not his personal life. She leaves "99 percent" because she remembers *Chicago*'s preference for using a numeral followed by "percent" (rather than the percentage sign, %) in nontechnical copy.

On to the fourth sentence:

> Unfortunately the remaining 1 percent are often the mistakes that not only cause embarrassment but trouble.

Kate adds a comma after "Unfortunately" because a sentence adverb (i.e., an adverb that modifies an entire sentence, not just a single word or phrase) is always followed by a comma. (*Chicago* does not discuss sentence adverbs as such but recommends the use of a comma to set off a transitional adverb that effects a "distinct break" in continuity.) Next, Kate moves "not only"— to yield "cause not only embarrassment but trouble"—because the items being contrasted are "embarrassment" and "trouble." (Compare: "These errors not only cause embarrassment but jeopardize our credibility." In this example, the items being contrasted are "cause embarrassment" and "jeopardize our credibility," so "not only" precedes "cause embarrassment.")

The fifth sentence brings Kate to a halt.

> For example, the wrong numbers for ordering merchandise or misspelled names.

This is a careless sentence fragment; that is, it is not a fragment serving some rhetorical purpose (which would be fine in the right circumstances). Kate decides that the least intrusive way to repair the fragment is to change the

Figure 1.   Samples of Light, Medium, and Heavy Copyediting

Murphy's Law assures us that no amount of proofreading will uncover all the errors in a work about to be published. The question is, how many re/readings are reasonable? In my ~~personal~~ professional experience I have found that two readings of galleys and two of page proofs will catch 99 percent of the errors. Unfortunately, the remaining 1 percent are often the mistakes that ~~not only~~ cause not only embarrassment but trouble—...¹for example, ~~the wrong numbers for ordering merchandise or~~ misspelled names or the wrong numbers for ordering merchandise.

Murphy's Law assures us that no amount of proofreading will uncover all the errors in a set of proofs. ~~work about to be published.~~ The question is, how many re/readings are reasonable? ~~In my personal experience~~ I have found that two readings of galleys and two readings of page proofs will catch 99 percent of the errors. Unfortunately, the remaining 1 percent are often the mistakes that ~~not~~ only cause not only embarrassment but trouble—~~for~~ For example, misspelled names or incorrect catalog numbers for merchandise. ~~the wrong merchandise or misspelled names.~~

~~Murphy's Law assures us that no~~ No amount of proofreading ~~will~~ can uncover all the errors in a set of ~~proofs. work about to be published. The question is, how many re-readings are reasonable? In my personal experience~~ I have found that two Two readings of galleys and two readings of page proofs will catch 99 percent of the errors, but ~~Unfortunately~~ the remaining 1 percent ~~are often the mistakes~~—incorrect phone numbers or misspelled names—often cause both ~~that not only cause~~ embarrassment and ~~but~~ trouble. ~~For example, the wrong numbers for ordering merchandise or misspelled names.~~

period before "for example" to a dash. (She turns to *Chicago* to confirm that either a comma or a dash may precede "for example," with the dash indicating a greater break in continuity.) She also changes the order of "wrong numbers for ordering" and "misspelled names" to prevent the misreading of "for ordering merchandise or misspelled names" as one unit of thought. The reordering prevents readers from thinking that one can "order misspelled names." When Kate is done, the last portion of the text reads: "Unfortunately, the remaining 1 percent are often the mistakes that cause not only embarrassment but trouble—for example, misspelled names or the wrong numbers for ordering merchandise."

Kate's light-handed copyedit is shown in figure 1, along with a medium and heavy copyediting of the same passage. The medium-handed and heavy-handed copyeditors, you'll notice, made all the necessary mechanical changes, but they also tried to improve the wording and syntax. In the name of conciseness, they pruned or cut several wordy locutions. But observe that although the heavy-handed copyeditor retained the key points, the edited version is drained of color and personality: Gone are Murphy's Law, the posing of the question to be answered, and the author's statement that the recommendation is based on experience. As you might guess, the author of the passage will be quite upset ("You've torn my writing to shreds! You've eliminated every syllable of humanity!") unless the editorial coordinator and the author have previously discussed the desirability of such wholesale cuts.

If your version of this passage looked more like medium or heavy copyediting, you will want to force yourself to lighten up. Do not machete a manuscript or rewrite a document unless you are explicitly asked to do heavy editing or rewriting. If the author's sentences are clear, correct, and serviceable (as this author's sentences are, with the few mistakes caught by our light-handed copyeditor), let them be. Don't rewrite an author's sentence simply because it is not the sentence you would have written. A reminder to this effect is posted on many bulletin boards in publishing offices around the world:

It's ~~hard~~ to *difficult*
resist the ~~urge~~ *temptation*
to ~~change~~ *improve*
someone else's writing.

Resisting this urge will make your life as a copyeditor easier in several ways. First, you will be able to devote more of your attention to your primary responsibilities: When you resist the urge to recast phrases in your own voice, you are more likely to catch mechanical errors, internal inconsistencies, and grammatical mistakes. Second, your relations with authors will be smoother because they will perceive you as an aide, not as a usurper of their authorial powers. Third, both the copyediting and the cleanup will take less time and be less frustrating. Finally, you will neatly sidestep an issue that often troubles novice copyeditors: "How do I maintain the author's style?" That issue will not arise if you focus on copyediting—not rewriting—and if you explain problems to your authors and ask them either to resolve the problems or to select among the alternatives you are posing.

❖ 2 ❖

Basic Procedures

Every copyeditor needs a system for marking changes to the author's text, a process for querying the author and the editorial coordinator, a method for keeping track of editorial decisions, and procedures for incorporating the author's review of the copyediting into the final manuscript or electronic files. The traditional procedures for marking, querying, recordkeeping, and cleanup were developed in the pre-computer era. Since then, these procedures have been adapted for editing on-screen. In this chapter, we'll look at both methods.

Even if you intend to do all your copyediting on-screen, there are several compelling reasons for learning the traditional hand-marking routines. First, some screening tests for employment and for freelance work are administered in paper-and-pencil form. Second, some authors will use traditional copyediting marks when reviewing the printout of your on-screen copyediting. Third, you will need manual skills to handle

material for which there are no electronic files or for which the author's files prove unusable.

documents that are exchanged by fax, photocopy, or PDF.

projects for authors who request hand-marked manuscript.

copy that has been poured into a sophisticated page-design program. (At advertising firms, for example, copyeditors work on printouts; only the graphic designers work on-screen.)

computer how-to books that entail testing the author's procedural instructions. (Typically, the copyeditor runs the program, or a student exercise DVD on his or her computer and edits the hard-copy manuscript.)

text (callouts, labels, captions) that accompanies maps or other graphics.

documents created in spreadsheet or presentation software programs that do not have a mark-revisions feature that enables the author to spot the copyeditor's proposed changes.

Also, as you'll see, the copyediting exercises in part 2 of this book entail editing on hard copy.

MARKING CHANGES ON HARD COPY

Every mark a copyeditor makes on the hard copy of a manuscript must be intelligible to the author (who must approve the copyediting), the word processor or typesetter (who must key in the handwritten changes), and the proofreader (who will read the proofs against the marked copy). To accommodate the needs of all these parties, copyeditors must work as neatly as they can. In this job, penmanship counts.

Copyeditors working on hard copy write their corrections in the text proper, reserving the margins for queries to the author (see figure 2). The choice of writing implement depends on how the manuscript will be handled after copyediting. If the entire marked-up copy will be sent to a typesetter for rekeying, the copyeditor may use an ordinary lead pencil. However, if the manuscript will be given to a word processor who will key in only the copyeditor's changes, the copyeditor may be asked to use a brightly colored pencil or pen. The bright color helps the word processor spot the changes without having to pore over every line of text.

No two copyeditors use identical markings, but the conventions shown in figure 3 are universally understood by publishing professionals. It's not safe, however, to assume that all authors will know the system. As a courtesy to your author, you can attach a list of symbols to the copyedited manuscript.

Figure 2. Hand-Marked Manuscript

One of the basic axioms of financial planing [n] is that
diversification [can] reduces volatility and risk. Apparently, many
investors agree, for their movement into asset allocation
mutual funds is making this group one of the fastest growing [=]
types of mutual funds.

[Add numbers on rate of growth?]

Asset allocation, though, can mean different things to
different investors as well as [to] different mutual fund
management companies. To survey the field, [I interviewed] fund managers ~~were~~
~~interviewed~~ from seven companies. Among them, a consensus
seems to be developing that an asset allocation fund is an
actively managed portfolio with assets in at least three
categories: U.S [.] stocks, U.S [.] bonds, and cash. Some funds also
invest in foreign stocks, foreign bonds, or precious metals.
Unlike the traditional "balanced funds," which perennially
allocated 50% of their holdings to stocks, 45% to bonds, and
5% to cash, the asset allocation funds continuously adjust
the proportions of asset classes [in their portfolios] to reflect economic
conditions.   [OK?]

[¶] This spring, for example, several of the funds ~~are at~~ [have] record
~~high points~~ [amounts] in cash. Citing unusually high short term interest [=]
rates and a yield cure [curve] that has been flat or ~~in a reverse~~ [inverted]
~~pattern~~ fund managers find cash quite attractive. The yield
curve has also prompted large positions in intermediate term [=]
bonds.

[Indicate what % is in cash?]

Figure 3.   Copyediting Marks

Mark	Name or Meaning	Example
∧	caret	Use a caret to add leters or words. _(t, entire)_
ℓ	delete	Use a delete sign to delete lettﬂers or a few pr words.
◡ or ⌢	close up	An easy way to remove ex⌢tra spá⌢ces.
⌡ or ⌠	delete and close up	Don't ask the typefsetter to guess af bout whether to close up the space.
# or ⊛	space	Sothe words don'trun together. Also used to add linespacing.
		Some copyeditors prefer to use a backslash—or a backslash and a space sign—to indicate a wordspace. Sothe words don'trun together.
∿	transpose	Transpose a lettﬂe or (misplaced) a word.
...	stet	Reinstates deleted material. ~~Also~~ used to mean _as is,_ to annotate an unusual spelling: Gorge Johnson cain't spell.
⟍ ⟎	run in	An easy way to correct typing errors or to delete a paragraph break.
¶ or ⊕	para	¶ Adds a new paragraph. No marking is needed when the text shows a paragraph indent.

(figure 3 continued)

Mark	Name or Meaning	Example

○ spell out

When an editor circles ① or ② numerals or an (abbrev), the ⑤Ⓟ compositor will spell out the circled items.

When an abbreviation is unusual or could be spelled in several ways, the copyeditor should write out the desired term.

Nineteen ninety   National Hockey
~~1990~~ was a good year for the ~~NHL~~ League○

⊙ period

Dr Kim L Jones delivered the report.

Copyeditors circle an inserted period to make it more visible; only handwritten inserted periods should be circled. Circling is also used to convert a typed comma into a period

Dr○ Kim L○ Jones delivered the report.

⌄ comma

Similarly for visibility editors place a roof over handwritten commas.

The roof makes the comma more visible. Do not mark a correctly typed comma; mark only handwritten commas and periods that are to be converted into commas.

She left But he did not.

⌄ apostrophe

Its just a matter of practice.

" " quote marks

You're doing well, she said.

(continued next page)

(figure 3 continued)

Mark	Name or Meaning	Example
⟮ ⟯	parens	⟮Parentheses always come in pairs.⟯
		The cross-hatches clarify that the character is not a *C* or an *l*.
=	hyphen	Copyeditors need to handmark hard end-of-line hyphens.
		Use the hyphen mark only to insert a hyphen or to indicate that a hyphen appearing at the end of a line is to be retained. Other hyphens need not be marked.
N̲	en dash	Used in numerical ranges: pp. 45–47.
		Most word processing programs can print an en dash (–) instead of a hyphen, but not all users take advantage of this feature.
M̲	em dash	Your everyday dash––see?
		Most word processing programs can print an em dash (—), but some users type two hyphens instead.
/	lowercase	To lowercase a letter or a WORD.
≡	capitalize	turns a lowercase letter into a capital.
=	small cap	So that B.C., a.m., P.M. will be set as B.C., A.M., P.M.
∨	superscript	Mark mc2 so that it will be typeset as mc^2.
∧	subscript	Mark O2 so that it will be set as O_2.

(figure 3 continued)

Mark	Name or Meaning	Example
___	italic	Use italics <u>sparingly</u>! Typists used to underline words that were to be set in italics, but now word processing programs can print *italic letters*.
◯	delete italic or bold	Instructs the typesetter to ignore the (underlining,) (printed italics,) or (**boldface type**.)
⌇	bold	The typesetter will set boldface type.
⌐	flush left	⌐Moves text to align at the left margin.
⌐	flush right	Moves text to align at the right margin: Jane L. Jones
⌐ ⌐	center	⌐This line will be centered. ⌐
|	align	Combine 2 cups fresh basil, chopped 1 cup olive oil 2 teaspoons chopped garlic 1 teaspoon salt

Don't worry about memorizing all the symbols in one or two sittings. Keep a list of the symbols on your desk whenever you are copyediting or doing the exercises in this book. It's easier to learn the symbols by using them than by staring at them. In addition to using conventional symbols, you should follow two guidelines:

1. If a word has several errors, cross out the entire word and rewrite it; don't expect others to correctly decode a cryptic string of markings.

Hard to read: Government must respect the

will of the p̶o̶e̶p̶e̶l̶.

Clearer: Government must respect the will

of the ~~poepel~~. (people)

2. When you insert a word or the final letters of a word, write in any punctuation marks that immediately follow.

Not: If you don't write in the

punctuation mark, the typesetter might

miss ~~it~~. (them)

But: If you don't write in the

punctuation mark, the typesetter might

miss ~~it~~. (them)

Copyeditors working on hard copy also mark the location of nonstandard characters, cross-references ("x-refs"), and in-text footnote or endnote numbers. These markings are known as *callouts,* and they are placed in the left margin of the manuscript.

Nitrate levels at the Shenandoah test

sites averaged 0.4µg/m^3 (see figure

36.7), among the highest in the state.[9]

In contrast, sulfate levels at the

Shenandoah test sites were well below

the average statewide readings (see

table 36.4).

MAKING CHANGES ON-SCREEN

The first step in an on-screen project is to copy the files from the author's or publisher's set. Keep the original files in a safe place, and work only on the duplicate files. Beyond the usual value of having the original set as a backup copy, you may also find that you need to consult the unedited original files while you are working on the project. In addition, some methods of generating redlined files—that is, files showing both the author's original text and the copyeditor's insertions and deletions (see figure 4)—require you to have both unedited and edited files. Under this system, the software "compares" the unedited and edited documents and generates the redlined copy as a third, separate document.

Word processing programs allow you to create redlined files as you work by using a mark-revisions feature. (In Microsoft Word, the term is *track changes*.) You can have the redlined text visible on screen at all times, or you can hide the redline markings and display them only when you want to review the changes you have made. If you do not want the author to be distracted by redlining that represents nondiscretionary corrections (e.g., misspellings and simple punctuation or capitalization errors), you can turn off the mark-revisions feature before you run the spellchecker and whenever you make a minor mechanical correction. However, you must have the mark-revisions feature on when you make any editorial intervention that could be vetoed or re-revised by the author.

Each word processing program provides various options for how editorial insertions and deletions are shown on the monitor and on the printout. For example, you can have the insertions shown in red on the screen and with double underlining in the printout; deletions can be shown in blue on the screen and with strikeout hyphens or slashes on the printout.[1] Some publishers supply their on-screen copyeditors with custom macros that set the format for insertions and deletions.

---

1. The reviser's name and the date and time of each revision are also embedded in the file. This information appears on the screen in a "sticky note" when a user allows the mouse to linger on a redlined word or passage. This feature enables all parties to determine who made each change to the document, an advantage when one document is sent to several reviewers in sequence (e.g., a technical expert, a second writer, and a copyeditor). This personal information, or metadata, can be deleted for security or other reasons.

Figure 4.   Redlined Text. In this sample the characters that the copyeditor has deleted are marked with horizontal strikeouts, and the characters that the copyeditor has added are double underlined. Even when color is used to differentiate the deletions and additions from the unchanged original text, both on-screen displays of redlined text and hard-copy printouts of redlined text are difficult to read. Thus copyeditors usually work on a clean display, rather than on the redlined display, and some authors forgo the advantage of reviewing a redlined printout—that is, the opportunity to see exactly what has been changed—for the ease of reading a clean printout.

~~Murphy's Law assures us that n~~<u>N</u>o amount of proofreading ~~will~~ <u>can</u> uncover all the errors in a <u>set of proofs.</u> ~~work about to be published. The question is, how many re-readings are reasonable? In my personal experience I have found that t~~<u>T</u>wo readings of galleys and two <u>readings</u> of page proofs will catch 99 percent of the errors<u>, but</u>~~. Unfortunately~~ the remaining ~~1 percent are often the~~ mistakes—<u>incorrect phone numbers or misspelled names—often cause both</u> ~~that not only cause~~ embarrassment <u>and</u> ~~but~~ trouble. ~~For example, the wrong numbers for ordering merchandise or misspelled names.~~

Your redlined screen display and printout will be more legible if you do not try to "save" part of a word:

Hard-to-read redlining: Th<u>e</u>~~is~~ reiteration~~ve~~ proce~~ss~~<u>dure</u>

Clearer: ~~The reiteration process~~<u>This iterative procedure</u>

You also need to be careful about the wordspacing before and after inserted words. The following markings may look correct on the screen:

It's ~~hard~~<u>difficult</u> to resist the ~~urge~~<u>temptation</u> to ~~improve~~<u>change</u> someone else's writing.

But the printout will read:

It'sdifficult to resist thetemptation tochange someone else's
writing.

Certain kinds of changes do not show up on the printout of a redlined document. For example, if you are using a horizontal line strikeout, a deleted hyphen may not appear to have been deleted because the strikeout mark prints over the hyphen; for clarity's sake, you can delete the entire word and type in the hyphenless form. The deletion or addition of a paragraph break will be visible only as a change in the color of the paragraph mark. To alert the author to such changes, you need to add a query.

Finally, watch what happens in redlined files if you move a portion of text that contains a correction:

Original	*Redlined printout*
Send your comments to	Send your comments to
P.O. Box 1	P.O. Box 1, <u>Anytown CA 94000</u>
Anytown CA 9400	~~Anytown CA 9400~~

Because the change in the zip code falls within a piece of transposed text, the addition of the fifth digit is not highlighted as a correction in and of itself. To call the author's attention to such a change, you must write a query. Note, as well, that when you move a piece of text the redlined version shows two changes: the deletion of the original words and the insertion of those same words. You may wish to warn your authors about this, lest an author scan the redlined version and think that you have made dozens of extra changes.

QUERYING

Often a copyeditor needs to address a question, comment, or explanation to the author. Some questions are so important—they pertain to the entire manuscript or to a large chunk of it—that the copyeditor must raise them with the author before completing the copyediting. In those cases, a phone call, fax, or e-mail is warranted. But other questions, comments, or explanations pertain only to a sentence or paragraph, or to a page or small section of the manuscript. These types of communications are collectively called *queries,* and they will accompany the copyedited manuscript when it is returned to the author for review.

For a copyeditor, good querying skills—knowing when to query (and when not to query) and how to query effectively—are as important as a solid grasp of punctuation and grammar. Query too often, and the author may become frustrated with the amount of time needed to read and respond to all your questions, comments, and explanations. Query too infrequently, and the author may not understand the problem you were trying to fix and may stet the error-laden original text, or the author may not catch a slight change in meaning that you inadvertently introduced, or the author may start to feel that you've taken over the manuscript without so much as a "may I?" Query in a way that confuses or insults the author, and you are unlikely to obtain the cooperation you need to resolve the problem at hand.

When to query.   Not every change in a manuscript requires a query. Copyeditors do not query routine mechanical changes that are not subject to the author's veto or re-revision; thus you need not explain the reason for every added or deleted piece of punctuation or for every lowercasing of a word that the author capitalized. You should, however, call the author's attention to any mechanical changes that may be controversial, and you must query any mechanical revisions that might affect the meaning of the sentence. For example, your author has written

> This directive is addressed to employees in the following departments: order fulfillment, customer service, marketing, media and print advertising.

If house style calls for the final serial comma (that is, the comma preceding *and* or *or* in a list), and you automatically place a comma after "media," you might be cutting the "media and print advertising department" in two. Here, you must ask the author whether the text should read "marketing, and media and print advertising" or "marketing, media, and print advertising."

A copyeditor also need not write a query to explain minor changes in wording or emendations to repair simple grammatical errors. If the grammatical issue is more esoteric or complex, however, it may be worth an explanation so that the author will know that you are fixing a mistake, and not tinkering for the sake of tinkering. For example, if a manuscript is replete with dangling participles, you might write a quick note at the first instance.

Although deciding when to write queries about mechanical and grammatical issues becomes second nature after a while, deciding when to pose substantive queries never becomes wholly routine. Each of the following substantive discrepancies and omissions definitely merits a query:

- Factual inconsistencies within the manuscript. For example, if the population statistics on page 5 do not match those on page 18, write a brief, polite query: "Population 17,000 on p. 5, but 12,500 on p. 18. Please reconcile."
- Points of fact about which you are certain that the manuscript is incorrect.
- Inconsistencies between the evidence presented and the author's interpretation of that evidence. For example, suppose your author writes: "Mean test scores for sophomores in the Artview district have risen steadily in the past ten years (see table 1)." You should look at table 1 to be sure that it shows the mean test scores for sophomores in the Artview district for each of the past ten years and that the mean score did rise each year.
- Inconsistencies between the manuscript and the accompanying diagrams, figures, or photographs.
- Incomplete or missing source notes, footnotes or endnotes, or bibliographical items. Sources should be given for all direct quotations other than proverbs, extremely familiar phrases, and literary allusions ("To be or not to be"). Sources should also be provided for facts outside the realm of common knowledge.

In deciding whether to pose a substantive query on issues other than these, you need first of all to consider the intended readers: Will readers be confused, frustrated, or misled by a sentence or passage that bothers you? Next, you need to think about the author and how much additional work you can reasonably expect the author to do at this stage of publication. Every request you make—no matter how polite—places demands on an author's time and patience. For some authors, an accumulation of requests—no matter how small—may be so upsetting that halfway through the manuscript they stop looking at the queries or become so demoralized that they miss their deadline for returning the manuscript. You should also think about the budget and schedule for the publication: Is there enough time for the author to respond to all the queries, for those answers to be reviewed, and for the author's additions to be copyedited?

Length of queries.   Sometimes, a query can be as simple as "OK?" Other times, you will need to write a longer query: an explanation of a proposed revision, a suggestion that the author clarify an ambiguous sentence, a request for the author to choose among alternative rewordings.

The best queries are succinct but still polite and specific. When queries are too brief or cryptic (e.g., "Logic?"), authors may not understand what the problem is, or authors may feel they are being chastised or attacked. Either way—whether you confuse the author's mind or hurt the author's feelings— the results will be counterproductive, and you will not get the information you asked for.

When queries are overly long and discursive, in contrast, authors may resent the imposition on their time. You might guess that it will take the author less than a minute to read the query and respond, but consider what happens when author Jack is trying to be conscientious in responding to copyeditor Jill's queries: First, Jack reads (and perhaps rereads) the query. Then he looks at the troublesome spot in the manuscript. Even though Jill's query concerns one sentence, Jack backs up and reads one or two paragraphs before the trou- blesome sentence and continues to read a paragraph or two past it. Next, he starts to consider the merits of Jill's query: Is Jill correct, or has she misun- derstood the text or misgauged the audience? This question prompts another rereading of a page or two of the manuscript and another rereading of the query. If Jack concludes that Jill's point is valid, then the time spent reach- ing that decision and the time to be devoted to revising the manuscript will be chalked up as time well spent. But if Jack concludes that Jill's query is irrel- evant or extraneous, he will harrumph (or worse) at having had to go to such lengths so that he could, in good conscience, stet his original sentence.

Think twice about queries that pose a substantive question and invite a yes or no answer. For example, the query "Could you add a sentence to explain what you mean by 'political correctness'?" meets the tests of succinctness, politeness, and specificity. In response to such a query, however, the author could simply scrawl NO. If that would be an acceptable response, then the phrasing of the query is fine. But if you believe that adding the explanation is essential to the readers' understanding of the document, then you will want to phrase your query in a way that helps the author understand the importance of providing the requested explanation. And so you might write: "Because 'political correctness' has become a Rorschach blot onto which everyone projects a personal meaning, readers will want to know what the term means here. Please add a sentence or two to define." Of course, the author is always free to ignore your requests, but this kind of query is harder to shrug off.

Tone of queries. Queries should never be sarcastic, snide, or argumentative, and queries should never have the tone of a schoolteacher lecturing a recalcitrant student, or a police officer interrogating a suspect. Above all, queries should not sound as though you might be challenging the author's expertise or intellectual ability. Queries are not the place for complaints or rebukes; use them to pose a problem and elicit the author's help in resolving it.

Here are some examples of do's and don'ts:

Instead of	*Write*
Fix these numbers.	Please reconcile.
Where's the referent for "this"?	"this" = the budget or the meeting?
"Picasso's portrait" is unclear.	"Picasso's portrait" could mean "the portrait of Picasso" or "the portrait by Picasso." Change?
Sometimes you say "pull-down menu," sometimes "drop-down menu." Please be consistent.	If "pull-down menu" and "drop-down menu" are equivalent, let's use the same term throughout this section. Which do you prefer?
You never explain how oil prices affected ordinary people.	Will readers follow the sequence here, or would it help them if you explain how soaring oil prices affected the cost of living?
Faulty transition; I don't see how this follows.	Will readers understand how this paragraph relates to the one preceding?

Instead of	*Write*
This example doesn't really illustrate the point; delete OK?	This example is striking, but it doesn't precisely match the principle. Move it to p. 145 (or delete it?) and supply a stronger example here? Or revise the example for a better fit here?
I don't find this convincing.	Will readers trained in structural analysis accept this conclusion as stated?
Surely, you can't mean this!	Is this "not" a typographical error (perhaps for "now")? Otherwise, this sentence doesn't seem to follow from what has preceded.
Your use of "he" throughout this section implies that all freight expediters are men. Certainly, that is no longer the case. In contemporary usage, the so-called generic he is inadequate. So I rewrote all the sexist sentences.	Scattered revisions to avoid gender bias. OK? Or please re-revise.

As several of the preceding examples illustrate, it is best to phrase a query in terms of what readers need, want, or expect. Queries worded in this way serve to remind the author that the primary purpose of a publication is to inform, persuade, or entertain and delight readers, and that all editorial decisions should be made with the readers' interests at heart. Also, the "readers first" wording can help you sidestep a potential author-copyeditor battle; instead, you and the author become a team working together for the good of the readers. In contrast, your "I don't get this" may provoke an author to mutter a nasty comment about your woeful lack of intelligence rather than to rewrite the confusing passage.

If you find yourself becoming annoyed with the author ("Didn't this guy

even reread what he wrote?" "How could she be so careless about her work?"),
do not write queries until your mood has improved. It helps to remember that
the author did not set out to make your life miserable by purposely mistyp-
ing or misspelling dozens of words, that the author may be working under
personal or professional constraints unknown to you, and—finally—that if
all authors were careful, diligent, and highly skilled, you would be out of work.

Another approach to query writing is to treat the manuscript, no matter
how poorly written or prepared, as though it were the author's ugly newborn.
That is, no matter how ugly you may think the baby is, you would never say
so to the new mother or father; no—surely, you would find something polite
to say. You don't have to coo over a manuscript, but you should remember
that it is the product of the author's labor and sweat, hopes and dreams, and
that you are being granted the privilege (along with the frustration) of par-
ticipating in its publication.

PROCEDURES FOR QUERYING ON HARD COPY

A pencil-and-paper copyeditor should ask the editorial coordinator about
the publisher's preferred method for queries:

- If the manuscript has generous margins and the queries are
  brief, the copyeditor can write *bubble queries* on the manuscript
  (as shown in figure 2). The advantage of this method is that the
  copyedited manuscript along with all of the queries can be photo-
  copied easily.
- Longer comments or questions can be placed on *flags* (also called
  query slips or *query tags*)—small gummed slips of paper that one
  attaches to the manuscript. The drawback of a flagged manuscript, however, is that it is time consuming to photocopy.
- Comments and questions can be placed on self-adhering notes
  (also known as Post-its or "sticky notes"), but these tend to fall
  off in transit and also pose difficulties in photocopying. These
  notes should always include the manuscript page number (and
  even the paragraph number) in the corner.
- Comments and questions (keyed to the manuscript by page
  number and paragraph) can be placed on separate pieces of
  paper interleaved with the manuscript or can be incorporated
  into a cover letter to the author.

Figure 5.   Bubble Queries in a Microsoft Word File. In Microsoft Word, copy-editors can write their queries as comments. The comments are automatically numbered and include the commenter's initials. Copyeditors and authors may each choose how they prefer to display the comments: as marginal bubble queries (as shown in this figure) or in a reviewing pane, a list that appears in a vertical split screen (alongside the document) or in a horizontal split screen (below the document).

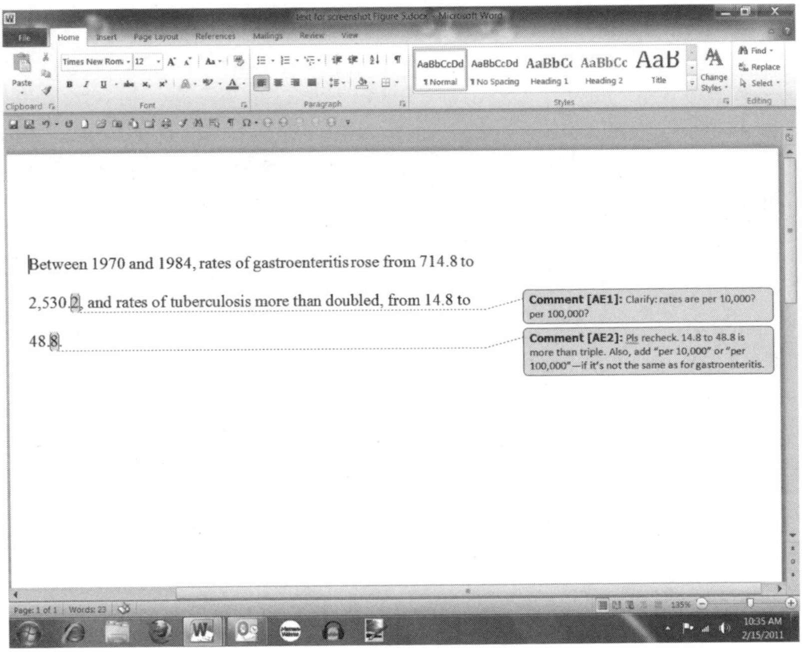

PROCEDURES FOR QUERYING ON-SCREEN

On-screen copyeditors have three choices for writing their queries:

- If the author will be reviewing the copyediting on screen, you can use the comment feature (see figure 5).
- You can use the footnote feature to place your queries in bottom-of-the page notes. If the manuscript itself contains numbered footnotes, you can use uppercase letters or nonalphabetical

characters (e.g., asterisks) to identify the query footnotes and reserve numerals for the author's footnotes.

- You can place your queries within braces in the text proper. Using
braces, rather than parentheses or brackets, which the author may
have used in the manuscript, will allow you or another editor to
search for all the queries during cleanup and remove them from
the file. To draw the author's attention to the queries, you can
make them boldface or use the color highlighting tool:

> Between 1970 and 1984, rates of gastroenteritis rose from
> 714.8 to 2,530.2, {**Clarify: 714.8 per 10,000? per 100,000?**}
> and rates of tuberculosis more than doubled, from 14.8 to
> 48.8. {**Pls recheck, 14.8 to 48.8 is more than triple. Also,
> add "per 10,000" or "per 100,000"—if it's not the same as
> for gastroenteritis**}

Although such in-text queries must be easy to spot, don't overdo
the typographical emphasis. If you type your queries in all caps,
for example, some authors will feel that you are screaming at
them. One disadvantage of this method is that it interferes with
the word count for the document.

Again, a copyeditor should ask the editorial coordinator which method is preferred. Some publishers provide copyeditors with custom macros that include
an insert-query feature.

STYLE SHEETS

For any copyediting project longer than a few pages, you will want to keep a
style sheet. If you are working for a publisher, the editorial coordinator will
give you a blank style sheet (either a hard-copy form or a file containing an
on-screen form). If you are working on your own, create a blank form based
on the sample shown in figure 6.

Figure 6.   A Copyeditor's Style Sheet

Author/Title   Smith, Big Book
Copyeditor   Amy Einsohn
Date   9/9/99

Special symbols
   European diacritics (é, è, ñ, etc.)

Permissions/credits needed
   4 lines of poetry by D. Terrell (MS p. 85)
   diagram from P. Ricardo (MS p. 172)

Tables, figures, captions
   Table 1. Title in Headline Style
   Figure 1. Artist, *Title of Work* (Museum)

Dates and numbers
   3 January 1996
   1955–1982 (en dash, repeat all digits)
   see pp. 123–125 (en dash, repeat all digits)
   see chapter 2, table 1, figure 4

Miscellaneous notes
   downstyle capitalization

page 1 of 4

Special symbols. Indicate special characters that appear in the manuscript: diacritic marks, foreign language characters, mathematical signs, and musical or scientific notation.

Permissions/credits needed. Indicate pages in the manuscript that contain long quotations of prose (more than 250 words from any source); quotations of song lyrics or poetry; and tables, charts, or photographs that are not the author's work. These notations will remind the author to request written permission from the copyright holder to reproduce the material.

Tables, figures, captions. Give examples of the punctuation and capitalization of the titles for tables and figures.

Dates and numbers. Record decisions about spelled-out numbers and the use of numerals for dates, ranges, sums of money, and cross-references to chapters.

Miscellaneous notes. This copyeditor noted the use of "downstyle" capitalization (see chapter 6).

(figure 6 continued)

Footnotes

P. Small, *Book Title* (City: Publisher, 1995), 36.

Q. Small, "Article Title," *Journal* 3 (1998): 23.

Bibliography

Small, Pablo. *Book Title.* City: Publisher, 1995.

Small, Quentin. "Article Title." *Journal* 3 (1998): 21–30.

Punctuation

serial comma (a, b, and c)
possessives: Erasmus's concepts
    but Moses' leadership

Abbreviations and acronyms

U.S.   U.N.
all other acronyms without periods: NATO, AFL-CIO

Spell out e.g., i.e., etc. (for example, that is, and so forth)

page 2 of 4

Footnotes. Provide samples of the format used in the footnotes.

Bibliography. Provide samples of the format for bibliographical entries.

Punctuation. Indicate whether the serial comma is to be used in this manuscript (see chapter 4). Give examples of the possessive form for proper names ending in *s* (see chapter 5).

Abbreviations and acronyms. Provide a sample of the abbreviations and acronyms that appear in the manuscript, and indicate whether each is to take periods or not.

(continued next page)

(figure 6 continued)

A
ad hoc (roman)
aide-de-camp
anti- compounds closed
    (antihistamine) *except*
    anti-aircraft
    anti-intellectual
    anti-utopian

B
BASIC (computer language)
the Bay Area (California)
Bible (roman)
booby-trap (v)
booby trap (n)
braille (lc)
breakdown (n)
break-in (n)

C
Capitol Hill
catalog
childcare (n)
coauthor
coordinate
co-opt
co-workers
Cubism, Cubists
curriculums (pl)

D
data (pl noun)
daycare (n)
decision makers
decision making (n)
decision-making (a)

E
early-twentieth-century (a)
engagé (rom)
entrepôt
ex officio members (rom)
ex parte conversation (rom)

F
federal government (lc)
firsthand (a)
focused (*not* focussed)
foreign exchange rates
foreign language dictionary
Forest v. *Doe* (court case)

G
glasnost (rom)
grade 3
gray (*not* grey)
the Great Depression
Great Society programs
great-grandparents

H
half-life (n)
halfway
homeowners association
houseboat
house rules

I-J-K
in-house position
inpatient (n, a)
interagency
IQs (pl)

page 3 of 4

Alphabetical ("alpha") list.
Enter choices about spelling,
plurals, hyphenation,
capitalization, and italics.
For example, choices
between

ad hoc	*ad hoc*
catalogue	catalog
coauthor	co-author
curriculums	curricula
day-care	daycare

Copyeditors often use the
following abbreviations in
the alpha list:

a = adjective
pa = predicate adjective*
n = noun
v = verb

s =singular
pl = plural

lc = lowercase
UC = uppercase

rom = roman type
ital = italic type

* Predicate adjectives are
those that follow the noun
(e.g., the play was well
received). For more ex-
amples, see the Glossary
of Grammar Terms, s.v.
"predicate adjective."

(figure 6 continued)

L
large-scale (a)
the Left Bank (Paris)
life cycle (n)
living room furniture

M
macroeconomic
mea culpa (rom)
microdot
microeconomic
Middle Ages
middle-aged (a)
middle-class (a)
millenniums (pl)
mind-set (n)
multitasking

N-O
New Year's Day
Ninth Ward
non- compounds closed:
    noncompliance
    nonnative fluency
    but non-English-speaking (a)
the North Atlantic states
online (a, pa)
outpatient (a, n)

P
PC-compatible (a)
pre-computer era
preenrollment
pretest
Purple Heart

Q-R
Ramadan
reelection
résumé

S
self- compounds hyphenated:
    self-important
    self-sustaining
Sesame Street
socioeconomic
the South (US region)
the Southwest (US region)
the Sun Belt (US region)
systemwide

T
t test
transatlantic
traveler (*not* traveller)

U-V
upper-middle-class (a)
the *Upton* case (court case)
v. (roman, in court cases)

W-Z
well-received (a)
well received (pa)
word processing (n)
word processing (a)
x-axis
y-axis
zlotys (pl)

page 4 of 4

As you copyedit, you must stop every time you make a choice or decision about a mechanical issue (spelling, capitalization, use of numbers, abbreviations, hyphenation) and enter that decision on your style sheet. As you continue to work your way through the manuscript, these entries will remind you of the choices you have made and will thus help you enforce mechanical consistency. And when the author's corrections and revisions to the copyedited manuscript arrive on your desk several weeks after you have moved on to another project, you will find yourself repeatedly consulting your style sheet in order to make sure that the author's additions to the text follow the editorial style of the copyedited manuscript. Your completed style sheet will also be used as a reference by the designer, typesetter, proofreader, and indexer whenever a question of mechanics arises during production.

To serve all these purposes, your style sheet should have an entry for each of the decisions and choices you have made. Do not stop to make an entry for every word that the author misspelled or mistyped; enter only those items that require a decision of some sort. For example, if you were copyediting the following sentence, you would correct the errors, but you would not make any entries on your style sheet:

```
The technical writer is solely
responsible for the factual accuracy
of the manuscript, but the editor is
expected to call the writers attention to
any internal disrepances.
```

In contrast, the following sentence doesn't require any corrections:

In 1980 the National Radio Astronomy Observatory (NRAO) completed the Very Large Array, a collection of twenty-seven portable antennas arranged in a Y-shape.

But this one sentence requires four entries on your style sheet:

NRAO (no internal periods)

the Very Large Array (caps, proper name of project)

antennas (plural, *not* antennae)

Y-shape (noun)[2]

Some terms require more than one entry on the style sheet. For example, the style sheet in figure 6 has one entry for the verb *booby-trap* and a second entry for the noun *booby trap*. Two entries are needed because the verb and the noun receive different editorial treatment. Similarly, the style sheet contains one entry to indicate that the noun *decision making* is not hyphenated and a second entry to indicate that this compound is hyphenated when used as an adjective (as in "decision-making skills"). There are also two entries for *well received* because this adjective is hyphenated when it precedes a noun ("a well-received proposal") but not when it follows a noun ("the proposal was well received"). When the same editorial treatment applies to more than one part of speech, the entry includes a notation for each (see the entries for *inpatient, online,* and *outpatient*).

For each entry, you can also indicate the page on which the term first appears. These notations can be helpful if you have to go back and change something.

ON-SCREEN STYLE SHEETS

When you are copyediting on-screen, the easiest way to compile a style sheet is to have a style sheet document open as you edit. Whenever you come upon an item that belongs on your style sheet, you can copy-and-paste the term from the manuscript to the style sheet. When you're done copyediting, you can use the sort feature to alphabetize the items in your alpha list. There's no need to keep track of page numbers, since you can use the global search feature to locate all mentions of a term.

You can also use the search feature to help you decide how to handle a particular item. For example, early in the manuscript you are puzzled by the author's having capitalized a particular term. You can immediately search

---

2. A serif or a sans serif typeface may be used for a letter that indicates a shape:

serif typeface: a V-shaped valley, an A-frame house, an S curve

sans serif typeface: a V-shaped valley, an A-frame house, an S curve

When the publisher's house style calls for sans serif, a copyeditor's style sheet entry would read: Y-shaped (sans serif "Y"). Most publishers, however, view the sans serif font as overly fussy unless the topic is visual acuity ("Three of the children tested could not distinguish a W from a W").

the manuscript to locate all the instances of the term and see whether the author has been consistent (indicating a definite preference) or not (indicating the author may not care about the term).

CLEANUP

PROCEDURES FOR HARD-COPY CLEANUP

For paper-and-pencil copyedits, the author is sent the marked manuscript, a copy of the style sheet, and a set of instructions for responding to queries, adding and deleting text, and restoring text that the copyeditor marked for deletion. Such instructions might read:

> *Copyeditor's queries.* Please be sure to answer all the queries. Often an "OK" or a check mark is all that is needed.
>
> *Additions.* Write any small changes on the manuscript in a color other than that used by the copyeditor; these changes must be readily visible and legible. To add a block of text, clip the newly typed passage to the manuscript page and indicate where the insert belongs: "Insert A (attached) goes here."
>
> *Deletions.* Do not erase or white out anything on the manuscript. If you want to delete text that the copyeditor has added, cross the words out. (Again, please use a color other than that used by the copyeditor.)
>
> *Restorations.* Use "stet" and a set of dots to indicate deleted copy that you wish to restore:

```
This masterly forgery passed unnoticed

until the  v̶e̶r̶y̶  end of the century.      (stet)
              · · ·
```

For the author's convenience, these instructions should be accompanied by a handout that explains the meaning of the copyediting symbols and the function of the style sheet.

During cleanup, the copyeditor scans each page of the manuscript to ensure that the author has not introduced mechanical errors into the manuscript by means of insertions, deletions, or restorations. Moving page by page, the copyeditor makes sure that

- Inserted and restored text follow the spelling, capitalization, and other mechanical preferences shown on the style sheet.
- All insertions and restorations are legible, and the location of every insertion is clear.
- The sequential numbering of footnotes, tables, figures, and other enumerated elements remains correct even after the author has added, deleted, or restored items.
- All cross-references to numbered items are correct.
- Additions to alphabetized lists are properly placed.

Cleanup also entails incorporating the author's responses to the copyeditor's queries. Any queries overlooked by the author should be re-posed and resolved.

Copyeditors should correct any nondiscretionary mechanical errors that they observe while cleaning up the manuscript. But the approval of the author must be sought for any other proposed changes at this stage.

PROCEDURES FOR ON-SCREEN CLEANUP

For on-screen copyedits, the author is sent either (1) *a redlined printout*[3] of the copyedited manuscript—that is, a printout showing the author's original text and the copyeditor's additions and deletions; or (2) a redlined printout and a *clean printout,* which shows how the manuscript would read if the author were to accept all of the copyeditor's changes; or (3) a printout (either redlined or clean) and a set of the copyedited files.

If files are sent to the author, one of three procedures should be used to prevent the author from silently incorporating changes into the edited files. One method is to lock (password-protect) the files so that no changes can be made to them and ask the author to write all additions and corrections on the accompanying hard copy. The second option is to password-protect the document for revisions; this type of protection allows the author to enter changes in the files, but these changes will appear on-screen as redlined copy in a color scheme other than the one used by the copyeditor. A third option is to password-protect the files for revisions and instruct the author to cast all revisions as comments or footnotes—but not to make any changes in the body of the text proper.

---

3. Some organizations save time, postage, and paper by sending authors PDFs instead of printouts. An author can then choose to review the document on-screen or to print a hard copy.

Incorporating the author's hard-copy corrections.   When the author supplies a hand-marked printout, the copyeditor must review the author's insertions, deletions, and restorations and transfer them to the files. The substantive issues are the same as those for cleaning up a hard-copy manuscript, but extra care must be taken in proofreading the new input, and it is prudent to run the spellchecker one final time, after all the changes have been entered. In addition, you need to be certain that no redlining marks or queries remain in the final files.

Incorporating the author's on-screen corrections.   The procedures for cleaning up on-screen corrections depend on the system that the copyeditor has used for querying and the author has used for responding. All changes requested by the author must be reviewed for mechanical correctness, and all traces of the editing process—annotations, queries, and redlining marks—must be deleted from the files.

❖ 3 ❖

Reference Books and Resources

The content of your reference collection will depend on the types of material you copyedit, but there are four books (or their digital equivalents) that should always be at your fingertips when you are copyediting: a dictionary, a copy of the publisher's preferred style manual, a thesaurus, and a usage guide. In this chapter we'll look at these basic reference works and then at various types of specialized resources and tools.

FOUR ESSENTIAL BOOKS

DICTIONARIES

A copyeditor must have a recent edition of a good dictionary—and must always keep this volume within easy reach. The most popular dictionaries are *Merriam-Webster's Collegiate, American Heritage College, Random House Webster's College,* and *Webster's New World.* In the publishing industry, these are called college (or collegiate) dictionaries; they are hardbound, roughly seven-by-ten inches, and about a thousand pages. A paperback dictionary simply won't do for copyediting. Nor can you depend on the dictionary that you received for high school or college graduation unless you are a recent graduate. Hundreds of words enter the language each year, and preferences regarding spelling, hyphenation, plurals, and other issues change from edition to edition.

For editors in corporate communications, one of the collegiate dictionaries is usually sufficient. But copyeditors working for book and journal publishers must also have access to an unabridged dictionary. *Webster's Third New International, Random House Unabridged,* and *American Heritage Dictionary of the English Language* are the three choices from American publishers. You don't have to have one of these twelve-pound monsters on your desk or bookshelf, but you should know where you can find one (public library, office reference room, website) when the need arises. The most comprehensive unabridged English dictionary is the twenty-volume *Oxford English Dictionary* (*OED*), which is also available in a two-volume photoreduced compact edition (packaged with the requisite magnifying lens), in several abridged one- and two-volume versions, and online by subscription. The *OED* has far more words and examples of historical usage than any of the American unabridged dictionaries, but watch out for British spellings.

The Internet offers access to general and specialized dictionaries in English and in foreign languages. A free online dictionary may be your only resource for the newest high-tech terms and other words that have not made their way into print or online-subscription dictionaries. For standard words, though, the entries in the free dictionaries tend to be skimpy.

Whichever dictionary you use, don't think of it just as a spelling list with definitions. Dictionaries also contain

> irregular forms (i.e., irregular plurals for nouns, past tenses and
>   past participles for verbs, comparative and superlative forms
>   for adjectives and adverbs)
> guidelines on capitalization, hyphenation, syllabication, and
>   pronunciation
> functional labels (parts of speech)
> usage notes, usage examples, and synonyms
> scientific (Latin) names for plants and animals
> spelled-out forms of common acronyms, abbreviations, signs,
>   and symbols
> biographical information for well-known people
> geographical information (location, population) for major cities
>   and countries
> translations of foreign words and phrases commonly used in English
> lists of common and scientific abbreviations and symbols

STYLE MANUALS

Next, a copyeditor needs a style manual. Among U.S. book publishers, the most widely used style manual is *The Chicago Manual of Style*. Another well-respected general-purpose style manual is *Words into Type,* which covers much the same material as *Chicago* and also includes helpful sections on grammar, usage, and spelling. The popularity of *Words into Type*, however, has suffered because the publisher has not brought out a new edition since 1974. *The New York Public Library Writer's Guide to Style and Usage* offers extensive discussions of usage and grammar as well as editorial style. This book is likely to make its mark in corporate publications departments; trade book publishers and scholarly presses are unlikely to surrender their *Chicago*s and *Words into Type*s.

If you are new to publishing and have never looked at an editorial style manual, either *Chicago* or *Words into Type* is the place to start. Both books are quite overwhelming because they include many topics not of direct concern to copyeditors (e.g., design, typography, composition, paper, and binding) as well as extremely detailed discussions of topics that are of direct concern to copyeditors. Take heart, however, in knowing that you are not expected to memorize every paragraph of the sections in your manual that treat editorial style. You need to read your manual carefully enough to learn the basic rules and conventions—the mechanical points that will arise whenever you copyedit. After all, when you are working on a manuscript, you can't stop at every comma, colon, and semicolon to consult your manual on the common uses of these punctuation marks. Rest assured, though, that even experienced copyeditors pause to check their style manual when they hit a thorny punctuation question.

You also need to read your style manual carefully enough to gain a sense of the kinds of esoteric issues that may arise from time to time in your work. For example, you don't have to remember whether your manual expresses a preference for "Ice Age" or "ice age." But after studying your manual over a period of several weeks, you should remember that, by convention, the names of some geological terms are capitalized. Then, if you come across "Ice Age" or "ice age" in a manuscript, you'll know that you need to pick up your manual, turn to the index, and locate the paragraphs that treat the capitalization of scientific terms.

Some people in corporate communications dismiss *Chicago* and *Words into Type* as overly pedantic and fussy.[1] But no other reference works cover such

---

1. Some of these departments rely on *The Gregg Reference Manual* or on one of various manuals published by Merriam-Webster. None of these books, however, is comprehensive enough for copyeditors working in scholarly or trade publishing.

a wide array of mechanical issues. Rather than ignore *Chicago* and *Words into Type*, corporate copyeditors can use these books strategically, as resources that can be followed, adapted, or ignored on a given point.

The other major style manuals are more specialized and used only by certain types of publishers and writers:

American Medical Association Manual of Style. Referred to as "AMA style" and used by medical journals and medical publishers.

Associated Press Stylebook. Referred to as "AP style" and used by many newspapers and some magazines.

MLA Style Manual and Guide to Scholarly Publishing. Referred to as "MLA style" (the acronym stands for Modern Language Association) and used by many writers in the humanities.

Publication Manual of the American Psychological Association. Referred to as "APA style" and used by many social scientists.

Scientific Style and Format: The CSE Manual for Authors, Editors, and Publishers. Referred to as "CSE style," after its publisher, the Council of Science Editors; used by writers working in biology, chemistry, physics, medicine, mathematics, earth sciences, and the social sciences.

United States Government Printing Office Style Manual. Referred to as "GPO style" and used by many government agencies and also by private sector businesses.

Your public library probably has copies of at least some of these books in its noncirculating reference section.

THESAURUSES

Most of the newer thesauruses arrange the main entries in alphabetical order; a few still follow Roget's nineteenth-century schema of categories. Pick any one you like. The best-sellers in this category include *Merriam-Webster's Dictionary of Synonyms, Random House Webster's College Thesaurus,* Rodale's *Synonym Finder,* and *Roget's International Thesaurus.* Most of these thesauruses are also published in digital format. If you are working on-screen, your word processing program probably includes a thesaurus feature, but the range of synonyms generated by these subprograms tends to be quite limited.

USAGE GUIDES

The best usage guide by far is *Merriam-Webster's Dictionary of English Usage*, a thousand pages of short articles, from "a, an" to "zoom." Each entry includes comments from the so-called language experts, examples from respected writers, and a good dose of commonsense advice.

You should also be aware of five usage guides, listed here from oldest to newest, which are so well known that they are often referred to simply by their author's surname:

> Henry Fowler, *Dictionary of Modern English Usage* (2d ed., rev.
> Ernest Gowers)
> Theodore Bernstein, *The Careful Writer: A Modern Guide to
> English Usage*
> Wilson Follett, *Modern American Usage: A Guide*
> R. W. Burchfield, *Fowler's Modern English Usage* (3d ed.)
> Bryan Garner, *Garner's Modern American Usage* (3d ed.)

On most issues, Fowler, Follett, and Garner tend to take a conservative position. Some of their strictures seem overly formal or dated. In the language wars (see pp. 335–39), they are known as "prescriptivists" (as in "prescribing what one ought to do"). In contrast, Bernstein and Burchfield lean more toward the "descriptivist" pole. They seem less interested in fault-finding and hair-splitting and more fascinated by examples of the variety of ways in which well-educated writers use, reinvent, and reinvigorate the language.

Another wrinkle: The "English" in Fowler's title refers to British English; the "English" in Bernstein's title refers to American English; and Burchfield's "English" covers British English, American English, and the differences between the two.

Also of interest is Theodore Bernstein's *Miss Thistlebottom's Hobgoblins: The Careful Writer's Guide to the Taboos, Bugbears, and Outmoded Rules of English Usage*, an effort "to lay to rest the superstitions that have been passed on from one generation to the next by teachers, by editors and by writers— prohibitions deriving from mere personal prejudice or from misguided pedantry or from a cold conservatism that would freeze the language if it could" (p. xi). Although many of the superstitions persist, the book has been successful enough that both Miss Thistlebottom (the archetypal archconservative English teacher) and hobgoblins routinely enter into conversations on editorial matters.

ON THE BOOKSHELF

GRAMMAR HANDBOOKS

The usage guides mentioned above discuss only controversial or difficult points. For a more general review of English grammar and usage, you might want to look at

> Edward D. Johnson, *The Handbook of Good English*
> *Words into Type,* parts V and VI (pp. 339–488)
> *The New Webster's Grammar Guide,* edited by Madeline
>   Semmelmeyer and Donald O. Bolander
> Margaret Shertzer, *The Elements of Grammar*

None of these is as complete as one might wish, but they will answer most of your questions. For a more comprehensive conceptual treatment of English grammar, you might explore

> Rodney Huddleston and Geoffrey K. Pullum, *A Student's Introduction*
>   *to English Grammar*
> Sidney Greenbaum and Randolph Quirk, *A Student's Grammar of*
>   *the English Language*

If you are not deterred by the look and feel of the newer college-level English handbooks (I find them too heavy on the color graphics, too light on the finer points, and mind-numbingly dull), there are at least a dozen to choose from.

You might also enjoy some of the more light-hearted books on grammar such as Bill Walsh's *Lapsing into a Comma* or *The Elephants of Style,* and Constance Hale's *Sin and Syntax.*

GUIDES FOR NEWCOMERS TO PUBLISHING

To learn more about traditional book publishing, from acquisitions to bound books, you might start by reading the chapters of *Chicago* that discuss how manuscripts are prepared, edited, designed, and manufactured. Marshall Lee's *Bookmaking: Editing, Design, Production* covers similar topics in greater detail.

One Book/Five Ways: The Publishing Procedures of Five University Presses documents an experiment in the late 1970s: A manuscript on house plants went through the prepublication process (acquisition, copyediting, production, design, marketing) at five university presses. The manuscript's odyssey is reproduced in the form of copies of all the in-house reports and correspondence. Because the experiment was conducted so long ago, the production processes are obsolete, but here is the rare opportunity to see substantial samples of how five experienced copyeditors handled the same manuscript pages.

Five books written by and for editors provide thoughtful discussions of the craft and practice. Edward Johnson worked in New York trade publishing houses for decades, and his *Handbook of Good English,* mentioned earlier as a grammar guide, discusses punctuation (over thirty pages on the comma alone!), diction, and other mechanical issues. Having worked on so many manuscripts, Johnson is exquisitely alert to the slightest nuance of each syllable and mark on the page. One drawback is that the book concludes with a lengthy, hard-to-use "Glossary/Index," rather than a traditional index.

Carole Fisher Saller's *The Subversive Copy Editor* also comes directly from the trenches. Saller, an in-house manuscript editor at the University of Chicago Press, has written with great care, tact, and humor about the day-to-day responsibilities and self-defeating perfectionism of an editor of scholarly books. Dealing with difficult authors, organizing streams of e-mail and computer files, bending rules and mending fences—Saller does it all, and tells you how to be a more productive and (dare I say it?) happier copyeditor.

As I noted in chapter 1, copyeditors are not expected to reorganize a manuscript. Scott Norton's *Developmental Editing,* however, deftly illustrates how many different ways a nonfiction book, chapter, or article may be structured. Norton's repertoire will help you formulate better queries and suggestions for authors who seem to have lost their way. (Norton will also inspire some of you to move into developmental editing.)

Jack M. Lyon's *Microsoft Word for Publishing Professionals* also benefits from being written by a practitioner specifically for editors. Lyon's mission is to teach you how to customize and turbocharge your version of Microsoft Word by using macros, personal toolbars, and wildcard search-and-replace routines to automate repetitive tasks. He is also the proprietor of Editorium .com, mentioned later in this chapter.

Judith A. Tarutz's *Technical Editing: The Practical Guide for Editors and Writers* is chock-full of copyediting examples, exercises, and advice about teamwork, picking your battles, and setting priorities. Many readers would welcome a revised edition that would speak to the newer technologies in publishing.

For an author's view of the problems caused by overly zealous copyeditors, read Jacques Barzun's "Behind the Blue Pencil: Censorship or Creeping Creativity?" If you can bear his scorn for the "laborious mole" whose "gratuitous tampering . . . knows no bounds," you will receive an excellent lesson in editorial restraint and judgment. To put yourself in a better humor, turn to William Bridgwater's essay "Copyediting."[2] After you pardon his use of the generic *he* (the essay was written in 1962), savor the amusing hyperbole of his concluding paragraph: "The professional copy editor, who sits at his desk with a manuscript planted squarely before him, is not superhuman. He is a humble man in a more or less humble job. Yet upon his shoulders lies the weight of centuries of learning. . . . The little marks he puts on paper are for the betterment of mankind."

GUIDES TO EFFECTIVE EXPOSITORY WRITING

Copyeditors are not expected to be skilled rewriters; indeed, heavy-handed copyeditors run into trouble when they take it upon themselves to rewrite a text rather than copyedit it. A copyeditor should, however, have some sense of what constitutes competent expository writing. It goes without saying that such writing is grammatically correct and that clarity, coherency, and conciseness are always valued. Beyond that, the characteristics of competent writing vary by field, purpose, and audience. Different standards apply to a journal article on biomedical technology, a monograph on metaphysics, a cookbook, an engineer's manual, and a history textbook for elementary school students.

One way to acquire a sense of the standards for a particular type of writing is to read and analyze excellent examples. If you intend to work primarily in one field, that approach would be reasonable. But if you aspire to be a jack or jill of all trades, you may want to begin by looking at some general guides for nonspecialized writers.

Many people swear by William Strunk Jr. and E. B. White's *Elements of*

2. Bridgewater's essay appears in *Editors on Editing: An Inside View of What Editors Really Do,* rev. ed., edited by Gerald Gross (New York: Harper & Row, 1985), pp. 68–88. The 1985 edition, now out of print, is superseded by *Editors on Editing: What Writers Need to Know About What Editors Do,* 3d ed., edited by Gerald Gross (New York: Grove Press, 1993); essays in this volume discuss the responsibilities and activities of various in-house book editors (e.g., editors in chief, acquisitions editors, and editorial assistants).

Style, often referred to simply as "Strunken-White." Copyeditors, however, must realize that *The Elements of Style* presents *a* vision of *a* style of English, one that freely mixes rules, outdated conventions, idiosyncratic preferences, and hokum. Before applying any Strunkian maxim, copyeditors must cross-examine the text: Is recommendation X a hard-and-fast rule that admits no exceptions? Or is it a convention that may or may not be appropriate to the manuscript at hand? Could it be a well-founded nicety, an antique preju-dice, or a curmudgeonly crotchet?[3]

Far more instructive for the beginning copyeditor is Claire Kehrwald Cook's *Line by Line: How to Improve Your Own Writing.* The author, a vet-eran copyeditor, works through hundreds of shaggy, baggy sentences to illustrate the basic principles of grammar and syntax. On a few points (e.g., the use of *hopefully* and use of *everyone . . . their*), time has overtaken Cook, but her examples and explanations are excellent.

If you're ready for a serious study of the principles of effective prose, look at E. D. Hirsch Jr., *The Philosophy of Composition,* or Joseph M. Williams, *Style: Toward Clarity and Grace.* Neither book is light bedtime reading, but both give detailed analyses of the structural and stylistic elements that en-hance or impede the readability of expository prose.

SPECIALIZED REFERENCE BOOKS

Many copyeditors regularly consult an encyclopedia, a gazetteer, or a dic-tionary of quotations. Depending on the types of materials you copyedit, you may also turn to a biographical dictionary, foreign language dictionar-ies, and technical dictionaries.

Every field also has its specialized reference books. Here are a few examples:

Chemistry. *The ACS Style Guide.*
Mathematics. Ellen Swanson, *Mathematics into Type;* Nicholas J.
    Higham, *Handbook of Writing for the Mathematical Sciences.*

---

3. If you are among those who revere *Elements of Style* as a sacred text, consider the following passage from co-author E. B. White, in his introduction to the volume (p. xv):

[Strunk] had a number of likes and dislikes that were almost as whimsical as the choice of a necktie, yet he made them seem utterly convincing. . . . He despised the ex-pression *student body,* which he termed gruesome, and made a special trip downtown to the *Alumni News* office one day to protest the expression and suggest that *studentry* be substituted—a coinage of his own.

Studentry?! Even White concedes that *studentry* is "not much of an improvement," but, he adds, "it made Will Strunk quite happy."

Medicine. *Dorland's Pocket Medical Dictionary; Stedman's Medical Dictionary.*

Physics. *AIP Style Manual.*

Psychiatry. *Diagnostic and Statistical Manual of Mental Disorders: DSM-IV.*

WEBSITES

Among the well-maintained websites that provide information about the practice and business of copyediting are

Bay Area Editors' Forum: www.editorsforum.org
Copyediting (McMurry): www.copyediting.com
Editorial Freelancers Association: www.the-efa.org
Editorium: www.editorium.com
Editors' Association of Canada: www.editors.ca
The Slot (Bill Walsh): www.theslot.com
Society for Editors and Proofreaders (U.K.): www.sfep.org.uk

Whatever your question about copyediting, grammar, or usage, one or more of the two thousand subscribers to Copyediting-L are likely to post an answer on this very-high-volume international electronic mailing list. Subscribers can also access the list's extensive archives. An introduction to the list is posted at www.copyediting-l.info.

Expansive answers to hundreds of frequently asked questions about grammar and usage are archived at www.alt-usage-english.org. You can also keep up with current grammar-related debates, myths, rants, and inquiries on the blog Language Log, languagelog.ldc.upenn.edu/nll, which is co-authored by more than a dozen of the foremost English-language linguists. The archives (going back to 2003) may be searched by keywords or by category; of the several dozen categories, my favorite is Prescriptivist Poppycock, the online heir to Bernstein's hobgoblins.

The websites of some of the professional editorial style manuals offer selected editorial tools—including FAQs, examples of citation style, and sample memos and documents—either free or by subscription:

The Chicago Manual Online: www.chicagomanualofstyle.com
APA style: www.apastyle.org
U.S. Government Printing Office: www.access.gpo.gov

Modern Language Association: www.mla.org
AP Stylebook Online: www.apstylebook.com

A CAVEAT

In the pre-Internet era, the rule of thumb was that copyeditors were expected to double-check items that appeared in standard desktop reference books: the spelling of the names of well-known people and places, the population of states and countries, the dates of major world events, and the wording of well-known quotations. Copyeditors were not expected to check any other types of facts, information, or quotations: responsibility for content lay with the author. The standard practice was to attach a cover note to the copyedited manuscript reminding the author to verify all facts, proper nouns, and quotations before returning the manuscript for cleanup.

Now that the Internet places terabytes of information at our fingertips, double-checking this or that item seems so easy and so quick that some copyeditors try to track down every detail they can. Indeed, some who are new to the field wrongly assume that verifying facts is among their principal responsibilities. But just as a little knowledge can be a dangerous thing, so can a little Googling.

First, revving up your search engine distracts your attention from mechanical editing and language editing. Second, unless your editorial coordinator has asked you to do some sleuthing, you run the risk of exceeding the project's budget or missing your deadline. Third, copyeditors usually do not have sufficient subject matter expertise to evaluate the accuracy or value of information on the Web. For example, your author may have chosen to cite editions of texts other than those that appear on the Web; if you repeatedly point out differences between your author's quotations and the text on the Web, you will be wasting your time and your author's. Fourth, even if you are extremely tactful in your queries about content, some authors may feel that you are second-guessing them every step of the way. Rather than applauding your diligence, they may resent your overreaching.

Even though it goes against a copyeditor's heart and soul to leave a stone unturned, I strongly caution copyeditors—especially those new to the field—from wandering into the thickets of content checking unless your editorial supervisor requests that you do so. Expectations and practices vary widely, of course, and so you will want to discuss this topic before you begin working on a project.

PART 2

❖ Editorial Style

In this part we first turn our attention to matters of editorial, or mechanical, style: punctuation, spelling, hyphenation, capitalization, numbers, quotations, abbreviations, acronyms, and symbols. We then look at the conventions and procedures used in copyediting material that is not running text: tables and graphs, notes and bibliographies, and front and back matter. The final chapter in this part addresses typecoding and design specifications ("specs").

These chapters are intended to raise your editorial awareness and to show you how copyeditors make decisions. They also clarify some of the more difficult points in the major style manuals, identify some of the principal differences among the manuals, and discuss vexing mechanical problems that are not addressed in the manuals.

Punctuation

Many people throw up their hands at the quirks of English punctuation, but no one would want to read an unpunctuated text. Look at this tiniest of examples:

tryitonotis

Doesn't that look like some kind of disease, perhaps a rare form of trichinosis? Now, let's add some wordspacing and punctuation:

"Try it on, Otis."

Suddenly, it's clear that someone is speaking (quotation marks), that the speaker is addressing someone named Otis (proper name, capital O; and his name is preceded by a comma indicating direct address), and that Otis is most likely being asked to try on an article of clothing.

Or what about something like:

what i had had was had began not had begun what was i thinking

Even with wordspacing, this string is hard to decipher until we add all the punctuation:

What I had had was "had began," not "had begun." What was I thinking?

Punctuation also serves to give structure and coherence to complex expressions. In chapter 114 of *Moby-Dick,* for example, Melville weaves the stages of life into one long carefully punctuated sentence:

> There is no steady unretracing progress in this life; we do not advance through fixed gradations, and at the last one pause: through infancy's unconscious spell, boyhood's thoughtless faith, adolescence' doubt (the common doom), then skepticism, then disbelief, resting at last in manhood's pondering repose of If.

Of course, even the most punctilious punctuation cannot rescue a sentence that is poorly constructed. And, as we will see, in some cases punctuation alone may be too subtle to convey the desired meaning.

This chapter focuses on the most common punctuation problems and will prepare you for a careful reading of the portions of your style manual that discuss punctuation. If you don't recognize one of the grammar terms, consult the Glossary of Grammar Terms at the back of this book.

CONVENTIONS, FASHIONS, AND STYLE

Eighteenth- and nineteenth-century English authors tended to be profligate in scattering commas and semicolons; their style is now called *close punctuation.* The contemporary preference, however, is to use as few commas and semicolons as possible, a style called *open punctuation.* For example:

> *Close:* The panelists included Dr. Ellen Reese, from Philadelphia; Dr. Jenia Peters, from Phoenix; and Dr. Redmond Smithers, from Omaha.

> *Open:* The panelists included Dr. Ellen Reese from Philadelphia, Dr. Jenia Peters from Phoenix, and Dr. Redmond Smithers from Omaha.

> *Or:* The panelists included Dr. Ellen Reese (from Philadelphia), Dr. Jenia Peters (Phoenix), and Dr. Redmond Smithers (Omaha).

Within the realm of open punctuation, some choices, particularly those related to the comma, are more subjective than objective. Some writers, for example, *hear* punctuation, and they use commas, semicolons, and colons to speed or slow the pace and rhythm of their prose. Aural punctuators tend to hear a comma as a one-beat pause, a semicolon as a two-beat pause, and a period as a three- or four-beat pause. Some also hear a colon as a pause; for others, a colon signals a sharp accelerando, a signal to speed ahead because something important is coming.

A second group of writers have a highly visual sense of punctuation, and they are most concerned about how their sentences look on the page, aiming for sentences that are not overly cluttered by punctuation yet not so sparsely punctuated as to look neglected or to be confusing.

A third approach—and the one taken by all the editorial style manuals—is to punctuate according to grammatical and syntactical units. The advantage of this method is that it does not rely on the ear or eye of the writer or copyeditor, and therefore tends to be less subjective. In a given sentence, the question that syntactical punctuators ask regarding the presence or absence of a comma is not "Do you hear a pause here?" or "Does this look too choppy?" but "Is this an introductory adverbial phrase?"

You will also encounter writers who regard punctuation as an esoteric art and freely combine the aural, visual, and syntactical methods. Most of these idiosyncratic punctuators take a wing-and-a-prayer approach and will be pleased by your imposition of order and reasonableness. A few, however, will defend to the death their eccentric ways, proclaiming that the First Amendment guarantees their freedom to punctuate without editorial interference.

When copyediting nonliterary texts, corporate documents, and scientific or technical reports, you can confidently apply the conventions set forth in your style manual. But if your author is an experienced literary or professional writer, you will want to interpret some of the conventions more liberally. Writers who care about punctuation may become quite upset if a copyeditor imposes conventions that are at odds with their own sense of cadence, appearance, or taste.

Editorial style manuals and grammar books typically discuss punctuation mark by mark, giving five or ten rules for the period, followed by fifteen or twenty rules for the comma, and so on. Although such a system makes for a tidy presentation, it tends to obscure the broad functional principles that govern punctuation. In this chapter, we'll look at four major functions and some common conventions before looking at the more troublesome individual marks.

To master the syntactical approach to punctuation, you must be able to identify various grammatical units. The most important are *independent clauses, dependent clauses* (which, as you'll see later in this chapter, come in two flavors: *restrictive* and *nonrestrictive*), and *phrases*. First, make sure you recall your schoolbook definitions:

A *subject* is the "doer" of a verb.
A *finite verb* is a verb that is not an infinitive (to be, to go, to walk), not a present participle (being, going, walking), and not a past participle (been, gone, walked).
A *clause* is a group of related words that includes both a subject and a finite verb.
    An *independent clause* is a clause that can stand alone as a complete sentence.
    A *dependent clause* is a clause that cannot stand alone as a complete sentence.
A *phrase* is a group of related words that does not contain both a subject and a finite verb.

With these definitions in mind, we can examine the first three principal uses of punctuation: to mark the end of sentences, to join independent and dependent clauses to form complicated sentences, and to set off phrases within sentences.

FUNCTION 1: TERMINAL PUNCTUATION

In English every sentence begins with a capital letter and ends with a terminal punctuation mark. The three most common terminal punctuation marks are the period, the question mark, and the exclamation point:

Statement: The experiment failed.

Question: The experiment failed?

Exclamation: The experiment failed!

As this trio illustrates, terminal punctuation marks not only indicate the end of a sentence but also contribute to the meaning of the sentence.[1]

---

1. Here is a more complex example of how a masterly writer can use punctuation to carry semantic meaning. The author, Adam Gopnik, is comparing the debate on modern art in Paris with

A sentence of dialogue may also end with an em dash (to indicate an interruption) or with a set of ellipsis points (to indicate a thought that trails off):

"We cannot allow—" Then the phone went dead.

His voice was weak. "I have only one regret . . ."

Pitfall: Sentence fragments.   Fragments should be used sparingly and to achieve special emphasis:

Must consumers accept this unfair ruling? Not necessarily.

If the project is approved, traffic will increase by 20 percent. Perpetual gridlock.

What does the legislature's perennial failure to pass the budget before the close of the fiscal year mean for the state's residents? Costly and severe headaches.

History has shown that there is only one cure for kleptocracy. More democracy.

Fragments that result from carelessness should be rewritten:

In the 1980s many farmers were on the verge of bankruptcy. ✗ Because wheat exports had declined.

In the 1980s many farmers were on the verge of bankruptcy because wheat exports had declined.

Moderate growth is usually positive for the stock market. ✗ The reason being that stable interest rates and low inflation provide favorable conditions for higher profits.

Moderate growth is usually positive for the stock market because stable interest rates and low inflation provide favorable conditions for higher profits.

---

that in New York; the former, he explains, is a debate between modernists and anti-modernists, the latter a debate between modernists and post-modernists.

This makes the debate in Paris at once more shallowly conservative—there are people who think it would have been better had Picasso never been born—and more interestingly radical: there are people who think it would have been better had Picasso never been born! ("In the Garden of Bien et Mal," *The New Yorker,* April 6, 1998, p. 62)

✗   The gifted copyeditor whose principal virtues include a command of spelling, punctuation, grammar, diction, and usage as well as an ear for idiom.

The principal virtues of a gifted copyeditor include a command of spelling, punctuation, grammar, diction, and usage as well as an ear for idiom.

Pitfall: Misuse of the terminal question mark.   A question mark indicates that the sentence is a direct question.

Should the project be funded?

The topic for debate was, Should this program be funded?[2]

Will this report be completed by Friday?

Indirect questions, requests politely phrased as questions, and one-word interrogatives take a terminal period.

Indirect question: The question is whether the project should be funded.

Request: Would you please complete your report by Friday.

One-word interrogative: Employees should not second-guess company policy by asking why.

Pitfall: Placement of terminal punctuation mark for sentences within parentheses.   When a parenthetical sentence stands on its own, the terminal punctuation mark goes inside the closing parenthesis.

Last year popular fiction accounted for half of all books purchased. (Business and self-help books were the second largest category.)

Three mice died. (They refused to eat.)

---

2. As this example illustrates, the first letter of a formal question is capitalized. Brief, informal questions are capitalized only when presented as dialogue:

He asked, "Why not?"

He asked himself, why not?

Note, too, that when a formal question is the subject of a sentence, it retains its question mark:

Should this program be funded? was the topic for debate.

When a parenthetical sentence is tucked inside another sentence, the parenthetical sentence does not take a terminal punctuation mark.

Last year popular fiction accounted for half of all books purchased (business and self-help books were the second largest category).

Three mice died (they refused to eat), and two others lost a third of their body weight.

Occasionally, a tucked-in parenthetical comment consists of two sentences. In that case, the first sentence carries a terminal punctuation mark, but the second does not:

The terse instructions ("Place tab A into slot B. Secure tab A") were not helpful.

Pitfall: Placement of terminal punctuation mark for quotations.   At the end of a quotation, the terminal punctuation mark is placed inside the closing quotation mark.

Jones stated that the manufacturing schedule was "entirely unrealistic."

Jones screamed, "I quit!"

Jones asked, "Where is everyone?"

"Who has the authority," Jones asked, "to change that?"

Who can forget his "Who doesn't like Nascar?" remark?

A question mark or exclamation point that is added as an editorial comment (i.e., an emphasis supplied by the writer) is placed outside the closing quotation mark.

Jones, of all people, said, "The manufacturing schedule is entirely unrealistic"!

Was it Jones who concluded that "the manufacturing schedule is entirely unrealistic"?

In some circumstances, however, it is preferable to adopt the British convention (also called the "logical convention"): Place a punctuation mark within the closing quotation mark only when that punctuation mark is part of the quotation. For example, in computer manuals, linguistic analyses, and some types of literary criticism, the British convention may be used to enable readers to distinguish between a punctuation mark that is part of the quoted material and a mark that is part of the quoter's sentence. The following pair of sentences illustrates this concern:

> To find all instances of "Judge," but not "judge," check the case-sensitive option and type "Judge."
>
> To find all instances of "Judge", but not "judge", check the case-sensitive option and type "Judge".

The first sentence invites confusion: Are we searching for the word *Judge* or only for *Judge* followed by a comma? Are we to type *Judge* or the word *Judge* followed by a period? Placing the punctuation outside the closing quotation marks prevents these kinds of misunderstandings.

FUNCTION 2: JOINING CLAUSES

JOINING INDEPENDENT CLAUSES

Commas, semicolons, colons, and dashes can all be used to join two independent clauses to form a compound sentence. The choice among these marks is dictated by the nature of the bond. From a grammarian's point of view, there are four types of bonding material—coordinate conjunctions, adverbs, transitional expressions, and punctuation alone—and the rules are:

> IND, coordinate conjunction IND.
> [A comma precedes the conjunction.]
>
> IND; adverb [,] IND.
> [A semicolon precedes the adverb; a comma usually follows the adverb.]
>
> IND; transitional expression, IND.
> [A semicolon precedes the transitional expression; a comma follows the transitional expression.]
>
> IND; IND. *or* IND: IND. *or* IND—IND.
> [Independent clauses may be directly joined by semicolons, colons, or dashes.]

The following paragraphs explain these rules and provide examples.

When independent clauses are joined by a coordinate conjunction—*and, but, for, nor, or, so, yet*—a comma precedes the conjunction. When both clauses are short and there is no chance that readers will misconstrue which elements are joined by the conjunction, the comma may be omitted.

> Ten people suffered minor injuries, and at least twenty homes near the creek were flooded.

> Ten people were injured, but all were released from the hospital by nightfall.

> Ten people were injured and twenty homes were damaged.

When independent clauses are joined by an adverb (e.g., *however, indeed, moreover, nevertheless, therefore, thus*), a semicolon precedes the adverb. A comma is usually placed after the adverb, but the comma may be omitted after *thus* or *therefore* when the transition is not abrupt and no emphasis is desired.

> The prosecution will appeal the exclusion of the videotape; however, the courts rarely overrule trial judges on evidentiary matters.

> The videotaped confession is essential to the prosecution's case; indeed, the government's entire case hinges on the defendant's confession.

> The videotape is essential to the prosecution's case; thus the prosecutor is appealing the exclusion of the tape.

When independent clauses are joined by a transitional expression (e.g., *for example, in addition, namely*), a semicolon precedes the transitional expression, and a comma follows the transitional expression.

> The price of airline tickets appears highly irrational; for example, a ticket from New York to Chicago (713 miles) is often less expensive than a ticket from Philadelphia to Detroit (443 miles).

Independent clauses can also be directly joined (with no intervening conjunction or adverb) by a semicolon, a colon, or a dash. The semicolon is the neutral choice. The colon is used when the second clause amplifies or illustrates the first. The dash signals an abrupt change of thought or tone.

> The past is not dead; it's not even past.

Minds are like parachutes: they function only when open.

Half of all advertising is wasted—but no one knows which half.

Pitfall: Run-on sentences.   Independent clauses can be joined solely by a comma only in those rare cases when one has a trio of short independent clauses that all have the same grammatical subject:

He came, he saw, he conquered.
[Note, however, that if there are only two independent clauses in the series, they cannot be joined solely by a comma: ✗ He came, he saw. Instead, these clauses must be joined by *and* or by a semicolon: He came and he saw. *or* He came; he saw.]

Read the instructions, fill out the form, and submit the completed form to the main office.
[Since the "implied person" of an imperative is always "you," there is no change of subject here. Again, a comma is incorrect when there are only two clauses in the series: ✗ Read the instructions, fill out the form.]

In all other cases, a comma is insufficient to join independent clauses to form a compound sentence.

✗ He came home, he saw that the refrigerator was empty, he conquered his craving for an anchovy pizza and ate three crackers for dinner.
[These independent clauses are too long to be joined by commas.]

✗ He came home, the refrigerator was empty.
[The change of subject precludes using a comma to join these independent clauses.]

There are many ways to repair a run-on sentence:

Replace each comma with a semicolon: He came home; he saw that the refrigerator was empty; he conquered his craving for an anchovy pizza and ate three stale crackers for dinner.

Add a conjunction after each comma: He came home, and he saw that the refrigerator was empty, and so he conquered his craving for an anchovy pizza and ate three stale crackers for dinner.

Punctuate each independent clause as a separate sentence: He came home. He saw that the refrigerator was empty. He conquered his craving for an anchovy pizza and ate three stale crackers for dinner.

Transform all but one of the independent clauses into dependent clauses: When he came home, he saw that the refrigerator was empty, which left him little choice but to conquer his craving for an anchovy pizza and eat three stale crackers for dinner.

Pitfall: Confusion between compound sentences and compound predicates. Punctuators must distinguish between compound sentences and compound predicates. A compound sentence contains two independent clauses; a compound predicate is one independent clause in which one subject governs two verbs.

Compound sentence: The committee will meet tomorrow, and the report will be mailed on Tuesday.

Compound predicate: The committee will meet tomorrow and will review the report.

A comma is placed before the "and" in a compound predicate *only* if there is a chance that readers will misconstrue which elements are being joined.

The committee will meet tomorrow, and on Tuesday will issue its report.
[Comma prevents misreading of "meet tomorrow and on Tuesday" as a unit of thought.]

Pitfall: Confusion about IND; IND and IND: IND. The choice between a semicolon and a colon depends on the relationship between the clauses. A colon is appropriate when the second clause amplifies the first and the desired traffic signal is "proceed." In most other cases, the semicolon is the better choice.

Pitfall: Overuse of IND—IND. The dash is best reserved for special effects: to prepare readers for a punchline or a U-turn.

APPENDING A LIST TO AN INDEPENDENT CLAUSE

When an independent clause introduces a list, a colon follows the independent clause.

Three buildings will be demolished: 12 Apple Street, 56 Cherry Drive, and 7 Peach Lane.

Scorers are asked to bring three items: a pencil, a pad, and a stopwatch.

Pitfall: Misuse of colon before a series.   As just noted, the colon is used to introduce a series that follows an independent clause. A colon is also used to introduce a series when the introductory clause contains a phrase like "the following":

Scorers are asked to bring the following: a pencil, a pad, and a stopwatch.

In all other cases, however, no colon precedes the list.

✗ Scorers are asked to bring: a pencil, a pad, and a stopwatch.

✗ Patients should: arrive by 10 A.M., check in at the desk, and go directly to the laboratory.

✗ The advertising campaign is aimed at: preteens, adolescents, and young adults.

In rare cases the independent clause and the list may be reversed:

A glass of iced tea, a peach, and an apple: his last meal was spartan and brief.

JOINING DEPENDENT AND INDEPENDENT CLAUSES

A dependent clause cannot stand alone as a complete sentence. Conventional punctuation relies on the punctuator's ability to distinguish between two types of dependent clauses:

A *restrictive clause* is one that is essential to the meaning of the sentence as a whole because it limits the meaning or extent of the independent clause.

A *nonrestrictive clause* is not essential to the meaning of the sentence as a whole; that is, it could be deleted from the sentence without changing the meaning of the sentence.

If you keep these definitions in mind, the punctuation of dependent clauses introduced by subordinate conjunctions (e.g., *after, although, because, except, if, unless, when, whether, while*) is a matter of applying three rules:

DEP, IND.
[A comma follows the dependent clause.]

IND R-DEP.
[There is no comma when the dependent clause is restrictive.]

IND, NR-DEP.
[A comma sets off the nonrestrictive dependent clause.]

The following paragraphs explain this stenographic set of guidelines.

When a dependent clause precedes an independent clause, a comma is placed after the dependent clause.

If the "disk is full" message appears, you must insert a new disk.

When the mail arrives, the receiving clerk should notify the bookkeeper.

Even though the software creates a backup copy of the active document, weekly tape backup procedures should be followed.

When a restrictive dependent clause follows an independent clause, no comma is used.

You must insert a new disk if the "disk is full" message appears.
[The *if* clause limits when "you must insert a new disk."]

This warranty covers all moving parts unless the owner is negligent in maintaining the equipment.
[The *unless* clause limits the cases in which "this warranty covers all moving parts."]

When a nonrestrictive dependent clause follows an independent clause, a comma follows the independent clause.

Weekly tape backup procedures should be followed, even though the software creates a backup copy of the active document.
[The *even though* clause does not limit when "weekly tape backup procedures should be followed."]

Sometimes the distinction between a restrictive and a nonrestrictive clause can be quite subtle:

He was annoyed when the phone rang.
[No comma, restrictive, means "The ringing of the phone annoyed him."]

He was annoyed, when the phone rang.
[Comma, nonrestrictive, means "He was annoyed and then the phone rang."]

This same restrictive-nonrestrictive principle governs the presence or absence of a comma before a *because* clause that is preceded by a negative independent clause:

The proposal was not sent to New York, because the meeting had been postponed.
[Nonrestrictive, means "The proposal was not sent, and the reason it was not sent was that the meeting had been postponed."]

The proposal was not sent to New York because of the impending merger.
[Restrictive, means "The proposal was sent, but the impending merger was not the reason it was sent." For clarity, this sentence should be reworded: "The proposal was sent to New York, but not because of the impending merger."]

When the independent clause preceding the *because* clause is affirmative, in contrast, the presence or absence of a comma effects a slight shift in emphasis. The presence of a comma emphasizes the assertion, while the absence of a comma emphasizes the reason:

All citations to the minutes of committee meetings must include the five-digit record number as well as the date, because the minutes are indexed only by record number.

The results of the third test are invalid because the protocol was not followed.

PUNCTUATING RELATIVE CLAUSES

Dependent clauses headed by a relative pronoun (*that, who, which*), a relative adjective (*whose*), or a relative adverb (*when, where*) are called relative clauses, and the restrictive-nonrestrictive distinction applies to these clauses as well. Here are some examples of restrictive relative clauses:

Dogs that have three legs need special medical care.
[*That* clause restricts "dogs" to only those dogs that have three legs.]

Adults who are functionally illiterate face many problems.
[*Who* clause restricts "adults" to those adults who are functionally illiterate.]

She rejected all of his suggestions that were impractical.
[*That* clause restricts "all of his suggestions" to those suggestions that were impractical.]

Here are some examples of nonrestrictive relative clauses:

Dogs, which are members of the canine family, are related to wolves and foxes.
[*Which* clause makes a statement true of all dogs.]

Individuals' federal tax returns, which are due April 15, may be filed electronically.
[*Which* clause makes a statement true of all individuals' federal tax returns.]

Relative clauses that function as appositives—that is, they rename the subject or add a new piece of information about a subject that has already been identified[3]—are always nonrestrictive.

Janetta Williams, who is directing the marketing campaign, is arriving tomorrow.

Liberty City, which is in the northeastern corner of the state, will host next year's conference.

The accountants will be busy until April 15, when federal tax returns are due.

---

3. Commas are also used to set off appositives introduced by *and* or *or:*

I want to thank my sister, and my co-author, for her commitment to this project.
[Means "I want to thank my sister, who is also my co-author."]

The soffit, or underside of the overhang, requires special treatment.
[The *or* phrase introduces a definition of "soffit."]

As the sample sentences illustrate, nonrestrictive clauses are set off with commas, and restrictive clauses are not. Lest the presence or absence of a comma be too subtle a cue as to the restrictive or nonrestrictive nature of the relative clause, many usage manuals recommend using "that" to signal a restrictive clause and reserving "which" for nonrestrictive clauses. Compare:

> Senator Smith opposes new state taxes that will increase the cost of doing business in California.
> [Restrictive *that* clause limits "new state taxes" to those taxes that will affect businesses.]

> Senator Jones opposes new state taxes, which will increase the cost of doing business in Maine.
> [Nonrestrictive *which* clause denotes that "increase the cost of doing business" is true of all the new state taxes.]

The usage manuals, however, admit two exceptions to this convention:

1. When a sentence contains the conjunction "that," it is preferable to use "which" to introduce a subsequent relative clause, even if it is a restrictive clause.

> Many writers have argued that the distinction which we have been discussing is trivial.

2. Euphony may override the that/which convention.

> It was a sparsely furnished flat which she had rented.

FUNCTION 3: SETTING OFF PHRASES

INTRODUCTORY PHRASES

The grammatical nature and the length of a sentence-opening phrase determine whether a comma is needed to set off the phrase from the rest of the sentence. A comma is not needed after a two- or three-word introductory phrase that functions as an adverb—that is, it indicates time, place, manner, or degree—unless there is a chance that readers may misinterpret the comma-less phrase.[4]

---

4. Although no comma is needed after a short introductory adverbial phrase, a comma is used after a sentence adverb or a transitional adverb. For example:

Time: At noon the staff will meet to discuss new software.

Place: Above the panel you will find the safety instructions.

Manner: In this way one can solve most quadratic equations.

Degree: At length they consented to the request made by the auditors.

For July Fourth the company is planning a picnic.

For July Fourth, Jetco is planning a company picnic.
[Comma prevents misreading of "July Fourth Jetco" as a unit of thought.]

In all more than 2,000 cases of typhus were reported in the region last year.

In all, cases of typhus decreased by 43 percent between 1991 and 1995.
[Comma prevents misreading of "In all cases" as a unit of thought.]

Each spring there is flooding in the valley.

Each spring, rain causes flooding in the valley.
[Comma prevents misreading of "Each spring rain" as a unit of thought.]

These are the general conventions; however, some authors prefer to place a comma after even a short introductory adverbial phrase, usually to enforce a pause that alerts readers that the sentence's main clause is to come. Whether a copyeditor deletes or retains these optional commas depends on house style and policy, on the copyeditor's intuitions about the strength of the author's convictions, and on the sentence and the context. For example, the absence or presence of a comma in the following sentences is likely to be of little or no concern to most authors and readers:

Last November, traffic accidents rose unexpectedly.

Over drinks, they made amends.

Sentence adverb: Unfortunately, the presentation was interrupted by a power outage.
Transitional adverb: Next, the recipes are tested in professional kitchens.

But when these optional commas cluster in a paragraph, they impose a tiresome stutter-step rhythm that places too much emphasis on the short adverbial phrases:

> Last September, we introduced a new quality standard for electric pencil sharpeners. In early December, this standard was reviewed and revised. Since January, the volume of consumer complaints has risen. Each month, between 250 and 350 consumers have requested refunds. At tomorrow's meeting, we must identify the source of the problem.

For longer adverbial phrases and all other types of introductory phrases, the convention is straightforward: Place a comma after the introductory phrase. The following examples illustrate this convention:

Phrase functions as an adverb and is longer than a few words:

On the first and third Mondays of every month, the reports must be copied and mailed.

In a small town near the Canadian border, hundreds of tourists come every summer to fish.

For the sake of his family and friends, he declined the job offer.

To the best of your ability, try to recall what happened.

Phrase functions as an adjective that modifies the subject of the subsequent independent clause:

Of the newer photocopiers, the P-12 is the fastest.

With one exception, the programs received excellent evaluations.

Phrase contains a present or past participle:

Before using the printer, the operator must check the paper supply and the toner gauge.

Having declined in January, stock prices rose in February.

Redesigned from top to bottom, the car won several awards this year.

This last rule, however, conceals two pitfalls. First: If the sentence uses an inverted word order—that is, if the finite verb precedes the subject in the independent clause—one does not use a comma after the introductory verbal phrase:

> Caught in the act of accepting the stolen goods was a clerk who had recently been fired.

Second: When a sentence begins with a gerund—a form that looks like a present participle but functions as a noun—the gerund is the subject of the sentence, and one does not want to set off the subject from the finite verb that follows.

> *Gerund:* Helping customers solve their problems is a company's most important mission.
> *Participle:* While helping customers, service representatives should be polite.

> *Gerund:* Driving down Fifth Avenue can be frustrating because the traffic is so heavy.
> *Participle:* Driving down Fifth Avenue, motorists should expect delays.

INTERRUPTERS

The category of interrupters includes all sorts of single words and phrases that flesh out the bare-bones skeleton of a sentence by providing detail, emphasis, transition, or commentary. Interrupters are set off from the surrounding sentence by a pair of commas, a pair of dashes, or a pair of parentheses. For short interrupters, a pair of commas is the neutral choice; dashes emphasize the interrupter, while parentheses de-emphasize it.

> Sales of software, according to the store-by-store report, fell sharply last month.

> The one—and only—reason to proceed is to recoup the investments we have already made.

> Nizhny Novgorod (called Gorky in the Soviet era) is the third largest city in Russia.

In addition to conveying emphasis, dashes are used when the interrupter contains internal punctuation, when the interrupter marks a break in syntax, or when the interrupter is lengthy.

Interrupter containing internal punctuation: Regarding the need for more classrooms, the panelists—Bill Jones of Oakland, Carlos Real of San Leandro, and Trey Lee of Hayward—agreed more often than they disagreed.

Interrupter marking break in syntax: I must plead the worst of authorial defenses—the perennial limitations imposed by time and space—but will offer several better reasons as well for not treating this issue in detail.

Lengthy interrupter: Too often the building's design—the element that will have the greatest effect on the costs and the most lasting effect on the residents—is left for the last minute.

In addition to de-emphasizing an interrupter that contains a relatively unimportant point, a trivial exception, or a brief list of examples, parentheses are used to supply an acronym, abbreviation, technical synonym, or translation; to set off a cross-reference; and to provide numerical equivalents. For example:

In draft mode the output from this printer is 300 dots per inch (dpi); in regular mode, 600 dpi.

The coast live oak (*Quercus agrifolia*) is the dominant native species in this region.

Newspapers in Japan complained about the intensity of American *gaiatsu* (external pressure).

In the first year after the moratorium on condominium conversions was lifted (see section 3), fifty applications for conversion were received by the Hunter County Planning Commission (HCPC; see table 4-1).

The highest point in the park is 1,500 meters (4,920 feet) above sea level.

Pitfall: Incorrect placement of commas.   The commas must be placed so that they enclose the interrupter and only the interrupter:

✗ Many of the processes that have contributed to the loss of biotic integrity, including dam construction and the stocking of lakes have been halted in recent years, or are slated for discontinuation.

Many of the processes that have contributed to the loss of biotic integrity, including dam construction and the stocking of lakes, have been halted in recent years or are slated for discontinuation.

You can test for the correct placement of commas preceding and following an interrupter by reading a sentence as though the words enclosed in the commas were not there; the abridged sentence should still make sense. In the preceding example, the incorrectly punctuated sentence fails the test: ✗ Many of the processes that have contributed to the loss of biotic integrity or are slated for discontinuation.

Pitfall: Interrupters within interrupters.   When an interrupter itself contains an interrupter, the boundaries of the nested interrupter must be clearly indicated by punctuation marks that are different from those marking the larger interrupter. When the main interrupter is set off by commas, place the nested interrupter in parentheses or dashes:

In the western region, according to Smith's most recent analysis (dated April 1) and the auditor's quarterly report, both shoplifting and returns of damaged merchandise decreased.

DataFlo, which now processes approximately 2,000 terabytes of data—or 10 percent of the market in North Carolina—at its three service centers, is planning to double its operating capacity.

When the main interrupter is set off by dashes, place the nested interrupter in parentheses or commas:

Only one manager—Dana Wilkes (vice-president for marketing) in Topeka—has resigned.

Only one manager—Dana Wilkes, vice-president for marketing, in Topeka—has resigned.

When the main interrupter is in parentheses, place the nested interrupter in brackets, commas, or dashes:

Mail the completed application form by October 15. (In-state residents must also submit Form 568 [Applicants' Statement of Residency] by December 1.)

Mail the completed application form by October 15. (In-state residents must also submit Form 568, Applicants' Statement of Residency, by December 1.)

Mail the completed application form by October 15. (In-state residents must also submit Form 568—Applicants' Statement of Residency—by December 1.)

FUNCTION 4: INDICATING OMISSION

The fourth principal function of punctuation is to indicate the omission of a letter, portions of a word, an entire word, or a phrase:

To indicate a(n)	*Use a(n)*
dropped letter	apostrophe
abbreviation of a word	period
excision of a portion of a word	em dash or two-em dash
ellipsis within a parallel construction	comma or semicolon
deletion of word(s) within a quotation	ellipsis points

The use of an apostrophe to indicate a contraction (can't) or a dropped letter (rock 'n' roll) causes few mechanical problems for copyeditors: just make sure that the character *is* an apostrophe and that the apostrophe falls in the correct place. Contractions do, however, raise a stylistic issue. Some publishers and writers insist that contractions have no place in formal writing—with the possible exception of "aren't I," since "am I not" sounds unnatural—but many publishers have dropped or loosened the ban. So be sure to ask your editorial coordinator about house policy. If your author's preferences strongly conflict with house policy, discuss the issue with your editorial coordinator before making wholesale changes; publishers will often waive house rules on these kinds of mechanical matters.

Regarding the use of a period to indicate an abbreviation (Dr.), the only issue is whether a particular abbreviation takes a period or not; this topic is discussed in chapter 9.

The use of an em dash (—) or a two-em dash (——) to indicate the excision of a portion of a word is of concern only to scholars (who use the dash to indicate a word that is illegible in a document) and to those publishers who rely on the dash to replace portions of so-called expletives ("This f—investigation!" he screamed.)

The punctuation of elliptical constructions (that is, constructions in which one or more words are understood and are thus not repeated) requires attention. In simple constructions, a comma suffices:

He was born and raised in Iowa City, she in Manitowoc.

In complex elliptical constructions, semicolons are preferable:

Along the south bank of the Grand River, 350 acres of valley oak have been replanted since 1995; along the north bank, 250 acres.

On the use of ellipsis points to indicate the omission of one or more words from a direct quotation, see "Ellipsis Points" in chapter 8.

MARK-BY-MARK PITFALLS

In addition to these principal functions, punctuation serves a variety of what we may call conventional purposes; these are summarized in table 3, and many of them are discussed elsewhere in this book. Here, we will look at the most common uses and misuses of the more troublesome punctuation marks: the comma, the semicolon, the colon, and the hyphen, em dash, and en dash.

TABLE 3.   Punctuation: Principal Conventions

To mark the possessive form of a noun	apostrophe *or* apostrophe *followed by* s
To mark the plural form of a(n)	
abbreviation that has an internal period	apostrophe *followed by* s
nonitalicized lowercase letter	apostrophe *followed by* s
word for which adding *s* alone would	
cause confusion (e.g., do's)	apostrophe *followed by* s

(*continued next page*)

(table 3 continued)

To link the members of compound terms	
simple compounds	hard hyphen
complex compounds (i.e., one or both members are themselves compound terms)	en dash

To indicate	
a word that continues on the next line	soft hyphen
ironic usage or slang	double quotation marks
a line break in a run-in quotation of poetry	slash
units within a run-in address	comma
an unfamiliar foreign term	italics
a word used as a word	italics or double quotation marks
omission	
a dropped letter	apostrophe
abbreviation of a word	period
excision of a portion of a word	em or two-em dash
ellipsis within parallel constructions	comma
deletion of words within a quotation	ellipsis points

Dialogue and quotations

To mark a direct quotation	double quotation marks
To mark quoted words within a quotation	single quotation marks
To introduce a long, formal quotation	colon
To set off the name of the person spoken to	pair of commas
To set off the speaker's tag (name and verb)	pair of commas
To indicate an interpolation within a quotation	pair of brackets
To set off a tag question (e.g., "He's here, isn't he?")	comma
Multiple-paragraph quotations	opening quotation mark at the start of each paragraph; closing quotation mark only at the end of the final paragraph

(continued next page)

(table 3 continued)

Run-in lists

To mark the end of an item	comma or semicolon
To signal enumerators (numerals or letters)	pair of parentheses
To append a summarizing statement to a list	em dash

Titles of works

Title of a short work (e.g., poem, song)	double quotation marks
Title of a long work (e.g., book, journal)	italics
Title of an unpublished work	double quotation marks
To set off a subtitle from a title	colon

With numerals

To set off thousands in long numerals	comma	12,345
In hour-minute expressions	colon	10:30 A.M.
In month-day-year expressions	comma	June 23, 1999
To indicate omission of the century	apostrophe	in the '80s
In ranges of years	en dash	1963–1969 (or 1963–69)
For successive years	en dash or slash	1998–99 or 1998/99
In chapter-verse or act-scene citations	colon or period	Genesis 4:2 or *Hamlet* 4.2.1
To indicate ratios	colon	a 3:1 mix
In fractions	slash	4/11
In phone numbers	hyphens or periods	510-555-1212 or 510.555.1212
In expressions of units per unit	slash	3 T/gal

COMMAS: THE COPYEDITOR'S NEMESIS

The preceding discussion covers many of the more treacherous perils involving the comma. For a complete inventory of comma rules, see *Chicago* or *WIT*. The most important of these rules and conventions are summarized in table 4, and two of the most troublesome are discussed below.

TABLE 4.   Principal Uses of the Comma

Compound sentence (two independent clauses joined by a conjunction)
Separate independent clauses by a comma unless they are very short and unambiguous.

> The air has become less polluted, and the incidence of respiratory disease has declined.

> In 1994 sales soared and profits rose.

Compound predicate (one subject governing two verbs)
Use a comma between the subject and the second verb only if needed for emphasis or clarity.

> Proofreaders must understand type specs and should learn to detect minute differences in horizontal and vertical spacing.

> Proofreaders must understand type specs and production and design constraints, and should learn to detect minute differences in horizontal and vertical spacing.

Dependent clause preceding an independent clause
Place a comma after the dependent clause.

> If the minimum wage is not increased, the purchasing power of low-wage earners will continue to decline.

Dependent clause following an independent clause
No comma after the independent clause if the dependent clause is restrictive.

> The purchasing power of low-wage earners will continue to decline if the minimum wage is not increased.

If the dependent clause is nonrestrictive, place a comma after the independent clause.

> Senator Poe voted to raise the minimum wage, if that addresses your concern.

Introductory phrase that contains a participle
Set off the phrase with a comma.

> Before reading the paper, I ate breakfast.

> Having finished reading the newspaper, I sat down to work.

(table 4 continued)

Sentence adverb
> Set off a sentence adverb with a comma.
>> Unfortunately, the results will not be available for another six weeks.

Transitional adverb
> Set off a transitional adverb.
>> However, the schedule is very tight.
>> The schedule, however, is very tight.
>> Thus, only one conclusion is logical.
> When the transition is not abrupt and no emphasis is desired, no punctuation is needed.
>> Thus the problem was resolved.
> Do not set off an adverb that is a qualifier, not an interrupter:
>> However hard she tried, he criticized her work.
>> We thus set out to meet our destiny.

Interrupter
> Set off an interrupter with a pair of commas.
>> Carla, to her credit, promptly reported the discrepancy.

Series of parallel items
> Use commas to separate the items in a list or series.
>> Bring your books, pens, and pencils.
>> A driver's license, passport, or other official photo ID must be shown to the clerk.
> The presence or absence of a comma preceding the *and* or *or* that introduces the final item in the series is a matter of house style. Even when house style does not call for the serial comma, some constructions require a comma to avoid ambiguity.
>> Please send invitations to Ann and Al, Barb and Bill, Carol, and Dina and Dan.

Pair or series of adjectives
> Use commas to separate coordinate adjectives.
>> She gave a thoughtful, constructive speech to a warm, appreciative, well-informed audience.

(continued next page)

(table 4 continued)

Do not use commas if the adjectives are not coordinate.

The new blue velvet drapes looked odd behind the overstuffed green leather chair.

Nor did the floor-length blue drapes match the slightly faded handmade wool rug.

Interdependent clauses

Separate interdependent clauses with a comma unless the clauses are very short.

The fewer the complications, the faster the project will be completed.

The more the merrier.

Antithetical elements

Separate antithetical elements with a comma.

That's my book, not yours, on the table.

Direct address

Set off the addressee.

"Let's eat, Grandma."

"Where, Alice, have you been?"

"Doctor, your next patient is here."

Direct quotation

Use a comma to separate the quotation from the speaker's tag.

I said, "Let's go."

"Let's go," I said.

Addresses

In running text, use a comma to separate the street address from the city, and the city from the state.

He lives at 123 Main Street, Oaks, Montana.

But: His address is 123 Main St., Oaks MT 59700.

(table 4 continued)

In expressions of the form "City, State," place commas before and after the name of the state.

Berkeley, California, is a university town.

Dates

Use a comma to separate the date from the year.

The headquarters was moved to Austin on June 1, 1998.

But: In June 1998 it didn't rain.

And: On 1 June 1998 the document was signed.

In expressions of the form "date, year," place commas before and after the year.

On June 1, 1998, they signed the document.

Lists and series.   The use of commas to separate items in a series or list causes a surprising number of problems. The first thing to remember is that these commas serve to separate the items; thus there is no comma before the first member of a series:

✗ This photocopier's features include, collating, double-sided copying, and reduction.

This photocopier's features include collating, double-sided copying, and reduction.

And there is no comma after the last member of a series:

✗ Yesterday, today, and tomorrow, are the semiannual inventory days.

Yesterday, today, and tomorrow are the semiannual inventory days.

The other issue concerns the so-called serial comma, which is the comma before the *and* or *or* that precedes the last item in a list. *Chicago, WIT, APA,* and *CSE* all either require or strongly recommend the serial comma, but most newspapers and magazines use the serial comma only when needed to avoid ambiguity. Ask your editorial coordinator about house policy.

Coordinate and noncoordinate adjectives.   The convention of placing a comma between coordinate adjectives seems to be fading, perhaps as part of the trend toward open punctuation, perhaps because the absence of this comma rarely confuses readers, or perhaps because the distinction between coordinate and noncoordinate adjectives is sometimes hard to apply.

In principle, coordinate adjectives are those that equally and independently modify a noun, and their coordinate status is marked by the presence of either the word *and* or a comma in between them; for example:

a dull and error-filled book *or* a dull, error-filled book

a cool and humid climate *or* a cool, humid climate

Conversely, noncoordinate adjectives do not equally and independently modify a noun; instead, the first adjective modifies the unit comprising the second adjective (or even a third adjective) plus the noun:

a thick green book

a battered old canvas fishing hat[5]

There are two "tests" for determining whether a pair of adjectives is coordinate. A pair of adjectives is coordinate if (1) one can place *and* between the adjectives or (2) one can reverse the order of the adjectives and still have a sensible phrase. The phrase "a long, restful vacation" passes both tests (a long and restful vacation; a restful, long vacation), and therefore these adjectives

5. This example comes from Wilson Follett; here is his analysis:

A battered old canvas fishing hat is not a hat that is (1) battered, (2) old, (3) canvas, and (4) fishing. The adjectives lie in different planes and bear unequal relations to one another and to their noun. One might truthfully say that each modifier belongs to everything that comes after it; that each is welded to what follows; that together they make a lengthening chain in which every link drags the following links. In reality the object—and hence the noun—is not "hat" but "canvas-fishing-hat." This single thought or object is described by the common adjective "old," to which is added the participial modifier "battered." There is no license that permits a comma between a single adjective and its noun. Hence none should go between "old" and "canvas." Next, analysis tells us that each descriptive word in the chain is attached to the following in such a way as to be integral with it; hence no comma between "battered" and "old." (*MAU,* pp. 401–2)

are coordinate. But "a long summer vacation" fails both tests (✗ a long and summer vacation; ✗ a summer long vacation), and therefore these adjectives are not coordinate.

Do-nots.   In addition to knowing when a comma is called for, copyeditors also need to know when *not* to use a comma.[6] The first three of the following do-nots repeat the syntactical rules discussed earlier in this chapter; the others follow from nonsyntactical conventions.

1. Do not use a comma to join independent clauses.

   ✗ The store is fully stocked, all we need are customers.

   The store is fully stocked; all we need are customers.

   Rare exception: When the clauses are very short and they have the same subject, a comma will suffice:

   Like Caesar, I came, I saw, I conquered.

2. Do not insert a comma between a subject and the second member of a compound predicate.

   ✗ This new method will simplify billing, and save us time.

   This new method will simplify billing and save us time.

3. Do not use commas to set off a restrictive appositive.

   ✗ The movie, *Casablanca,* is being re-released this year.

   The movie *Casablanca* is being re-released this year.[7]

4. Do not use commas before an indirect quotation.

   ✗ Senior management asked, whether appliance sales were slowing.

   Senior management asked whether appliance sales were slowing.

---

6. This list of do-nots is adapted from Harry Shaw, *Punctuate It Right!* (New York: Harper & Row, 1986), and from Joan I. Miller and Bruce J. Taylor, *The Punctuation Handbook* (West Linn, Ore.: Alcove, 1989).

7. For comparison's sake, note that the film's title functions as a nonrestrictive appositive in the following sentences:

Their favorite movie, *Casablanca,* is being re-released this year.

The film that introduced Ingrid Bergman to American audiences, *Casablanca,* was released in 1942.

5. Do not use a comma after a *that* that precedes a quotation:

✗ The prospectus states that, "historical returns are not indicative of future performance."

The prospectus states that "historical returns are not indicative of future performance."

6. Do not use a comma before a quotation that is the direct object of a verb:

✗ The sign said, "No Trespassing."

The sign said "No Trespassing."

✗ The group's motto is, "All for one, and one for all."

The group's motto is "All for one, and one for all."

7. Do not allow a comma to interrupt a *so . . . that* construction.

✗ The upcoming negotiations are so crucial, that all vacations are canceled.

The upcoming negotiations are so crucial that all vacations are canceled.

8. Do not place a comma before an opening parenthesis that introduces a comment.[8]

✗ Many readers dislike double pronouns, ("he or she") and so we do not use them.

Many readers dislike double pronouns ("he or she"), and so we do not use them.

Nuance versus clutter.   Sometimes an author will insert a pair of commas to provide a slight degree of de-emphasis; for example:

The older conventions for using commas, at times, can produce an unpleasant choppiness.

---

8. A comma may, however, precede a set of parentheses that encloses a numeral or letter in an in-text list.

The minimal installation requires (a) a Pentium processor, (b) 40 MB of available hard disk space, (c) 16 K RAM, and (d) a VGA or higher-resolution graphics card.

The older conventions for using commas are, for the most part, yielding to a more open style.

Although no commas are required in either of these sentences, no harm is done by their presence, and some writers would argue that the commas improve the cadence of these sentences. But watch what happens if the writer combines these sentences and keeps the commas before and after "at times" and "for the most part":

The older conventions for using commas, which, at times, can produce an unpleasant choppiness, are, for the most part, yielding to a more open style.

In this longer sentence, it is preferable to reduce the number of commas to two, both to eliminate the stutter-step cadence and to visually clarify the boundaries of the nonrestrictive *which* clause:

The older conventions for using commas, which at times can produce an unpleasant choppiness, are for the most part yielding to a more open style.

Preventing misreadings.   Sometimes the syntactical structure of a sentence does not in itself call for a comma, but a comma is needed nonetheless to prevent misreading. For example:

Whenever possible, actions should be taken to ensure clients' privacy.

To Jane, Harry had nothing to say.

Soon after, the company declared bankruptcy.

Judgment and taste.   Even after you have mastered all the comma do's and don'ts, you will continually come across sentences that are not covered by any of the rules. Then you need to ask yourself whether the presence or absence of a comma will best serve the writer's purposes and the readers' needs: Will the addition or deletion of a comma facilitate or impede the readers' understanding of the sentence? suggest the desired nuance of meaning or tone? call undue attention to itself or be perceived as a typographical error? For example, consider the following sentences:

Her brief, eloquent tribute appears in this month's newsletter.

[Comma separates the pair of coordinate adjectives.]

Her brief and eloquent tribute appears in this month's newsletter.

Her brief but eloquent tribute appears in this month's newsletter.

[No comma is required since the adjectives are joined by a coordinate conjunction.]

Her brief yet eloquent tribute appears in this month's newsletter.

Her brief, yet eloquent tribute appears in this month's newsletter.

Her brief, yet eloquent, tribute appears in this month's newsletter.

[Writer's choice: No comma is required; inserting one comma emphasizes the contrast conveyed by "yet"; inserting a pair of commas de-emphasizes "yet eloquent."]

SEMICOLONS

Confusion about the use of semicolons arises from the semicolon's dual personality: Sometimes a semicolon serves as a weak period that joins independent clauses more closely together than a period would. But at other times a semicolon functions as a strong comma that separates syntactical elements more definitively than a comma would.

"Weak period" semicolons.   As we have seen, one use of semicolons is to bind independent clauses together into one sentence. For example, an author writes:

> In most community property states, the income from separate property remains separate property. In a few states, however, the income from separate property is deemed to be community property.

On rereading these sentences, the author feels that they are so closely related—because each sentence makes only part of the point—that they should be joined into one sentence. So the author substitutes a semicolon for the period at the end of the first sentence (and lowercases the first letter of the second sentence):

In most community property states, the income from separate
property remains separate property; in a few states, however,
the income from separate property is deemed to be community
property.

In theory, any terminal period can be replaced by a semicolon, and any
semicolon that joins two independent clauses can be replaced by a period.
The artfulness comes in deciding which sentences are so closely linked in
meaning that a semicolon is preferable to a period. Rhythm and sentence
length also enter into the choice. When the independent clauses are long or
complex, a semicolon will technically hold them together, but readers may
be confused. When the independent clauses are simple and short, a comma
and a conjunction can hold them together, while a semicolon may seem too
heavy-handed:

An anaphylactic reaction is a medical emergency. Prompt care
is needed.

An anaphylactic reaction is a medical emergency, and prompt care
is needed.

An anaphylactic reaction is a medical emergency; prompt care
is needed.

"Strong comma" semicolons.   The semicolon's second personality is that of
a strong comma. For example, an author writes:

The itinerary includes Venice, Florence, and Parma, the jewels of
northern Italy, Rome, Naples, and Ravello, in southern Italy, and the
islands of Sicily, Sardinia, and Corsica.

In this kind of complex series, the commas are not adequate to help the reader
distinguish the different items. If we replace some of the commas with semicolons, readers can see that the trip has three parts:

The itinerary includes Venice, Florence, and Parma, the jewels of
northern Italy; Rome, Naples, and Ravello, in southern Italy; and the
islands of Sicily, Sardinia, and Corsica.

Similarly, semicolons are used to mark off the segments of a complex elliptical construction:

In 1996 we raised $120,000 from 525 donors; in 1995, just under $80,000 from 406 donors.

The Labor Party won 125 seats; the Freedom Party, 58; and the Dignity Party, 46.

COLONS

As we have seen, colons can be used to join two independent clauses to form one sentence or to append a list to an independent clause. It is this second function that causes most of the problems, but the rule is simple enough: Use a colon to append a list to an independent clause; do not use a colon if the words that precede the list do not form an independent clause. Thus the colon should be deleted in these sentences:

✗ We have to: conduct the inventory, calculate the profits, and submit our proposal.

✗ She will write: a production memo, the jacket copy, and a press release.

✗ This budget does not include such activities as: proofing, editing, and indexing.

There are two other common uses for the colon: to introduce a formal quotation (see "Punctuation of Quotations" in chapter 8) and to introduce a set-off list (see "Lists" in chapter 13).

HYPHENS, EM DASHES, AND EN DASHES

Soft hyphens.   A hyphen that appears at the end of a line of text to indicate that a word continues on the next line is called a soft hyphen. The epithet "soft" refers to the fact that the hyphen must disappear should the entire word fall on one line. The placement of a soft hyphen is governed by the syllabication of the word and various conventions regarding line breaks; for example, it is incorrect to strand a single letter of a word at the end or the beginning of a line of text.

Copyeditors working on hard copy usually need not concern themselves with whether the soft hyphens are correctly placed, since the line breaks that appear in the manuscript will not appear in the final document. Thus, rather than checking for the correct hyphenation of a word, the copyeditor marks all soft hyphens with a "close-up and delete" sign. Copyeditors working on-screen will not encounter soft hyphens in well-prepared manuscripts because authors are instructed not to use soft hyphens. If the author has used soft hyphens, the editorial coordinator will usually ask the copyeditor to turn off the hyphenation feature, which will delete the soft hyphens from the files.

You may, however, have occasion to copyedit a manuscript in which the line breaks will carry over to the final document. In that case, you should correct any misplaced soft hyphens. Dictionaries differ somewhat in their syllabication principles, so it's important to consult the house dictionary to confirm the proper location for a soft hyphen. You may also wish to consult *Chicago* or *WIT* on conventions concerning line breaks in long numerals, proper names, and hyphenated words.

The newest wrinkle in end-of-line hyphenation is how to break an e-mail address or a URL. One should never insert an end-of-line hyphen in these clusters, and one should never break a cluster after a hyphen that is part of an address or URL. For e-mail addresses, line breaks may appear *before* the at sign (@) or a dot (because a break after the dot may cause the reader to construe the dot as a sentence-ending period). For URLs, one can break the line after a single or double forward slash (/ or //), a backslash (\), a colon, or a pipe (|); before a dot; or between the syllables of a word in the path name.[9]

Hard hyphens.   Hard hyphens are used to join certain compound words (e.g., self-respect). The epithet "hard" indicates that the hyphen must always appear in print, even when the hyphenated term appears on one line. (The conventions for hyphenating compound words and phrases are discussed in chapter 5.) Copyeditors working on hard copy are expected to mark all hyphens that appear at the end of a line of text so that the compositor or word processor will know whether the hyphen is hard or soft.

```
Clean-Fuel Vehicles. For details,

see IRS Publication 535, Busi⁀
```

9. For clarity's sake, some publishers italicize e-mail addresses and URLs. A few use boldface for these items or set them in a font that contrasts with the surrounding text. Decisions about such strategies should be made in consultation with the publication's designer.

> ness Expenses. If you claim part
> of your deduction on Schedule C,
> C-EZ, or E, identify as "Clean⌐⌣
> Fuel."

Em dashes.   Em dash is the technical term for what most people call "a dash." Typists and word processors often type an em dash as two hyphens (--), but in typeset text the em dash appears as one character (—). Copyeditors working on hard copy need not mark em dashes that are consistently typed as either -- or —. On-screen copyeditors may be instructed to replace the em-dash character with two hyphens or to replace it with a specified code to meet the requirements of the typesetting system. By convention, there is no wordspace before or after an em dash.

En dashes.   The quirky creature in this set is the en dash. You have doubtless seen many en dashes in print, although newspapers and some magazines do not use them. An en dash is longer than a hyphen but shorter than an em dash:

hyphen:-   en dash: –   em dash: —

The en dash is used in three situations. First, it replaces the hyphen in compound terms when one element of the compound is itself a hyphenated or an open (nonhyphenated) two- or three-word element:[10]

Europe's post–World War II economic recovery was primed by the Marshall Plan.

The San Francisco–based company posted higher-than-expected earnings for the second quarter.

She presented the report at the New York–New Jersey symposium on regional air pollution.

El Niño–related storms caused $200,000 in property damage last week.

---

10. To avoid "awkward asymmetry," *Chicago* prefers a hyphen, not an en dash, in complex compounds that admit no ambiguity: wheelchair-user-designed environment.

These lead soldier–size bronze sculptures will be on display through August.

In compound adjectives formed by attaching a prefix to a hyphenated element, however, a hyphen is used:

The airlines are demanding more training for non-English-speaking air traffic controllers.

Wages in these semi-labor-intensive industries are not keeping pace with inflation.

Second, the en dash is used as a substitute for the word *through* in a range of inclusive numbers or months.

The life of John Smith (1873–1945) is discussed on pages 44–47.

The budget for January–April 1997 appears in the May-June issue of the company newsletter.

Note that in the last of these examples, "January–April 1997" takes an en dash because it represents an inclusive range of months (i.e., the en dash is a substitute for *through*), but "the May-June issue" takes a regular hyphen because these two months do not represent a range (one would not say "the May through June issue").

Third, the en dash may be used to report scores or tallies: "The Mets won, 5–3" or "The court split 5–4."

A howler publicized by Strunk and White in *The Elements of Style* illustrates the value of the en dash, but also its limitations. When the *Chattanooga News* and the *Chattanooga Free Press* merged, "someone introduced a hyphen into the merger, and the paper became *The Chattanooga News-Free Press,* which sounds as though the paper were news-free, or devoid of news" (p. 35). Using an en dash to join the open two-word *Free Press* to its new partner would have helped, though *Chattanooga News–Free Press* still invites snickers.

When marking manuscripts by hand, copyeditors indicate any hyphens in a manuscript that are to be set as en dashes:

                              N
    The budget for January-April 1997 appears

    in the May-June issue of the bulletin.

On-screen copyeditors may be asked only to ensure that the en dash character is correctly typed, or they may be instructed to code en dashes as <–> or <n> or <en>. (Coding is discussed in chapter 13.)

QUOTATION MARKS: SINGLE AND DOUBLE

The most common use of double quotation marks (to indicate a direct quotation) and of single quotation marks (to set off a quoted word within a direct quotation) cause few problems; these are discussed in "Punctuation of Quotations" in chapter 8.

Double quotation marks are also used to set off a word that the author is using in some special sense—for example, a piece of slang or technical jargon or a neologism:

> Inevitably, the debate over "squawk radio" turns into a debate about the First Amendment and whether limits may be placed on the freedom of speech.

> The proposed bill would ban "drive-by" deliveries and require insurers to cover the cost of at least a forty-eight-hour hospital stay.

> Emoticons, or "smileys," are those odd combinations of punctuation marks that harried e-mail writers use to indicate their mood at the nanosecond of composition.

> Before a single reporter could ask a single question, the press secretary launched into a well-rehearsed "prebuttal."

Over time, as a word or phrase is naturalized into the language, these quotation marks will disappear.

Double quotation marks may also be used to indicate that a word or phrase is being used ironically.

> Copyeditors should not overlook such "minor details" as punctuation.

> The "evidence" for this claim consists of anecdotes from disgruntled former employees.

A similar effect can be achieved by the use of "so-called," in which case the suspect word is not placed in quotation marks:

The so-called evidence for this claim consists of anecdotes from disgruntled former employees.

Note, however, that quotation marks should not be used to set off clichés:

✗ Why do so many Americans persist in struggling to "keep up with the Joneses"?

Why do so many Americans persist in struggling to keep up with the Joneses?

✗ Every young entrepreneur is convinced that he or she can "build a better mousetrap."

Every young entrepreneur is convinced that he or she can build a better mousetrap.

MULTIPLE PUNCTUATION

Sometimes more than one punctuation mark is required at a particular spot in a sentence. The following conventions describe American practice in these matters.

PUNCTUATION WITH CLOSING QUOTATION MARKS

All the principal style manuals except *CSE* recommend what is called American style:

A period or a comma goes *inside* the closing quotation mark.
A colon or a semicolon goes *outside.*
An exclamation point, question mark, or dash goes *inside* if the mark belongs to the quoted material; *outside* if the mark is not part of the quotation.

CSE, however, follows what is called British (or "logical") style: A period, comma, exclamation point, question mark, or dash goes inside a closing quotation mark if it is part of the quoted material, outside if it is not. Since a section of quoted matter never ends with a semicolon or a colon (if these are in the original, they are suppressed in the quotation), these marks always go outside the closing quotation mark.

PUNCTUATION WITH A CLOSING PARENTHESIS

Here is a summary of the placement of punctuation marks relative to a closing parenthesis:

The period goes *inside* when the parenthetical comment is its own complete sentence; otherwise, the period goes *outside.*

Punctuation marks that are part of the parenthetical comment go *inside;* for example, a parenthetical comment may end with an exclamation point or question mark.

Since a parenthetical comment cannot end with a comma or a semicolon, these marks always go *outside* the closing parenthesis.

STRONGER AND WEAKER PUNCTUATION MARKS

When two punctuation marks are called for at the same location, only the stronger is retained. In this sense, a question mark or an exclamation point is "stronger" than a comma or a period.

✗ "Why are you here?," he asked. "Really!," she said.

"Why are you here?" he asked. "Really!" she said.

✗ His latest book is *Why Are We Here?.*

His latest book is *Why Are We Here?*

Clarity, however, sometimes demands that this rule be waived. For example, when a title ends with a question mark or an exclamation point, syntactically required commas are not suppressed:

✗ Her best-selling books include *Who Was That Man? Here We Go Again!* and *Don't Be Late.*

Her best-selling books include *Who Was That Man?, Here We Go Again!,* and *Don't Be Late.*

✗ "Do You Have a Future in Banking?" the latest pamphlet in the series, is now available.

"Do You Have a Future in Banking?," the latest pamphlet in the series, is now available.

In the first of these pairs, the serial comma is required to prevent readers from conceiving of *Who Was That Man? Here We Go Again!* as one title; in the second, the comma clarifies the function of "the latest pamphlet in the series" (a nonrestrictive appositive). In other cases, however, the comma may be safely deleted because the question mark alone is sufficient and unambiguous; for example:

✗ When customers ask "Do you have this in my size?", you should help them.

When customers ask "Do you have this in my size?" you should help them.

EYEBALLING EVERY MARK

If you are working on a manuscript that will be rekeyed by the compositor, you can trust the compositor to insert the proper characters for apostrophes and opening and closing quotation marks. If you are working on-screen on files that will be processed by a typesetter, you will usually receive files that conform to the typesetter's equipment; for example, the files will contain either typeset-style quotation marks (e.g., " " ' ') or plain marks (e.g., " ').

However, if you are working on documents that will be printed without any intervention from a compositor (e.g., documents produced on the office laser printer), you will have to carefully scrutinize every piece of punctuation to be sure that the document contains the correct character (see table 5). You should also delete any extra wordspacing before or after punctuation marks. The conventions are:

- One space follows a sentence-ending punctuation mark (period, question mark, or exclamation point).
- One space follows a comma, colon, or semicolon.
- There is no space before or after an em dash or en dash.
- There is no space before or after a hyphen with the exception of suspended compounds, which are followed by a space: "a two- or three-day delay." When suspended compounds appear in a series, there is no space between the hyphen and the comma: "a two-, three-, or four-day delay."

- There is no space between enclosures (quotation marks, parentheses, brackets) and the enclosed words.
- There is no space between a symbol (dollar sign, cents sign, percentage sign) and a numeral.
- No space precedes or follows a slash in a stenographic construction: and/or, 1997/98.
- One space precedes and follows a slash that indicates the end of a line in a quotation of poetry: "Buffalo Bill's / defunct."

You may also be asked to regularize the punctuation marks that follow italicized or boldface words. Some book publishers still follow what have come to be called traditional conventions:

- Periods, commas, colons, and semicolons are set in the same typeface as the preceding word.
- Question marks and exclamation points are set in the same typeface as the preceding word when they are part of the italicized or boldface term; otherwise they are set in roman.
- Both members of paired punctuation marks (e.g., parentheses, brackets, quotation marks) are set in the same typeface. These paired marks are italic (or bold) only if the material within them begins and ends with italicized (or bold) words.

Alternatively, newer house styles call for roman punctuation after italicized or bold words except for a question mark or an exclamation point that belongs to an italicized title: Is *Who Did It?* or *Viva!* better than *Doom*? (Squint hard and you'll see that this terminal question mark is roman.)

TABLE 5.   Typewriter and Typeset Punctuation Marks

	Typewriter Characters	Typeset Characters
Apostrophe	I can't go.	I can't go.
Single quotes	The 'gestalt'	The 'gestalt'
Double quotes	"Go," she said.	"Go," she said.
En dash	Edit pages 2-5.	Edit pages 2–5.
Em dash	Here--take it.	Here—take it.

CONTROVERSIAL TECHNIQUES

Two techniques intended to save space are widely used in corporate writing but are open to criticism because they sacrifice clarity.

Slashed constructions.   Some people dislike the appearance of slashed constructions, but the deeper issue concerns the meaning of the following types of constructions:

and/or	are/were
writer/editor	inner/outer limits
high altitude/low temperature gear	

First used in British maritime contracts in the mid–nineteenth century, "and/or" has spread far beyond law offices, sowing confusion and doubt wherever it lands.[11] Today, the sleight-of-hand "*a* and/or *b*" is usually interpreted to mean "*a* or *b* or both," but often the intended meaning is simply "*a* or *b*," or even "*a* and *b*." Rather than ask readers to piece together the desired relationship between the two items, careful writers and copyeditors avoid the Janus-like "and/or" and supply whatever words are needed to clarify the sentence.

Similarly, the multiple-choice construction "are/were" can be replaced by a short string of words—"are or were," "once were and still are"—or by a verb that denotes continuity ("remain"). For the bivalent "writer/editor," one can substitute the compound "writer-editor" (to denote a person who is both a writer and an editor) or the disjunctive "writer or editor" (to denote a task that may be performed by either a writer or an editor). And "inner/outer limits" can be transformed into "inner and outer limits," "inner or outer limits," "limits, both inner and outer," or "limits, either inner or outer," depending on the intended meaning.

Note also that when a two-word phrase appears on either side of the slash (e.g., "high altitude/low temperature gear"), a layer of visual confusion

---

11. The first judicial review of a contract dispute over "and/or" (in England, in the 1850s) concluded with the three-judge panel offering three different interpretations of the meaning of "and/or." In subsequent litigation, three new judges again reached three different opinions— none of which agreed with any of the earlier three. See *DEU,* s.v. "and/or."

("altitude/low" looks like a syntactical unit) is added to the denotational ambiguity (at high altitudes *and* low temperatures? at high altitudes *or* low temperatures?). For appearance' sake, some publishers add a thin space: high altitude / low temperature gear.

A few multiword slashed constructions have become so well entrenched that there is no risk of misunderstanding; for example, "Here's another good news/bad news quarterly report," "This is one more he said/she said controversy." (Anti-slashers, however, will prefer "another good news, bad news report" or "another good-news, bad-news report.")

Parenthetical plurals.   The second stenographic technique open to censure is the use of (*s*) after a noun to indicate that the statement may apply to one or more than one member of the category; for example:

> The insured person(s) must take reasonable care in securing the
> vehicle(s).

When such shorthand migrates from insurance contracts into other contexts, it can not only confuse the reader but also stump the careful writer or copyeditor. The first riddle is whether "person(s)" takes a singular verb or a plural verb. In documents that make sparing use of parenthetical plurals, one can finesse this difficulty by avoiding the verb *be* and using only those verbs that have the same form in the third-person singular and the third-person plural (e.g., *can, may, must, should, will*). The corollary issue is one of pronoun-antecedent agreement for antecedents such as "person(s)." The better course is to write around the problem and not use pronouns; in a pinch, however, "they" usually works.

A final conundrum concerns the form of the parenthetical plural for nouns that take *-ies* or *-es* in the plural. For nouns in the first group, adding (*s*) is sufficient: beneficiary(s). For nouns in the second group, (*es*) is added: loss(es). For nouns whose plurals are wholly irregular, even the most inventive writers yield: no one has yet lobbied for ma(e)n, woma(e)n, or child(ren).

EXERCISE A

Punctuate the following sentences. The answer key is on pages 459–62.

1. The man wearing the long-sleeved red gingham shirt told amusing tall tales

2. The accountant asked whether the receipts were in order

3. The accountant asked "Are the receipts in order"

4. School curriculums have traditionally been the domain of politicians and educators not judges

5. The promoter said that if no more ticket requests came in the concert would be canceled

6. Harvard freshmen who have reading scores below the national average performed better than expected on the math aptitude test

7. You can teach yourself basic computer skills using a how-to book but a better

choice is to ask a knowledgeable sympathetic friend for tutoring

8. Each hospital has a service office whose staff members will answer your questions about hospital policies

9. From June 1 through June 3 1998 the Chamber of Commerce of Oakland California hosted its third annual conference for small businesses

10. All part-time employees who are not covered by the new contract will be laid off

EXERCISE B

The following paragraphs are from a manuscript on editing. You are being asked to do a light copyedit. The answer key is on pages 463–66.

Some overly zealous copyeditors will pour over a manuscript, and change every "till" to 'until' or vice versa, depending on their training, their grammatical ear, and their ideas about prose style. Although editors must try to forestall the deprecation of English into colloquial swill, they should never adopt a self-styled purism that does not allow for some vareity of expression. When a tyrranical editorial coordinator waves Fowler, Wilson Follett, and other venerable guardians, his staff should wave back Theodore Bernstein's *Miss Thistlebottom's Hobogoblins,* a thoughtfull debunking of scared cows in usage, or William Morris and Mary Morrris's *Harper Dictionary of Contemporary Usage* which explores the differences of opinion among the so-called "experts."

A second danger: Some novice copyeditors misinterpret the recommendations in *The Elements Of Style* as a mandate to change such sentences as "the outcry was heard round the world" to "every-one in the world heard the outcry." True, the active voice is more forceful, and a procession of passive constructions is a sure cure for insomnia. But the passive voice is preferable when the writer's goal is variety or emphasizing an important word in a sentence.

❖ 5 ❖

Spelling and Hyphenation

Good spelling skills are essential for a copyeditor. Although copyeditors who work on-screen are rescued from some misspellings by the spellchecking feature, spellcheckers do not distinguish between homophones (*principal* and *principle*), do not account for spellings determined by usage (*resume* and *résumé*), and may allow variant spellings (*catalog* and *catalogue*) in the same document. And, of course, spellcheckers do not highlight a misspelled word if the misspelling is itself a word (*from* and *form*). Thus spellchecking would not detect any errors in the following sentence: "Too bee oar knot two beet, what is the question."

People who are good spellers not only know how to spell many commonly misspelled words but also

> readily look up unfamiliar or unusual words
> know which words they *always* have to look up
> know that usage affects spelling
> are not fooled by homophones
> double-check a word in the dictionary before changing it
>   on the manuscript
> do not introduce misspellings into a manuscript

The following list should give you a little trouble—but only a little—if you're a strong speller. Don't look at the dictionary yet. Place an X next to the words you know are misspelled and put a ? next to the words you're not sure about.

accordian	fallacy	occurrence
achievement	leisure	privilege
adolescence	lillies	reference
antiquated	maintenance	separate
athlete	mischievious	sophomore
calendar	non sequitur	vaccuum
disastrous	occasion	weird
environment	occurred	withhold

(The answers appear in the next section.)

One more list—this one intended to bedevil even excellent spellers. Again, place an X next to the words you know are misspelled and put a ? next to the ones you're not sure about.

accommodate	hemorrhage	predilection
acknowledgment	hierarchy	prejudice
Albuquerque	idiosyncrasy	proceed
anomaly	indiscernible	proffered
cemetery	indispensable	publicly
consensus	inoculate	resistance
dachshund	iridescence	restaurateur
decaffeinated	judgment	rococo
desperate	liaison	sacrilegious
ecstasy	lightning	sergeant
embarrassment	liquefy	shepherd
exhilarate	millennium	siege
Fahrenheit	minuscule	skepticism
fluorescent	nickel	stratagem
foreword	niece	supersede
fulfill	parallel	temperament
gauge	persistent	tendinitis
guerrilla	Portuguese	tenement
harassment	preceding	tranquillity

Don't read ahead until you've finished this list.

IMPROVING YOUR SPELLING SKILLS

Unless you are a letter-perfect speller, you probably didn't get everything right on the first list. There, four words are misspelled; the correct spellings are:

accordion, lilies, mischievous, vacuum. And you were probably stymied by at least five or ten words on the second, longer list. All the words on that list are spelled correctly. (Foreword = opening section of a book; not to be confused with "forward.")

Don't be dismayed by your mistakes. The purpose of these lists is not to trick you but to remind you that you can't always trust your eyes. It is better to take a moment with your dictionary and look up a word rather than assume (or hope) that you know the correct spelling. Here are seven suggestions for improving your spelling skills.

Stare at lists of hard words.   You can begin with the list on the preceding page. Tape up a photocopy near your desk and skim it once a day (e.g., when you first sit down to work, or when you return from a lunch break).

Keep a list of all the words you look up.   Whenever you look up a word in the dictionary, jot it down. Wait until you have ten or fifteen words and then put *that* list up near your desk. Make a conscious effort to add to your list: Whenever you have the dictionary open to look up a word, skim that page to see if there isn't another word worth learning.

Learn spelling rules and exceptions.   A fair number of books have been written for poor spellers, but not for good spellers who want to improve. *WIT* has a section of helpful tips, as does Harry Shaw's *Errors in English and Ways to Correct Them,* 4th ed. (New York: Harper & Row, 1993).

Learn something about the etymology of difficult words.   Etymology accounts for many of the oddities of English spelling, as the following examples show.

Why *supersede* but *precede?* Both words are derived from Latin, but

supersede = super (above) + sedere (to sit; cf. sedentary)
precede = pre (before) + cedere (to go; cf. secede)

Unfortunately, etymology cannot account for the fact that three verbs derived from *cedere* are -*ceed* (exceed, proceed, succeed) while all the others are -*cede* (accede, concede, intercede, recede, etc.).

Why one *r* in *iridescence* but two in *irregular? Iridescence* is derived from the name of the Greek goddess Iris (one *r*), the deity associated with the rainbow. *Irregular* is the prefix *ir-* attached to *regular; ir-* is the form the prefix *in-* (= not) takes before a stem beginning in *r.*

Why only one *n* in *inoculate* but two in *innocent*? Both are derived from Latin, but

inoculate = in (within) + oculus (eye; cf. ocular)
innocent = in (not) + nocens (wicked; cf. noxious)

Why *bisect* but *dissect*? The root of both words is the Latin *sectus* (the past participle of the verb *secare*, to cut). But

bisect = bi (two; cf. bicycle) + sect
dissect = dis (apart; cf. discern) + sect

Those two *l*'s and two *n*'s in *millennium*? Another word derived from the Latin, and again the etymology points to the correct spelling:

millennium = mille (thousand; cf. millimeter—two *l*'s) + annum
   (year; cf. annual—two *n*'s)

Pay special attention to suffixes that contain unstressed vowels.   Unless your memory is flawless, take a moment to look in the dictionary when you encounter a word that ends in *-able* or *-ible; -ance* or *-ence;* or *-ar, -er,* or *-or.*

Pay special attention to doubled consonants.   Words that have several consonants, only one of which is doubled, cause a disproportionate number of problems: battalion, Caribbean, desiccated, graffiti, Mediterranean, occasion, Philippines, vaccination.

Learn some mnemonic devices.   Here are some mnemonic devices I was taught in elementary school and have never quite been able to forget:

amend = alter
emend = edit out errors (= improve)

complement = to complete
compliment = I like hearing them

principle = rule
principal = is your pal; is the main agent or actor; is the adjective

stationary = stay still
stationery = for letters

accommodate surely has room for two *c*'s and two *m*'s

VARIANT SPELLINGS

Some words can be spelled more than one way: likable *and* likeable, *or* tying *and* tieing. Such pairs are called equal variants, and either spelling is acceptable in a manuscript. For equal variants, the copyeditor's job is to note on the style sheet which variant the author has used and to enforce consistency throughout the manuscript.

For other words, your dictionary will show one spelling as the preferred spelling, another as a secondary variant or as a British variant. American publishers expect copyeditors to change British variants (e.g., metre), but some publishers will accept American secondary variants (e.g., epilogue *and* epilog).

Read the explanatory notes at the beginning of your dictionary to understand how the editors treat variant spellings. In *M-W Collegiate*, for example, equal variants are separated by *or*, and secondary variants are separated by *also*:

Equal variants: Shakespearean *or* Shakespearian

Primary and secondary variants: cancellation *also* cancelation

Because dictionaries list words in alphabetical order, the first spelling shown for a pair of equal variants is usually determined by alphabetization, not by the prevalence of usage. For a variant spelling, the entry will refer you to the preferred spelling:

jibe *var of* GIBE

metre *chiefly Brit var of* METER

The following pairs are shown as equal variants in *M-W Collegiate*. Nonetheless, many book publishers have unshakable preferences among these pairs; these industrywide preferences are indicated by an asterisk.

acknowledgment*	acknowledgement
afterward	afterwards
catalog	catalogue
diagrammed*	diagramed
excludable	excludible
fulfill*	fulfil
judgment*	judgement
programming*	programing

résumé*	resume
salable	saleable
theater*	theatre

The following list is also based on *M-W Collegiate;* other dictionaries may show different preferences for some of these words.

Preferred spelling	*Secondary variants*
adviser	advisor
anesthetic	anaesthetic (chiefly British)
descendant	descendent
epilogue	epilog
forgo ("do without")	forego (but *forego* is correct when the meaning is "come before" or "precede": a foregone conclusion)
gray	grey
medieval	mediaeval
mustache	moustache
naïveté	naivete, naiveté
skeptic	sceptic (chiefly British)
skillful	skilful (chiefly British)
toward	towards

Of course, a self-reinforcing effect is in play here. The lexicographers' decision to label a spelling as a secondary variant is based on the prevalence of that spelling in publications from which evidence of usage is culled. But once a spelling is labeled a secondary variant, it is less likely to appear in print.

BRITISH SPELLING

If you have read many books and publications printed in Britain or Canada, British spellings may look correct to you. But, as noted above, the house style of most American publishers calls for using the American spelling. Table 6 indicates some of the major differences. Another distinctively British convention is to double the consonant in words such as *focussed, marvellous,* and *traveller.* In American spelling, however, the consonant is doubled only when the stress falls on the syllable containing the consonant; thus *focused, marvelous,* and *traveler.*

TABLE 6. Differences between American and British Spelling

Lexical Feature		Examples	
American	British	American	British
-am	-amme	program	programme
-ction	-xion	connection	connexion
-e-	-ae-	anemia	anaemia
-e-	-oe-	fetus	foetus
-ed	-t	misspelled	misspelt
-ense	-ence	offense	offence
-er	-re	caliber	calibre
-eu-	-oeu-	maneuver	manoeuvre
-ice	-ise	practice	practise
-ize	-ise	recognize	recognise
-f-	-ph-	sulfur	sulphur
-ol-	-oul-	smolder	smoulder
-or	-our	color*	colour
-ow	-ough	plow	plough
-yze	-yse	analyze	analyse

*American spelling calls for *color, honor, labor, neighbor,* and the like, but note the trio *glamour, glamorous,* and *glamorize.* Practice is divided on retaining the British spelling for proper nouns: *Chicago* favors "the Labour Party," but *The Associated Press Stylebook* recommends "the Labor Party."

HOMOPHONES

A copyeditor must also be aware of homophones (words that are pronounced identically or quite similarly but that are spelled differently). You are probably a whiz at the simpler homophone pairs and triplets, able to spot misuses of *there* and *their,* or of *to, two,* and *too.* You should also be able to distinguish between more troublesome pairs and triplets:

accept	except	
adverse	averse	
affect	effect	
allusive	elusive	illusive
ascent	assent	

baited	bated	
bazaar	bizarre	
canvas	canvass	
capital	capitol	
censure	censor	sensor
complement	compliment	
disc	disk[1]	
discreet	discrete	
eminent	immanent	imminent
ensure	insure	
gorilla	guerrilla	
grisly	grizzly	
hoard	horde	
incidence	incidents	
mantle	mantel	
palate	palette	pallet
rack	wrack	
review	revue	
troop	troupe	
undo	undue	

If you are unsure about any of these words, grab your dictionary and bone up. (My favorite homophonic mix-up: an author who wrote about a doctor cutting the "naval chord.")

Note, too, that confusion among homophones is quite prevalent in set phrases whose original meaning may now seem obscure:

bated breath	bated = held in abeyance; restrained
just deserts	deserts = deserved reward or punishment
hue and cry	hue = outcry
beyond the pale	pale = an area enclosed by pales, or stakes
hold one's peace	peace = silence (The phrase is from *The Book of Common Prayer*, "Solemnization of Matrimony.")
free rein	rein = strap used by a rider to control an animal

1. In the computer industry, *disk* is reserved for *hard disk, floppy disk,* and *diskette,* while *disc* is the preferred spelling for the newer storage media: *compact disc, laserdisc, magneto-optical disc,* and *videodisc.*

toe the line   toe = to place one's toe at or on
vale of tears   vale = valley

FOREIGN WORDS AND PHRASES

Foreign words and phrases now naturalized into English retain their original spelling (when imported from a language that uses the Latin alphabet), often retain their diacritical marks, and are set in roman type.

> From French: carte blanche, de rigueur, déjà vu, fait accompli, faux pas, hors d'oeuvre, laissez faire, raison d'être (*secondary variant:* raison d'etre), vis-à-vis
> From German: ersatz, gestalt, realpolitik, weltanschauung, zeitgeist
> From Italian: a cappella, al fresco, cappuccino, espresso, punctilio, virtuoso
> From Japanese: hara-kiri, hibachi, samurai, tempura
> From Latin: ad nauseam, de facto, in loco parentis, modus operandi, sine qua non, sui generis
> From Spanish: aficionado, gringo, guerrilla, junta

In contrast, non-naturalized foreign terms are set in italics. When a non-naturalized import appears repeatedly in the text, it is set in italics on first mention and usually set in roman thereafter.

One test of naturalization is whether the term appears in the main section of the dictionary. Yet some entries in the "Foreign Words and Phrases" appendix to *M-W Collegiate* would pass muster in roman type for certain audiences: de profundis, dies irae, sans souci, sayonara. Here again, a copyeditor must gauge the readership: If the term is set in roman, will readers be confused? If the term is set in italics, will readers be surprised?

Longer foreign phrases may be set in roman and enclosed in quotation marks; the translation may be appended in parentheses.

> The poem is a meditation on the proverb "Una mano no se lava sola" (A single hand cannot wash itself), although the phrase never appears in the poem itself.

If you are unable to verify the spelling and grammar of foreign phrases, remind your author to double-check the quotations.

PROPER NOUNS AND ADJECTIVES

Copyeditors are expected to verify or to query the spelling of every proper noun (person, place, organization, etc.) and proper adjective that appears in a manuscript. The spelling of well-known names can be verified in the dictionary—either in the main section or in separate biographical and geographical listings at the back of the book. On some projects, it is more efficient to consult basic or specialized reference books rather than to query the author or to hope that the author will identify all errors during the review of the copyediting.

For a manuscript containing relatively few proper nouns whose spelling you cannot verify, you should query each unverified spelling with a simple "Spelling OK?" For a manuscript with dozens of unfamiliar, unverifiable proper nouns, you need not bother querying each. Instead, explain to the author in a cover note that he or she should take extra care to double-check the spelling of all proper nouns.

Proper nouns that are translated into English from foreign languages may have more than one form or spelling. In articles and books addressed to nonspecialists, Spanish kings and princes may be called Peter, Charles, Philip, or James; readers of scholarly texts, however, will expect to see Pedro, Carlos, Felipe, and Jaime. Transliterated names pose many additional choices; the variants on "Tchaikovsky" (the form shown in *M-W Collegiate*) are legendary.

Sometimes the choice of variants is political rather than orthographic. For example, after the breakup of the Soviet Union, some of the newly independent states changed the spelling of their names to reflect the local preferences; thus, Belarus (formerly Byelorussia), Kyrgyzstan (formerly Kirgizia), Moldova (formerly Moldavia), and Tajikistan (formerly Tadzhikistan). Politics and ideology are also at issue in some controversies over names (the Falkland Islands or the Malvinas). In such cases, when the author's spelling or choice of names differs from that in your reference books, it is better to query the author rather than change the manuscript.

Authors of historical works usually retain the place names that prevailed during the period under discussion. The city today known as St. Petersburg would be called Petrograd in a study of the Russian Revolution, but Leningrad in a study of World War II.

Unlike other foreign words, foreign proper nouns are not italicized.

The Biblioteca Nacional is in Madrid.

The Rue des Ursins is on the Ile de la Cité.

PLURALS

All the major style manuals discuss the conventions regarding the formation of plurals. Here are some explanations and pointers to complement those discussions.

Common nouns.   Your dictionary is your best source for the spelling of common nouns and their plurals. The nouns most likely to cause trouble are those ending in *f* (halves, leaves, wolves, *but* roofs), in *fe* (knives, lives, wives, *but* safes), or in *o* (echoes, heroes, potatoes, *but* egos, embryos, and portfolios). When your dictionary lists two plurals for a common noun, read the entire entry to discover if the two forms have different uses. For example, *staff* has two plurals: *staffs* for groups of people and *staves* for musical notation; *indexes* are alphabetical lists, but *indices* are mathematical expressions; and *mediums* are persons claiming to have paranormal powers, but *media* are artistic materials. Also, although some dictionaries show *appendixes* and *appendices* as equal variants, many book publishers prefer *appendixes* for denoting the back sections of a book.

Other difficulties arise for nouns borrowed from the classical languages but naturalized into English. For some of these nouns, the regular and irregular plural forms are labeled as equal variants in *M-W Collegiate*: millennia *or* millenniums, *and* memoranda *or* memorandums. The following nouns always take a Latin- or Greek-style plural.

-a → -ae	alga	algae
	alumna	alumnae
	larva	larvae
	minutia	minutiae
-is → -es	axis	axes
	basis	bases
	crisis	crises
	ellipsis	ellipses
	hypothesis	hypotheses
	oasis	oases
	parenthesis	parentheses
	thesis	theses

-on → -a	criterion	criteria
	phenomenon	phenomena
-um → -a	addendum	addenda
	erratum	errata
	ovum	ova
	phylum	phyla
-us → -i	alumnus	alumni
	fungus	fungi
	locus	loci
	radius	radii
	stimulus	stimuli
but	ignoramus	ignoramuses (after the hero of the play *Ignoramus*)
-us → -era	genus	genera
	opus	opera

Allegiances remain divided about the singular or plural nature of several borrowings from Latin and Greek. The debate over *data* (see chapter 1, footnote 2) is the best known of these. Other squabbles concern *insignia* (the Greek plural of *insigne*, but often treated as a singular in English and given the English plural *insignias*) and *media* (a plural in Latin, often treated as singular in such phrases as "the print media"). The case of *kudos*, a singular noun in classical Greek, is more curious. Sometime in the 1940s English speakers, believing that the final *s* indicated a plural, invented a singular form (kudo) and began to treat kudos as a plural. Both forms appear in *M-W Collegiate*, which upholds the singular as an example of a back-formation.

For nouns derived from languages other than Latin and Greek and now naturalized into English, check your dictionary for irregular plurals; for example:

adieu	adieus *or* adieux
beau	beaus *or* beaux
cherub	cherubim (though "cherubs" is preferred when the meaning is figurative—that is, to denote chubby, rosy-faced people or images of winged children)
concerto	concertos *or* concerti
faux pas	faux pas

libretto	librettos *or* libretti
seraph	seraphim *or* seraphs
weltanschauung	weltanschauungs *or* weltanschauungen

For foreign nouns that have not been naturalized into English, the plural is formed by adding a roman *s* after the italicized noun:

the *keiretsus* [Japanese for "distribution conglomerates"]
the *sottopassaggios* [Italian for "underpasses"]

Or one may revise the wording to avoid pluralizing the foreign word: the *keiretsu* associations.

Compound nouns.   The plural of a hyphenated compound noun is usually formed by adding *s* to the noun member of the compound: sisters-in-law *and* courts-martial. The plurals of solid compounds, however, are regular: handfuls, spoonfuls, tablespoonfuls, *and* teaspoonfuls. For open compounds, the preference is to pluralize the key noun: attorneys general. When in doubt, consult your dictionary.

Proper nouns.   The plural of most proper nouns is regularly formed:

The property is owned by the Arroyos, the Bachs, the Beaches, and the Roths.

But the plural of a proper noun ending in *y* takes an *s:*

There are three Marys and two Larrys in this department.

Exceptions: the Rocky Mountains, the Rockies; the Allegheny Mountains, the Alleghenies; Teletubby, Teletubbies.

The plural of a proper noun ending in *s* takes *es:*

We invited the Joneses and the Wellses to dinner.

Nonetheless, to add *es* to form the plural of *McDonald's* seems to invite an odd pronunciation. Sometimes, one can write around the problem by adding a noun after the proper name: "Two new McDonald's restaurants opened last week—in Belarus and Tahiti." In other situations, it seems best to treat *McDonald's* as an invariant:

Large corporations—the Intels, the IBMs, and the McDonald's—can achieve significant economies of scale.

Abbreviations and initialisms.   Most abbreviations and initialisms are made plural by adding an *s:* vols., IDs, CDs, HMOs. However, when a publisher's style calls for initialisms to carry internal periods, an *'s* is added to form the plural: H.M.O.'s. An *'s* is also added to form the plural of an abbreviation that contains internal periods: M.D.'s. Such plurals are rarely used in formal writing; in most cases, a copyeditor would substitute the spelled-out form:

> *Overly colloquial:* She has two M.A.'s.
>
> *Better:* She has two master's degrees.
>
> *But:* A panel of M.B.A.'s gave their opinions of the new auditing procedures.

In this last example, one has to retain the abbreviation because there are no graceful substitutes: "a panel of people holding master's degrees in business administration" is far too clunky.

Letters of the alphabet.   Some letters can be made plural by adding an *s* (the three Rs), but often an apostrophe is needed:

> How many students received A's?
>
> Are all the i's dotted and the t's crossed?
>
> Mind your p's and q's.

POSSESSIVES

Possessive form of common nouns.   All the style manuals agree on the following principles for creating the possessive forms for common nouns:

> Singular common noun that does not end in *ess:* Add an apostrophe and an *s.*[2]

---

2. However, both *Chicago* and *WIT* advise dropping the *s* in some set expressions ("for goodness' sake"). *Chicago* also advises dropping the *s* in the possessive form of an uninflected singular noun that ends in *s* (e.g., corps, measles, series, species), or else rewording to avoid the possessive: this species' survival *or* the survival of this species.

Plural common noun that does not end in *s:* Add an apostrophe and an *s.*

Plural common noun that ends in *s:* Add an apostrophe only.

But there is some dissension about forming the possessive of a singular common noun that ends in *ess. WIT* notes that "some prefer *witness*, *countess*, and the like," but recommends *witness's* and *countess's* as more accurately reflecting spoken English. *The Associated Press Stylebook* advises looking at the word that follows and recommends "the witness's answer" but "the witness' story," to avoid a sibilant hiss. Writers and copyeditors in corporate publications departments usually avoid *business's* as the singular possessive by substituting another noun (firm, company) to produce a more euphonious and less controversial sentence.

Possessive form of proper nouns.   The formation of the possessive for proper nouns that end in *s* or *z* is fraught with peril. In the opinion of the editors of *Chicago* 14, "How to form the possessive of polysyllabic personal names ending with the sound of *s* or *z* probably occasions more dissension among writers and editors than any other orthographic matter open to disagreement" (p. 201). *Chicago* 15 offered two pages of rules, exceptions, and options, but *Chicago* 16 offers one simple principle: Form the possessive of all singular proper nouns by adding an apostrophe and an *s*; form the plural possessive by adding an apostrophe to the plural proper noun. Examples of singular possessive forms include Illinois's policy, Marx's essay, Jesus's parables, Moses's anger, Euripides's plays, Camus's novels. Examples of plural possessive forms include the Obamas' daughters, the Lopezes' home, the Coxes' ranch.

A more traditional convention is to add an apostrophe and an *s* to form the possessive of all proper nouns except *Jesus, Moses,* and classical names with "an unaccented ending pronounced *eez.*" Thus: Dylan Thomas's poems, Jasper Johns's paintings, *but* Jesus' parables, Moses' anger, Achilles' heel, Euripides' themes.

Some in-house style guidelines, however, call for adding only an apostrophe to form the possessive of any proper name ending in *s:* Dylan Thomas' poems, Jasper Johns' paintings.

Possessive form for inanimate objects.   In some quarters, a peculiar hobgoblin is afoot: Since inanimate objects cannot own anything, one should not attach an *'s* to an inanimate noun. The origin of this hobgoblin is uncertain (see *DEU,* s.v. "genitive"), but Wilson Follett and his disciples have insisted on it with such fervor that some copyeditors become queasy when they spot such common forms as "Florida's governor" and "the nation's capital." Follett (*MAU,* p. 254) vilifies both expressions as "newfangled and false [possessives]"—he is wrong on both counts. They are venerable instances of the genitive case (the traditional name for the possessive), and they cannot be *false* possessives because they are not possessives at all. *DEU* (p. 475) blesses them and even supplies a set of fancy names (objective genitive, descriptive genitive, genitive of purpose, group genitive). Trust your ear and your sensibility: the car's engine *and* the tree's roots, *but not* the computer's user *or* the eggs' carton.

Possessive for duration.   The possessive form is used for units of time that indicate duration.[3]

> We took three weeks' vacation.

> *But:* She handed in her paper two weeks early. *And:* She is five months pregnant.

You can test for the correct form by imagining a sentence in which the unit of time is singular:

> I took a week's vacation. [*Not* "a week vacation"] *So:* I took three weeks' vacation.

> I finished my paper a week early. [*Not* "a week's early"] *So:* I finished my paper two weeks early.

WIT, however, concludes that in some expressions "the idea of possession is so remote" that the unit of time functions as an adjective: "a two weeks waiting period." But surely that is better put as "a two-week waiting period."

Possessive form of words in italics or in quotation marks.   To form the possessive of an italicized word, *Chicago* recommends adding a roman apostrophe followed by a roman *s: Newsweek*'s circulation. If one cannot rewrite a

---

3. One also hears this use of the possessive in "ten dollars' worth of gas" or "a dollar's worth." In print, however, this expression is rarely used: rather than "millions of dollars' worth of devastation," one usually sees "millions of dollars in devastation."

sentence to avoid using the possessive form for a word that appears within quotation marks, the apostrophe and the *s* are placed outside the closing quotation marks: "Lord Randal"'s rhymes and rhythms.

Attributive nouns. The apostrophe is sometimes omitted when a plural head noun ending in *s* functions as an adjective rather than as a possessor; in other words, when the relation between the plural head noun and the second noun could be expressed by the prepositions "for" or "by" rather than the possessive "of": carpenters union, New York Mets first baseman. If the plural form of the head noun does not end in *s*, however, the apostrophe is always used: the people's republic, a children's hospital. This convention explains the absence of an apostrophe in such proper nouns as *Teachers College* (in New York City), *Department of Veterans Affairs,* and *Consumers Union.*

ONE WORD OR TWO?

Open, hyphenated, and *solid* (or *closed*) are basic terms in copyediting jargon:

An *open compound* is written as two words: high school, near miss, common sense.
In a *hyphenated compound,* the words are linked by a hard hyphen: half-life, self-confidence.
A *solid compound* is written as one word: schoolteacher, headache, textbook, commonsensical.

The treatment of some compounds is fixed, but the treatment of many others is determined by their grammatical function. For example, *problem solving* is open when used as a noun (engage in problem solving), but hyphenated when used as an adjective preceding a noun (problem-solving approach); the adjective *time consuming* is hyphenated when it precedes a noun (time-consuming tasks) but not when it follows the noun (these tasks are time consuming). Hyphens also help readers sort out complex modifiers: her all too brief letter *but* her all-too-brief public service career.

A copyeditor's first resource on the treatment of compounds is the dictionary. But, as the editors of *M-W Collegiate* explain, "Variation in the styling of compound words in English is frequent and widespread. It is often completely acceptable to choose freely among open, hyphenated, and closed alternatives (as *life style, life-style,* or *lifestyle*). However, to show all the stylings that are found for English compounds would require space that can be better used for other information. So this dictionary limits itself to a single styling for a compound" (p. 10A). Copyeditors then turn to their style manual. Some editors say, "When in doubt, add a hyphen," while others say, "When in doubt, leave it out."

It is also worth noting that the hyphenation of compounds changes over time. New compounds typically enter the language in open or hyphenated form; if the term gains currency, the wordspace or hyphen disappears and the term becomes solid. Thus *copy editor* and *copy-editor* yield to *copyeditor*. Citing this principle, some tech editors advise "when in doubt, close it up": *email, homepage, menubar.*

Above all, copyeditors must remember that hyphenation alone cannot rescue a writer's careless or compulsive agglomerative clusters. A bushel of hyphens won't clarify indecipherable strings of adjectives and nouns; rewriting is the only solution.

COMPOUND ADJECTIVES: ATTRIBUTIVE AND PREDICATE

Adjectives that precede the noun they modify are called *attributive adjectives;* adjectives that follow the noun are called *predicate adjectives.* When an attributive adjective is two words or longer, the possibility of misreading often arises. For example, a sign outside a restaurant reads "No Smoking Section." Some patrons will assume that the restaurant does not have a section in which diners can smoke ("there is no smoking section"); others will assume that the restaurant has a section in which smoking is prohibited ("there is a no-smoking section").

Here is another example of the difference a hyphen can make:

He is taking care of four year-old boys.

She is taking care of four-year-old boys.

Every style manual has a long section on compound adjectives, and each has its peculiarities and preferences. The following guidelines summarize the most important concepts.

Two-word attributive adjectives.   Two-word attributive adjectives are usually hyphenated:

low-rent district	hot-water faucet	working-class families
tax-free trade	full-service bank	freeze-dried coffee
sad-eyed gaze	all-out effort	acid-forming compounds

There are, however, three principal exceptions to this rule.

Exception 1. When the attributive adjective is a common open compound noun, a hyphen is used only when needed to avoid ambiguity:

income tax refund	word processing files
real estate transaction	city planning department
mass transit routes	baby boom generation
high school student	social service providers
post office regulations	

But:
end-user manuals	free-trade agreement
hard-sell tactics	real-number theory
short-story writer	top-dog status
free-market system	secret-police organization
loose-cannon mentality	

Exception 2. When the first member of the compound adjective is an adverb ending in -ly, the compound is open: highly developed sense of irony *and* openly hostile attitude.

Exception 3. Adjectives derived from foreign phrases are not hyphenated (in any position) unless the term is hyphenated in the original language:

à la carte menu	per capita consumption
ex parte motion	

But:
beaux-arts style	papier-mâché construction
tête-à-tête negotiations	

Do hyphenate a multilingual attributive adjective: *béisbol*-crazed teenagers, *flâneur*-inspired style.

Phrases used as adjectives. Adjectives that consist of short common phrases are hyphenated when used attributively:

off-the-record remark	spur-of-the-moment decision
over-the-counter drugs	black-and-white photographs

Unusual short phrases may be hyphenated or placed in quotation marks:

> big-box stores *or* "big box" stores
>
> strong-comma semicolon *or* "strong comma" semicolon

When a longer commonplace phrase is pressed into service as an attributive adjective, practice varies. The goal is to provide clarity with a minimum of clutter. To this end, writers and copyeditors have enlisted commas, hyphens, en dashes, quotation marks, and even the ever-controversial slash.

> Tickets will be distributed on a first come, first served basis.
>
> It was a typical he-said, she-said dispute.
>
> We need a high-touch–low-tech solution.
>
> His lips curled into a "been there, done that" sneer.
>
> This is another good news/bad news story.

Adjectives of quantity.   Compound adjectives that consist of a number and a unit of measurement are hyphenated:

> a one-word reply   a late-tenth-century relic
> a 105-pound dog   a twenty-six-mile race
> thirteenth-century art   a 5-percentage-point decline
> a twelve-ounce can   a twenty-first-century notion
> a 350-page book

There is no hyphen, however, in between a numeral and an abbreviation for a unit of measurement:

> a 10 km race   a 7.75 oz bottle

Suspended compound adjectives.   A space follows the hyphen in a suspended compound adjective:

> right- or left-handed users   micro- and macroeconomics
> fifteen- and thirty-year mortgages   125- and 185-pound cartons

In a series of suspended compounds, no space intervenes between the hyphens and the commas:

> first-, second-, and third-graders   35-, 45-, 55-, and 65-year-olds

(*Note:* In a phrase like "ten-to-fifteen-minute traffic delays," the "ten to fifteen" constitutes a unit—an approximation of length of the backup—and it is therefore not a suspended compound.)

Suspended compounds of the form "water-based and -soluble paint" are licit but likely to confuse readers; substitute "water-based and water-soluble paint."

COMPOUND ADVERBS

Compound adverbs rarely cause problems, but be on the lookout for ambiguous combinations:

He too readily agreed.
[*Means* He also agreed.]

He too-readily agreed.
[*Means* He agreed too readily.]

She is requesting yet more arcane information.
[*Means* additional information that is arcane]

She is requesting yet more-arcane information.
[*Means* information that is more arcane]

COMPOUND NOUNS

There isn't much rhyme or reason to many of the conventions for compound nouns; for example, *M-W Collegiate* shows *crossbones, cross-purpose,* and *cross section; break-in, breakout, breakup; walk-in, walk-on, walkout, walk-up.* And since few writers pause to check the preferred hyphenation of a word that is easy to spell (e.g., *girl friend* or *girlfriend? half hitch* or *half-hitch?*), even good writers tend to mix various forms within a document. To ensure consistency within a document, the copyeditor should always take a moment to look up compound nouns in the dictionary and to enter the desired form on the style sheet.

Sometimes, though, copyeditors must break with convention and depart from the dictionary in order to avoid compounds that will call attention to themselves or appear inconsistent. For example, *M-W Collegiate* shows *backseat.* But it would seem odd to read "Test drivers and their passengers report that the backseat feels roomier than the front seat." Here, "back seat" would call less attention to itself.

Sometimes, too, it is worthwhile to think about how a compound noun is pronounced and how it functions. As Nicholson Baker points out, "'Backseat' wants to be read as a trochee, BACKseat, like 'baseball,' when in reality we habitually give both halves of the compound equal spoken weight." Baker's thoughts about function coalesced in a discussion with a copyeditor over *pantyhose, panty hose,* and *panty-hose.* Baker had used the closed compound, and the copyeditor proposed the open form, which is the only form shown in *M-W Collegiate:* "My feeling was that . . . *pantyhose* . . . constitutes a single, interfused unit of sense, greater than the sum of its parts, which ought to be the criterion for jointure."[4]

PREFIXES AND SUFFIXES

Most words formed with common prefixes (e.g., *anti-, bi-, mid-, multi-, non-, over-, post-, pre-, re-, sub-, un-, under-*) and suffixes (e.g., *-fold, -less, -like*) are usually closed up—unless the closed form would be ambiguous or hard to read:

anti-intellectual, semi-independent (to avoid a double *i*)
co-edition, co-op, co-opt
de-emphasize, de-escalate, de-ice
guru-like, hobo-like, lava-like
mid-ocean, mid-thirties, mid–thirteenth century (noun),
    mid-thirteenth-century (adjective)

---

4. Both comments appear in Baker's "The History of Punctuation," in *The Size of Thoughts: Essays and Other Lumber* (New York: Random House, 1996), which describes the hyphenation minefield from the point of view of a careful, fastidious writer:

> And yet, though the suggested space [in *pantyhose*] seemed to me mistaken, I could just as easily have gone for *panty-hose* as *pantyhose*—in fact, normally I would have campaigned for a hyphen in this sort of setting, since the power-crazed policy-makers at Merriam-Webster and *Words into Type* have been reading too much Joyce in recent years and making condominiums out of terms . . . that deserve semi-detachment. . . . Evolution proceeds hyphen by hyphen, and manuscript by manuscript—impelled by the tension between working writers and their copy-editors, and between working copy-editors and their works of reference. (pp. 81–82)

Here again, if writers and copyeditors are completely deferential to the choices shown in the dictionary, the lexicographers' observations about which forms are most frequently used will not reflect the actual preferences of writers *(pantyhose)* but rather the compromises writers make with the dictionary entry *(panty-hose)* or their copyeditors' suggestion to abide by the dictionary entry *(panty hose).*

pro-democracy, pro-choice, pro-government, pro-life
re-aerate, re-interview
re-cover, re-form, re-sign (as distinct from *recover, reform,*
    and *resign*)
un-ionized (as distinct from *unionized*)

The "hard to read" standard, of course, introduces a subjective element. Here, many writers and copyeditors find *Chicago* and *M-W Collegiate* far too stingy in the allocation of hyphens. *Chicago* does mention the difficult-to-read test but recommends "neoorthodox," "nonevent," and "proindustrial." The list of *co-* compounds in *M-W Collegiate* is almost bizarre: cocaptain, cochair, coconspirator, cocurator, coheir, costar, coworker. Fortunately, *The Associated Press Stylebook* (s.v. "co-") offers a sane alternative: "Retain the hyphen when forming nouns, adjectives and verbs that indicate occupation or status." Thus: co-captain, co-chair, co-conspirator, co-curator, co-heir, co-star, and co-worker.

Compounds consisting of a prefix and a hyphenated term are hyphenated:

non-English-speaking students   post-cease-fire negotiations
un-air-conditioned auditorium   preflight-de-icing equipment

Compounds consisting of a prefix and a proper noun or a proper adjective are hyphenated:

anti-American sentiments   in mid-July   pre-Newtonian physics

If the proper noun is itself a two-word item, an en dash is used:

anti–New York sentiments   pre–World War II borders

CYBERJARGON

Dozens of computer-related compounds have entered everyday life, and current practice is sharply divided, with preferences changing as technologies mature. For example, "E-mail" was common in the mid 1990s, but has since all but disappeared, leaving editors and writers to haggle over "e-mail" versus "email."

If cyberjargon is covered in the publisher's in-house guidelines, you will of course follow the conventions shown there. But if you have to make an independent decision, look to the author's preference and the strength of the author's feelings as well as to the intended readership and the purpose of the document. Most often your overriding concern should be, Which forms are likely to be clearest to the readers? In corporate publishing, however, conveying an up-to-date image is sometimes deemed more important than clarity; in these cases, the publications department may prefer the sleeker all-lowercase closed compounds (homepage, voicemail, website).

SPELLCHECKERS

All word processing programs include a spellchecking feature. For short documents that contain few unusual words and few proper nouns, spell-checking is fast and convenient—though not reliable. As noted at the beginning of this chapter, spellcheckers do not identify a misspelled word if the misspelling is itself a word, do not distinguish between homophones, do not account for spellings determined by usage, and may allow variant spellings and hyphenations that may not be compatible with the house dictionary.

To save yourself some embarrassment, you can create an exclude dictionary: a list of words that you want your spellchecker to flag even though they are legitimate words. For example, if you add *pubic, thee,* and *widows* to your exclude dictionary, your spellchecker will stop three times in the following sentence: The pubic library ordered thee licenses for Widows XP.

For long documents that contain many unusual words, spellchecking can be tedious. You can save some time by clicking the "ignore all" option, which instructs the computer to ignore all instances of the word in the current document. Or you can click "add," which permanently adds the word to the main dictionary or to a supplementary dictionary that you have created. Add-on spelling modules are available for some technical fields and many foreign languages.

Because bibliographies and reference lists are filled with proper names, spellchecking these sections is a slow process, and some copyeditors do not run the spellchecker on these sections.

On-screen edits.   When you copyedit on-screen, running the spellchecker is one of your routine tasks. Most copyeditors run the spellchecker before editing the file—so that they will not have to correct each misspelling as it arises—and again after editing the file. The spellchecker is run one final time during cleanup, after the author's changes have been incorporated into the file.

Hard-copy edits. If you can obtain the author's files, running the spellchecker before or after you copyedit may help you catch a few hard-to-spot typos.

EXERCISE C

"Sprinkle" hyphens, close-up marks, and wordspaces in the following sentences. The answer key is on pages 467–71.

1. There was an above average turnout by middle aged working class voters in the south eastern states.

2. He submitted a hastily written report that documented his half baked effort to revise his predecessor's ill conceived cost cutting plan.

3. To replicate this early nineteenth century experiment, the high school students needed two gallon test bottles, a four inch long tube, a six or seven foot plank, and two to three teaspoons of salt.

4. The ideal candidate will have strong skills in problem solving, decision making, film making, book keeping, and proof reading.

5. He is self conscious about his 45 percent productivity decline and five fold increase in tardiness.

6. As a comparison of the pre and post test scores for the fourth, fifth, and sixth grade students showed, highly motivated young students can learn the most basic aspects of socio economic theory.

7. He sat cross legged at the cross roads cross questioning the pollster about the cross over vote and the cross fire over the nomination.

8. The state of the art amplifier is over there with the other out of order equipment that the under appreciated copy editors and their anti intellectual co workers left behind.

EXERCISE D

The following capsule reviews will be published in a mail-order catalog. You are being asked to do a light copyedit. Write your queries in the margins, and keep a style sheet on a piece of paper. The answer key is on pages 472–77.

A FROLIC OF HIS OWN. William Gaddis. Poseidon. $25.00

A *Frolic of His Own,* William Gaddiss' long anticipated fourth novel, is a funny, accurate tale of lives caught up in the toils of law. Oscar Crease, middle-aged college instructor, savant, and playwright is suing a Hollywood producer for pirating his play *Once at Antietam,* based on his grandfather's experiences in the Civil War, and turning it in to a gory block-buster called *The Blood in the Red White and Blue.* Oscar's suit, and a host of other lawsuits--which involve a dog trapped in an outdoor sculpture, wrongful death during a river baptism, a church versus a soft drink company, and even Oscar himself after he is run over by his own car--engulf

all who surround him, from his free-wheeling
girlfriend to his draconian, nonagenarian
father, Federal Judge Thomas Creese. Down
this tortuous path of depositions and
decrees, suits and countersuits, the most
lofty ideas of our culture are rung dry in
the often surreal logic and language of the
law.

THE BIRD ARTIST. Howard Norman. FSG. $20
Howard Norman's spellbinding novel is set in
Newfoundland in 1911. The novel not only
shares its place, but also its tone and
passion, with *The Shipping News*. Fabian Vas's
story, told with simplicity and grace, takes
place against a spare beautiful landscape. At
age 20, Fabian is working at the boatyard,
taking a correspondence course in bird
painting, and sleeping with Maraget Handle, a
woman of great beauty, intelligence, and
waywardness. When his father leaves on a long

hunting expedition and his mother takes up with the lighthouse keeper, Fabian looses his bearings. The author's intense observation of people and nature make for a remarkably good novel.

A PERSONAL MATTER. Kenzaburo Oë. $7.95

A Personal Matter, here translated by John Nathan, is probably Oë's best known novel. It is the story of a man's relationship with his severely brain-damaged child. As he plots the child's murder, he finally realizes that he must take responsibility for his son. The novel, written out of Oé's profound despair after the birth of his own disabled child (now a 31-year-old successful composer) is original, different, tough in its candor and beautiful in its faithfulness to both intellectual precision and human tenderness.

❖ 6 ❖

Capitalization

Proper nouns and proper adjectives are always capitalized, but there are two conventions for treating words that are not indisputably proper. *Down style* favors the sparse use of capital letters; in *up style* many more nouns and adjectives are uppercased:

Down style	*Up style*
The president announced	The President announced
The Truman administration	The Truman Administration
After the secretary of state left	After the Secretary of State left

Up style is used by some newspapers and magazines, but down style predominates in book publishing.[1]

You can save yourself a lot of time if you raise questions about capitalization with your editorial coordinator or the author after you've skimmed the manuscript and before you begin working on it. *Chicago* 14 asserts that "most authors . . . do not feel strongly about capitalization" (p. 236), but the editor of the Cambridge University Press style manual offers the opposite advice: "Many authors have strong feelings about capitalization. . . . Do not carry logic too far, or you will find yourself with too many capitals or too

---

1. In "Let's Kill All the Copy Editors" (*New York Times,* October 6, 1991), William Safire takes a gleeful poke at book publishers' preference for down style, which he labels "a case of the lowers": "We are not going to turn into slaves of e. e. cummings." In November 1999, however, the *New York Times* abandoned up style for down. Also, Cummings used unconventional capitalization in his poems, but he did not lowercase his name; see "NOT 'e. e. cummings,'" by Norman Friedman, in *Spring* 1 (1992): 114–21.

few" (Judith Butcher, *Copy-editing: The Cambridge Handbook,* 2d ed. [Cambridge: Cambridge University Press, 1981], p. 89).

The truth may well lie somewhere in the middle: Most authors do not have strong opinions about capitalization; for others, however, capitalization is not merely a matter of typography but an issue of according or denying status to a term. The conventions in some academic, professional, and technical fields also differ from the down-style preferences shown in *Chicago* and *WIT.* Thus you should use your style manual as a starting point but always be willing to accommodate current conventions in the author's field. Making reasonable, consistent choices is more important than adhering to every preference stated in a general-purpose style manual. So that you and others can keep track of your decisions about capitalization, you should always record those decisions on your style sheet.

Here are some pointers about the most common headaches that arise in the area of capitalization.

PERSONAL NAMES AND TITLES

By convention, all personal names (first, middle, and last names as well as nicknames and the suffixes *Jr.* and *Sr.*) are capitalized. The suffixes *Jr.* and *Sr.* were traditionally preceded and followed by a comma, but the newer convention eliminates these commas:

> *Older convention:* Pemberton Smythe, Jr., was appointed chairman of the board.

> *Newer convention:* Pemberton Smythe Jr. was appointed chairman of the board.

Policies vary, however, in the treatment of individuals who prefer that their names be lowercased. Here's Bill Walsh's spirited defense of using standard capitalization despite the individual's preference (but on Cummings's preference, see page 151n):

> Sure, before "k.d. lang" there was "e.e. cummings." But, as most good dictionaries . . . and *New York Times* style recognize, these are logos. The names are K.D. Lang and E.E. Cummings. To bow to the artists' lowercase demand . . . deprives readers of a crucial visual cue. . . . [Although] when you print "K.D.

Lang" or "E.E. Cummings" without a footnote explaining your departure from the norm . . . many readers will simply assume you made a mistake.

But Bill, you may ask, don't people have the right to be called whatever they choose? Well, ideally, yes. . . . [But] how about another ordinary citizen . . . who insists that his name is I'M!!!A!!!NEAT!!GUY!!? . . . It's impossible to be a consistent liberal on this issue—you have to draw the line somewhere, and I choose to draw it quicker than most.[2]

Some publishers, however, respect the lowercasers' preference. When a lowercased name appears occasionally in a text, one tries to avoid having the name at the start of a sentence. Thus:

Awkward: bell hooks is the pen name of Gloria Watkins.

Preferable: Gloria Watkins uses the pen name bell hooks.

This strategy is cumbersome, however, for lowercased names that appear frequently throughout a document. In such cases, the copyeditor should consult with the author and the editorial coordinator before deciding whether to uppercase the first letter of the name at the beginning of a sentence.

Initials.   Most style manuals call for spacing between initials in a personal name: A. B. Cherry (*not* A.B. Cherry).[3] There are no spaces, however, between personal initials that are not followed by periods (FDR, LBJ). Some manuals also recommend closing up initials that follow a first name (Thomas A.J. Castle), and initials that come in a set of three (J.R.R. Tolkien). In *CSE* style— which eliminates periods whenever possible—personal initials in running text carry internal spacing (Dr S E Ralph), and in bibliographical citations are closed up (SE Ralph).

Some publishers expect their copyeditors to ask the author to supply the full name (not just the initials and surname) of an individual the first time

2. Bill Walsh is a copyeditor at the *Washington Post;* this passage comes from the "Curmudgeon's Stylebook" section of his website (www.theslot.com), a vast, eclectic collection of rules, pointers, and rants on matters editorial. The eagle-eyed reader will notice that Walsh closes up personal initials (k.d. and K.D.), which is the treatment mandated by *The Associated Press Stylebook.* Other conventions for the spacing of personal initials are discussed in the next subsection.

3. Some publishers prefer a thin space, rather than a regular wordspace, between personal initials. If you are working on hard copy, you may be asked to add the instruction "thin #" for the typesetter. If you are working on-screen, you may be asked to insert a special code or to use your word processing program's *hard space* character (also called a *nonbreaking space*). The hard space will prevent the line from breaking in between the initials.

that person is mentioned in the document. Excepted from this convention are extremely well known people whose surnames are distinctive (Shakespeare, Darwin, Poe), persons who are best known by their initials rather than their full names (T. S. Eliot, A. A. Milne, J. D. Salinger, H. G. Wells, E. B. White), and persons best known by only one name (Michelangelo).

In addition, the sensitive copyeditor will consider the intended audience, the function of the name within the document, and the cadence of the sentence. In a scholarly book about a twentieth-century Spanish poet, for example, there is no need to insert the first names of artists who appear in a whirlwind cluster like the following:

> When he returned to Madrid, he resumed his acquaintances with Picasso, Dali, Buñuel, Salinas, Jiménez, Guillén, and Aleixandre. That winter, at a conference in Moscow, he met Eisenstein, Gorky, Prokofiev, and Malraux.

Since the author's purpose here is simply to suggest the number and variety of artists that her subject knew, and since readers of this kind of specialized work are likely to recognize all these surnames, there is no reason to clutter the text with a rash of given names.

Particles.   There are no surefire rules for the capitalization of particles (de, de la, van, von) in personal names. The capitalization of the names of well-known individuals can be found in a dictionary or a desktop encyclopedia; for more obscure personal names, you should ask the author to verify the capitalization. When a lowercased particle appears as the first word in a sentence, it is capitalized. When a lowercased particle appears at the beginning of an entry in an alphabetical listing (e.g., a directory, index, or bibliography entry that uses an inverted order), the particle remains lowercased.

Titles and offices.   In down style, a person's title or office is capitalized only when it directly precedes a personal name and is part of the name:

> In 1862 President Lincoln announced . . .
>
> In 1862 the president announced . . .
>
> In 1862 the American president announced . . .
>
> In 1862 American president Lincoln announced . . .
>
> Lincoln, before he was elected president, announced . . .

Adjectives based on personal names.   The most common suffixes for transforming a personal surname into an adjective are *-esque, -ean, -ian,* and *-ic.* The proper adjectives are always capitalized:

Audenesque, Disneyesque, Lincolnesque, Reaganesque

Aeschylean, Lockean, Sartrean

Aristotelian, Chekhovian, Emersonian, Freudian, Hegelian

Aristiophanic, Byronic, Napoleonic, Pindaric, Platonic, Ptolemaic

Surnames ending in *w* and *eau* call for some adjustment: Shaw, Shavian; Thoreau, Thoreauvian. For the adjectival forms of well-known names, consult your dictionary; for other names, consult with your author and trust your ear. Some names can take different suffixes, with a slight difference in tone: To most Americans, *Clintonesque* sounds a bit grander than *Clintonian.* This device should be used with care. If the individual is not of sufficient stature to merit adjectivalization, some readers will take the usage to be satiric or parodic.

Terms derived from personal names.   Many terms derived from personal names are lowercased: braille, caesarean birth, fallopian tube, molotov cocktail. Units of measurement named after individuals are also lowercased: joule, newton, pascal, watt. In medical terminology, however, the possessive form of the name (but not the adjectival or other forms) is usually capitalized: Achilles' tendon, Huntington's disease, Parkinson's disease, *but* parkinsonian, parkinsonism.

GEOGRAPHICAL NAMES

All style manuals offer detailed discussions of place names. The following pointers address the most common issues.

Proper names and nicknames.   Both the proper names and nicknames of places are capitalized: the Bay Area, the Big Apple, the Big Easy, the Twin Cities, Euroland.

Directions.   Directional nouns and adjectives are capitalized when they are used to refer to a distinct region (the Midwest, the South, the East Coast, Western Europe) but not when they merely indicate direction (southern Texas, eastern Pennsylvania, central Europe, northern Oregon).

Terms derived from place names.   Most terms derived from place names are lowercased: arabic numerals, french fries, manila envelope, *and* venetian blinds. The capitalization of *Scotch tape* has nothing to do with Scotland; by convention, brand names are capitalized.

Name changes.   In Europe, in particular, the map has been remade in recent years. Thus you may need recourse to such terms as "the former West German capital," "the former East Germany," and "the former Soviet Union."

Names for residents of states in the United States.   The *United States Government Printing Office Style Manual* recommends the following forms for state residents:

Alabamian	Louisianian	Ohioan
Alaskan	Mainer*	Oklahoman
Arizonan	Marylander	Oregonian
Arkansan	Massachusettsan*	Pennsylvanian
Californian	Michiganite*	Rhode Islander
Coloradan	Minnesotan	South Carolinian
Connecticuter*	Mississippian	South Dakotan
Delawarean	Missourian	Tennessean
Floridian	Montanan	Texan
Georgian	Nebraskan	Utahn (adj.: Utahan)
Hawaiian	Nevadan	Vermonter
Idahoan	New Hampshirite	Virginian
Illinoisan	New Jerseyite	Washingtonian
Indianian*	New Mexican	West Virginian
Iowan	New Yorker	Wisconsinite
Kansan	North Carolinian	Wyomingite
Kentuckian	North Dakotan	

* For these somewhat awkward forms, other books suggest Nutmegger (Connecticut), Hoosier (Indiana), Down Easter (Maine), Bay Stater (Massachusetts), and Michiganian or Michigander (Michigan). These controversies, among others, are discussed by Paul Dickson in *Labels for Locals: What to Call People from Abilene to Zimbabwe,* a dictionary of nouns and adjectives, which Dickson terms "demonyms," that denote residents of cities, states, and countries around the world. (For good measure, the book also has entries for hypothetical residents of the planets in our solar system.)

Names for residents of countries.   Here's a selection from the recommendations in the *United States Government Printing Office Style Manual* for nouns denoting nationality:

Afghan(s)	Mozambican(s)
Argentine(s)	Nepalese (*sing. and pl.*)
Bahamian(s)	Nigerois (*sing. and pl.*)[†]
Bangladeshi(s)	Pakistani(s)
Belizean(s)	Portuguese (*sing. and pl.*)
Briton(s) (*collective pl.*, British)[*]	Salvadoran(s)
Filipino(s)	Senegalese (*sing. and pl.*)
Greenlander(s)	Swiss (*sing. and pl.*)
Icelander(s)	Thai (*sing. and pl.*)
Iraqi(s)	Togolese (*sing. and pl.*)
Lao *or* Laotian (*pl.*, Laotians)	Vietnamese (*sing. and pl.*)
Liechtensteiner(s)	Yemeni(s)
Luxembourger(s)	Zimbabwean(s)

[*] *Briton* and *British* are used to denote the residents of England as well as those of the United Kingdom. (The United Kingdom comprises the island of Great Britain—England, Scotland, and Wales—and Northern Ireland.)
[†] Refers to residents of Niger, not Nigeria (Nigerians).

RACIAL AND ETHNIC GROUPS

The capitalization of racial and ethnic groups remains a contentious topic. (On controversies over the names themselves, see "Bias-Free Language" in chapter 15.) *Chicago* and *WIT* both recommend lowercasing designations based on skin color (*black, white*), though *Chicago* notes that at times these terms can be capitalized. All the manuals recommend capitalizing the names of ethnic and national groups: African Americans, Chicanos, Hispanics, and Native Americans.

Sometimes such capitalization decisions are purely political, but at other times the issue is one of achieving an editorial consistency that looks consistent to readers who are unfamiliar with the strictures enunciated in the style manuals. Thus, when the name of one group is capitalized, a copyeditor may decide to ignore the style manual and capitalize the names of all analogous groups:

Original: The number of black, Latino, and Native American applicants rose last year.

Revision: The number of Black, Latino, and Native American applicants rose last year.

Or: The number of African American, Latino, and Native American applicants rose last year.

If group names repeatedly arise in your work, you may want to read the extensive discussion provided by Marilyn Schwartz and others, *Guidelines for Bias-Free Writing* (Bloomington: Indiana University Press, 1995).

COMPANY NAMES, TRADEMARKS, AND BRAND NAMES

Always ask your author to reverify the spelling and capitalization of business names and terms, especially those that have unusual typographical features.

All capitals: UMAX Technologies[4]

Midcap or intercap: WordPerfect, LaserJet

Numerical character: 7-Eleven

Lowercase letter: eBay (in headlines or at the start of a sentence: eBay or EBay)

No internal periods: IBM, AT&T, Dr Pepper

Although novelists often use (and overuse) brand names as an aid to characterization, careful expository writers use generic names unless they are discussing a particular product.

Careless usage: Please keep all kleenexes and cokes away from the xeroxing machine.

Better: Please keep all tissues and cans of soda away from the photocopier.

But: We are ordering three new Xerox copiers and two LaserJet printers.

---

4. As Bill Walsh points out: "Your credit card may say VISA, your athletic shoes may say NIKE, but this is just because the companies chose an all-caps presentation for the brand names. That doesn't mean you write the words that way, any more than you would write WEBSTER'S NEW UNIVERSAL UNABRIDGED DICTIONARY just because that's what it says on the spine" (www.theslot.com).

All editorial style manuals recommend that trademarks be capitalized. But strict adherence to this convention is likely to startle readers, many of whom are unaware that Dacron, Dumpster, Formica, Frisbee, Jell-O, Mace, Muzak, Orlon, Ping-Pong, Post-it, Styrofoam, Teflon, and Touch-Tone are trademarks. Once a trademark is so common as to be perceived as a generic term that is used metaphorically ("that's no more than a band-aid approach"; "the teflon president"; "he shook like jello"), some editors will lowercase the name.[5]

The more common trademarks appear in the dictionary, with "trademark" in the slot used to indicate the part of speech. *M-W Collegiate* shows "xerox" as a transitive verb ("to copy on a xerographic copier"), and "Xerox" as a trademark for a xerographic copier.[6] You may also wish to consult the website of the International Trademark Association (INTA)—www.inta.org—which features an alphabetical list of some four thousand trademarks and service marks and their generic equivalents.

There is no need to include such designations as ™ (trademark), ˢᴹ (service mark), ® (registered trademark), or © (copyright) in running text. Indeed, it is preferable not to use these symbols because they may interfere with the linespacing of the final document.

CYBERJARGON

The following forms are conventional:

CD-ROM, CD-ROMs

e-book; e-commerce; e-mail (*or* email)

> At the beginning of a sentence: E-books

> In headline-style titles: E-Books *or* E-books

hypertext markup language; HTML

the Internet, the Net

---

5. Because all the style manuals are so insistent on capitalizing trademarks and brand names, I have always felt a bit guilty (or defiant, depending on my mood) when I lowercased them. But it seems that I am in excellent company: Edward D. Johnson, who proudly upholds many proprieties that others dismiss as overly finicky, confesses: "When I find a figuratively used trademark lowercased in a book I am editing, I am apt to pretend I don't know it should be capitalized, though I can't conscientiously recommend this course" (*The Handbook of Good English,* p. 233).

6. *M-W Collegiate* does not have an entry for the noun *xerox* ("a photocopy"). All the manuals advise using the generic terms (copy, photocopy).

local-area network; LAN

multipurpose Internet mail extensions; MIME

portable document format; PDF (*or* .pdf file)

the World Wide Web; the Web; Web site *or* website;

> Web browser *or* web browser; webcast; webmaster

Publishers of computer manuals have devised various conventions for capitalizing the names of items on the screen display and on the keyboard:

> *Names of keys:* ALT, CTRL, ESC, TAB, ENTER *or* Alt, Ctrl, Esc, Tab, Enter
>
> *Names of cursor keys:* Down Arrow, Up Arrow, Home, PgUp, PgDn
>
> *Labels on the menu bar:* File, Edit, View, Table, Help

TITLES OF WORKS

The conventions regarding the capitalization of titles apply to the capitalization of complete works (books, corporate reports, magazine articles), chapter titles, and headings within books and documents. There are two basic styles for capitalizing these titles. The first is called either *headline style* or *UC/lc* (shorthand for "uppercase and lowercase"), and the second is called *sentence style* or *initial cap only.*

Both styles are acceptable as long as they are used consistently throughout a document. Here, "consistently" does not mean "exclusively." The two styles may be combined in one document—major headings in headline style, subheadings in sentence style—as long as all items in a given class are treated consistently. *Exception:* When a chapter title or heading contains a quotation, the quotation may be set in sentence style, even if the other chapter titles and headings are set in headline style:

> Redefining Patriotism: "Ask not what your country can do for you"
>
> "Shall I compare thee to a summer's day?": Metaphors and Clichés of Our Time

Headline style.   In headline style, one capitalizes the first and last words of a title or subtitle. Subtitles are most often introduced by a colon (*Sticks and Stones: The Magic of Names*), but sometimes a dash is used ("Willa Jan— The Greatest Player").

In addition, one capitalizes all interior words except articles (a, an, the), coordinate conjunctions (and, but, or, for, nor),[7] prepositions, scientific terms that begin with a lowercase letter (pH, mRNA), and scientific (Latin) names that are lowercased in running text (*E. coli*).

Regarding prepositions, however, there are contending conventions. *Chicago* recommends lowercasing prepositions regardless of length, some publishers use a "four-letter rule," and others use a "five-letter rule":

Chicago *style* (lowercase all prepositions)	Four-letter rule (uppercase preposi- tions of four letters or longer)	Five-letter rule (uppercase preposi- tions of five letters or longer)
Running for Cover	Running for Cover	Running for Cover
Life with Father	Life With Father	Life with Father
Driving through Maine	Driving Through Maine	Driving Through Maine

Whichever preposition rule you adopt, you need to remember that many common prepositions sometimes function as nouns, adjectives, or adverbs, and when they do, they should be capitalized in a title.

Lowercase the prepositions: *Poverty in America in the 1960s*

Uppercase the nouns: *The Ins and Outs of Office Etiquette*

Uppercase the adjectives: "The In and Out Trends This Year"

Uppercase the adverbs: "Taking In the Sights, Taking Over the City"

As this last example shows, an erstwhile preposition that is an inseparable part of the verb (take in, take out, take up, take over) is capitalized in a title. *WIT* also recommends capitalizing compound prepositions (apart from, just before, out of, owing to) in titles.

Another pesky little word is *as,* which may function as a preposition, adverb, subordinate conjunction, or pronoun. *Chicago* advises always lowercasing *as* in a title. Or you can parse the title:

---

7. For correlative conjunctions, the leading element is capitalized, and the trailing element is lowercased: Mayor Urges Either Fare Hikes or Service Cuts; Riders Demand Both Fare Cuts and Better Service; Riders Demand Not Only Fare Cuts but Better Service.

Lowercase the preposition: *Working as an Editor*

Uppercase the adverb: *Twice As Good*

Uppercase the conjunction: "Do As the Pros Do"

Uppercase the pronoun: "Tears Such As Angels Weep"

The style manuals differ in their approach to hyphenated words in a title. *Chicago* calls for capping all elements of a hyphenated term except for the articles, coordinating conjunctions, prepositions, and elements attached to a prefix (unless the element is a proper noun or adjective):

Over-the-Counter Remedies

"An Up-and-Down Ride for Investors"

Anti-intellectualism in Post-Restoration Drama

Twenty-First-Century Architecture

"E-mail and Texting among Non-English-Speaking Students"

As noted in chapter 4 (see "Controversial Techniques"), slashed constructions pose various semantic problems. When they appear in titles, however, the slash does not interfere with the regular rules for capitalization:

"Capitalization Quandaries for the Modern Writer/Editor"

Peace and/or Justice

"The Slash/Slant/Virgule: Boon or Bane?"

When slashed constructions are printed in display type, a thin space may be inserted before and after the slash for appearance' sake.

Sentence style.   In sentence style, one capitalizes the first word of the title, the first word of a subtitle, and those words that would be capitalized in regular text (i.e., proper nouns, proper adjectives, and the word *I*). The following examples illustrate the treatment of hyphenated and slashed words:

"Self-esteem in the American workplace"

"The post–World War II economic miracle"

"Slash/slant/virgule: Boon or bane?"

Typographical treatment.   Within running text, the titles of books, newspapers, magazines, journals, movies, operas, and works of art are set in italics.

The titles of short literary works (poems, essays, short stories, and magazine and journal articles) and short musical works (songs) are set in roman type and placed in quotation marks. Some newspapers and magazines, however, set all titles in roman type, enclosed within quotation marks.

NAMES OF PLANTS AND ANIMALS

The capitalization of the common names of plants and animals is somewhat anarchic, and copyeditors should always consult a dictionary. Copyeditors who routinely work on scientific papers, field guides, and similar projects will want to acquire specialized reference books.

By convention, the scientific (Latin) names of plants and animals are always italicized, and the genus is capitalized, while the species and subspecies are lowercased: *Escherichia coli; Ursus americanus; Heteromeles arbutifolia macrocarpa.* On second reference, the genus name is usually abbreviated, and only its first letter is given: *E. coli; U. americanus; H. arbutifolia.*

The abbreviations *sp.* (species; plural, *spp.*), *var.* (variety), and *cv.* (cultivar) are set in roman type: *Ceanothus* sp.; *Acer negundo* spp. *californicum; Delphinium decorum* var. *patens; Pelargonium peltatum* cv. Claret Crousse. Note that variety names are lowercased and italicized, while cultivar names are capitalized and set in roman type. In some editorial styles, cultivar names are placed in single quotation marks (and the abbreviation *cv.* is not used): *Pelargonium peltatum* 'Claret Crousse.' Hybrids are indicated by a multiplication sign: *Salvia* × *superba.*[8]

Phylum, class, order, and family names are capitalized and set in roman type: Hominidae, Mammalia.

---

8. A space always precedes the ×, but whether or not a space belongs after the × depends on how the hybrid name was derived (see *CSE*).

EXERCISE E

Copyedit the following capsule biographies. The answer key is on pages 478–80.

After serving for five years as President Eisenhower's Staff Secretary, General Andrew J. Goodpaster assumed many of the duties of Chief of Staff in 1958. During Eisenhower's administration, General Goodpaster supervised the National Security Council Staff, briefed the President on intelligence matters, and was White House Liaison for defense and national security.

Before being appointed special assistant and counsel to President Johnson in 1965, Harry McPherson had served as counsel to the Democratic policy committee in the Senate, Deputy Undersecretary of the Army, and assistant Secretary of State. He is now an attorney in Washington, D.C., and vice-chairman of and general counsel to the John

F. Kennedy Center for the performing arts.

General Alexander Haig was deputy to

national security adviser Henry Kissinger

during the early days of President Nixon's

administration. He became Nixon's chief of

staff in 1973. In 1974 he was named Supreme

Commander of NATO, a post he held until 1979

when he retired to enter private industry. He

returned to Government service as Secretary

of State during the first eighteen months of

President Reagan's first term.

EXERCISE F

This exercise is the text of a short handout addressed to people seeking entry-level editorial jobs. You are being asked to do a light copyedit and to complete a style sheet (use a blank piece of paper). If you have queries, write them in the margin. The answer key is on pages 481–91.

If you want to break into publishing, you probably know that the center of book publishing in the United States is New York City. But you don't have to move to New York to work in book publishing. Go to the Public Library and look at the most recent edition of *Literary Market Place* (*LMP,* published annually by R.R. Bowker, New York). Use the geographical index to locate book publishers in your town. Then turn to the full entries for each publisher and take note of how many titles the company publishes. A company that produces fewer than eight or ten titles a year is most likely a two-or-three-person operation, staffed by it's owners. But the names of any larger publishers should go on your job hunting list.

While you have *LMP* in hand, turn to the subject index and notice how many different kinds of book publishers there are, not just fiction and nonfiction but el-hi (elementary and high school) and college textbook publishers, legal and medical publishers, science and math publishers, foreign language publishers, and publishers of children's books, art books, scholarly books, wilderness books, computer books, gardening books, cook books, and every stripe of how-to-books.

While you're at the library, you might also also look at the current edition of *Magazine Industry Market Place* (R. R. Bowker) or *Writer's Market* (Writer's Digest Books). You'll be surprised to see how large the universe of magazine publishers is. There are

hundreds of small trade magazines, and
hundreds of local and regional magazines.
Check the directories to see which magazines
have editorial offices in your town.

As you're compiling your list, don't forget
the corporate sector. The obvious employers
in the corporate sector are direct-mail and
catalogue companies, but many firms whose
primary business lies elsewhere do an
enormous amount of publishing: banks, law
firms, phone companies, hospitals,
universities, museums, manufactures of high-
tech equipment, and consulting firms in all
fields. Any business that provides client
manuals, documents, or reports, or that
produces a newsletter for employees or for
clients needs editors. Some companies do not
advertise, but post their openings at the
company's Personnel Office. Call that office
and ask how openings are publicized.

Finally, there's the government sector. Hordes of editors are employed in almost every department of municipal, county, state, and federal goverments. Some of these positions require subject-matter expertise, but others do not. Check with nearby government offices to find out whether you need to take a Civil Service Exam and how openings are posted.

In all four sectors, there is stiff competition for entry-level jobs. To improve your chances of landing a job:

1. Make sure your résumé and cover letter are easy to read, error free, and have a consistent editorial style (punctuation, treatment of dates, use of abbreviations, etc). Don't just list your previous job titles-- take a sentence or two to describe what you did in those positions. Be sure to include any relevant subject-matter expertise

and auxiliary skills (pasteup, graphic design, type-setting).

2. Don't dwell on your writing skills (unless the job callls for writing)--most managing editors believe there is little or no correlation between writing skills and editing skills. And don't dwell on your academic credentials unless you're applying to a scholarly press or journal.

3 If you have work samples, bring them to an interview. Attach a Post-It to each sample describing the work you did on the project.

4. Be prepared to take proofreading and copyediting tests. Some employers will also test your word-processing skills.

Numbers and Numerals

A publication's editorial style for the treatment of numbers includes guide-lines for

when to spell out a quantity and when to use a numeral
how to treat common numerical expressions (e.g., fractions,
    percentages, money, time)
how to express units of measurement
how to treat inclusive numerical ranges
how to style mathematical expressions

The two broad sets of conventions for the treatment of numbers are called *technical* (or *scientific*) style and *nontechnical* (or *humanistic*) style. Techni-cal style is used in technical and scientific writing, of course, but also in other types of documents that typically have many numbers and quantities in them, including statistical and financial material, cookbooks, and do-it-yourself car-pentry books. Nontechnical style, in contrast, is often used for pieces that have relatively few numbers in them.

WORDS OR NUMERALS?

In both technical and nontechnical documents, one rule is absolute: A sen-tence must never begin with a numeral. Thus a copyeditor must either spell out the numeral or reword the sentence.

Original: 10,500 pages of depositions were submitted by the plaintiff.

Revision: Ten thousand five hundred pages of depositions were submitted by the plaintiff.

Or: Some 10,500 pages of depositions were submitted by the plaintiff.

Original: 1998 was a disappointing year for wheat exporters.

Revision: The year 1998 was a disappointing one for wheat exporters.

Or: Nineteen ninety-eight was a disappointing year for wheat exporters.

[*The Associated Press Stylebook* does permit "1976 was a very good year," but no other manuals endorse this practice.]

Beyond this restriction, technical and scientific publishers—and most newspapers and magazines—prefer numerals to spelled-out numbers because numerals are easier to read and locate (they stand out from the sea of surrounding words) and because they take up less space than spelled-out numbers.[1] Most style manuals and in-house guides for technical texts prescribe spelling out only whole numbers less than ten that do not represent precisely measured quantities.[2] Thus, in "We performed the five experiments within a 6-week period," a numeral appears before the unit of measurement "weeks," but a spelled-out word is used for the number of experiments, which is deemed to be a matter of counting rather than the specification of a precisely measured quantity.

In nontechnical texts, in contrast, the convention is to spell out whole numbers less than 101—except for percentages, years and dates, page numbers, and chapter numbers—and to spell out large numbers that can be spelled out in two words (e.g., thirty-three thousand, five million).

---

1. In some banking and legal documents, sums of money are expressed by a numeral followed by the spelled-out form: The underwriting fee will be $2,500,000 (two and a half million dollars).

2. *APA* also calls for numerals to be used for quantities that "denote a specific place in a numbered series" (e.g., grade 8, trial 3) and for "each number in a list of four or more numbers" (e.g., Participants were allowed to make 1, 2, 3, or 4 choices). *CSE* calls for numerals for anything that can be counted or measured; thus: "We performed the 5 experiments within a 6-week period." For ordinal numbers, *CSE* recommends spelling out "first" through "ninth."

Scientific or technical text	Humanistic or nontechnical text
Students were tested at ages 5, 7, and 9.	Students were tested at ages five, seven, and nine.
The satellite traveled 23 million miles.	The satellite traveled twenty-three million miles.
The average speed of the test vehicles was 25 mph.	The average speed of the test vehicles was twenty-five miles per hour.

In spelled-out numbers, hyphens are used only to join the parts of a two-digit number: forty-five, forty-five thousand, forty-five million, nineteen forty-five, twenty forty five.

In both technical and nontechnical documents, all numerical values of the same class or type are treated similarly in the text.

Technical document: We ran 5 trials in January, 9 in February, and 12 in March.

[Since numerals are used for all two-digit numbers in a technical document, the twelve trials in March must be expressed as a numeral. Because the five trials in January and the nine in February are numerical values of the same class—number of trials run—these must also be expressed as numerals, even though they are less than ten.]

Nontechnical document: Next year 325 local officials will attend the national meeting. California is expected to send the largest contingent, 28 delegates; Rhode Island, the smallest, 2 delegates. The meeting will last two days and will include six hours of workshops.

[The 325 in "325 local officials" has to be a numeral, so numerals must be used for all numbers that refer to the officials (28 delegates, 2 delegates). But the number of days and the number of hours of workshops are not in the same category as officials and delegates, and these small numbers are spelled out.]

In nontechnical documents one tries to avoid having two unrelated numerals in a row. (Many technical documents also observe this convention in order to prevent misreading.) A copyeditor can add a word between the two numerals, or spell out one of the numerals, or reword the sentence.

Original: In 1968 125,000 marchers protested the decision.

Revision: In 1968 about 125,000 marchers protested the decision.

[*About, approximately,* and *some* are the usual choices here. The context may also permit *an estimated, more than,* or *less than.*]

Original: We ordered 120 12V batteries.

Revision: We ordered 120 twelve-volt batteries.

[The decision to spell out "twelve" precludes the use of the abbreviation for volt. The convention is: Always use a numeral before an abbreviated unit of measurement.]

Original: The 2002 162-game schedule will be announced next week.

Revision: The 162-game schedule for 2002 will be announced next week.

But: Her scores on the four tests were 85, 88, 84, and 93.
[Here the back-to-back numerals are fine because they are of the same class—test scores.]

You may also encounter some nontechnical authors who follow *WIT* in spelling out all numerals other than years when they appear in dialogue or any other transcription of speech. *WIT* is the only style manual that makes this recommendation, but some authors feel strongly about it, arguing that speakers speak in words, not numerals. Although the logic of this argument is shaky—speakers speak sounds, which may be transcribed in various ways—copyeditors are usually expected to honor the author's preference in the matter.

PUNCTUATION OF NUMERALS

All style manuals recommend placing a comma to set off the last three digits of a five-digit numeral; some manuals also recommend placing a comma in four-digit numerals, except those that represent addresses, page numbers, and years (*thus* 2000 *but* 20,000 B.C.E.). The five-digit convention tends to prevail in technical documents, the four-digit convention in nontechnical documents.

If you work with non-American authors, you should be aware of two other conventions for punctuating long numerals. In what is called British style, a period is used in lieu of a comma in long numerals, and a raised dot is used in lieu of a decimal point. In what is called Continental style, a space is used in long numerals, and a comma is used to indicate decimals.

Style	Long numerals	Decimal numerals
American	12,345,678	3.1416
British	12.345.678	3·1416
Continental	12 345 678	3,1416

All the style manuals recommend placing a zero before a decimal expression that is less than one (e.g., 0.2) unless the numeral is of a category whose value cannot exceed one (e.g., probabilities, correlations, levels of statistical significance). The leading zero offers a friendly alert that the subsequent numeral is less than one (because readers may easily overlook a decimal point, especially in smaller type sizes). When such a decimal appears before a unit of measurement, the unit is stated in the singular:

0.25 inch   0.75 square foot   0.2 kilometer   0.5 liter

The number of digits expressed after the decimal point depends on the context. In nontechnical work, rounding off to one or two decimal places is usually sufficient. In technical work, however, some values are conventionally expressed to three, four, or more decimal places, and copyeditors working on technical documents should not delete any digits from these lengthy decimals. When an author has been inconsistent in expressing values of the same class or type, the copyeditor should query the internal discrepancy ("Two decimal places or three for test values? Revise for consistency").

FRACTIONS

Nontechnical text.   In nontechnical text, fractions are treated like other numbers: Those that can be spelled out with one-word or two-word numerators and denominators are spelled out. But *Chicago, WIT,* and *APA* each have slightly different recommendations for the hyphenation of spelled-out fractions; these require careful study. If house style does not mandate strict adherence to one of these manuals, you might want to adopt the following rules:

- Place a hyphen between the numerator and denominator of a spelled-out fraction when neither of these numbers is itself hyphenated: one-third, two-fifths, fifteen-sixteenths, eleven-hundredths, three and three-quarters, twenty-five and one-half.
- Omit the hyphen between the numerator and denominator when either of these itself contains a hyphen: twenty-five hundredths, five sixty-fourths.
- Apply these two rules to all fractions, whether they function as nouns, adjectives, or adverbs:

  Noun: Two-thirds of the children answered the question.
  Adjective: A two-thirds majority is required.
  Adverb: The work was two-thirds completed.

Mixed numbers (i.e., a whole number followed by a fraction) may be spelled out (if short) or set as numerals:

The final report was five and one-half inches thick.

Or: The final report was $5\frac{1}{2}$ inches thick.

Converting a mixed fraction into a decimal expression (5.5 inches thick) produces neater copy but may imply a finer degree of precision than desired.

Common fractions are usually set as a single character (e.g., $\frac{1}{2}, \frac{1}{3}, \frac{1}{4}, \frac{3}{4}$); these are called *case fractions,* or *piece fractions.* Unusual fractions may be set as *built-up fractions* (e.g., 11/16, 27/64); a space (not a hyphen) is used to separate a built-up fraction from a whole number: 5 9/32 inches.

Technical text.   Fractions rarely appear in technical text; usually the decimal form is preferred. When fractions are used, the fraction is spelled out if it is not a precisely measured quantity.

In one-third of the trials, the results were not statistically significant.

Two-thirds of the subjects received a placebo.

But: The test cards were $2\frac{1}{2}$-by-$4\frac{1}{4}$ inches.

Or: The test cards were $2\frac{1}{2}$-by-$4\frac{1}{4}$ in.

PERCENTAGES, PERCENTAGE POINTS, BASIS POINTS, AND PERCENTILES

To express percentages, a numeral and the percentage sign are used in technical documents; in nontechnical text, the convention is to use a numeral and the word *percent*.

> *Technical:* Over the 6-month period, the cost of employee benefits declined by $50 per employee, which reduced overhead by 2.5%.

> *Nontechnical:* Over the six-month period, the cost of employee benefits declined by fifty dollars per employee, which reduced overhead by 2.5 percent.

Ranges should be treated consistently within a document:

> *Technical:* 20% to 30% *or* 20%–30% *or* 20–30%

> *Nontechnical:* 20 percent to 30 percent *or* 20 to 30 percent *or* 20–30 percent.

Copyeditors who work with documents that contain percentages should remember the following:

- When a quantity doubles, that is an increase of 100 percent (*not* 200 percent); when a quantity triples, that is an increase of 200 percent.
- When a quantity decreases by half, that is a drop of 50 percent.
- A quantity can increase by more than 100 percent, but it cannot decrease by more than 100 percent (because once the quantity has decreased by 100 percent, it is reduced to zero).

Percentage points are also expressed in numerals.

> *Technical:* In one 18-month period (mid-1979 to late 1980), the prime rate rose by 9 percentage points, from 11.5% to 20.5%.

> *Nontechnical:* In the past month, the governor's popularity rating dropped by 12 percentage points, from 57 percent to 45 percent.

As these examples illustrate, percentage points are used to quantify the change between two percentages by subtracting the smaller percentage from the larger (e.g., 20.5 − 11.5 = 9). But to say that the prime rate increased by 9 percentage points is *not* the same as saying it increased by 9 percent: Had the prime rate increased by 9 percent, the higher rate would have been only 12.5% (11.5 + [9% × 11.5] = 12.535).

Basis points, which are used in the banking and financial industries, are also expressed in numerals. A basis point is one-hundredth of a percentage point. When interest rates rise by half a percentage point (e.g., from 5.50 percent to 6.00 percent), that is an increase of 50 basis points, and when rates rise by a quarter of a percentage point (e.g., from 6.00 percent to 6.25 percent), that is an increase of 25 basis points.

Percentiles are also expressed in numerals:

> Students in the Eden district scored in the 75th percentile on the statewide reading test.

Note that percentiles are measured "from the top": To score in the 99th percentile is to score better than 99 percent of all the people who were tested. Thus no one is ever in the 100th percentile, and those in the 10th percentile down through the 1st percentile are those who performed the worst.

MONEY

Monetary units.   Monetary units are lowercased: dollar, franc, mark, peso, euro. Proper adjectives that modify these units are, of course, uppercased: the Canadian dollar, the Turkish lira, the Malaysian ringgit.

Some financial publications use three-letter codes to refer to those units of currency that are heavily traded on international markets. These codes are uppercased:

> The CAD is expected to decline against the USD as the JPY strengthens this winter.
> [CAD = Canadian dollar; USD = U.S. dollar; JPY = Japanese yen.][3]

---

3. Other codes in this system include AUD (Australian dollar), CHF (Swiss franc), EUR (euro), GBP (British pound), HKD (Hong Kong dollar), MXN (Mexican new peso), NZD (New Zealand dollar), and SGD (Singapore dollar).

Amounts of money.   In technical or scientific text, sums of money are expressed in numerals, accompanied by the symbol for the unit of currency.

85¢ (*or* $0.85) $25,000 $33 million $1.5 billion to $1.8 billion

Commonly used symbols and abbreviations for overseas currencies include:

British pound	£100
Canadian dollar	Can$100 *or* C$100
euro	€100
Japanese yen	¥100

Most style manuals show no space between a foreign currency symbol and the numeral that follows (£100, €100, ¥100) but a wordspace or thin space after an abbreviation for a foreign currency (Fr 100, R 100).

In nontechnical text, the occasional mention of a sum of money that can be expressed in one or two words is spelled out:

A subscription to the local newspaper costs less than thirty-five cents a day.

The manufacturer is requesting a five-dollar increase in the wholesale price per unit.

The rental fee is thirteen hundred dollars a month.

However, when round sums of money cluster in a sentence or paragraph, numerals are used:

The initiation fee has tripled, from $200 to $600, and monthly dues have doubled, from $40 to $80.

Similarly, large sums of money are expressed in numerals:

Last year the median price of a home in San Francisco exceeded $260,000.

For arranging the $8 billion buyout, the brokerage firms earned $80 million in fees.

The surplus for this fiscal year is estimated at $53 billion to $71 billion.

As this last example shows, clarity requires that ranges not be condensed unless space is at an absolute premium. In running text, "$53 billion to $71 billion" is preferable to "$53 to $71 billion" or "$53–71 billion."

TIME

Noon and midnight.   A persistent point of confusion—not only among copyeditors but also in the world at large—concerns the relationship between noon, midnight, 12 A.M., and 12 P.M. Many of us were taught

    12:00 P.M. [noon]   12:00 A.M. [midnight]

But one also sees

    12:00 M. [noon]   12:00 P.M. [midnight]

or even

    12:00 N [noon]   12:00 M [midnight]

The source of the confusion can, in part, be attributed to etymology. Since A.M. and P.M. stand for *ante meridiem* (literally, "before midday") and *post meridiem* ("after midday"), neither abbreviation serves to express the exact moment of noon or midnight.

To avoid confusion, the airlines, railroads, and other time-sensitive organizations never use the precise hour of 12:00 in their schedules: planes and trains arrive at 11:59 A.M. or 12:01 P.M. The solution for copyeditors, however, is to spell out "noon" and "midnight":

The meeting was scheduled to begin at noon, but it did not start until 12:25 p.m.[4]

Between 10 p.m. and midnight, four emergency calls were received.

Redundant expressions—"2 A.M. in the morning" or "11 P.M. at night"— should be revised. House style dictates the choice of A.M., AM, A.M., or a.m.

---

4. *Or* twelve twenty-five. Other spelled-out forms: ten *or* ten o'clock *or* ten in the morning; two in the afternoon, six in the evening, nine at night; five after ten, ten fifteen, ten thirty, ten forty-five.

Time zones.   Time zones are styled as follows:

The speech will air at 9:15 p.m. EST (6:15 p.m. PST).

The plane landed in Paris at 6 p.m. (noon EST).

The abbreviations for time zones within the continental United States are

EST, EDT	eastern standard time, eastern daylight time
CST, CDT	central standard time, central daylight time
MST, MDT	mountain standard time, mountain daylight time
PST, PDT	Pacific standard time, Pacific daylight time

There are no abbreviations for Alaska standard or daylight time (one hour earlier than Pacific time) nor for Hawaii standard time (two hours earlier than PST; three hours earlier than PDT).[5]

The other common time-zone abbreviation is GMT (Greenwich mean time), the time at the Royal Observatory in Greenwich, England, located at 0° longitude. Local times may be expressed in relation to GMT; for example, GMT + 8 or GMT − 2. Astronomers and other physical scientists often use the notation UTC (universal time coordinated) in lieu of GMT.

Dates.   In running text, a full date is usually written in the following form: June 1, 1997. Some publishers, however, prefer or will accept what is called the European convention: 1 June 1997. In both styles the day of the month is expressed as a cardinal number, not an ordinal: on June 1, on 1 June.

In tables, footnotes, and other places in which space is at a premium, dates may be expressed wholly in numerals: 6/1/97 or 06/01/97. If you are working with non-American authors, you may encounter dates styled according to the European convention, in which 1 June 1997 is shortened to 1/6/97, 01/06/97, or 1.vi.97. When in doubt, you should ask the author which convention applies, although scanning the manuscript will usually supply the answer: If you spot numerals between 1 and 31 in the first position and only the numerals 1 through 12 appear in the second position, then the author has used the European system.

---

5. If you are copyediting materials that mention times in different parts of the country or the world, be sure to account for the vagaries of daylight savings time, which is not uniformly observed. Hawaii, for example, does not switch to daylight time in the spring.

Depending on the type of materials you copyedit, you may also come across the following notations:

FY 98–99	FY stands for "fiscal year" and is used when an organization's fiscal year spans two calendar years (i.e., July 1, 1998, through June 30, 1999). Typically only the final two digits of the year are used in this construction: FY 00–01, FY 01–02.
AY 1998–99	AY stands for "academic year" and is used by educational institutions. Typically, four digits are used for the first year in the range, and two digits or four digits for the last: AY 1999–2000, AY 2001–2002 *or* AY 2001–02.
1997-06-01	A ten-character format (eight numerals, two hyphens) is used in computer documents that follow the conventions of the International Standards Organization (ISO). The sequence is year-month-day.
dd-mm-yy	An eight-character format (six numerals, two hyphens) is used in some software programs. The example here signals that dates are expressed as day-month-year, with two characters allotted to each factor (01-06-97). Alternatively, dates can be formatted mm-dd-yy or yy-mm-dd.

Dates as attributive adjectives.   Some writers and copyeditors have been taught never to use a date or year as an attributive adjective; for example, they would not write "the November 4 election" or "the 2002 election," but instead "the election on November 4" and "the election of 2002." The taboo may stem from an overly broad interpretation of a subtle point made by Jacques Barzun: the phrase "her 1972 fall from a horse" implies that she had a series of falls, just as "the 1920 marriage of Countess Haha" suggests repeated marriages at suitable intervals.[6] Barzun traces the "vulgar practice" to a "legitimate one" used by scientific journals (e.g., In his 1905 paper on relativity, Einstein . . .) but still pleads for the "more elegant" use of "of" (In his paper

6. "Vulgar, Vulgarity, Vulgarisms," in *A Word or Two Before You Go* . . . (Middletown, Conn.: Wesleyan University Press, 1986), p. 66.

of 1905, Einstein . . .). It would seem, then, that one is free to use a date or year as an attributive adjective as long as the event *is* one of a repeated series (the 2002 election), the adjective is not overly long or awkward, and the document does not require Barzunesque elegance.

STREET NUMBERS AND PHONE NUMBERS

Numbered street names.   In running text, numbered street names are spelled out or expressed as numerals according to the publication's general rule for numbers.

> *Technical style:* We interviewed 15 men aged 18 to 35 who were waiting for the bus at 12th Street.

> *Nontechnical style:* The center of the neighborhood's business district is Twelfth Street.

In lists or directories of addresses, numerals are usually used, although numbered street names may be spelled out:

123 First Street	*or*	123 1st Street
45 Fortieth Street	*or*	45 40th Street
1 Sixty-Eighth Street	*or*	1 68th Street

Phone numbers.   There are several conventions for expressing American phone numbers:

> 212-555-1234   (212) 555-1234   212.555.1234   212 555 1234

Phone numbers may be preceded or followed by an indication of the type of transmission available:

> Fax 212-555-1919   212-555-1818 (phone)

When a made-up phone number is needed as an example, the convention is to use the three digits reserved for information (555) followed by four digits between 0100 and 0199.

For phone numbers that are expressed in words, the text should include the numerical equivalent as a courtesy to readers who have telephones on which the letters are less legible than the numerals:

Call 555-NEWS (555-6397).

For toll-free phone numbers, the long-distance access code 1 is usually included (because all callers must dial the 1):

1-800-123-4567   1 888 123 4567   1.877.123.4567

If the publication is to be distributed outside the United States, a non-toll-free number should be added, because 1-800, 1-888, and 1-877 numbers are not accessible outside the country.

For overseas phone numbers in publications addressed to U.S. readers, the listing may include the international access code (011), the one- through three-digit country code, the one- through four-digit city code, and the local phone number:

(011) 39 42 123 4567   011-39-42-123-4567   011.3942.123.4567

Overseas local phone numbers may contain six, seven, or eight digits, and different countries have developed different conventions for printing local phone numbers:

123 456   1234 567   1234 5678   12 34 56 78   12345678

For documents that will be circulated abroad, the phone number should begin with a + (the international placeholder for the overseas-access prefix), followed by the country code, city code, and local phone number: + 39 42 123 4567.

Calling instructions may also make mention of the two nonalphanumeric keys on the phone pad: the pound sign (#) and the star (*).

In all cases, the copyeditor should scrutinize all instances of 1 (one) and I (capital *i*) and 0 (zero) and O (capital *o*).

UNITS OF MEASUREMENT

Technical text.   In technical text, a quantity is expressed as a numeral, and the unit of measurement may be spelled out or abbreviated. Depending on conventions in the author's field and the units in which the measurements were taken, quantities may be expressed in U.S. units, in metric or SI units,[7] or in both. If a field team took measurements in feet, for example, the text would read:

The sample was taken 190 feet north of Starkweather Pond.

Or: The sample was taken 190 ft (58 m) north of Starkweather Pond.

But if the surveyors took the measurements in meters, the text would read:

The sample was taken 58 meters north of Starkweather Pond.

Or: The sample was taken 58 m (190 ft) north of Starkweather Pond.

When metric equivalents are given, the copyeditor may be asked to spot-check the equivalents; table 7 provides rough conversion factors for this purpose.

TABLE 7. Rough Metric Conversion Factors

	From U.S. to Metric	From Metric to U.S.
Length	1 mile = 1.6 kilometers	1 kilometer = 0.6 mile
	1 yard = 0.9 meter	1 meter = 1.1 yards
	1 foot = 0.3 meter	1 meter = 3.2 feet = 39 inches
	1 inch = 2.5 centimeters	1 centimeter = 0.4 inch
Area	1 square mile = 2.9 square kilometers	1 square kilometer = 0.4 square mile
	1 acre = 0.4 hectare	1 hectare = 2.5 acres
Weight	1 pound = 0.5 kilogram	1 kilogram = 2.2 pounds
Capacity	1 liquid quart = 0.9 liter	1 liter = 1.1 liquid quarts
	1 gallon = 3.8 liters	1 liter = 0.3 gallon
Temperature	To convert Fahrenheit to Celsius, subtract 32 and multiply by 5/9.	To convert Celsius to Fahrenheit, multiply by 9/5 and add 32.

Note: These rough conversion factors should be used only to spot-check equivalences that appear in a manuscript. They are not accurate enough for calculating conversions.

7. SI (Système international d'unités, or International System of Units) is an expanded version of the metric system that is used by scientists. *Chicago, APA,* and *CSE* all discuss SI conventions; see also "Units of Measurement" on pages 223–25.

Scientific notation.   Scientific notation allows writers to express very small and very large numbers in a succinct format. The system is based on the powers of ten:

$$10^1 = 10 \qquad 10^{-1} = 0.1$$
$$10^2 = 100 \qquad 10^{-2} = 0.01$$
$$10^3 = 1,000 \qquad 10^{-3} = 0.001$$
$$10^4 = 10,000 \qquad 10^{-4} = 0.0001$$

(*Note:* When 10 is raised to a positive power, the number of zeros after the 1 is the same as the power: the long form of 10^8 has eight zeros after the 1. When 10 is raised to a negative power, the number of digits after the decimal point is the same as the power: the long form of 10^{-8} has seven zeros followed by a 1.)

In scientific notation, a large or small quantity is expressed as a numeral between 1 and 10 multiplied by the desired factor of 10.

$$6.25 \times 10^{11} = 6.25 \times 100,000,000,000 = 625,000,000,000$$
$$4.53 \times 10^{-8} = 4.53 \times 0.00000001 = 0.0000000453$$

Nontechnical text.   In nontechnical text, round quantities under 101 are usually spelled out, as are the units of measurement:

He is six feet four inches. *Or:* He is six feet four. *Or:* He is six four.

We need fifty-five pounds of flour and twenty-two pounds of butter.

Names of large numbers.   Large numbers are usually expressed in numerals and words; here are the terms for large numbers:

million	1,000,000	[6 zeros]
billion[8]	1,000,000,000	[9 zeros]

---

8. In British English 1,000,000,000 was traditionally called a milliard or a thousand million, and a billion was equivalent to a million million (1 followed by twelve zeros). According to the *Oxford English Dictionary,* however, the American value for a billion has been increasingly used in Britain since 1951, though the older sense is still common. R. W. Burchfield recommends that "it is best now to work on the assumption that [a billion] means 'a thousand millions' in all English-speaking areas, unless there is direct contextual evidence to the contrary" (*New Fowler's,* s.v. "billion"). Similarly: "[Trillion] normally means now a million million . . . both in AmE and BrE" (s.v. "trillion").

trillion	1,000,000,000,000	[12 zeros]
quadrillion	1,000,000,000,000,000	[15 zeros]
quintillion	1,000,000,000,000,000,000	[18 zeros]

The numeral that precedes the word should be larger than 1, unless the use of a decimal facilitates comparisons within a sentence or a paragraph, as in the second of the sentences shown here.

The cost overruns to date are $800,000. [*Not* $0.8 million]

The project was budgeted at $3.5 million, but cost overruns to date are estimated at $0.8 million.

Prefixes for very small and large numbers.   In expressions of very small or large quantities, prefixes may be used to modify the unit of measurement:

A millisecond is 0.001 second (one-thousandth of a second).
A microsecond is 0.000001 second (one-millionth of a second).
A nanosecond is 0.000000001 second (one-billionth of a second).

A kilobyte is 1,000 bytes (one thousand bytes).
A megabyte is 1,000,000 bytes (one million bytes).
A gigabyte is 1,000,000,000 bytes (one billion bytes).
A terabyte is 1,000,000,000,000 bytes (one trillion bytes).

ROMAN NUMERALS

Roman numerals are rarely used in regular text, unless the topic is kings (Louis XIV), popes (Leo V), historic inscriptions (the cornerstone reads MDCCLVI), Super Bowls (Super Bowl XII), or the front matter of a book (on page ix). Some journals use roman numerals on their covers for the volume number, but the arabic form is always used in citations and bibliographies.

The system has seven basic units, which may be written in uppercase or lowercase:

I (*or* i) = 1	C (*or* c) = 100
V (*or* v) = 5	D (*or* d) = 500
X (*or* x) = 10	M (*or* m) = 1,000
L (*or* l) = 50	

These basic units are combined in the following ways:

When a unit is followed by an identical or a smaller unit, the two
values are added.

When a unit is followed by a larger unit, the smaller unit is
subtracted from the larger unit. This rule prevents the appearance
of four identical units in succession; thus IV (*not* IIII) = 4.

The units I, X, C, and M may be repeated in succession; the units V,
L, and D are not.

When a bar appears over a unit, the unit's value is multiplied by one
thousand.

Table 8 shows a representative sample of roman numerals.

TABLE 8.   Roman Numerals

I	1	L	50	DCCC	800
II	2	LX	60	CM	900
III	3	LXX	70	M	1,000
IV	4	LXXX	80	MCD	1,400
V	5	XC	90	MD	1,500
VI	6	C	100	MDCCC	1,800
VII	7	CL	150	MCM	1,900
VIII	8	CC	200	MCMXCIX	1,999
IX	9	CCC	300	MM	2,000
X	10	CD	400	MMI	2,001
XX	20	D	500	$\overline{V}$	5,000
XXX	30	DC	600	$\overline{X}$	10,000
XL	40	DCC	700	$\overline{C}$	100,000

INCLUSIVE NUMERALS

There are three conventions for treating inclusive numerals. In most contexts, any of these systems is acceptable as long as it is used consistently in a
document. The first style is to simply repeat all the digits in the range:

See pages 22–25, 100–102, 105–109, 441–449, 481–503, and
1000–1004.

The second style, which conserves a bit of space, calls for repeating only those digits that change:

See pages 22–5, 100–2, 105–9, 441–9, 481–503, and 1000–4.

The third style is a bit more complex, with the repetition and elision of digits depending on the nature of the first numeral in the range:

For a two-digit numeral, show all digits: See pages 22–25.

For a multiple of 100, show all digits: See pages 100–102, 300–315, and 1000–1004.

For a numeral that exceeds 100 and ends in 01 through 09, show the changed digits only: See pages 105–9 and 1001–9.

For a numeral that exceeds 100 and ends in 10 through 99, show at least the last two digits and show all digits that change: See pages 441–49, 481–503, 1333–35, and 1388–402.

In ranges that consist of roman numerals or of dates labeled B.C. or B.C.E., all digits should be repeated:

pp. xiv- xvii   195–120 B.C.   20,000–15,000 B.C.E.

In technical copy that includes signs, the sign is usually repeated:

10%–12% $35–$55 million   44°–48°F

If house style calls for no repetition of signs in ranges, the sole sign should be logically placed:

10–12% $35–55 million   44–48°F

Inclusive ranges should not be used when one of the quantities is a negative number.

MATHEMATICAL SIGNS AND SYMBOLS

If you work extensively with mathematical texts, you will want to consult a specialized style guide (several are mentioned in chapter 3). All copyeditors, however, may come across simple mathematical expressions and should be aware of a few conventions governing them.

Operation signs should be preceded and followed by a wordspace or a thin space:

$$2 + 2 = 4 \qquad 8 \times 8 < 100 \qquad 6 \cdot 5 = 30 \qquad 99 \div a = 33$$

But when signs do not represent an operation, there should be no space between the sign and the numeral:

The low temperature for the day was $-13°F$, and the high was $+2°F$.

The central bank kept the peso within its $±2.5\%$ trading band.

All the samples exceeded the standard of $<10,000$ ppm.

When a lowercase letter represents an unknown quantity, it is italicized:

$$x - 5 = 23 \qquad y + z^2 = 125$$

When a lowercase letter is used as an abbreviation, it is set in roman:

Gift boxed. $16w \times 5d \times 11h$. 4 pounds.

In mathematical expressions, parentheses appear within brackets—the reverse of the convention for prose:

Math: $[(25 - a) \times (b/2)]$

Prose: The study was attacked for "chaotic design" and "slapdash follow-up" (Briggs, *Guide to Evaluation* [Big Press, 1972], 382).

Copyeditors working on hard copy should clarify for the word processor or typesetter which symbols are intended.

$$5 - 2 \qquad 5 \times 3 \qquad 1 + w = 1 \qquad A' > D' \qquad O < 0$$

(minus) (mult) (el) (one) (prime) (oh) (zero)

STYLE SHEET ENTRIES

To ensure consistency throughout the manuscript, copyeditors should make entries on their style sheets that state the principles applied and that provide examples of the different categories of numbers, numerals, and quantities that appear in the manuscript.

First, you should note a general principle for which numbers are to be spelled out:

Spell out all numbers under 10 (*or* under 11).

Or: Spell out all numbers under 101 and all large numbers that can be expressed in two words, except for percentages, dates, and page numbers. Also, use numerals when quantities cluster in a paragraph.

Or: Treatment of numbers (spell-outs vs. numerals) follows the in-house style manual, pages 11–18.

Then, for each type of numerical expression that appears in the manuscript, you should provide an example and, as needed, a guiding principle:

Dates: June 1, 1997   June 1   June 1997

Decades   the 1990s   the mid-1960s   the late 1940s

Academic years: 1997–98   2000–01 *but* 1999–2000

Abbreviations: A.D. 100   300 B.C.   a.m.   p.m.

Inclusive page ranges: pp. 123–125 (include all digits)

Cross-references: see chapter 12   see part 5   see figure 17

Money: Spell out round amounts under $100,000:
   twenty-five dollars, thirty thousand dollars
Use numerals for amounts $100,000 and over:
   $900,000, $1 million, $2.5 million

Percentages: 72 percent   72.5 percent

Decimals: Include leading 0 for decimals less than one (0.5 percent)

Latitude and longitude: 23°52' W

EXERCISE G

Using the conventions that apply to nontechnical text, copyedit the following sentences. The answer key is on pages 492–95.

1. The mortgage loans in default range from $35 to $500,000.

2. For more information, see Degas's article in volume xlii of the *Journal of Higher Studies.*

3. From 1991–1994, the town's population increased by ten percent.

4. The new fighter planes cost $.25 billion each.

5. The insurance surcharge is $.75 for twenty-five-dollars' coverage, $1.40 for $25–50, and $1.80 for $50–100.

6. The atmosphere weighs 5,700,000,000,000,000 tons.

7. The sales data for the 3d quarter of '94 are presented on pages 113–5, 300–8, and 201–09.

8. Amendments 1 through 10 of the Constitution are known as the Bill of Rights.

9. The vote in the Electoral College was 185 to 184 in 1876.

10. 1492 is the one year most American schoolchildren can identify correctly.

11. Using Carbon-14 dating, scientists have determined that the Hopewell earthworks first appeared in Southern Ohio in about 100 B.C, and that the last elaborate valley earthwork was constructed in about 550 A.D.

12. The burial mounds on the Hopewell farm range from 160 to 470 feet (48 to 141 km.) in length and from 20 to 32 feet (6 to 10 m) in height.

EXERCISE H

The following economic summary will appear in an informal in-house report that will be distributed to the seven people who work at the international trading desk. The answer key is on pages 496–98.

Bobonia's economy contracted sharply in the 2d quarter. Exports declined by 14.5%, the worst monthly performance in 12 and a half years. Electronic manufacturers were particularly hard hit. Imports, however, continued to rise, which plunged the trade deficit to $1.25 billion. This deficit is likely to worsen before it improves and the revised government forecast calls for it to reach $1.75 billion by late Fall.

Domestically, inflation remains almost nonexistent, at an annual rate of only 1%. Unemployment rates--6.5% in June, compared to 6.8% in March--also continued to move lower. On the good news, consumer confidence measured by the Univeristy of Bobonia

National Feelgood Scale rose from 105.5 in March to 109 in June.

Short-term interest rates were unchanged: the overnight rate is 5.25%, and the average yield on 30-year government notes is 5.35%.

The currency has strengthened since mid-March when the Bobonian Bobble traded at 5.4550 to the U.S. dollar. On June 30, the Bobble closed at 5.580 to the dollar on the London Worthless Currency exchange.

❖ 8 ❖

Quotations

The author of a manuscript is responsible for the accuracy of direct quotations from printed matter, interviews, and speeches. Rarely are copyeditors provided with the original documents and asked to verify (or spot-check) the word-by-word accuracy of quotations in a manuscript, although well-known quotations can be quickly verified in *Bartlett's Familiar Quotations* or a similar compendium.

Whenever a direct quotation appears in a manuscript, copyeditors are expected to

> query or correct any obvious spelling errors in the quotation
> call to the author's attention any odd wording within the quotation that suggests that words were mistyped, deleted, or otherwise miscopied
> enforce consistency in deciding which quotations are run into the text and which quotations are set off as extracts (block quotations)
> make sure that opening quotation marks have closing mates and that quotation marks within quotation marks are handled correctly
> make sure that the syntax of the quoted matter fits the surrounding text
> mark ellipsis points correctly and delete unnecessary ellipsis points
> ensure that the quotation is attributed to its source

All the major style manuals offer extensive guidelines on these issues; here, we will survey the principal points.

MISSPELLINGS IN THE SOURCE DOCUMENT

A direct quotation need not reproduce innocent misspellings or typographical errors that appear in the original document; instead, these errors may be silently corrected.

> *Source document containing a typo:* Copyeditors are expected to delete unnecessary elipsis points.

> *Manuscript quoting source document:* The guidelines call for deleting "unnecessary ellipsis points," but they do not define "unnecessary."

In a work of literary criticism or historical analysis, however, the original spelling is usually reproduced. Alternatively, the author should explain—in the preface, in a footnote, or in a parenthetical comment—that the spelling has been modernized or standardized.

A misspelling in the original document should also be reproduced when the fact that there was a misspelled word is at issue—for example, in a document that discusses the carelessness with which the original document was prepared. To alert readers that the misspelling occurred in the original, an author may insert an italicized *sic* (Latin, meaning *thus*) within brackets:

> The memo from the principal included a request that teachers "devote less time to science and arithmatic [*sic*] and more time to reading, penmanship, and spelling."

If there are many misspellings in the original document, it is usually preferable to insert a footnote or a parenthetical comment to that effect rather than to sprinkle *sics* throughout the quotations from that document. Such a comment might read

> I have here reproduced all the misspellings contained in the original document.

> *Or:* The original document is replete with misspellings, and these are reproduced here.

ODD WORDING IN THE SOURCE DOCUMENT

Direct quotations from printed material must be reproduced verbatim; a copyeditor may never revise the wording of a direct quotation from a printed source. If a quotation sounds awkward or incorrect, ask the author to recheck the quoted material against the source. Should the transcription prove to be accurate, the author's choices are to (1) let the quotation stand, however odd it may sound; (2) add a bracketed *sic* after the troublesome phrase; (3) add clarifying words and place these within brackets; (4) add a comment, either in the text proper or in a footnote, stating that the transcription, however awkward, is correct; or (5) replace all or part of the direct quotation with a paraphrase.

When the material being quoted is spoken—not written—language, acronyms and abbreviations should be rendered in their conventional written form.

> *Transcript:* "Mister Ralph Snider the third will now discuss the newest scuzzy technology."
>
> *Print version:* "Mr. Ralph Snider III will now discuss the newest SCSI technology."

Some publishers also encourage, or even require, copyeditors to make minor changes to correct a speaker's grammar, to eliminate false starts, and to delete voiced hesitations ("uh," "well," "you see").

> *Original comment:* "The number of consumer complaints about our products are decreasing."
>
> *Print version:* "The number of consumer complaints about our products is decreasing."

> *Original comment:* "The introduction of the 405 line, I mean, uh, the 4055 line, of course, is expected to increase revenues by 10 percent."
>
> *Print version:* "The introduction of the 4055 line is expected to increase revenues by 10 percent."

It is never acceptable, however, to tamper with the truth under the guise of editorial cleanliness. Under no circumstances should copyeditors make changes in direct quotations that alter the speaker's meaning or that serve only to make the speaker "look better."

If the original quotation is horribly mangled by false starts, labyrinthine syntax, jargon, or grammatical errors, the text should paraphrase the speaker's point.

Original: Addressing the council, General Smith said, "High tech—spy satellites and computer-enhanced infrared photography and electronic intercepts and all those Star Wars gadgets—well, we live in an age where that kind of envelope-pushing technology affects decision-making at the national security–type level, and then we begin to downgrade human judgment, but technology is no substitute for well-informed, well-trained officers."

Revision, using paraphrase: General Smith warned the council of the dangers of allowing advanced technological gadgetry to supersede human judgment in national security decisions. "Technology," he said, "is no substitute for well-informed, well-trained officers."

RUN-IN AND SET-OFF QUOTATIONS

Short quotations are usually run into the text, and longer quotations are usually set off as extracts (block quotations). The distinction between "short" and "longer" in this case is rather arbitrary: *Chicago* suggests setting off quotations that are eight lines or longer, *WIT* puts the cutoff at five lines, and *APA* calls for setting off quotations longer than forty words. Many publishers have in-house rules that define "longer" as more than, say, six or eight lines. Sometimes even shorter quotations are treated as extracts so that readers can easily compare them.

CREATING AN EXTRACT

To change a run-in quotation into an extract, a copyeditor who is working on hard copy must

indicate where the set-off block is to begin and end
typecode the block to indicate that it is an extract (a typical code is EX)[1]
delete the opening and closing quotation marks that surround the block
change any single quotation marks within the block to double quotation marks

---

1. Typecodes are used to alert the designer and compositor to the presence of patches of text that require special formatting: extracts, lists, chapter titles, and headings, for example. (Typecoding is discussed in detail in chapter 13.) Extracts may be differentiated from the running text by one or more typographical devices: extra indention (from the left, right, or both); extra lead-

For example, the manuscript reads:

> "Whatever infrastructure is provided
> will be used to capacity," Gilliam
> argues. "Traffic, for example, always
> expands to fill the capacity of a
> freeway, creating a 'demand' for
> more freeways. And the population
> inevitably expands to the limit set
> by the infrastructure--no matter how
> high that limit is."

Here, the author has correctly used double quotation marks to indicate the beginning and end of the words quoted from Gilliam, and the single quotation marks indicate quotation marks that appeared in Gilliam's original statement. If this quotation is to be set as a run-in quotation, you would not need to mark anything. But for the sake of example, let's turn this run-in quotation into an extract. The marked hard copy would look like this:

> "Whatever infrastructure is provided
> will be used to capacity," Gilliam
> argues. Traffic, for example, always
> expands to fill the capacity of a
> freeway, creating a "demand" for
> more freeways. And the population

(EX)

---

ing above and below the extract; reduced leading within the body of the extract; or a smaller type size. Decisions about the typographical treatment are made by the publication's designer.

```
    inevitably expands to the limit set

    by the infrastructure--no matter how

  ⌐ high that limit is.⟿
  └───────
```

The compositor will then follow the designer's specifications (specs) for the EX code; the resulting printed text might look like this:

"Whatever infrastructure is provided will be used to capacity," Gilliam argues.

> Traffic, for example, always expands to fill the capacity of a freeway, creating a "demand" for more freeways. And the population inevitably expands to the limit set by the infrastructure—no matter how high that limit is.

The copyeditor working on-screen will achieve the same results by inserting hard returns before and after the extract, inserting the starting and ending codes for the extract (see "Typecoding On-Screen" in chapter 13), and fixing the quotation marks.

Notice that when a quotation is set as an extract, opening and closing quotation marks are not added; instead the typography indicates that the material is a direct quotation. Thus an extract will begin with an opening quotation mark only if the material being quoted happens to begin with an opening quotation mark:

Source:
"That dog don't hunt" has become an all-too-familiar refrain in Washington this year, nuzzling out all other animals in the Capitol Hill menagerie. What accounts for the migration of the dependable duck, which for decades has been relied on to "look like a duck and quack like a duck"? Where are our 800-pound gorillas? (And why do they never weigh in at 700 or 900 pounds?)

Quotation from source:
After expressing relief at the disappearance of the "soccer moms," Whitson turns to another set of clichés:

> "That dog don't hunt" has become an all-too-familiar refrain in Washington this year, nuzzling out all other animals in the Capitol Hill

menagerie. What accounts for the migration of the dependable duck, which for decades has been relied on to "look like a duck and quack like a duck"? Where are our 800-pound gorillas? (And why do they never weigh in at 700 or 900 pounds?)

CREATING A RUN-IN QUOTATION

To change an extract into a run-in quotation, a copyeditor working on hard copy must

> add a run-in curlicue and write a circled "run-in" instruction
> add opening and closing double quotation marks around the entire quote
> change any internal double quotation marks to single quotation marks

For example, the manuscript reads:

```
"Whatever infrastructure is provided

will be used to capacity," Gilliam

argues.
```

```
Traffic, for example, always expands

to fill the capacity of a freeway,

creating a "demand" for more

freeways. And the population

inevitably expands to the limit set

by the infrastructure--no matter how

high that limit is.
```

Here, the author has correctly formatted the extract and has correctly used double quotation marks to set off the word that was in quotation marks within the original. To turn this extract into a run-in quotation, you would mark your hard copy as shown here:

"Whatever infrastructure is provided
will be used to capacity," Gilliam
argues.   (run in)

"Traffic, for example, always expands
to fill the capacity of a freeway,
creating a 'demand' for more
freeways. And the population
inevitably expands to the limit set
by the infrastructure--no matter how
high that limit is."

And the resulting printed text would look like this:

> "Whatever infrastructure is provided will be used to capacity," Gilliam
> argues. "Traffic, for example, always expands to fill the capacity of a
> freeway, creating a 'demand' for more freeways. And the population
> inevitably expands to the limit set by the infrastructure—no matter how
> high that limit is."

The copyeditor working on-screen can effect a run-in of a set-off quotation
by deleting the author's hard return, deleting any coding and extra indention before the extract, and fixing the quotation marks.

PUNCTUATION OF QUOTATIONS

PUNCTUATION PRECEDING A QUOTATION

Run-in quotations may be introduced by a comma or a colon. The choice
reflects the syntax of the introductory phrase, the length of the quotation,
and the degree of formality that is desired. A comma is the usual choice to
introduce a short quotation.

As Heraclitus wrote, "Nothing endures but change."

A colon is the usual choice to introduce a lengthy quotation.

> As Thomas Paine wrote: "These are the times that try men's souls. The summer soldier and the sunshine patriot will, in this crisis, shrink from the service of their country; but he that stands it *now,* deserves the love and thanks of man and woman."

A colon is also used when the introductory tag contains "the following" or "thus."

> Heraclitus wrote the following: "Nothing endures but change."

Set-off quotations may be introduced by a comma, a colon, or a period, depending on the syntax of the introductory tag.

> As Carolyn Heilbrun notes,

> > To denounce women for shrillness and stridency is another way of denying them any right to power. . . . Ironically, women who acquire power are more likely to be criticized for it than are the men who have always had it. (*Writing a Woman's Life* [W. W. Norton, 1988], p. 16)

> Despite all that these women accomplished, their autobiographies downplay or ignore the very qualities that enabled them to be successful:

> > Well into the twentieth century, it continued to be impossible for women to admit into their autobiographical narratives the claim of achievement, the admission of ambition, the recognition that accomplishment was neither luck nor the result of the efforts or generosity of others. . . . Their letters and diaries [reflect] ambitions and struggles in the public sphere; in their published autobiographies, however, they portray themselves as intuitive, nurturing, passive, but never—in spite of the contrary evidence of their accomplishments—managerial. (Carolyn Heilbrun, *Writing a Woman's Life* [W. W. Norton, 1988], p. 24)

> "Above all," Carolyn Heilbrun explains, in women's autobiographies "the public and private lives cannot be linked."

> > We hardly expect the career of an accomplished man to be presented as being in fundamental conflict with the demands of his marriage and children; he can allow his public life to expand occasionally into the private sphere without guilt or disorder. These women are therefore unable to write

exemplary lives: they do not dare to offer themselves as models, but only as exceptions chosen by destiny or chance. (*Writing a Woman's Life* [W. W. Norton, 1988], p. 25)

SINGLE AND DOUBLE QUOTATION MARKS

When a quotation occurs within running text, an opening double quotation mark appears at the beginning of the quotation and a closing double quotation mark appears at the end. If a quotation extends over a paragraph break, an opening double quotation mark appears at the beginning of each paragraph, and a closing double quotation mark appears only at the end of the last paragraph in the quotation.[2] (In expository works, however, a multiparagraph quotation is usually printed as an extract.)

In addition to making sure that each opening quotation mark has its closing mate, the copyeditor must ensure that the author has used the correct mark. In American practice, the outermost marks are double quotation marks, and single quotation marks are used to indicate a quotation within a quotation.

> According to Gilliam, traffic "always expands to fill the capacity of a freeway, creating a 'demand' for more freeways."

In the rare event that a third level of quotation is embedded within the other two, double quotation marks are used:

> At his deposition, Mr. Vine stated: "John asked, 'Shall I change "unaccustomed" to "not accustomed" in the Miller contract?' I replied, 'Suit yourself. You always do.'"

SYNTACTICAL FIT

When a quotation is embedded within an author's sentence, the copyeditor should ascertain that the syntax of the quotation meshes with the surround-

2. A refinement of this principle is offered by *The Associated Press Stylebook*, which requires a closing quotation mark at the end of the first paragraph of a multiparagraph quotation if the words within quotation marks at the end of that first paragraph do not constitute a complete sentence.

ing sentence and that placement of the quotation marks does not fracture the phrasing of the sentence or the quotation. In the following example, the shift in tenses is unsettling:

> *Awkward:* In devising their classification scheme, Potrero and Sanchez wanted to ensure that it "accounts for patterns of intraspecific genetic variation measured by DNA analysis, allozyme analysis, and virulence studies."

In revising the sentence to fix the tense shift, the copyeditor must not introduce a new problem by interrupting the inseparable "account for":

> *Awkward:* In devising their classification scheme, Potrero and Sanchez wanted to ensure that it would account "for patterns of intraspecific genetic variation measured by DNA analysis, allozyme analysis, and virulence studies."

The better solution here is to move the quotation marks to a less intrusive location:

> *Revision:* In devising their classification scheme, Potrero and Sanchez wanted to ensure that it would account for "patterns of intraspecific genetic variation measured by DNA analysis, allozyme analysis, and virulence studies."

In some cases, revising the quoter's wording will produce the best fit between quotation and context:

> *Awkward:* Occasionally, Hugo promulgates silly, idiosyncratic preferences as though they were divinely inspired rules. He insists that writers use "no semicolons. Semicolons indicate relationships that only idiots need defined by punctuation. Besides, they are ugly."

> *Revision:* Occasionally, Hugo promulgates silly, idiosyncratic preferences as though they were divinely inspired rules. "No semicolons," he insists. "Semicolons indicate relationships that only idiots need defined by punctuation. Besides, they are ugly."

Another approach is to interpolate a bracketed syllable or word so that the quotation fits the context.

Awkward: As early as the 1950s, "middle-class Americans' twin obsessions with automobiles and single-family homes conspire to make housing less affordable."

Revision: As early as the 1950s, "middle-class Americans' twin obsessions with automobiles and single-family homes conspire[d] to make housing less affordable."

Notice that the syntax of the sentence as a whole determines the punctuation immediately preceding and following the quotation:

In Emerson's words, "A foolish consistency is the hobgoblin of little minds, adored by little statesmen and philosophers and divines."

In Emerson's words, "A foolish consistency is the hobgoblin of little minds."

"A foolish consistency," Emerson says, "is the hobgoblin of little minds."

Emerson argues that "a foolish consistency is the hobgoblin of little minds."

Emerson disparages "a foolish consistency" as "the hobgoblin of little minds"; this sort of consistency, he explains, is motivated by "a reverence for our past act or word."

As these examples show, in most instances authors may silently change the capitalization of the first word in a quotation to suit their own syntax. Thus, if a brief quotation is embedded within a sentence, the author will lowercase the first word of the quotation, regardless of how it appeared in the source document. Similarly, if the quotation appears at the head of the author's own sentence, the author will uppercase the first word of the quotation.

Source: Proper words in proper places, make the true definition of a style.

Quotation from source: Swift defines style as "proper words in proper places."

Or: "The true definition of a style," according to Swift, is "proper words in proper places."

In literary criticism, legal documents, and other texts in which precise reproduction is important, the changed letter is placed in brackets.

> *Source:* Rule 5.8.1. Proof of service may be made by declaration of
> the person accomplishing the service.

> *Quotation from source:* According to Rule 5.8.1, "[p]roof of service
> may be made by declaration of the person accomplishing the
> service."

> *Or:* "[D]eclaration of the person accomplishing the service" consti-
> tutes proof of service under Rule 5.8.1.

ELLIPSIS POINTS

Sometimes an author wishes to quote only a portion of a sentence. By convention, ellipsis points (three spaced periods) replace the omitted words.

> *Source:* The half-year convention does not apply to residential real
> property, nonresidential real property, and railroad gradings and
> tunnel bores. It treats all property placed in service (or disposed of)
> during any tax year as placed in service (or disposed of) on the mid-
> point of that tax year.

> *Quotation from source:* Under the half-year convention, the company
> must treat "property placed in service . . . during any tax year as
> placed in service . . . on the midpoint of that tax year."

But no ellipsis points are needed when the abridged quotation consists of
words that are contiguous in the source document—that is, when no intervening words have been omitted.[3]

> *Source:* But all copy editors show a common bias: vigilance breeds
> suspicion, and the suspect is the writer. What he has set down
> is ipso facto questionable and incomplete; anything not utterly
> usual is eccentric and reprehensible; what the editor would
> prefer is preferable.

---

3. Leading ellipsis points (e.g., " . . . and for no other purpose") and trailing ellipsis points
(e.g., "the limitation shall be disallowed . . . ") are used only in textual criticism and legal work
in which precise reproduction is crucial.

Quotation from source: In "Behind the Blue Pencil: Censorship or Creeping Creativity?" Jacques Barzun warns copyeditors against what he calls "a common bias," the source of which is the very vigilance that copyeditors covet: "Vigilance breeds suspicion, and the suspect is the writer." Mistrustful of "anything not utterly usual," the copyeditor wrongly turns into an intrusive semi–ghost writer. [No ellipsis points are needed before or after any of the quoted phrases here because each phrase is intact.]

On hard copy, the periods in an ellipsis are spaced:

Correct manuscript: `"property placed in service . . . during any tax year"`

Incorrect manuscript: `"property placed in service...during any tax year"`

Marked hard copy: `"property placed in service`|.|.|.|`during any tax year"`

Will be typeset as: "property placed in service . . . during any tax year"

Copyeditors working on-screen may be asked to insert an ellipsis code or a special ellipsis character that consists of three tightly spaced dots (...).[4]

Some publishers, including most scholarly and academic presses, retain an older convention regarding what are sometimes called three-dot and four-dot ellipses. Under this convention, when the cut material is located within one sentence in the original document, the quoter inserts a three-dot ellipsis. But when the cut material spans a sentence boundary in the source document, a four-dot ellipsis (that is, a period followed by a three-dot ellipsis) is used.

Source: The limitations on lines 5 and 11 apply to the taxpayer, and not to each separate business or activity. Therefore, if you have more

---

4. In traditional typesetting, the space before and after each dot in an ellipsis is one-third of an em wide (see the entry for *em* in the Glossary of Copyediting Terms), in other words, narrower than a wordspace.

than one business or activity, you may allocate your allowable section 179 expense deduction among them.

Quotation from source: According to the instructions for Form 4562, "the limitations on lines 5 and 11 apply to the taxpayer. . . . If you have more than one business or activity, you may allocate your allowable section 179 expense deduction among them."

Authors who are unaccustomed to working with quoted material may use three dots or four dots willy-nilly. Sometimes you will be able to tell from the context whether a three-dot or a four-dot ellipsis is called for. Otherwise, write a query that explains the convention and ask your author to revise the manuscript as necessary.

In the relatively unusual situation in which ellipsis points appear in the original document, this fact should be indicated in a footnote or in a bracketed or parenthetical comment.

His last letter to his son began, "Dear Sonny, Lead . . . and they will follow [ellipsis in the original]. But don't never ever look back—not because someone might be gaining on you, but because there might not be anyone there. Hah! Ain't that rich!"
[Here the comment is placed in brackets because it falls within a set of quotation marks.]

Just as Jetsen is on the verge of revealing who committed the heinous crime, he turns to his cousin and says, "But I digress . . . " (ellipsis in the original), and the chapter ends.
[Here the comment follows the direct quotation and is placed in parentheses.]

BRACKETS

Brackets—not parentheses—are used to enclose any material that the quoter wishes to interpolate into the quotation or to add for the purposes of clarification or explanation.

The principal's memo called for greater attention to "spelling and reading comperhension [*sic*]."

Merriam-Webster's Dictionary states that the noun is "often attrib[utive]."

A local aid worker said, "The UNHCR [United Nations High Commissioner for Refugees] could have done more to avert this disaster."

"Errare humanum est [To err is human]" was his sole defense.

According to the press release, "The assistant vice-mayor in charge of community relations [Dinai Smithers] will be reassigned for the duration of the investigation."

The start-up company's motto is "A terabyte [one trillion bytes] on every desktop."

Heine's last words were "Of course he [God] will forgive me; that's his business."

"We must never forget it is a *constitution* we are expounding [emphasis in the original]."

"The power to tax involves the power *to destroy* [emphasis added]."

"Vision requires distance; one cannot see a thing if one is too close to it [translation mine]."

In contrast, parentheses appear within quotation marks only when parentheses were used in the source document.

The tax code is quite clear on this point: "The contribution must be made by the due date (including extensions) for filing the tax return."

Sometimes you will be able to tell that your author has used parentheses where brackets are called for; otherwise, write a query that explains the convention and ask the author to revise the manuscript as necessary.

CITING SOURCES

Quotations of extremely well known phrases need not be formally attributed to their source, but all other quotations—with the exception of casual snatches of conversation—must be. In documents that contain many quotations, a formal system of attribution (either footnotes or endnotes, or in-text references keyed to a reference list) is used; see chapter 11.

In documents that contain few quotations, however, sources may be cited in the text proper. These citations must include the author and title of the work; the publisher, city of publication, date of publication, and the page number may also be provided.

> In *The Devil's Dictionary,* Bierce defines "accordion" as "an instrument in harmony with the sentiments of an assassin."

> "Why do you sit there looking like an envelope without any address on it?" (Mark Twain, quoted by Nancy McPhee, *The Book of Insults, Ancient and Modern*).

> The Russian word *razbliuto* denotes "the feeling a person has for someone he or she once loved but now does not" (Howard Rheingold, *They Have a Word for It* [Los Angeles: Tarcher, 1988], 62).

As shown in these examples, the parenthetical citation is punctuated as part of the sentence; thus the terminal period follows the closing parenthesis. In contrast, when a parenthetical citation accompanies an extract, the citation is placed after the final period in the quotation.

> From his reading of many of the explorers' accounts, Barry Lopez concludes:

>> The literature of arctic exploration is frequently offered as a record of resolute will before the menacing fortifications of the landscape. It is more profitable I think to disregard this notion—that the land is an adversary bent on human defeat, that the people who came and went were heroes or failures in this. It is better to contemplate the record of human longing to achieve something significant, to be free of some of the grim weight of life. That weight was ignorance, poverty of spirit, indolence, and the threat of anonymity and destitution. This harsh landscape became the focus of a desire to separate oneself from those things and to overcome them. In these arctic narratives, then, are the threads of dreams that serve us all. (*Arctic Dreams,* p. 310)

EXERCISE I

You are being asked to do a light copyedit on the following short piece, which is to appear in a consumer newsletter. Keep a style sheet on a separate piece of paper. The answer key is on pages 499–503.

Every month the It's Our Money Institute

in New York city publishes a list of

particularly outrageous, ironic or ridiculous

wastes of tax-payers taxes. Here are some of

last years winners:

The Economic Developement gave Bedord,

Indiana $.7 million dollars to build a model

of the pyramid of Cheops and a 800-feet

replica of The Great Wall of China to

"attract tourists and "demonstrate the value

of limestone in the building industry".

The National Science Foundation spends

$14,4012 to test the affects of inflation on

the behavior of rats and pigeons. The

studies' conclusions: when given a choice

animal "consumers" opt for cheaper goods,

just as people do.

The Federal Highway Administration broke
the record for cost over-runs on a civilian
project. The Intestate Highway System now
cost $ 100,300 million or 267% of what
congress originally approved, due to
inflation, delay, and mismanagment.

The Department of Agriculture spent fourty-
thousand dollars on a year-long study of food
preferences and popular stereotypes. Results ?
The public sees fast-food-addicts as
patriotic, conservative, and hard workers.
Vegetarians are intellectual and creative,
gourmets like small families, mixed doubles
in tennis, and "live in the fast lane"
The National Endowment For the Arts granted
$7,000 for a sound and light show to make
Wisconsins' state capital building in
Milwaukee "send forth human and planetary
energies in a massage of world peace.' The
one performance was marred when half the

lights failed to work and the recorded
broadcast from the dome was illegible.

The U. S. Army's Materiel Development and
Readyness Command (DARCON) spent $38 million
and 13 years to develop a new gas mask, the
XM30, that usually malfunctions within 48
hours. The Army's training and Doctrine
Command found the XM-30s generally inferior
to the 17-year old M17AL mask it was designed
to replace.

The Defense Department paid #13,000 to
test the possible side-effects of extremely-
low-frequency radio waves on a hereford bull
named Sylvester. After 6 years, Sylvestre was
autopsied and judged "essentially a normal
bull though somewhat obese." A Navy Vice
Admiral admitted that the experiment has no
value due "to the limited size of the sample
data base."

Abbreviations, Acronyms, and Symbols

Abbreviations, acronyms, and symbols are shortcuts that help authors save space. By uncluttering the text, these shortcuts can also facilitate comprehension. Consider, for example, the following sentence, which is to appear in a document for the general public:

> Researchers are examining samples of deoxyribonucleic acid in an effort to determine why some people who test positive for human immunodeficiency virus do not develop acquired immune deficiency syndrome.

Here, replacing the three scientific terms with acronyms[1] will help readers because most nonscientists are more familiar with the acronyms than with the spelled-out forms.

> *Revision:* Researchers are examining DNA samples in an effort to determine why some people who test positive for HIV do not develop AIDS.

Indeed, despite the schoolbook injunction "Never use abbreviations in formal writing," some abbreviations, acronyms, and signs are routinely used in formal writing.

---

1. Some authorities reserve *acronym* for those initialisms that are pronounced as words, rather than as a series of letters. Thus HIV, DNA, and AIDS are all initialisms, but only the last is an acronym. In general usage, however, *acronym* is used to denote both groups.

Abbreviations

The courtesy titles Mr., Mrs., and Ms. are never spelled out when they precede a proper name. (In any case, there is no spelled-out equivalent for Ms.)

Military, political, and other titles are commonly abbreviated when they precede a full name—Gen., Lt. Col., Sen., Rep., Dr.—though the full title is usually spelled out when only a surname is given.

Following a proper name, suffixes (Jr. and Sr.) are always abbreviated, as are academic degrees (B.A., M.S., Ph.D.) and the designation Esq.

The following designations related to time are always abbreviated: A.M. (or a.m.), P.M. (or p.m.), B.C., A.D.

The adjectives U.S. and U.N. are always abbreviated, although the noun forms are spelled out.

Business suffixes (Inc., Co., Ltd.) are almost always abbreviated.

Most style manuals recommend or accept the abbreviation St. in the names of cities (St. Louis, St. Paul).

Acronyms

Acronyms are routinely used for the names of many corporations (ABC, A&P, CBS, IBM); indeed, for some companies (AT&T, 3M, USX) the acronym is the official corporate name.

Some high-tech products (CD-ROM, VCR) and scientific terms (DNA, LSD) are routinely referred to by their initials or acronyms, and dictionaries label these terms as ordinary nouns. Similarly: AM and FM radio, UHF and VHF television channels, and UFOs.

In some contexts the initials for well-known phrases are used: RIP (or R.I.P.), QED (or Q.E.D.).

Signs

The dollar sign ($) is used when sums of money are expressed in numerals.

The percentage sign (%) is used in technical and financial documents, and in tables in nontechnical documents (see "Words or Numerals?" in chapter 7).

The ampersand (&) is used in the names of companies.

The section sign (§) and paragraph sign (¶) are used in references to legal documents.

The various style manuals each recommend slightly different editorial conventions for the treatment of abbreviations, acronyms, and symbols. As in all matters of editorial style, the three overarching concerns for the copyeditor are that (1) the document is internally consistent, (2) the document conforms to recognized conventions in the author's field, and (3) the editorial style facilitates readers' comprehension of the document.

In this chapter we'll look at some of the everyday problems that abbreviations, acronyms, and symbols pose for copyeditors. Copyeditors who work on scientific and technical documents should consult *CSE* and the specialized style manuals listed in chapter 3.

ABBREVIATIONS

In the editorial styling of abbreviations, the three issues are capitalization, punctuation, and plural forms. Before looking at the conventions for specific types of abbreviations, we can make some generalizations about these three issues.

Capitalization: Typically, the capitalization of an abbreviation follows the capitalization of the spelled-out term. For example, the abbreviations of personal titles and proper nouns are capitalized, but the abbreviations of most common nouns are not:

The report was submitted by Dr. John Osgood Jr.

Gusts along the coast exceeded 72 knots (83 mph).

The police arrested Hapgood Smythe (a.k.a. Sticky Fingers).

Contemporary scholarly style discourages the use of "op. cit." in notes.

Punctuation: Most abbreviations take terminal periods;[2] the following do not:

French courtesy terms: Mme Dupris, Mlle Dupris (*but* M. Dupris)

---

2. In British style, no period follows an abbreviation whose last letter is the same as the last letter in the full word: Dr Smith *but* Capt. Smith, *and* vol. 1 *but* vols 2–4. American publishers typically instruct their copyeditors to Americanize a document that follows the British convention.

Units of measurement: ft, sq ft, mi (*but* in.—to avoid confusion
with the word *in*),[3] cm, kg, mL, kHz

Rates of measurement: mph, dpi (dots per inch), cps (cycles per
second)

Abbreviations that have internal periods do not take internal spaces:[4]

U.S.   U.N.   Washington, D.C.   at 8 A.M.   e.g.   i.e.

Plural forms: Some abbreviations have regular plural forms (vol., vols.;
chap., chaps.); others have irregular plurals (p., pp.; f., ff.; Mr., Messrs.) All
units of measure are invariant: in., ft, cm, g.

COMMON LATIN ABBREVIATIONS

Many publishers allow the common Latin abbreviations (etc., e.g., i.e.) only
in parenthetical references and in footnotes. Copyeditors working under this
policy are expected to substitute for the abbreviation or delete it, depending
on the context. The standard substitutes for these Latin abbreviations are English phrases:

For	*Substitute*
e.g.	for example
etc.	and so on *or* and so forth *or* and the like;
	less often: et cetera [*no italics*]
i.e.	that is

The following examples illustrate several ways to handle these abbreviations:

Original: Consider planting evergreens, e.g., pines, firs, and cedars.

Revision: Consider planting evergreens—for example, pines, firs,
or cedars.

Or: Consider planting evergreens: pines, firs, and cedars, for example.

3. In nonscientific texts, *Chicago* recommends periods after all American units of measure
(in., sq. ft., mi.) but notes that when these abbreviations are used in scientific copy they usually
appear without periods.

4. *Chicago* 16 recommends not using periods within abbreviations that are set in capital
letters, even if lowercase letters appear within the abbreviation: US, UN, DC, PhD. Nonetheless, *Chicago* retains internal periods in traditional state abbreviations: N.Y, N.J., N.M. (see pp.
221–22).

Or: Consider planting pines, firs, cedars, or other evergreens.

Original: Arrange the reports in chronological order: January, February, etc.

Revision: Arrange the reports in chronological order: January, February, and so on.

Or: Arrange the reports in chronological order, from January through December.

Original: Connect the 15-pin output to the DIS port, i.e., the display adapter.

Revision: Connect the 15-pin output to the DIS port (i.e., the display adapter).

Or: Connect the 15-pin output to the DIS port (that is, the display adapter).

When house style allows these abbreviations to appear in running text, you must make sure that the abbreviations are correctly used and punctuated; for example:

Consider planting evergreens, e.g., pines, firs, and cedars.

Consider planting evergreens (e.g., pines, firs, and cedars).

Connect the 15-pin output to the DIS port, i.e., the display adapter.

Connect the 15-pin output to the DIS port (i.e., the display adapter).

Wilco ships nuts, bolts, hand tools, etc., by overnight mail.[5]

Wilco ships small orders (nuts, bolts, hand tools, etc.) by overnight mail.

The abbreviation etc. requires special care. Since etc. is short for the Latin *et cetera,* which means "and the others" or "and the rest," the expression "and etc." is always incorrect:

---

5. Traditional editorial style recommends that *et cetera, etc., and so on,* and similar expressions be set off by commas, but some minimalist punctuators style these expressions like any other final element in a series: Wilco ships nuts, bolts, hand tools, etc. by overnight mail.

✗ Reread the front matter (title pages, copyright page, contents page, preface, and etc.).

Reread the front matter (title pages, copyright page, contents page, preface, etc.).

Moreover, etc. should not come at the end of a list introduced by a form of *including* or by *such as*, both of which denote that the list is not exhaustive:

✗ The analyses account for factors that include age, sex, marital status, etc.

The analyses account for factors that include age, sex, and marital status.

The other Latin abbreviation in common use is v. (versus), which may be set in roman or italic:

Wilkins v. *California* is a landmark case in patent law.

Or: Wilkins v. California is a landmark case in patent law.

In contexts other than lawsuits, "versus" is usually spelled out; the abbreviation vs. may be used in parenthetical expressions, however.

A few other Latin abbreviations sometimes appear in manuscripts (for bibliographical abbreviations, see "Documentation" later in this chapter).

c. *or* ca.	circa	approximately (used before a date: c. 1530)
fl.	floruit	flourished (used before a date: fl. 900 B.C.)
N.B.	nota bene	note (used before a caveat or explanation)
viz.	videlicet	namely, to wit

ABBREVIATIONS FOR STATES

There are two systems for abbreviating the names of states and territories. In what has come to be called the traditional system, most of the shorter names are not abbreviated (Alaska, Guam, Hawaii, Idaho, Iowa, Ohio, Utah), and the longer names have two- to five-letter abbreviations (Calif., Conn., N.Y., Wash.). The second system uses the postal codes, a set of two-letter, all-uppercase, no-internal-period abbreviations: AK, GU, HI, IA, UT, CA, CT, NY.

Some publishers use the postal abbreviations in all cases in which abbreviations are permitted; other publishers use the following conventions:

1. Running text. No abbreviations of states in running text except for addresses and parenthetical expressions of political affiliation (see items 2 and 3 below):

   The new factory will be built in Worcester, Massachusetts.

2. Addresses. Use the postal abbreviations in addresses:

   Send questions and comments to PO Box 101, Anytown MA 01222.

3. Political affiliation. In parenthetical expressions, use the traditional abbreviations for states:

   Senators Jeanneanne Mei (D-N.J.) and Carla Hoving (R-Nev.) are sponsoring the bill.

   Note: This journalistic convention uses D (or D.) for Democrats, R (or R.) for Republicans, and I (or I.) for independents, followed by a hyphen and an abbreviated state name.

4. Notes and bibliography. Use the traditional abbreviations for states in a note (footnote or endnote) or a bibliographical entry:

   Footnote: Keith Wilson, *Life Goes On* (Marshall, Mass.: Little Press, 2000), pp. 11–12.

   Bibliography: Wilson, Keith. *Life Goes On.* Marshall, Mass.: Little Press, 2000.

TIME

The following abbreviations are never spelled out: A.M., P.M., B.C., A.D. Some publishers prefer small capital letters (small caps) for these abbreviations (A.M. or AM); some set them uppercase (A.M. or AM); and some set the times of day lowercase (a.m. or am).

A traditional publishing convention calls for B.C. to follow the year, but A.D. to precede the year:

The shrine was built in 50 B.C. and destroyed in A.D. 40.

Outside of scholarly publishing, this convention seems to be losing ground to a preference for placing the abbreviation after the year: 50 B.C. and 40 A.D.

Note that the designation A.D. is used only when B.C. appears nearby in the text.

In works addressed to general readers, some of the less common abbreviations for eras may be spelled out on first mention:

B.C.E.	before the common era (a synonym for B.C.)
C.E.	common era (a synonym for A.D.)
B.P.	before the present (used in astronomy and cosmology; by convention, "present" = A.D. 1950)
A.H.	*anno Hegirae* (used in the Islamic calendar; the Hegira occurred in A.D. 622)
J.D.	julian date (used in astronomy; represents the number of days between January 1, 4713 B.C. and the date in question)

There is no need to spell out these abbreviations in texts addressed to specialists, however.

UNITS OF MEASUREMENT

In nontechnical text, units of measurement are abbreviated only when space is at a premium (e.g., in tables) or when the abbreviations facilitate comprehension (e.g., when numerical data cluster thickly in a paragraph). In technical text, abbreviations are used more freely.

Abbreviations of units of measure named after people are capitalized. The abbreviations of other units of measure are lowercased—except the abbreviation for liter, which is an uppercase L (a lowercase l is too similar to the numeral 1).

A	ampere	ft	foot
Hz	hertz	kg	kilogram
J	joule	m	meter
K	kelvin[6]	mi	mile
L	liter	mol	mole
Pa	pascal	s	second (SI unit)
W	watt	sec	second (American unit)

---

6. The unit kelvin is lowercased, but both the abbreviation (K) and the scale (the Kelvin scale) are capitalized. Temperatures expressed in kelvins do not carry a degree sign: Water freezes at 273 K (32°F) and boils at 373 K (212°F).

Care must be taken in the capitalization of abbreviations for prefixes used in the metric and SI systems.[7] The prefixes larger than kilo- are uppercased; the others are lowercased:

T	tera-	(1 trillion × the base unit)
G	giga-	(1 billion × the base unit)
M	mega-	(1 million × the base unit)
k	kilo-	(1,000 × the base unit)
c	centi-	(0.01 × the base unit)
m	milli-	(0.001 × the base unit)

Nonetheless, in computer publications kilobyte is usually abbreviated Kb or K.

Uncommon units of measurement should be spelled out on first mention in documents intended for general readers, but such units need not be spelled out in documents intended for specialists.

For general readers: The best of the dot-matrix printers produced noticeably stippled text at 72 dots per inch (dpi); today, the standard laser printer provides a crisp 600 dpi.

For general readers: The lead levels in 102 of the 150 samples exceeded 8 parts per million.
[The abbreviation ppm should be supplied only if the document contains further references to this unit.]

For specialists: The lead levels in 102 of the 150 samples exceeded 8 ppm.

When measurements are given in both American and SI units, the equivalences are enclosed in parentheses.

The shards were found 328 ft (100 m) from the fence.

The shards were found 100 m (328 ft) from the fence.

The boiling point of this compound is 800°F (445°C).

The boiling point of this compound is 445°C (800°F).

---

7. SI (Système international d'unités; International System of Units), which is based on the metric system, is the international standard in science and technology. *Chicago, APA,* and *CSE* all discuss SI conventions.

When an abbreviated unit of measurement appears in a compound adjective preceding a noun, the compound is not hyphenated:

a 20 ft wall   a 13 m tube   a 10 km race   a 5 kg carton

DOCUMENTATION

If you are copyediting text that contains footnotes, in-text references to source materials, or a bibliography, you may encounter or want to use the abbreviations shown in table 9.

TABLE 9.   Bibliographical Abbreviations

Singular	Plural	Meaning
cf.		compare. Used to direct readers to compare (not simply to "see" or "see also") a source that presents an alternative interpretation or point of view: Cf. Ludi, *Rights and Privileges,* p. 35.
chap.	chaps.	chapter
ed.	eds.	edition; edited by
et al.		and others. Used in some styles of documentation to refer to a work that has multiple authors: Barton et al. repeated this experiment. There is no period after "et" because the Latin *et* (and) is a complete word.
f.	ff.	and following. Used to refer to pages: See pp. 67f. and pp. 234ff. (the plural "pp." because the reader is being referred to more than one page). Or, if the publisher's style calls for the omission of "p." and "pp.": See 67f. and 234ff. There is no space between the numeral and "f." or "ff."
fig.	figs.	figure
ibid.		"in the same place." Used in some styles of documentation to indicate that the source of a quotation or piece of evidence is the same as the source previously cited. Usually appears only in notes and is capitalized when it is the first word in a note: 8. Ibid., p. 15. Or, if "p." is not used: 8. Ibid., 15.

(continued next page)

(table 9 continued)

Singular	Plural	Meaning
l.	ll.	line. Many publishers discourage authors from using l. and ll. because these abbreviations too closely resemble the numerals 1 and 11.
n.	nn.	note (i.e., footnote or endnote)
no.	nos.	number (i.e., issue of a magazine or journal)
p.	pp.	page
pt.	pts.	part
s.v.	s.vv.	see under. Used to refer the reader to an entry in a dictionary or an encyclopedia: *Webster's New World,* s.v. "comprise."
vol.	vols.	volume

ACRONYMS

All the major style manuals recommend that acronyms be set in uppercase letters with no internal periods: WHO, MRI, CPR. A newer convention for styling acronyms has been adopted by many newspapers, however, and it is likely to spread to corporate and book publishing:

> Full caps for acronyms that are pronounced as letters: NFL, HMO, NAACP.
> Full caps for three- or four-letter acronyms that are pronounced as words: RAM, GATT.
> Initial cap only for acronyms five letters or longer that are pronounced as words: Nafta, Erisa.

Familiar versus unfamiliar.   Acronyms that appear in the alphabetical section of a standard dictionary (e.g., AIDS, DNA, LSD, REM, VCR) need not be introduced or spelled out, even on first mention in a document. This principle also applies to the acronyms of extremely well known organizations (e.g., AFL-CIO, CIA, FBI, IRS, NATO, YMCA). Nonetheless, if the intended audience includes readers in other countries, it is preferable to spell out all acronyms on first use. The watchword is "When in doubt, spell it out."

In documents addressed to scientists, technical specialists, and other professional experts, acronyms that are standard in the field may usually be used without any introduction. For example, an accountant writing a report addressed to other accountants can confidently use FASB, IRR, and ROI.[8] But when the intended audience for the document is broader (say, readers in other specialties or in other countries), all acronyms should be formally introduced.

Parenthetical introduction.   The traditional way to introduce an acronym is to place it in parentheses after the first mention of its spelled-out equivalent.[9]

> The International Monetary Fund (IMF) will announce its decision next month. Analysts predict that the IMF will reinstate the funding package only if the government presents a credible budget that includes substantial cuts in social welfare programs.

> The technology for optical character recognition (OCR) has improved in the last five years. But even when OCR is 99.99 percent accurate, scanned documents will contain 1 error per 10,000 characters, or about 1 error on every third page.

When introducing an acronym on first mention would interrupt a compound or force an otherwise awkward parenthetical expression, either the sentence should be rewritten or the introduction of the acronym should be delayed until the second mention of the term.

> *Awkward:* State law requires that all Department of Conservation (DC)–mandated water testing be performed by a state-certified laboratory.

> *Revision:* State law requires that all water testing mandated by the Department of Conservation (DC) be performed by a state-certified laboratory.

---

8. FASB = Financial Accounting Standards Board, IRR = internal rate of return, ROI = return on investment.

9. Under the influence of *The Associated Press Stylebook,* some nonjournalists have adopted a convention that does away with the parenthetical introduction of acronyms. The AP rule is to spell out the term on its first mention in the text and to use the acronym thereafter; if the acronym standing alone will be puzzling to readers, then the spelled-out term is always used. Under this system, the examples would read:

> The International Monetary Fund will announce its decision next month. Analysts predict that the IMF will reinstate the funding package . . .

> The technology for optical character recognition has improved in the last five years. But even when OCR is 99.99 percent accurate, scanned documents will contain . . .

Awkward: Any retirement plan opened by an account executive (AE, except those who hold Series 11 licenses) must be reviewed by the AE's branch manager.

Revision: Any retirement plan opened by an account executive (AE)—except those who hold Series 11 licenses—must be reviewed by the AE's branch manager.

Or: Any retirement plan opened by an account executive (AE) who does not hold a Series 11 license must be reviewed by the AE's branch manager.

For terms better known by their acronym than by their full name, some publishers prefer that the acronym precede the spelled-out term on first mention:

The CPU (central processing unit) is often called the brain of the computer.

Newcomers are advised to read the list of FAQs (frequently asked questions).

As all the preceding examples illustrate, only proper nouns and proper adjectives are capitalized in the spelled-out version of an acronym.

Ideally, an acronym is introduced shortly before it is repeatedly used in the document. For example, an organization may be mentioned in a long list on page 5 of the text, but if that organization is not discussed in detail until page 25, it is preferable to introduce the acronym on page 25 rather than on the first mention of the organization. Alternatively, the acronym can be introduced on page 5 and re-introduced on page 25. In very long documents, especially those using many unfamiliar acronyms, readers will appreciate seeing the spelled-out term on the first mention in each chapter or long section.

There is usually no need to use an acronym at all if the full term appears only a handful of times in a document, because the space to be saved is not worth the strain placed on the reader's memory. Occasionally, however, an author may introduce an acronym solely so that readers who come across it in another context will recognize it.

"Alphabet soup." Writers and copyeditors must guard against "alphabet soup," strings of confusing nonce acronyms that will confuse readers.

Alphabet soup: MDFs scored higher than MDMs on the DI.

Revision: Moderately dysthymic females scored higher on the depression inventory than moderately dysthymic males.

Alphabet soup: The CDF-SPP map shows both the CCDs and the smaller CBGs within the LAWD.

Revision: The map produced by the Strategic Planning Program of the California Department of Forestry shows both the county census divisions and the smaller census block groups within the Los Angeles Water District.

This last example could be rewritten to introduce one or two acronyms, but readers will be overwhelmed by five new acronyms in one sentence:

Confusing: The map produced by the Strategic Planning Program (SPP) of the California Department of Forestry (CDF) shows both the county census divisions (CCDs) and the smaller census block groups (CBGs) within the Los Angeles Water District (LAWD).

Revision: The map produced by the Strategic Planning Program of the California Department of Forestry shows both the county census divisions (CCDs) and the smaller census block groups (CBGs) within the Los Angeles Water District.

Or: The map produced by the Strategic Planning Program of the California Department of Forestry (CDF) shows both the county census divisions and the smaller census block groups within the Los Angeles Water District (LAWD).

Overseas organizations. Some international organizations are best known by acronyms that are derived from their non-English names. In such cases, it is preferable to include both the organization's proper name as well as the English translation of the name. Although a bit cumbersome, this system prevents readers from puzzling over the relationship between the acronym and the translated name.

The PRI (Partido Revolucionario Institucional; Institutional Revolutionary Party) has ruled Mexico for decades.

The initial study was conducted by researchers at CERN (Conseil Européen pour la Recherche Nucléaire; European Laboratory for Particle Physics).[10]

Some publications use a less formal construction to provide the additional information:

The conference is being sponsored by the GSI (which stands for the German Gesellschaft für Schwerionenforschung, or Society for Heavy Ion Research).

In Sunday's election the Institutional Revolutionary Party, best known by its Spanish acronym PRI, lost its majority in the House of Deputies.

A or an?   When an indefinite article precedes an acronym, the choice between "a" and "an" follows from the pronunciation:

a FAQ file ("fack"—though sometimes pronounced "ef-a-cue")
an FTC commissioner ("ef-tee-cee")
an IRA plan (both "eye-ar-a" and "eye-ra" are used; either way, the
    article is "an")
an LED display ("el-ee-dee")
an MPEG application ("em-peg")
an NAACP spokesman ("en-double-a-cee-pee")
an ROTC program (officially, "ar-oh-tee-cee"—though many people
    say "rot-cee")
an SEC ruling ("ess-ee-cee")
a SEP-IRA plan ("sep-eye-ra")
a UNESCO project ("you-nesco")
a URL ("you-ar-el")

If you do not know how an acronym is pronounced, ask your author or editorial coordinator for help.

Redundonyms.   In speech, people often use an acronym followed by a word that is actually a part of the acronym:

10. The acronym CERN reflects the organization's original French name, shown here. The acronym was retained after the organization changed its name (to avoid the end-of-the-world connotations of *nuclear*). As a result, the English translation of the organization's current name does not match the French name that explains the acronym.

ATM machine (ATM = automated teller machine)
GRE exam (GRE = Graduate Record Examination)
HIV virus (HIV = human immunodeficiency virus)
PIN number (PIN = personal identification number)
UPS service (UPS = United Parcel Service)

In writing, such redundancies are best avoided. A former redundonym, SAT test, however, is no longer a redundonym. In 1997 the College Board, the company that administers the exam, announced that "SAT is not an initialism. . . . The SAT has become the trademark; it doesn't stand for anything."[11]

Pronunciation cues.   There are several conventions for representing the pronunciation of an acronym:

ASCII (pronounced "ass'-key")   ASCII (pronounced ASS-key)
ASCII (rhymes with "passkey")   ASCII (rhymes with *passkey*)

As in all other matters, consistency within a document is crucial, whichever convention is used.

List of acronyms.   As a kindness to readers, long documents that incorporate many acronyms often include an alphabetized list of acronyms or abbreviations. In a book this list may appear in the front matter or in the back matter; in a shorter document, the list may appear in a footnote or an endnote or in a separate section that precedes or follows the main text.

SYMBOLS AND SIGNS

A handful of symbols and signs are in common currency:

Nonalphanumeric characters found on the standard keyboard:
@ # $ % & *
Degree sign, for temperature and longitude and latitude: °
Single and double prime signs, for feet and inches as well as longitude and latitude: ' "

11. Scott Jeffe, in Peter Applebome, "Insisting It's Nothing, Creator Says SAT, Not S.A.T.," *New York Times*, April 2, 1997, p. A16, national edition. Originally, SAT stood for "Scholastic Aptitude Test"; after years of dispute about whether the test measures aptitude, as opposed to skills, the exam was rechristened the "Scholastic Assessment Test."

Section and paragraph signs, for citations from legal and technical
documents: § ¶

No spacing intervenes between the sign and the numeral in the following types
of expressions.

Currency:	$525	65¢	£123	¥10,568 €110 million
Percentages:	15%	8.4%	0.5%	2½%
Citations:	§1457(a)	¶5(c–e)		
Prime signs:	6'	5' 2"	3' 6" × 2' 8"	

Latitude and longitude:
   50°45'35" N (*or* 50-45-35 N)   85°20'10" E (*or* 85-20-10 E)
Degree sign: 61°F   16°C
   (*or* 61 °F *and* 16 °C, *with a thin space before the degree sign*)

Copyeditors working on hard copy may need to call out for the compositor
the names of the following signs and symbols:

#	number sign, pound sign, hash mark (formerly called octothorp)
£	pounds sign (British currency)
€	euro glyph (single European currency)
¥	yen sign
&	ampersand
@	at sign
*	asterisk
( )	parentheses
[ ]	brackets, square brackets
{ }	braces, curly brackets
< >	angle brackets
« »	guillemets (a style of quotation marks used in some European languages)
/	slant, slash, virgule, solidus
\	backslash
|	pipe, vertical bar
†	dagger
‡	double dagger
¶	paragraph sign (formerly called pilcrow)
§	section sign

°	degree sign
‖	parallels
☚ ☛	index symbols, hands

α	Greek lowercase alpha (in editorial shorthand: Gr lc alpha)
β	Greek lowercase beta
Γ	Greek uppercase gamma
γ	Greek lowercase gamma
Δ	Greek uppercase delta
δ	Greek lowercase delta
ε	Greek lowercase epsilon
λ	Greek lowercase lambda
μ	Greek lowercase mu
Π	Greek uppercase pi
π	Greek lowercase pi
Σ	Greek uppercase sigma
σ	Greek lowercase sigma
χ	Greek lowercase chi
Ω	Greek uppercase omega

Chicago discusses other symbols in chapters on foreign languages and mathematics, and *APA* has several lists of symbols used in the social sciences. Copyeditors who work with scientific or technical material should consult *CSE* or a specialized handbook.

APA offers the following guidelines about beginning a sentence with a symbol: "Never begin a sentence with . . . a symbol that stands alone (e.g., α). Begin a sentence with . . . a symbol connected to a word (e.g., β-Endorphins) only when necessary to avoid indirect and awkward writing. In the case of chemical compounds, capitalize the first letter of the word to which the symbol is connected" (p. 111). For example:

In regular running text: The effects of λ-hydroxy-β-aminobutyric acid were measured.

At the start of a sentence: λ-Hydroxy-β-aminobutyric acid has several unusual properties.

EXERCISE J

This manuscript is the opening section of a magazine article written by an experienced writer. You are being asked to do a light copyedit, one that respects the author's somewhat idiosyncratic style, and to prepare a style sheet. The answer key is on pages 504–13.

Until recent times, doctors spoke a magic language, usually Latin, and mystery was part of your cure. But modren doctors are rather in the situation of modern priests; having lost their magic language, they run the risk of losing the magic powers too.

For us, this means that the doctor may lose his ability to heal us by our faith; and doctors, sensing powerlessness, have been casting about for new languages in which to conceal the nature of our afflictions and the ingredients of their cures. They have devised two dialects, but neither seems quiet to serve for every purpose. For this is a time of transtion and trial for them, marked by various strategies, of which the well known illegible handwriting on your prescription is but one. For doctors themselves seem to have lost faith too, in themsevles and in the old mysteries and arts. They have been taught to think of themselves as scientists, and so it is first of all to the language of science they they turn, to control, and confuse us.

Most of the time scientific language can do this perfectly. We are terrified, of course, to learn that we have "prolapse of the mitral valve"--we promise to take our medicine and stay on our diet, even though these words describe a usually innocous finding in the investigation of an innocent heart murmur. Or we can be lulled into a false sense of security when the doctor avoids a scientific term: "You have a little spot on your lung"-- even when what he puts on the chart is "probable bronchogenic carcinoma."

With patients, doctors can use either scientific or vernacular speech, but with each other they speak Science, a strange argot of Latin terms, new words, and acronyms, that yearly becomes farther removed from everyday speech and is sometimes comprised almost entirely of numbers and letter: "His pO_2 is 45; pCO_2, 40; and pH 7.4.' Sometimes it is made up of peculiar verbs originating from the apparatus with which they treat people: "well, we've bronched him, tubed him, bagged him, cathed him, and PEEPed him" the intern tells the attending physician. ("We've explored his airways with a bronchoscope, inserted an endotrachial tube, positioned a cathater in his bladder to monitor his urinary output, provided assisted ventilation with a resuscitation bag, and used positive end-expiratory pressure to improve oxygenation.") Even when discussing

things that can be expressed in ordinary

words, doctors will prefer to say "he had a

pneumonectomy," to saying "he had a lung

removed."

One physician remembers being systematically

instructed, during the fifties, in scientific-

sounding euphemisms to be used in the

presence of patients. If a party of interns

were examining an alcoholic patient, the

wondering victim might hear them say he was

"suffering from hyperingestation of ethanol."

In front of a cancer patient they would

discuss his "mitosis." But in recent years

such discussions are not conducted in front

of the patient at all, because, since

Sputnik, laymen's understanding of scientific

language has increased so greatly, that

widespread ignorance cannot be assumed.

Space exploration has had its influence, especially on the *sound* of medical language. A CAT-scanner (computerized automated tomography), *de rigueur* in an up-to-date diagnostic unit, might be something to look at the surface of Mars with. The resonance of physical rather than biological science has doubtless been fostered by doctors themselves, who, mindful of the extent to which their science is really luck and art, would like to sound microscopically precise, calculable and exact, even if they cannot. Acronyms and abbreviations play the same part in medical language that they do in other walks of modern life. We might be irritated to read on our chart "that this SOB patient complained of DOE five days PTA." (It means: "this Short Of Breath patient complained of Dyspnea on Exertion five days Prior To

Admisssion.") To translate certain syllables,
the doctor must have yet more esoteric
information. Doctor A, reading Doctor B.'s
note that a patient has TTP, must know
whether Dr. B is a hematologist or a chest
specialist in order to know whether the
patient has thrombotic thrombocytopoenic
purpura, or traumatic tension pnuemothorax.
That pert little ID means identification to
us, but Intradermal to the dermatologist,
Inside Diameter to the physiologist, and
Infective Dose to the bacteriologist.

But sometimes doctors must speak vernacular
English, but this is apparently difficult for
them. People are always being told to discuss
their problem with their doctor, which,
considering the general inability of doctors
to reply except in a given number of reliable
phrases, must be some of the worse advice

ever given. Most people, trying to talk to the doctor--trying to pry or to wrest meaning from his evasive remarks ("I'd say you're coming along just fine.")--have been maddened by the vague and slightly inconsequential nature of statements which, meaning everything to you, ought in themselves to have meaning but do not, are noncommittal, or unengaged, have a slightly rote or rehearsed quality, sometimes a slight inappropriateness in the context ("it's nothing to worry about really"). This is the doctor's alternative dialect, phrases so general and bland as to communicate virtually nothing.

This dialect originates from the emotional situation of the doctor. In the way passers-by avert their eyes from the drunk in the gutter or the village idiot, so the doctor must avoid the personality, the individuality, any involvement with the destiny,

of his patients. He must not let himself

think and feel with them. In order to retain

objective professional judgment, the doctor

has long since learned to withdraw his

emotions from the plight of the patient.

❖ 10 ❖

Tables, Graphs, and Art

The problems that copyeditors encounter in handling tables, graphs, and art depend on how well the author understands the construction of these elements and on how much care the author has taken in their preparation. Ideally, tables and graphs offer an efficient way to present a large amount of information, most often numerical data. And various types of art—line drawings, maps, charts, photographs—can be used to present information or to provide ornamentation.

However, because tables, graphs, and art are more expensive to produce than running text, most publishers ask authors to exercise some restraint, with the number and complexity of these items depending on the nature of the project. Although a field guide to Pacific coast birds, for example, will contain many illustrations (line drawings, black-and-white photographs, color photographs, and maps), the biography of an ornithologist may have no illustrations or just a handful of photographs.

The two questions a copyeditor should always ask about any table, graph, chart, map, or photograph are: What specific purpose is this item intended to serve? and Is this particular item the best way to serve that purpose? You must be able to answer these questions in order to correctly handle the item. You need not, however, concern yourself with the technical quality of an illustration; the publisher's production staff will evaluate that. The production staff will also arrange to have charts or maps redrawn by graphic artists.

TABLES

All the major style manuals discuss the construction and formatting of tables and provide some tips on simplifying complex tables. Copyeditors who deal with relatively simple tables may need no guidance beyond that offered in *Chicago* or *WIT*. *CSE* and *APA* offer more sophisticated treatments of various types of scientific and statistical tables.

When working on a manuscript that contains more than a few short tables, you will usually have to make three passes through the tables—either on-screen or on hard copy:

Pass 1. Look at a table when it is first mentioned in the text.

- Make sure that the table "tells" a worthwhile and intelligible story. Although tables are meant to be read in conjunction with the text, a table should be understandable on its own.
- Check the relationship between the text and the table: Does the table present the information that the text says it presents? Is all the information in the table relevant to the discussion in the text? Does any information in the table seem to contradict the text?

Pass 2. At a convenient point, stop reading the manuscript and copyedit the table.

- Check the numbering and location of the table.
- Impose mechanical consistency (spelling, capitalization, punctuation, use of abbreviations).
- Scan the data in the table for internal inconsistencies.
- Verify that all information taken from other sources is attributed.
- Query an unusually small or large table that may need to be reconceptualized.

Pass 3. Read all the tables in the manuscript as a batch.

- Make sure all elements (e.g., table numbers, titles, column heads, footnotes) are consistent in format. (The elements of a table are illustrated in figure 7.)

Let's look at each of these tasks in turn.

Figure 7.   Parts of a Table

| Table number | Table 1. Virus-Neutralization Tests on Sera from Mammals and Birds | | | Table title |

Column heads

Spanner head

Decked heads

Stub head	Species	Number Tested	Positive N	%	
Cut-in head	Mammals				
	Camel	9	7	78	
Stub entries	Cow	36	6	17	Cells
	Donkey	15	7	47	
	. . .	. . .	. . .	. . .	
	Sheep	64	15	23	
Subtotal	Total mammals	466	187	40	
	Birds				
	Chicken*	24	4	16	Indicator for foot-note that applies to an entire row
	Crow	163	102	65	
	Duck	14	2†	14	Indicator for foot-note that applies only to one cell
	. . .	. . .	. . .	. . .	
Subtotal	Total birds	420	170	40	
Grand total	Grand total	886	357	40	

Source note

Source: Chris T. Author, *Book Title* (New York: Big Books, 1990), 536–37.

Footnotes

Note: All tests and retests were performed under IASA standards.

*Chickens were retested by PSA-3 analysis.
†Retest results were inconclusive for 2 additional ducks.

EVALUATING THE STORY

The function of a table is to provide information in a format that is more efficient or effective than a prose description would be. For example, the information presented in the table in figure 7 would be harder to comprehend if presented in a sentence-by-sentence, animal-by-animal report of the experiment: "Of the 9 camels tested, 7 (or 78%) tested positive. Of the 36 cows tested, 6 (or 17%) tested positive . . ."

When a table does not appear to be efficient or effective, however, the copyeditor should suggest that the information be given in the text proper and that the table be dropped. For example, consider table 10.

TABLE 10.	Turnout in Anytown Mayoral Elections, 1994–1998, by District		
	1994	1996	1998
District 1	58.4%	54.0%	58.3%
District 2	69.8	67.9	70.0
District 3	67.7	68.8	70.1

Because this array is both short (four lines of text) and narrow (four columns), all the information could easily be displayed in a multicolumn list:

	1994	1996	1998
District 1	58.4%	54.0%	58.3%
District 2	69.8	67.9	70.0
District 3	67.7	68.8	70.1

A different type of difficulty is presented by table 11. Although the table sorts the numbers of voters and nonvoters by sex—as promised by the table's title—the raw numbers do not tell the entire story. Readers cannot easily ascertain whether voting is more common among men or among women, nor how great the gender gap might be.

In other words, the real story in table 11 lies in the percentages (not the raw numbers) of voters and nonvoters. One could improve the table by adding columns that supply the percentages or by replacing the raw numbers with the percentages, as shown in table 12.

TABLE 11. April Primary Election: Turnout among Registered
Voters, by Sex

	Voted	Did Not Vote	Total
Men	2,111	1,404	3,515
Women	1,904	1,440	3,344
Total	4,015	2,844	6,859

TABLE 12. April Primary Election: Turnout among Registered Voters, by Sex

	Number of Registered Voters	Voted	Did Not Vote
Men	3,515	60.0%	40.0%
Women	3,344	56.9%	43.1%
Total	6,859	58.5%	41.5%

But consider how easily the information in table 12 could be conveyed in a single sentence:

In the April primary election, 60.0 percent of the registered men, but only 56.9 percent of the registered women, voted.

Or: Registered men were more likely to vote than registered women: 60.0 percent of the men, but only 56.9 percent of the women, cast ballots in the April primary.

Or the information could be presented as a multicolumn list:

Among registered voters, men were more likely than women to turn out for the April primary.

	Voted	*Did Not Vote*
Men	60.0%	40.0%
Women	56.9%	43.1%

Sometimes you will face the opposite problem: a table that contains too much information. If you come upon a table that contains many different types of data and that is referred to repeatedly in the manuscript over a series of pages, you could suggest to the author that the table be broken into two less complicated tables. (Problems related to a table's physical size, rather than its complexity, are discussed later in this chapter.)

RELATIONSHIP BETWEEN TEXT AND TABLE

The discussion of a table should not simply describe the table nor repeat vast portions of the data given in the table. Rather, the discussion should, as needed, prepare the reader to understand the table; summarize the importance, meaning, or value of the data presented in the table; or explain the implications of the data. Suppose your author writes the following:

> For each member of the OECD, table 2.2 shows the population (column 1), population density per square mile (column 2), per capita gross national product (column 3), per capita annual income (column 4), and life expectancy (column 5).

Since the table does show all these items, and each column in the table carries a heading that identifies it, this entire sentence could be deleted.

Another example. Your author writes:

> For at least a decade after the depression, the rate of population growth declined substantially. The birthrate dropped (see table 13), from 31.5 per thousand in 1920, to 28.7 per thousand in 1930, to 24.7 per thousand in 1935, and began to recover modestly only in 1945 (25.2 per thousand). In addition, emigration increased and immigration came to a halt.

TABLE 13. Birthrates and Death Rates, 1915–1950 (Rates per 1,000 inhabitants)

	Birthrate	Death Rate		Birthrate	Death Rate
1915	35.1	15.5	1935	24.7	12.5
1920	31.5	14.7	1940	24.0	10.7
1925	30.9	13.6	1945	25.2	10.3
1930	28.7	12.2	1950	28.9	10.1

You could delete the redundant data in the text and write a query to the author to explain the change:

> For at least a decade after the depression, the rate of population growth declined substantially. The birthrate dropped (see table 13),

~~from 31.5 per thousand in~~ between 1920, ~~to 28.7 per thousand in~~ and 1930, ~~to 24.7 per thousand in 1935,~~ continued to decline through 1940, and began to recover modestly only in 1945 ~~(25.2 per thousand).~~ (see table 13). In addition, emigration increased and immigration came to a halt.

> [Query] No need to repeat statistics in the text proper; they're clearly presented in the table. Add some mention of death rate in the text?—or else drop those figures from this table?

In-text cross-references.   *Chicago* recommends lowercasing in-text references to tables and portions of them: see tables 3 and 4; see tables 1.6 through 1.9; see table 12, column 2. *WIT, APA,* and *CSE* uppercase in-text references to tables (e.g., see Tables 3 and 4) and are silent on the issue of how to treat portions of tables.

Percent versus *percentage.*   When referring to percentages that are shown in tables, conservative usage favors the noun *percentage* (not *percent*): The percentage of absentee voters has continued to increase.

NUMBERING AND PLACING TABLES

All tables in a manuscript must be numbered consecutively, by either single numeration (Table 1, Table 2, Table 3) or double numeration (Table 1.1, Table 1.2, Table 1.3, where the first digit represents the chapter number and the second digit represents the table's location within that chapter).[1] The numbering should match the order in which the tables are first referred to in the text. In other words, it is not acceptable to have the first in-text reference to table 3 precede the first in-text reference to table 2. Once a table has been introduced, it may be referred to again at any time.

For hard-copy manuscripts, all the tables must be removed from the running text and gathered in a separate batch, one table to a page, at the end of the manuscript. If the tables are interspersed throughout the manuscript, you may need to photocopy the originals (one table to a page), mark for deletion the tables interspersed in the manuscript, and call out in the left margin the

---

1. Under both systems, tables that appear in an appendix take the lettered designation of the appendix as their first element. Thus the tables in Appendix A are numbered Table A.1, Table A.2, and so on; the tables in Appendix B are labeled Table B.1, Table B.2, and so on.

approximate location of each table. These callouts are usually done in red pencil (so they can be easily spotted) and are placed in boxes (like other editorial instructions):

> For many working-class families, real
> wages fell by as much as 50 percent
> between the depression of 1913 and the
> Armistice in November 1918 (see table
> 8.4). The falling standard of living,
> accompanied by a tightening labor
> market, proved a politically explosive
> combination.

table
8.4
about
here

For on-screen manuscripts, the procedure is similar: All the tables are gathered in a separate file (or several files when there are many long tables), and an in-text code is inserted at the end of a paragraph to alert the compositor to the location of each table:

> For many working-class families, real wages fell by as much as 50 percent between the depression of 1913 and the Armistice in November 1918 (see table 8.4). The falling standard of living, accompanied by a tightening labor market, proved a politically explosive combination. <Table 8.4>

For the compositor's convenience, the location of each table is called out on the hard copy that accompanies the files. When the tables are complex or not well prepared, you may be asked to copyedit the tables on the hard copy rather than on-screen.

MECHANICAL EDITING

Table numbers.   Some publishers have a preferred house style for the format and terminal punctuation of the table numbers that precede the table title:

All caps, followed by a period: TABLE 1. World Population, 1996

Upper- and lowercase, followed by a colon: Table 1: World Population, 1996

Uppercase and small caps, followed by one or more wordspaces:
TABLE 1   World Population, 1996

Other publishers allow authors to use any reasonable style for table numbers, as long as it is applied consistently.

Table titles.   Titles should be accurate and brief. If the table is part of a scholarly or serious nonfiction work, the table title should be an objective statement of the table's contents and should not express value judgments or conclusions about the data (*not* "SAT Scores Drop between 1960 and 1995," *but* "SAT Scores, 1960–1995"). In business reports and newsletters, in contrast, a table title may function as an eye-catching interpretive headline ("Sales Soar in 1999").

The capitalization and terminal punctuation of the table titles should follow house style. If there is no house style, be sure the author has been consistent in these matters. Typically, the title is set in one of the styles shown here, with no terminal punctuation following.

Headline style: Per Capita Personal Income in Canada, Mexico, and the United States, 1995

Sentence style: Per capita personal income in Canada, Mexico, and the United States, 1995

All caps: PER CAPITA PERSONAL INCOME IN CANADA, MEXICO, AND THE UNITED STATES, 1995

As these examples illustrate, long titles are cumbersome and hard to read when set in all caps, and so an all-caps style is best reserved for a piece in which all the table titles are short. (The rules for headline style and sentence style are discussed under "Titles of Works" in chapter 6.)

Squibs.   A squib is a short parenthetical indicator placed after the table title to indicate an element that pertains to the table as a whole. For example, in a table itemizing a state's annual budget, it is preferable not to clutter the table with six-, seven-, eight-, and nine-digit numbers. Instead, a squib— ($ Millions)—is placed after the table title. Tables 14 and 15 illustrate how much space this device can save.

TABLE 14. State Budget, 1995–1997

Department	1995	1996	1997
Education	$14,500,000	$16,700,000	$17,300,000
Health	800,000	900,000	1,100,000
Transportation	125,600,000	141,100,000	136,400,000

TABLE 15. State Budget, 1995–1997 ($ Millions)

Department	1995	1996	1997
Education	14.5	16.7	17.3
Health	0.8	0.9	1.1
Transportation	125.6	141.1	136.4

Some publishers prefer to set squibs in headline style, and others prefer sentence style:

Headline style

(in Constant 1985 Dollars)
(in Thousands of Persons)
(in Japanese Yen)

Sentence style

(In constant 1985 dollars)
(In thousands of persons)
(In Japanese yen)

Whichever style is used, all squibs in the manuscript must be treated consistently. (Another use for squibs, to express the baseline for a statistical index, is discussed later in this chapter.)

Stub.   The items in the stub should be arranged in a logical order. Depending on the purpose and content of the table, the items in the stub may be arranged

    in chronological or reverse chronological order (earliest to latest;
        most recent to oldest)
    in alphabetical order
    in size order (largest to smallest; smallest to largest)
    in geographical order (northeast to southwest; north to south;
        distance from the sun)
    according to a conventional series (colors of the spectrum;
        zoological families)

When the stub consists of a set of numerical ranges (e.g., age cohorts), these ranges should not overlap. For example, because the ranges shown here in stub A overlap, readers cannot tell whether the 20-year-olds were counted in the 15–20 group or in the 20–25 group. A copyeditor would have to ask the author to review the data presented in the table and to select the correct ranges (either stub B or stub C).

A (illogical)	B (logical)	C (logical)
15–20	15–20	15–19
20–25	21–25	20–24
25–30	26–30	25–29

The capitalization of stub entries should also follow house style; if there is no house style, either headline style or sentence style may be used. *Exception:* Scientific terms that begin with a lowercase letter (pH, mRNA) should not be capitalized in the stub.

Column heads.   Column heads should be brief and logically arranged. If all cells in a column contain percentages, the percentage sign (%) may be placed in parentheses after the column heading. Similarly, if the numbers in a column represent dollars, a dollar sign ($) may be placed in parentheses after the column heading. (Alternatively, the % or $ may be placed in the first cell in the column or in each cell.)

If different units are used in different columns, the units are placed in parentheses after the column headings, as in table 16. Everyday units of measurement may be abbreviated and placed in parentheses after the column head; unusual abbreviations should be spelled out in a footnote to the table.

If you copyedit science or social science manuscripts, you are likely to come across tables in which N, *N*, or N appears in a column head. By convention,

TABLE 16.   Oceans of the World

	Area (sq mi)	Average depth (ft)	Greatest depth (ft)
Pacific	164,000,000	13,215	35,820
Atlantic	81,815,000	12,880	30,246
Indian	75,300,000	13,002	24,460
. . .	. . .	. . .	. . .

N is used to indicate the number of subjects or participants in an experiment or survey. Some publishers call for an italic *N;* others prefer a small cap N. Always ask your editorial coordinator which convention to follow.

Body of a table.   Although the author is responsible for the accuracy of the data in a table, copyeditors are expected to scan the entries, looking for any obvious typographical errors and querying any apparent inconsistencies or illogicalities. For example:

- All cells in a column should be of the same type and unit.
- If decimal numbers are used, all items in a column should be given to the same number of decimal places, and the column should be marked to align on the decimal point. *Note:* A copyeditor cannot simply add zeros to fill out a column; the editor must ask the author to decide how many decimal places are appropriate to the table and ask the author to supply the correct numbers.
- If four-digit and larger numbers appear in a table, the commas in each column must align.
- Any words in the body of a table must match the editorial style of the document (capitalization, hyphenation, spelling, and the like). Any unusual abbreviations or symbols should be defined; these explanations are usually placed in a footnote to the table.
- The notation n.a. (or na, *na,* or NA) may be used to mean "not applicable" or "not available," but this abbreviation should not be used for both meanings in the same table or series of tables. When n.a. stands for "not applicable," n.av. can be used for "not available." In tables intended for readers familiar with statistical data, there is no need to spell out these abbreviations. In tables intended for less sophisticated readers, *Chicago* recommends leaving the cell blank or inserting an em dash. Some publishers add an unnumbered footnote to the table: N.a. = not applicable.

Source notes.   If the information presented in a table is not the result of the author's research (lab experiments, fieldwork, surveys), the source(s) of the data must be stated in a note directly below the table (see figure 7). Source notes are not needed, however, for standard mathematical and financial tables (e.g., tables of square roots, logarithms, geometric functions, or mortgage amortizations). Multiple sources are usually listed in the order matching the appearance of the data in the table (either column by column, from left to right; or row by row, from top to bottom).

Source notes are labeled Source (or Sources when more than one source is named). Depending on the designer's preference, the label Source may be set in italics or in boldface, in uppercase and small caps, or in some other distinctive style. Some designers prefer a colon after the label Source; others use a period.

Footnotes.   When copyediting the footnotes to a table, you must first determine which columns, rows, or cells the note refers to. If you are not sure, you must query the author.

Notes that apply to an entire table are placed directly below any source note and are introduced by the label Note (or Notes when there is more than one). This convention avoids the placing of a footnote superscript or an asterisk after the title of the table. (Most publishers discourage or ban the placement of footnote indicators in display type; *CSE,* however, permits footnote indicators in table titles.) The location of other footnote indicators depends on the content of the note:

When a footnote applies to	*Place the footnote indicator*
all entries in a column	in the column heading for that column
all entries in a row	in the stub entry for that row
only one cell	in that cell

When the same footnote text applies to more than one column, row, or cell, the same footnote indicator should be repeated in all the relevant locations in the body of the table (see table 17).

Once you have sorted out where each footnote indicator belongs (column head, stub, or cell), make sure that the order of the footnotes matches their appearance in the table, reading from left to right across the column heads, the column subheads, and then the cells; for an example, see table 17. (*CSE,* however, calls for an entirely different hierarchy for assigning footnotes to tables.)

The content of the table determines the system most appropriate for numbering or lettering the footnotes. Three systems are in common use:

Numbering: 1, 2, 3, 4, 5, 6

Lowercase lettering: a, b, c, d, e, f

Asterisk-dagger system: *, †, ‡, §, ‖, #

The number, letter, or character within the table is conventionally set as a superscript (e.g., [1], [a], [*]). At the beginning of the footnote itself, the marker may be set as a superscript, with no punctuation following it (see figure 7); numerals and lowercase letters may also be set as regular characters followed by a period (see table 17).

TABLE 17.   Unemployment and Mean Annual
Wages, 1954–1957

	Unemployed as % of Labor Force[a]	Mean Annual Wages	
		Urban[b]	Rural[c]
1954	10.4	n.a.	n.a.
1955	11.5	$6,221[d]	$5,258
1956	17.7	6,717[d]	5,527
1957	13.4	7,049	6,342[e]

Source: Jan Smith, *The Economy of Dystopia* (New York: Economics Institute Press, 1965), 122–23.
   a. Males over age 16.
   b. Urban index based on ten largest cities and their suburbs.
   c. Rural index based on provinces of Jefferson, Adams, and Fillmore.
   d. Estimated from incomplete data.
   e. Extrapolated from data collected in March 1958.

When a table contains numerals, it is preferable to use lowercase lettering or the asterisk-dagger system because numbered footnotes invite confusion: 123.56[7]. But the asterisk-dagger system cannot be used if any of the tables in the manuscript contain probability footnotes of the form $*p < .05$ (discussed in the next subsection). In such tables, the asterisk is reserved for the probability footnotes, and it is best to use lowercase letters for the other footnotes.

Whichever system is used, the footnotes in each table begin at the start of the sequence (i.e., the first footnote in each table is labeled 1, a, or *). In other words, the sequence of footnote indicators is never carried over from one table to the next, and the sequence of footnote numbers in the running text is never interrupted by any numbered footnotes in a table.[2]

---

2. If the author integrated the tables into the manuscript (rather than treating them as separate items) and if the text and the tables both contain numbered notes, then—most unfortunately—

Footnotes stating probabilities.   When scientists conduct experiments to determine the correlation between two or more variables (i.e., the frequency with which those variables are observed to accompany one another), they subject the correlation to statistical tests in order to ascertain whether the correlation is meaningful (significant) or is merely the result of coincidence. The statistical strength of a correlation is expressed in terms of its probability level, which is conventionally represented as *p* (a lowercase italic p). If the statistical test of significance (a complex set of mathematical operations) shows that a correlation has a 5 percent or smaller chance of being a random coincidence, that correlation is said to have a *p* that is less than 5 percent; in scientific shorthand, this level of confidence in the result is expressed as $p < .05$. If the correlation has a 1 percent or smaller chance of being random, then $p < .01$, and so on. (No zero precedes the decimal point in these expressions because *p* by definition is always less than one.) In the body of a table, the correlations that are not statistically significant carry no marker; the correlations that are statistically significant at the weakest level of confidence are marked by a single asterisk; two asterisks mark correlations that have a stronger level of confidence. The *p* levels are stated in footnotes that follow the table. Notice that in the following example, a portion of a table showing correlations, each probability footnote carries a terminal period.

.670*	.879**	.612	.345
.322	.823*	.989**	.278
.415	−.124	.455	.977*

* $p < .05$.   ** $p < .01$.

Statistical indexes.   You may also come across tables that have squibs or footnotes containing a year or date, an equals sign, and the numeral 100, for example: $(1990 = 100)$. This kind of shorthand—used by economists, historians, and financial writers—indicates the base year (here, 1990) for a statistical index.

In constructing a statistical index, one assigns the value 100 to a specific point in time (either a year or a month and a year), and values for other peri-

the word processing program will have conflated all the numbers, and you will have to segregate the tables and renumber all the notes in the running text and in each table.

ods of time are expressed relative to that baseline. This system enables readers to make immediate comparisons: An index number of 200 means that whatever quantity is being measured has doubled since the period when the baseline was set at 100. For example, if 1980 is the base year for wheat exports, and the index number for 1995 is 200, then wheat exports doubled between 1980 and 1995.

Among the most widely cited indexes is the U.S. Consumer Price Index (CPI), the monthly indicator of the level of retail prices based on the cost of everyday goods and services. Each month the U.S. Bureau of Labor Statistics adds up the cost of a fixed list of consumer items, which is then represented in relation to the cost in the baseline year. Consider these hypothetical figures:

	Dollar Cost	Index
March 1984 (baseline)	$250	100.0
March 1985	$265	106.0
March 1986	$277	110.8

By dividing each month's price by the baseline and multiplying the quotient by 100, one arrives at the index equivalent ($265/$250 = 1.06; 1.06 × 100 = 106), which expresses the percentage increase or decrease relative to the baseline:

106 = 6% increase since the baseline date
110.8 = 10.8% increase since the baseline date
90 = 10% decrease since the baseline date

A table that presents index numbers must indicate the baseline period. By convention, this statement of the baseline is always placed in parentheses, and it appears in one of three places: as a squib following the title of the table; after the appropriate column heading; or as an unnumbered, unasterisked footnote to the table.

Baseline as squib:	Table 8.1. Retail Gasoline Prices, 1965–1995 (1965 = 100)
Baseline in column head:	Consumer Price Index (1984 = 100) Real Wages (1984 = 100)
Baseline in footnote:	(January 1988 = 100)

Horizontal and vertical rules.   Typically, horizontal rules are placed above and below the body of a table, below spanner heads, and below the column heads (see figure 7). Most publishers ask their copyeditors to delete vertical rules; but sometimes the rules are retained (or added) for tables that have many columns. Check with your editorial coordinator regarding the convention to be observed.

ODD-SIZE TABLES

Exactly how a table will look on the printed page is the responsibility of the designer, who will select the typeface, type size, margins, column widths, and so on. But if you copyedit books, you will need some general sense of how large a table can fit on a typeset book page. That way, you can make suggestions to the author for revising overly large tables, avoid making suggestions that will result in cumbersome tables, and alert the designer to potential difficulties. Here are some rules of thumb based on a typical 6-by-9 book page. Of course, small pages will accommodate less text, and large pages will accommodate more. (If you are puzzled by the mention of fonts and point sizes in these guidelines, return to this list after you have read chapter 13.)

Width

- A table typed in an 11-point font that fits on an $8\frac{1}{2}$-by-11 manuscript page (with 1-inch margins left and right) will comfortably fit on a 6-by-9 book page.
- If the body of the typeset table will be in 8-point type, a 6-by-9 book page can accommodate 80–85 characters per line. A character count of the widest lines in a table should allow at least 2 characters for the spacing in between adjacent column heads.
- If necessary, the table can be set in 8-point type and photoreduced by a small percentage.
- An overly wide table may be run broadside (also called landscape), although some publishers discourage or ban broadside tables. A broadside 6-by-9 book page can accommodate a table that is 125–135 characters wide and 20–25 lines long.
- A very wide table cannot be run across two pages; such an arrangement poses almost insurmountable difficulties in binding.
- A very narrow table can be run doubled up (see table 13 earlier in this chapter).

Length

- A double-spaced typed table that fits on two 8½-by-11 manuscript pages (with 1-inch margins top and bottom) will fit comfortably on one book page.
- If the body of the table will be set in 8-point type, a 6-by-9 book page can accommodate 50–55 lines of text.
- Very long tables can be continued over to the next page, and the column heads are repeated at the top of the continuation page.

ODD-SIZE COLUMNS

Tables that have many words may pose special problems in composition. For example, although the text of table 18 fits across the page, the last column is so narrow that the table looks ungainly. To produce a better-looking table, one could

decrease the number of columns by combining compatible items
decrease the number of characters in any column head that is sub-
    stantially wider than the data in the column
use common abbreviations
use common symbols

Table 19 shows the result of applying these techniques to table 18. (A fine point: The titles of tables 18 and 19 are capitalized according to sentence style, reflecting the preference of most scientific journals and books.)

READING TABLES AS A GROUP

During your final pass, you want to look at all the tables as a group in order to double-check the consistency in the treatment of titles, squibs, use of measurement units in column heads, use of horizontal and vertical rules, styling of source notes, placement of dollar and percentage signs, and the like.

TABLE 18.   Genetic variation within populations of mammal species in the western United States

Taxonomic Name	Common Name	Heterozygosity*	Sampling Range	Number of Sites	Researchers
Dipodomys agilis	Pacific kangaroo rat	0.040	Western United States	12	Wilson, Kline, and Stonefield (1995); Wilson and Kline (1996)
Dipodomys deserti	Desert kangaroo rat	0.010	Western United States	14	Alvarez and Messinger (1993)
Canis latrans	Coyote	0.052	Southern California	17	Singh, Yarnell, and Whapper (1992); Singh and Rosen (1993)
Microtus californicus	California vole	0.220	California Coast Range	21	Eden and Paradise (1991); Johnson (1992)

*Heterozygosity is the proportion of heterozygous genotypes per site per individual.

TABLE 19.   Genetic variation (heterozygosity) within populations of mammal species in the western United States

Taxonomic Name (Common Name)	H*	Sampling Range/ Number of Sites	Researchers
Dipodomys agilis (Pacific kangaroo rat)	0.040	Western U.S./12	Wilson, Kline & Stonefield (1995); Wilson & Kline (1996)
Dipodomys deserti (Desert kangaroo rat)	0.010	Western U.S./14	Alvarez & Messinger (1993)
Canis latrans (Coyote)	0.052	S. Calif./17	Singh, Yarnell & Whapper (1992); Singh & Rosen (1993)
Microtus californicus (California vole)	0.220	Calif. Coast Range/21	Eden & Paradise (1991); Johnson (1992)

*H = heterozygosity, the proportion of heterozygous genotypes per site per individual.

GRAPHS

All graphs must be read for sense, consistency, and editorial style.[3] The procedures are similar to those for tables:

- Make sure that the information or conclusions stated in the text match the data shown in the graph.
- Check the sequence and numbering. Graphs are usually labeled with other visual elements as Figure 1, Figure 2, Figure 3, and so on. When a manuscript contains many graphs, charts, photographs, drawings, or maps, each type may be labeled in a separate sequence: graphs labeled Graph 1, Graph 2, and so on; charts labeled Chart 1, Chart 2, and so on; photographs and line drawings labeled Figure 1, Figure 2, and so on; maps labeled Map 1, Map 2, and so on.
- Call out the location of each graph in the margin of the manuscript:

  GRAPH 5 ABOUT HERE

  If you are working on-screen, insert a callout code at the end of a paragraph:

  <Graph 5>

- Edit the titles and captions for consistency and mechanical style (spelling, hyphenation, capitalization).
- Make sure every graph has a source line. If the graph is reproduced from a published work that is under copyright, the author should also request written permission to reprint the graph from the copyright holder.
- Check to see that each part of each graph is clearly and correctly labeled:

3. Copyeditors are usually not expected to comment on the construction of an author's graphs; these construction issues include the selection of graph type (e.g., pie, line, bar), selection of scale values, and use of linear or logarithmic scales. However, if you are interested in these topics, you might look at Edward R. Tufte's *The Visual Display of Quantitative Information.* In addition to describing the principles that govern graphical excellence, Tufte illustrates numerous ways to maximize what he calls "data-ink" (the ink in a graph or chart that represents nonredundant information) and to eliminate what he calls "chartjunk" (overly busy or excessive graphical decoration).

Pie charts: Each slice of a pie chart (see figure 8) should have a label identifying the sector and the percentage it comprises, and the percentages should total 100 (slightly more or less if the percentages have been rounded).

Bar graphs: For bar graphs (see figures 9 and 10), the tabs should be in a logical order, the scale line must be labeled and the units (dollars, tons) stated, and the scale line must begin at zero and have tick marks at reasonable intervals.

Line graphs: For line graphs (see figures 11 and 12), the different types of lines must be sufficiently distinctive and legible at the size the graph will be printed; the lines may be of different weights or of different character (solid, dashed, dotted). When the units on an axis represent numerical quantities, the scale line for that axis usually begins at zero (for example, see the price data represented on the Y-axis in figure 11). However, the range of the numerical values sometimes makes it impractical to start the scale line at zero (for example, see the two Y-axes in figure 12). When the units on an axis do not represent numerical quantities, the scale line does not begin at zero (for example, see the time-interval data on the X-axis in figure 11).

Scatter charts: For scatter charts (see figure 13), the symbols for each variable, in both the chart and the legend, must be distinctive and legible at the size the chart will be printed.

Glyphs: All the glyphs in a pictogram should be equal in width and height; unequal glyphs produce a misleading impression. For example, each of the following lines contains five glyphs, but the glyphs in the second line are noticeably smaller.

☎ ☎ ☎ ☎ ☎

⊠ ⊠ ⊠ ⊠ ⊠

▪ ▪ ▪ ▪ ▪

- Read through the graphs as a batch to be sure that they are consistent.

Figure 8.   Copyediting a Pie Chart. The copyeditor must make sure that

1. The pie chart is correctly numbered and appropriately titled.
2. Each slice is labeled, and the labels are consistent with the manuscript's editorial style (e.g., spelling, capitalization, hyphenation, use of italics).
3. The percentage share is shown for each slice, and all percentages are shown to the same number of decimal points.
4. The percentages total 100 or very close to 100. (Sometimes the percentages do not equal 100 because the numbers are rounded.)
5. The size of each slice appears to match its percentage of the pie.
6. Contiguous slices are visually distinctive.
7. A source line is included. (For any chart reproduced from a published or unpublished work, the author must obtain written permission from the copyright holder; see "Publishing Law" in chapter 15.)

Figure A. Educational Background of AXY Employees   Chart number and title.

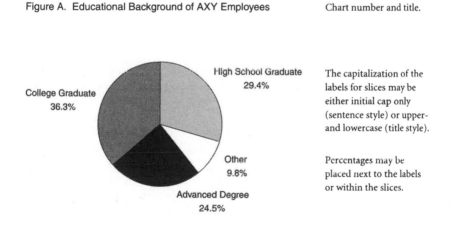

The capitalization of the labels for slices may be either initial cap only (sentence style) or upper- and lowercase (title style).

Percentages may be placed next to the labels or within the slices.

Source: AXY Company survey, June 1995.   Source line.

Figure 9.   Parts of a Bar Graph

Figure number
and title.

Items in the tab,
here arranged from
largest to smallest.

Axis begins at zero;
tick marks guide
the reader; label
indicates unit of
measurement.

Source line.

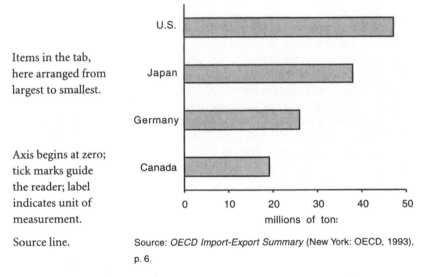

Figure B. World's Largest Gizmo Exporters, 1993

millions of ton:

Source: *OECD Import-Export Summary* (New York: OECD, 1993),
p. 6.

Figure 10.   Sliding-Bar Graph. Sliding-bar graphs can depict complex relation-ships. Figure C, for example, shows the variation in the company's total sales from quarter to quarter, the variation in each region's sales from quarter to quarter, and the share of sales achieved by each region during each quarter. Note how much more difficult it is to discern the various relationships when the same information is presented in tabular form.

| | Sales ($ million) | | | |
	1Q96	2Q96	3Q96	4Q96
North	85	65	50	90
South	70	45	40	50
East	20	40	30	25
West	45	30	20	10
Total	220	180	140	175

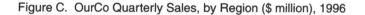

Figure C. OurCo Quarterly Sales, by Region ($ million), 1996

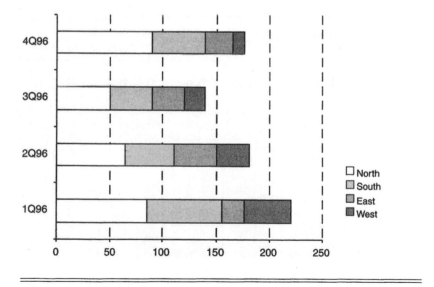

Figure 11.   Line Graph. Line graphs are useful for depicting trends or changes over time. Figure D-1, for example, shows the stock prices for four companies over the course of a trading day. A bar graph, in contrast, can present only selected, discontinuous data points for each stock; figure D-2 presents the prices at four moments during the day. Note also that trends in each stock are easy to track from reading the line graph but hard to discern from the bar graph.

Figure D-1. Intradaily Stock Prices for Companies A, B, C, and D on July 1, 1998

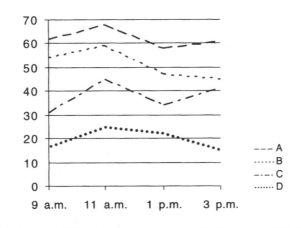

Figure D-2. Intradaily Stock Prices for Companies A, B, C, and D on July 1, 1998

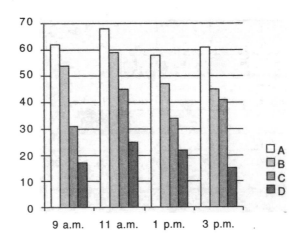

Figure 12.   Line Graph with Two Y-Axes. Figure E shows the trading range of the Italian lira against the U.S. dollar (USD) and the German mark (DEM) over a five-month period. The number of lire per dollar is shown on the vertical axis to the left (called Y-1), and the number of lire per mark is shown on the vertical axis to the right (called Y-2).

Figure E. Trading Range of the Italian Lira vs the USD and the DEM

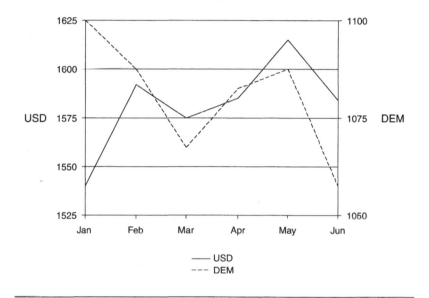

Figure 13.   Simple Scatter Chart. Figure F-1 is a scatter chart that shows the competitive rankings of three mutual funds in the four quarters of 1998. Because the X-axis data points are discontinuous (the funds were ranked once a quarter) and the Y-axis data points are discontinuous (no fractional rankings are possible), the scatter chart presents the data accurately, while a line graph (figure F-2) distorts the data.

Figure F-1. Quarterly Performance Rankings of Mutual Funds AA, BB, and CC in 1998 (3 = best-performing fund)

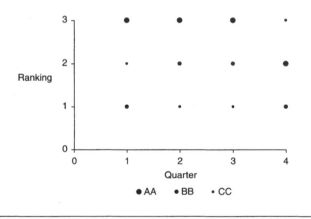

Figure F-2. Quarterly Performance Rankings of Mutual Funds AA, BB, and CC in 1998 (3 = best-performing fund)

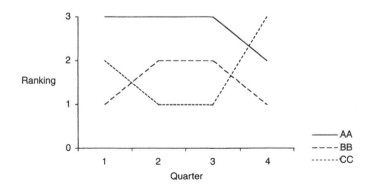

ART

When a manuscript contains drawings, maps, or photographs, photocopies of all the illustrations should accompany the manuscript that is given to the copyeditor. The procedures are similar to those for tables:

- Make sure that the author's comments on the illustration reflect what is shown in the illustration. If the text turns our attention to "the building in the upper right of figure 6," check to see that there is a building in the upper right of figure 6. If the author mentions the blue circle in figure 12, verify that the illustration is to be printed in color; if not, the text should be reworded.
- Check the sequence and numbering of the illustrations, and call out the location of each illustration in the margin of the manuscript:

  FIG 2 ABOUT HERE

  If you are working on-screen, insert a callout code at the end of a paragraph:

  <Figure 2>

- Make sure every substantive illustration has a caption and edit the captions for consistency and mechanical style (spelling, hyphenation, capitalization). Decorative illustrations, in contrast, usually do not carry captions.
- Make sure every substantive illustration has a credit line and edit the credit lines for consistency and mechanical style. Credit lines for decorative illustrations, in contrast, are usually placed on the copyright page, in the acknowledgments, or elsewhere in the text.
- Copyedit any text that appears within an illustration (e.g., labels of parts, cities on maps, legends and keys) that is being newly drawn for the author. If "Seville" appears throughout the text, then the label for that city on the map of Spain should read Seville, not Sevilla. However, if a historical map is being photographically reproduced (and not redrawn), the labels on the old map must suffice.
- Make sure the illustration and caption supply all the information readers need in order to interpret the illustration

(e.g., magnification for a microscopic view, legend for a map, identification of principal persons in a photograph).

- If a list of illustrations is to appear in the front matter, correlate the numbering and captions for the art against that list. Shortened captions may be used in the list of illustrations.

EXERCISE K

Even if you have no idea what "present value" means, you should spot six items to query or correct in the following section of a larger table. The answer key is on page 514.

TABLE 20.	Present	Value	of	One Dollar
Year	5%	6%	8%	9
1	0.952	0.943	.0926	0.917
2	0.907	0.890	0.857	0.842
3	0.864	0.840	0.794	0.772
3	0.823	0.592	0.735	0.708
5	0.784	0.747	0.681	0.65

EXERCISE L

Suggest a way to combine tables 21, 22, and 23 into one table (to be labeled table A). The answer key is on pages 515–16.

TABLE 21. Department of History, Degree
            Recipients, 1993–1995

	Bachelor's Degree	Master's Degree	Doctoral Degree
1993	456	87	5
1994	778	95	8
1995	892	106	12

Source: Office of the President, *Utopia University Data Profile, 1995,* p. 13.

TABLE 22. Department of English, Degree
            Recipients, 1993–1995

	Bachelor's Degree*	Master's Degree	Doctoral Degree
1993	745	47	9
1994	798	52	11
1995	695	65	9

Source: Office of the President, *Utopia University Data Profile, 1995,* p. 15.

*Does not include students in the dual-major program.

TABLE 23. Department of Psychology, Degree Recipients, 1993–1995			
	Bachelor's Degree	Master's Degree	Doctoral Degree
1993	275	32	4
1994	298	29	7
1995	302	30	9

Source: Office of the President, *Utopia University Data Profile, 1995,* p. 18.

❖ 11 ❖

References

___

An author must provide a source for every direct quotation (other than an extremely well known quote) and for every table, graph, and illustration that is reproduced from someone else's work.[1] Sources must also be cited for all facts, statistics, conclusions, and opinions that the author obtained from someone else's published or unpublished work. Sources are not needed, however—and should not be given—for facts that are in general circulation.

The means by which an author cites the source of a quotation, paraphrase, or piece of evidence taken from another work depends on

> the conventions within the author's profession or field
> the intended audience for the work (e.g., scholars, professionals, general readers)
> the number and complexity of citations within the author's manuscript
> the preferences, if any, of the publisher

For uniformity within their issues, all journals and magazines impose their house style on contributors. Some book and corporate publishers do so as well, especially for multi-author collections and works in a series. Other publishers allow authors to use whatever citation system they prefer, as long as it is not too idiosyncratic and is applied consistently.

___

1. Lengthy quotations and the reproduction of tables or illustrations require permission from the copyright holder in addition to a reference citation or credit line; see "Publishing Law" in chapter 15.

When a document has only a few citations, these may be incorporated into the running text (see "Citing Sources" in chapter 8). For documents that contain many citations, one of three systems of attribution is used: *author-date* (also called *name-year*), *reference notes*, or *citation-sequence*. As you will see, each of these systems has complicated conventions governing the order, punctuation, and capitalization of items as well as the use of italics, quotation marks, and parentheses; and each system admits many variations in editorial styling.

For copyeditors, then, reference citations require an almost excruciating attentiveness to detail. Always consult with your editorial coordinator about the publisher's preferred style and the publisher's policy for manuscripts that do not conform to that preference. Also, ask whether you are expected to verify or spot-check the accuracy of the citations. Usually the answer to this last question is no, and you should not spend your time verifying entries unless you find a knotty tangle that you simply must resolve before you return the manuscript to the author.

AUTHOR-DATE SYSTEM

In the author-date system, the source is cited in the running text. The in-text citation includes the surname of the author, the year of publication, and, as needed, a page, chapter, or table number.

> British usage differs from American usage: "the educated American's strong feeling [is] that *different from* is idiomatic and hence inviolable" (Follett 1966, 129).

> Similar findings have been reported in the rain forests of Brazil (Johnson 1991, chap. 5; Peters and Lynn 1996).

> Jones (1988, table 6.6) observed no relation between megadoses of vitamin C and resistance to influenza.

At the end of a document containing author-date citations, there must be an alphabetized reference list (or a list of works cited) that supplies the complete publication data for each citation.

The author-date system is quite common in the social sciences and the natural sciences but is rarely used in the humanities. *Chicago, APA,* and *CSE* all present detailed advice on the formatting of in-text citations and the reference list. Each book, however, takes a slightly different approach to the editorial styling of these items. In editorial jargon, the three variants are called *Chicago* author-date, *APA* author-date, and *CSE* name-year.

FORMATS FOR IN-TEXT CITATIONS

The syntax and content of the author's sentence govern the location of the in-text citation. Here are some of the most common formats, shown in *Chicago* style with notes that highlight the most important differences between *Chicago, APA,* and *CSE.*

> Complete citation in parentheses. *Chicago* and *CSE* recommend the following formats; *APA,* however, always requires a comma after the surname in a parenthetical citation: (Gallegos, 1993).
>
> *Reference to an entire work:* A report on the *m* allele (Gallegos 1993) . . .
>
> *Reference to a chapter in a work:* A report on the *m* allele (Gallegos 1993, chap. 1) . . .
> *Note:* In *APA* style: (Gallegos, 1993, Chapter 1)
>
> *Reference to specific pages in a work:* A report on the *m* allele (Gallegos 1993, 11–13) . . .
> *Note:* *APA* uses "p." before a page number and "pp." before a page range. *CSE* uses "p" before all page numbers and page ranges.
>
> *Reference to specific pages in a volume:* A report on the *m* allele (Gallegos 1995, 2:211–15) . . .
>
> *Reference to a work that is in press:* A report on the *m* allele (Gallegos forthcoming) . . . *or* A report on the *m* allele (Gallegos in press) . . .
>
> *Reference to an undated work:* A report on the *m* allele (Gallegos n.d.) . . .

> Author's name in the text proper
>
> Gallegos (1993) describes the *m* allele.
>
> Gallegos (1993, chap. 1) describes the *m* allele.
> *Note:* In *APA* style: Gallegos (1993, Chapter 1)

Gallegos (1993, 11–13) describes the *m* allele.

Note: In *APA* style: Gallegos (1993, pp. 11–13). In *CSE* style: Gallegos (1993, p 11–13).

Gallegos (1995, 2:211–15) describes the *m* allele.

Gallegos (forthcoming) describes the *m* allele.

Note: In APA style: Gallegos (in press)

Gallegos (n.d.) describes the *m* allele.

Multiple citations

Two later studies (Wong 1996, 1997) report . . .

Note: In *APA* style, a comma would follow each surname in a parenthetical citation: (Wong, 1996, 1997).

Two later studies (Wong 1996, 15; 1997, 27) report . . .

Note: In *APA* style: (Wong, 1996, p. 15; 1997, p. 27). In *CSE* style: (Wong 1996, p 15; 1997, p 27).

The reanalyses of these data (Ellington 1994a, 1994b) show . . .

Other studies (Mays 1989, 1996; Byrd 1995) have shown . . .

As both Mays (1989, 1996) and Byrd (1995) have shown . . .

Multiple authors

The findings of Willy and Wally (1994) were not confirmed by later testing (Apple and Berry 1996; Apple, Berry, and Cherry 1997).

Note: Within parenthetical references *APA* substitutes an ampersand for "and": The findings of Willy and Wally (1994) were not confirmed by later testing (Apple & Berry, 1996).

Institutional author

A nationwide survey by the National Food Institute (1997) . . .

A nationwide survey (National Food Institute 1997) . . .

Personal communications (including letters, interviews, telephone conversations, and e-mail)

As I. R. Felix (personal communication, July 31, 1996) suggests, . . .

Unattributed book or article

> One other intriguing hypothesis has been suggested (*Book Title* 1996, 215–35), but . . .

> According to a recent report ("Article Title" 1999), . . .

> *Note:* In *CSE* style, "Anonymous" is placed in the author slot for an unattributed work: According to a recent report (Anonymous 1999), . . .

REFERENCE LIST

An alphabetized reference list must appear at the end of a document that contains author-date citations. Each item in the list contains four blocks of information: (1) the name of author(s) or editor(s), inverted for ease of alphabetization, (2) the year of publication, (3) the title of work, and (4) the place of publication and the publisher's name. The formats shown here are typical, but they admit many variations.

Author(s) and year.   Each entry begins with the name of the author(s) or editor(s) and the year of publication; these blocks are separated by a period. *Chicago* encourages the use of authors' full names in citations and recommends inverting only the first name in a multiple-author citation:

> *One author:* Babble, Alan B. 1992.

> *Two authors:* Banana, Quincy, and Susan L. Cream. 1993.

> *Three authors:* Berle, Merle M., Lyndon D. Mindon, and Paul Olds. 1995.

> *Institution:* Canadian Broadcasting System. 1994.

> *Unattributed work: Concise Columbia Encyclopedia.* 1994.

> *Editor:* Dylan, Dee, ed. 1997.

In *APA* style for reference lists, (1) the author's first and middle names are replaced by initials, (2) all authors' names in a multi-author citation are inverted, (3) an ampersand replaces "and," (4) the notation "ed." (or "eds." for multi-editor works) is treated as a separate block (i.e., it begins with a capital letter and ends with a period) and is placed in parentheses, and (5) the year is placed in parentheses:

> Babble, A. B. (1992).
> Banana, Q., & Cream, S. L. (1993).

Berle, M. M., Mindon, L. D., & Olds, P. (1995).
Canadian Broadcasting System. (1994).
Concise Columbia encyclopedia. (1994).
Dylan, D. (Ed.). (1997).

(The lowercase "e" in "encyclopedia" is not an error; *APA* style uses sentence capitalization for book and article titles.)

In *CSE* style (1) no periods appear after personal initials, (2) all names are inverted, (3) the surname and initials are not separated by a comma, (4) "and" is not used in multi-author cites, and (5) the notation "editor" (or "editors" for multi-editor works) is treated as part of the name block (i.e., it is preceded by a comma and followed by a period):

[Anonymous]. 1994.
Babble AB. 1992.
Banana Q, Cream SL. 1993.
Berle MM, Mindon LD, Olds P. 1995.
Canadian Broadcasting System. 1994.
Dylan D, editor. 1997.

(In *CSE* style, "[Anonymous]" appears in the author slot for an unattributed work, such as the *Concise Columbia Encyclopedia.*)

When two or more works by an author were published in the same year, a lowercase letter is appended to the date in the reference list:

Rightsalot, Abby. 1989a.
Rightsalot, Abby. 1989b.
Rightsalot, Abby. 1989c.

(In *Chicago* style, the second and subsequent instances of the author's name would be replaced by a three-em dash: ———. 1989b.)

The corresponding in-text citations would be

Only one study (Rightsalot 1989a) examined . . .
Note: In *APA* style: (Rightsalot, 1989a)

Rightsalot (1989b, 1989c) concludes that . . .

Title.   The third block consists of the title of the work. The two principal styles for formatting titles are called humanities style (in which the headline style of capitalization is used) and scientific style (in which sentence-style capitalization is used).[2] When the cited work is an article, the name of the journal, volume number, and page numbers follow the article title.

Humanities style

Book: Petrographic Analysis of Cherts.

Article: "Anorexia Nervosa in Teenage Boys." *Journal of Anatomy* 33 (July): 514–24.

Scientific style, *APA* version

Book: Petrographic analysis of cherts.

Article: Anorexia nervosa in teenage boys. *Journal of Anatomy,* 33, 514–524.

Scientific style, *CSE* version

Book: Petrographic analysis of cherts.

Article: Anorexia nervosa in teenage boys. J Anat 33:514–24.

As these examples illustrate, the various author-date styles also differ in the typographic treatment of book, article, and journal titles.

Publication data.   The fourth block of the entry consists of the publication data, which is intended to provide interested readers with sufficient information to locate the source.

For a book, one supplies the city of publication and the name of the publisher. (Variant: All entries provide only the publisher's name.) When the place of publication is not a major city, the abbreviated name of the state or the full name of the country is given:

---

2. Newspapers take headline style a step further in capitalizing the first word of every line in a headline. This design choice should not be imitated in references to the article. For example:

New Wines   *Citation:* "New Wines from France and Spain," *Daily Planet,*
From France   March 8, 1998, p. 14.
And Spain

Major city

New York: Bigtop Books.

Washington, D.C.: Topnotch & Wheedle.

Paris: Livres populaires.

Other places

Williams, N.D.: Great Plains Press.

Lublin, Poland: Katowice.

For an article in a journal, magazine, or newspaper, the place of publication is given only when needed to help readers locate obscure publications.

Reference list entries for electronic resources.　Editorial conventions for citing electronic resources continue to evolve as more documents are published online and as DOIs (digital object identifiers) replace URLs. (DOIs help readers locate an online document even after the document "moves" to a new URL.) Some publishers prefer that entries include access dates (the date on which the author last consulted the online source); other publishers see little value in these dates or request them only for certain types of online documents. Ask your editorial coordinator about house policy, and consult your editorial style manual or in-house style guide for current practices. Here are sample entries from *Chicago* and *APA*:

Chicago author-date reference list

Kossinets, Gueorgi, and Duncan J. Watts. 2009. "Origins of Homophily in an Evolving Social Network." *American Journal of Sociology* 115:405–50. doi:10.1086/599247.

Stolberg, Sheryl Gay, and Robert Pear. 2010. "Wary Centrists Posing Challenge in Health Care Vote." *New York Times*, February 27. http://www.nytimes.com/2010/02/28/us/politics/28health.html.

APA author-date reference list

Herbst-Damm, K. L., & Kulik, J. A. (2005). Volunteer support, marital status, and the survival times of terminally ill patients. *Health Psychology, 24,* 225–229. doi:10.1037/0278-6133.24.2.225

Sillick, T. J., & Schutte, N. S. (2006). Emotional intelligence and self-esteem mediate between perceived early parental love and adult happiness. *E-Journal of Applied Psychology, 2*(2), 38–48. Retrieved from http://ojs.lib.swin.edu.au/index.php/ejap

COPYEDITING PROCEDURES

If you are working on the hard copy of a manuscript that uses the author-date system, you must copyedit the reference list *before* you work on the text. (The reason will become apparent when you read steps 2 and 3 below.) If you are working on-screen, however, you may choose to ignore this precaution, since you can always use the global search to locate entries that require further attention.

Step 1. Scan the entire reference list to verify that the entries are in alphabetical order. Special conventions govern the alphabetization of multiple surnames, foreign names, and names beginning with particles (e.g., *de, Della, von*), *Mac, Mc, St.,* and *Saint.* For example, hyphenated American and British surnames are alphabetized under the first element of the surname, but nonhyphenated American and British surnames are alphabetized under the last element. Thus *Jean Dorr-Winston* is alphabetized under *Dorr,* while *Ann Smith Jones* is alphabetized under *Jones.* Other special conventions are described in *Chicago* and *CSE;* for an extended discussion, see Nancy Mulvany, *Indexing Books.*

Step 2. Scan the entire list again and notice whether there are two works by the same author(s) in the same year, for example:

Blythe, A. L. 1988. *In Praise of Proofreaders.* New York: Ashcan Press.

Blythe, A. L. 1988. *In Praise of Copyeditors.* Chicago: Veritas Press.

In this case, you need to rearrange the two entries so that the titles are in alphabetical order and then label the first entry 1988a and the second entry 1988b. When you are copyediting the manuscript, you must remember to call your author's attention to all in-text citations that refer to Blythe 1988 so that your author can change them to either Blythe 1988a or Blythe 1988b.

Step 3. Scan the entire list again and notice whether there are two authors with the same surname, for example:

Roberts, Ellen M. 1995. *Paranormal Psychology.* Boston: ESP Press.

Roberts, Jack L. 1989. *Psychometrics.* Los Angeles: Southland Books.

When you are copyediting the manuscript, you will have to make sure that all in-text references to these authors include an initial:

E. Roberts (1995) and J. Roberts (1989) provide differing views of this phenomenon.

Step 4. Copyedit the entries. Read each entry slowly so that you can spot any typographical errors. (Because reference lists contain so many proper names, on-screen copyeditors usually do not run the spellchecker on the reference list.)

Then read the entry a second time to make sure that it is properly formatted and styled. Follow your editorial coordinator's recommendation for either imposing the house style or using the style the author has chosen. If the author's style is not one you are familiar with, write out sample entries based on the first few in-text citations and entries and annotate each style choice and piece of punctuation:

In-text citation: (Doe 1999, 125–129)
[No comma after surname; comma after date; no p. or pp.; repeat all numerals in ranges.]

Reference list entry, book: Doe, A. A. 1999. *Title of book: Subtitle of book.* City, Sta.: Publisher.
[Author's initials only; title and subtitle in sentence style, italic; nonpostal state abbrevs.]

Reference list entry, article: Doe, A. A. 1999. Title of article: Subtitle included too. *Journal title* 5(2): 125–129.
[Title and subtitle in sentence style, roman; journal title in sentence style, italic; roman for volume(issue); space after colon; repeat all numerals in ranges.]

These samples will help you learn the style and make it easier for you to spot inconsistencies.

As you are reading, pay special attention to the logic of page ranges (an article cannot have appeared on pages 45–32 or pages 45–45 of a journal) and the consistent styling of the page ranges. (The ranges should follow one of the three systems described in "Inclusive Numerals" in chapter 7.) Be alert, as well, for internal inconsistencies. For example, the following discrepancy in volume numbers (3 or 13?) merits a query:

Babs, R. R. 1997. "Study Skills for High School Students." *Teachers Journal* 3: 12–18.

Morgenstern, L. 1997. "Journal Writing." *Teachers Journal* 13: 115–26.

Step 5. Make notations on your style sheet about the styling of in-text citations and reference list entries. If the author has followed one of the formats in *Chicago, APA* or *CSE,* write a note to that effect on your style sheet, under Footnotes and Bibliography—or Citations and Reference List (see figure 6 in chapter 2). But if you had to select a format and impose it on the manuscript, record sample entries on the style sheet. These samples will be helpful to the author during the review of the copyediting, when he or she may need to add entries; the samples will also refresh your memory during cleanup.

When you have finished copyediting the reference list, begin working on the manuscript. Each time you come across an in-text author-date citation, check it against the reference list. If there is no corresponding entry in the reference list, ask the author to supply one.[3] Also, query any discrepancy between an in-text citation and the reference list (e.g., author's name, date, page ranges).

REFERENCE NOTES

In the note system, the sources are placed in notes keyed to the running text by asterisks or superscript numerals. The notes themselves may appear at the bottom of the page (footnotes) or gathered together at the end of the article, document, book chapter, or book (endnotes). For example:

Running text: British usage differs from American usage: "the educated American's strong feeling [is] that *different from* is idiomatic and hence inviolable."[1]

Note: 1. Wilson Follett, *Modern American Usage: A Guide* (New York: Hill & Wang, 1966), p. 129.

---

3. Personal communications (letters, interviews, phone conversations, e-mail), however, are usually not listed in the reference list, since readers will not be able to locate these items.

Running text: Similar findings have been reported in the rain forests of Brazil.[2]

Note: 2. See, for example, A. R. Johnson, "Microclimatology in the Southern Rain Forests," *Journal of Meteorological Studies* 3 (1987): 35–42; S. S. Peters and W. Lynn, "Mating Habitats of the South American Zao-zao," *Journal of Avian Studies* 2 (1988): 58–63.

Running text: Jones observed no relation between megadoses of vitamin C and resistance to influenza.*

Note: *K. C. Jones, "Vitamin C Revisited," *Journal of the Institutes of Health* 32 (1988): 45.

Notice that reference notes are written and punctuated so that all the information about the source is contained in one sentence. As these examples show, the in-text note indicator is set as a superscript, but the number in the text of the note is not. Unfortunately, the default setting in some word processing programs produces superscripts in both locations.[4] The use of "p." and "pp." to indicate page numbers is optional, and many authors and publishers prefer to eliminate these indicators.

When a document contains a bibliography that lists all the works cited in the document, complete publication data need not be given in the notes. Instead, each note may contain the author's surname, a short form of the title, and the relevant page number(s):

1. Follett, *Modern American Usage,* p. 129.

2. Johnson, "Microclimatology," p. 38; Peters and Lynn, "Mating Habitats," p. 61.

*Jones, "Vitamin C Revisited," 45.

Some publishers, however, prefer that a full citation appear in the first note that mentions a source. In subsequent notes, only the surname and short title are given.

---

4. To fix these errant superscripts, copyeditors working on hard copy can write a global instruction for the typesetter ("Within the notes, set all note numbers on the line followed by a period") and also hand-mark the first example or two in each chapter or section of the manuscript. Copyeditors working on-screen for a publishing house will usually find that the production editor has already updated the author's files to correct the improperly placed superscripts. Copyeditors

To reduce the number of notes that refer to one or more often-cited works, an author may (1) provide a complete citation to the work in a note on the first reference to the work, (2) mention in that note that future references to the work appear in the text and are indicated by a short title or acronym, and (3) thereafter reference the work in parenthetical in-text citations. For example:

> *Running text:* British usage differs from American usage: "the educated American's strong feeling [is] that *different from* is idiomatic and hence inviolable."[1] . . . Cross-Atlantic differences in the choice of prepositions lead Americans to "tinker with," while the British "tinker at" (*MAU,* 259).

> *Note:* 1. Wilson Follett, *Modern American Usage: A Guide* (New York: Hill & Wang, 1966), p. 129. Future references to this work are denoted by *MAU* and are cited in the text.

Here's an alternative wording for the note and an alternative treatment of the title:

> 1. Wilson Follett, *Modern American Usage: A Guide* (New York: Hill & Wang, 1966), p. 129; hereafter cited as *Usage.*

As this example illustrates, a short title need not include the first word(s) of the full title; also, although a short title may contain an adjective, it must contain a noun. In addition, all the words in a short title must appear in the same order as in the full title:

> Full title: *A Manual for Writers of Term Papers, Theses, and Dissertations*

> Short title: *Manual for Writers* or *Manual* but not *Manual for Term Paper Writers*

A short title is usually preferable to an unwieldy acronym. For example, *Metaphors We Live By* could be shortened to *Metaphors* rather than *MWLB.*

Notes are the preferred citation system for writers in the humanities, and

---

working on-screen for unsophisticated corporate publishers or for self-publishing authors should consult their word processing program's help files for advice on redefining the numbering style for footnotes or endnotes.

they are favored by some historians and social scientists. *Chicago* offers the most detailed discussion of the various formats. In the humanities another widely used style guide for notes is the *MLA Style Manual*. (Since *APA* requires the author-date system and *CSE* calls for either author-date or citation-sequence, neither manual discusses reference notes.)

LOCATION OF IN-TEXT NOTE INDICATOR

The in-text superscript or asterisk is preferably placed at the end of a sentence or, if necessary, at the end of a clause.

> *Awkward:* Many educators,[5] working in diverse settings, report considerable success with this method.

> *Revision:* Many educators, working in diverse settings, report considerable success with this method.[5]

Only in the rarest of cases should a sentence contain more than one note indicator.

> *Incorrect:* Scores improved in math classes,[6] science classes,[7] and history classes.[8]

> *Revision:* Scores improved in math classes, science classes, and history classes.[6]
> [Within this new note 6, the references would be divided by subjects: On scores in math, see . . . ; on science, see . . . ; on history, see . . .]

Each chapter of a book (or section of a long document) begins with note 1. Numbered footnotes in tables are not integrated into the sequence of notes to the text (see the discussion of table footnotes in chapter 10).

Many publishers prohibit the placement of an in-text note indicator in a line of display type (e.g., a chapter title, author byline, first- or second-level head, table title), although *Chicago* accepts note indicators in the title of a journal article and in a subhead within an article or a book chapter. The remedy for a misplaced indicator depends on the context and the content of the note.

> *Problem:* Manuscript has a note indicator after the chapter title, article title, or author byline. *Solution:* Delete the note indicator but retain the text of the note and treat it as an unnumbered note. If the notes are to be printed as footnotes, this unnumbered note

should be placed at the bottom of the first page of the chapter or article. If the notes are to be printed as endnotes, this unnumbered note precedes the numbered notes in the endnote section.

Problem: Manuscript has a note indicator within or at the end of a display heading. *Solution:* Move the note indicator to the end of the first sentence of text under that heading.

Problem: Manuscript has a note indicator within or at the end of a table title. *Solution:* Delete the indicator from the table title. If the note applies to the entire table, label it Note and place it before the numbered, lettered, or asterisked footnotes to the table. If the note applies to only a portion of the table, place the note indicator in the appropriate stub line, column heading, or cell. (See figure 7 and table 18 in chapter 10 for examples.)

Some trade publishers use the note style for documentation but without having note indicators appear in the text. Instead, the references appear at the end of the book, keyed to the text by page number and phrase:

5   In national polls . . . : *New York Times,* "Taxes and the Middle Class," Sept. 5, 1997, p. 12.

8   Judges proposed . . . : Allegra Thom, "Legal Rights of Pregnant Women," *Reproductive Rights,* 2 (10), July 1995, p. 17.

9   "Improving prenatal care . . .": Dr. Corinna Somes, letter to author, Aug. 15, 1997.

On this type of project, the hard-copy copyeditor may be asked to indicate which lines in the manuscript are linked to the reference notes; the final page and line listings can be completed only after the final page proofs are available. On-screen copyeditors may be asked to code the text so that the correct cross-references can be generated automatically.

PLACEMENT OF NOTES: FOOTNOTES VERSUS ENDNOTES

Some journal and book publishers routinely favor either footnotes or endnotes (also called *backnotes*). Other publishers make the decision case by case, weighing various editorial and design issues. These decisions are usually made before the manuscript is released for copyediting, but sometimes copyeditors are asked to participate in them. There are three primary editorial considerations:

- Intended readership: Readers of academic and scholarly books usually prefer footnotes to endnotes because the former allow them to skim the notes without losing their place in the text. Popular wisdom, however, says that nonscholarly readers are either reluctant or unwilling to purchase a nonfiction trade book whose feet are hemmed with ribbons of tiny type; thus most trade books place (the shop term is "bury") the notes containing sources and references at the back of the book.[5]
- Content of the notes: Footnotes are preferable for notes that include material other than references and sources, because readers will be able to glance at, if not scrutinize, this material without jumping to the back of the book. However, tables, charts, complex math and musical examples, and similar elements cannot be run as footnotes. There are four ways to handle such elements: (1) the author can move the element into the text proper; (2) the author can decide to delete the problematic element; (3) all the notes can be run as endnotes, which can easily accommodate complex elements; (4) a table or chart can be treated as an appendix, and a cross-reference to the appendix can be placed in a footnote or in the text proper.
- Demand for offprints: Some anthologies and collections of articles are designed so that instructors and professors can order multiple copies of individual selections for their students. When such offprints are a possibility, all the notes must be run either as footnotes or as end-of-chapter notes, not as backnotes at the end of the entire volume.

In terms of design, the choice between footnotes and endnotes depends on the quantity and length of the notes as well as the desired visual style for the publication. If the notes are few, short, and widely dispersed, treating them as footnotes will not substantially affect the overall look of the final document or book. But if the notes are many, long, or densely clumped at vari-

---

5. If the text contains substantive notes—commentary, asides, or brief excurses—the author may be asked to integrate them into the text proper. Or the publisher may decide to run the substantive notes as footnotes under the asterisk-dagger system and to run the reference notes as endnotes (either numbered notes or notes keyed to the text by page and line number).

ous intervals, designers favor endnotes. In oversize books that have wide margins, the notes may be run in the outer margin.

BIBLIOGRAPHIES

A bibliography is a list, alphabetized by the authors' surnames, of the works cited in a document, article, or book. When the notes include all the information a reader needs to locate the work being cited, the author need not provide a bibliography. Some publications, however, particularly those intended for classroom use, include a bibliography as an additional tool for readers.

Bibliographical entries provide the same information as notes, but in a different form. In a bibliographical entry, the author's name is inverted for ease in alphabetizing the list, and each of the three blocks—author's name, title of the work, publication data—is followed by a period.

> *Note:* 1. Wilson Follett, *Modern American Usage: A Guide* (New York: Hill & Wang, 1966), p. 129.
>
> *Bibliography:* Follett, Wilson. *Modern American Usage: A Guide.* New York: Hill & Wang, 1966.

> *Note:* 2. See, for example, A. R. Johnson, "Microclimatology in the Southern Rain Forests," *Journal of Meteorological Studies* 3 (1987): 35–42; S. S. Peters and W. Lynn, "Mating Habitats of the South American Zao-zao," *Journal of Avian Studies* 2 (1988): 58–63.
>
> *Bibliography:* Johnson, A. R. "Microclimatology in the Southern Rain Forests." *Journal of Meteorological Studies* 3 (1987): 35–42.
>
> Peters, S. S., and W. Lynn. "Mating Habitats of the South American Zao-zao." *Journal of Avian Studies* 2 (1988): 58–63.

Chicago and the *MLA Style Manual* give detailed advice about the formatting of entries for online documents. You can also adopt the following simpler formats:

Individual work

> Author. *Title of Work.* Publisher, 19xx. URL [access date].
>
> Ortega, Marilena. *Four Corners.* Sylvan Online, 1996. http://www.sylvan.org/corners/ [April 1, 1996].

Part of a work

Author. "Title of Selection," *Title of Complete Work.* Publisher, 19xx. URL [access date].

Weber, Israel. "GUIs," *Encyclopedia of Design.* ComputerForm Publications, 1996. ftp://cfp.com/encycd/218/html [January 30, 1997].

Journal, magazine, or newspaper article

Author. "Title," *Periodical Title* volume:issue (19xx), paging or indicator of length. URL [access date].

Dennison, Michael. "Selecting a Web Browser," *Online Consumer Review* 2:3 (1997), 5 paragraphs. http://www.ocr.com/ brow~denn/html [March 8, 1997].

COPYEDITING PROCEDURES

At some point during the copyediting, you need to make a separate pass through all the notes in order to make sure the numbering is correct and the styling is consistent. The best time to do this pass is usually after you have finished your first pass through the entire manuscript, including the bibliography (if there is one). Here's one way to proceed:

Step 1. Copyedit the manuscript. When you come upon an in-text note indicator, turn to the text of the note. Read the note for sense and relevancy, and correct any obvious errors. Also, some publishers ask copyeditors who work on hard copy to call out all in-text note markers (superscript numbers or asterisks):

British usage differs from American

usage: "the educated American's strong

feeling [is] that *different from* is

 idiomatic and hence inviolable."[1]

Similar findings have been reported in

the rain forests of Brazil.[2]

Many copyeditors call out the notes (whether asked to or not) because the callouts make it easier to page through the manuscript and verify that all numbered notes are in sequence.

Step 2. Copyedit the bibliography. First, scan the bibliography to make sure the entries are in alphabetical order.[6] Then read entry by entry and correct or query all typographical errors, illogical items (e.g., a page range of 45–43), and incomplete entries.

Step 3. Copyedit all the notes. During this pass, read each reference citation in the notes against the bibliography. Query any inconsistencies, discrepancies, and incomplete entries.

Step 4. If the in-text note indicators are numbers, page through the manuscript and the notes to make sure the numbering is correct.

Step 5. Make your second pass through the manuscript. If you add or delete any notes during your second pass, recheck the numbering sequence when you are done.

If the manuscript has an unwieldy number of notes and if time permits, you may want to try to reduce the number of notes by combining notes that fall in the same paragraph or by introducing short titles and in-text citations, as described earlier in this section.

CITATION-SEQUENCE SYSTEM

The citation-sequence system uses in-text superscripts for references, but—unlike the reference note system—only one work appears in each numbered note and that number serves to identify that source throughout the entire document. In other words, 1 is assigned to the first source mentioned in the text, 2 is assigned to the second source, and so on. In the reference list at the end of the document, the items appear in order of their first mention in the text (i.e., the reference list is not alphabetical).

If you've never seen a document that uses the citation-sequence system,

6. Some authors divide their bibliographies into sublists by topic or by chapter, and such divisions are sometimes helpful for readers. When an author has arranged the items by type (e.g., primary sources, secondary sources) or has separate lists for books, articles, and archival materials, you should ask your editorial coordinator whether to retain the sublists or ask the author to consolidate them.

you will at first be puzzled: Multiple superscripts may be clustered together, and superscripts may appear out of numerical sequence.

> Occupational injuries are underreported for agricultural workers in all regions of the country.[1-3] Underreporting is most serious for itinerant workers,[2,4] and for younger workers.[3]

The [1-3] after the first sentence refers the reader to items 1, 2, and 3 in the reference list. The sources for the comment about itinerant workers are items 2 and 4 on the reference list, and the source for the comment about younger workers is item 3.

The principal advantage of the citation-sequence system is that the running text is not interrupted by long strings of parenthetical references. Look what happens, for example, when the two earlier sentences about occupational injuries are rewritten in author-date style:

> Occupational injuries are underreported for agricultural workers in all regions of the country (Angeles 1997; US Department of Labor 1996a; Myrmia and Wilkerson 1998). Underreporting is most serious for itinerant workers (US Department of Labor 1996a; Hollingshead 1998) and for younger workers (Myrmia and Wilkerson 1998).

The principal disadvantage of the citation-sequence system is that the entire reference list and all in-text superscripts must be renumbered if the author adds or deletes a reference at the last minute.

The citation-sequence system is used by some natural scientists and social scientists, especially in articles for professional journals. *CSE* presents a comprehensive description of the system and the formatting of the reference list; neither *Chicago* nor *APA* mention the citation-sequence system.

COPYEDITING PROCEDURES

The citation-sequence system poses the fewest problems for the copyeditor: There are no in-text citations to be checked against the reference list, and there is no alphabetization task (since the items in the reference list appear in the order they have been cited in the document). All of the following tasks may be done before or after copyediting the manuscript.

Step 1. Check the numerical order in the reference list. Make sure that no numerals are skipped or repeated.

Step 2. Scan the document to check the sequence of the in-text superscript numerals. Look for the first appearance of each numeral; these first appearances must be in sequence, although any numeral may reappear at any time. Also, make sure that multiple citations are correctly punctuated: inclusive numerals (e.g., [2–5]) are linked by an en dash; noninclusive numerals (e.g., [2,3,8]) are separated by commas without any wordspacing after the commas.

Step 3. Copyedit the reference list. Read each entry carefully so that you can spot any typographical errors. Then reread the entry to check the format. These entries should be styled according to the models presented in *CSE*, another specialized scientific style manual, or in an in-house style guide. For example, in *CSE* style:

1. Winters AA. Air pollution, water contamination, and public health. New York: Eco Books; 1998. 525 p.

2. Spring BY, Fall CZ, editors. Genetic diversity within species. Boston: T Riley, 1996. 1234 p.

3. Summers DE, Mamori I, Jackson J. A controlled trial of quality assurance. Am J Clin Lab 1995 Jan;85(2):125–37.

4. Hunter Applied Physics Laboratory. Standards for mapping subatomic particle behavior. Int J Phys 1997;12:785–804.

EXERCISE M

Copyedit the following portion of an author-date reference list using these sample formats:

> Surname, First name. 19xx. *Book Title: Book Subtitle.* City: Publisher. [Traditional state abbrevs.]
> Surname, First name. 19xx. "Article Title." *Journal Title* 1:123–35.
> For multiple authors: Surname, First, and First Surname. 19xx.

The answer key is on pages 517–20.

Abben, Pilar. 1985. "A Modern Approach to Algebra," *Mathematical Monthly* 17: 55–68.

Adder, William and Mary. 1980. *Statistics in the Social Sciences.* Evanston Illinois: Schoolbooks Press, 1980.

Adder, William and Mary. *1982. How To Write Social Science Papers.* New York: Wise Owl.

Akmore, G. 1983, "A Study of the Affects of Peer Teaching in College Remedial Mathematic Courses." *American Mathematical Monthly* 18: 149–67.

Aiken, Lydia, ed., *Probelms in English Grammar.* Boston, Tiara Books.

Allen, Pattrick. 1993. *Composition for Beginnning ESL Students.* New York: Language Laboratory

Allen, P. and Anita Zamorra, 1994. "Error Analysis in Quasi-Experimental Designs." *Analytic Quarterly* 9:63–53.

Ammonds, Carolyn. 1794. *A Short Course in Speedwriting.* Santa Barbara, Santa Luisa Community College.

Anderson, Vito. 1991. "A Response to President Clinton's Proposal for Head Start." *Preschool Reporter* 15:1.

Front and Back Matter

Copyeditors who work on books and book-length documents may be called upon to handle front matter (the materials that appear before the first page of the text proper) and back matter (the materials that appear at the end of the volume). For the sake of brevity, in this chapter *book* is used to refer to any publication that is printed in the form of a traditional book.

FRONT MATTER

All books have at least four pieces of front matter (also called *preliminaries* or *prelims*):

The half-title page (bastard title page) displays the main title of the book only. (Sometimes the half-title page is eliminated to save space.)

The title page gives the title, subtitle, edition, author's name, publisher's name, and the cities in which the publisher's main offices are located.

The copyright page includes the copyright notice, Library of Congress Cataloging-in-Publication (CIP) data, and the book's publishing history (e.g., earlier editions).

The contents page, which carries the heading "Contents" (rather than "Table of Contents"), lists all the chapters or sections and the opening page number for each.

The prelims for technical reports and other book-length documents often use condensed formats: no half-title page, title and copyright data placed on the cover or on a title page, and a contents page.

In traditional book design, the half-title, title, and contents pages are printed on right-hand pages, and the copyright page appears on the back side of the title page. By convention, all front matter is numbered with lowercase roman numerals, and page numbers (also called *folios*) are suppressed (that is, not printed) on the half-title, title, and copyright pages. Thus for a book having only these four elements, the order and paging would be

Right page	half-title page	i	(folio suppressed)
Left page	[blank]	ii	(folio suppressed)
Right page	title page	iii	(folio suppressed)
Left page	copyright page	iv	(folio suppressed)
Right page	contents page	v	(folio expressed)
Left page	continuation of contents or blank	vi	(folio expressed if text appears on the page; folio suppressed if page is blank)

If the book is part of a series, a list of other books in the series may be placed on page ii. Page ii may also be used for a list of contributors (for a multi-author work) or a frontispiece (illustration).

When the manuscript contains a dedication page or an epigraph, it is usually placed on page v, and the contents page appears on the next right page, which would be page vii.

After the contents page, any or all of the following items may appear, in the following order:

list of illustrations
list of tables
foreword
preface
acknowledgments
introduction
list of abbreviations

The copyeditor's tasks are to

- Check the order and page numbering of the front matter.
- Proofread the half-title, title, and copyright pages. Although these pages contain few words, they are important words, and careful proofreading is essential.
- Read the contents page against the manuscript, making sure that every section of the manuscript (front matter, chapters, back matter) is listed on the contents page and that the chapter titles and subtitles on the contents page exactly match those that appear at the opening of each chapter.
- Make sure that the pieces of front matter are correctly titled.

    The table of contents should be titled "Contents" (*not* "Table of Contents"). Similarly, a list of illustrations should be titled "Illustrations"; a list of tables, "Tables"; and an acknowledgments page, "Acknowledgments." (Note the preferred spelling: no *e* between the *g* and the *m*.)

    An introductory piece written by someone other than the author is labeled "Foreword." (Note the spelling and remember the mnemonic "a *word* that comes be*fore*.")

    An introductory piece written by the author is titled either "Preface" or "Introduction." Typically, a preface is a short piece (one to three book pages) containing remarks of a personal nature (reasons for writing the book, acknowledgments). A longer piece is usually treated as an introduction. An introduction that includes substantive material essential to the book, however, is not placed in the front matter; instead, it is treated as the first (unnumbered) chapter of the body of the book, and it carries arabic page numbers.

- Correlate any list of illustrations, tables, or maps against the caption copy for those items. Is everything numbered correctly? Are the entries on the list consistent in content, format, and editorial style?
- Advise the author of ways to consolidate the amount of front matter: If the acknowledgments are brief, they can be moved to the end of the preface or the introduction. If the book has only a few tables, charts, or maps, the front matter need not include lists of these elements.

BACK MATTER

Back matter is traditionally presented in the following order, with each item beginning on a right-hand page unless space is at a premium:

Appendix(es)   Instead of being given a chapter number, appendixes are labeled Appendix A, Appendix B, and so on. The title of the appendix follows:

> Appendix A. Field Data from Malaysia
>
> Appendix B. Field Data from Thailand

Notes   If the book has endnotes, they are printed here, chapter by chapter. When the endnotes include many acronyms or short titles for often-cited texts, a list of abbreviations precedes the notes.

Glossary

Bibliography   May also be called Selected Bibliography, References, or Works Cited

Index

All back matter pages carry arabic numerals.

For the copyeditor, working on an appendix is just like working on regular text, but other types of back matter require special attention. In chapter 11, we discussed copyediting notes and bibliographies; here are some tips for working with glossaries and indexes.

GLOSSARIES

The copyediting of a glossary usually requires four passes. The first pass is a quick skimming of the manuscript to get a general sense of the author's definition-writing style. Typically, a definition opens with a concise sentence fragment that captures the essence of the term being defined. Subsequent sentences in a definition may be fragments or grammatically complete; when a term has more than one definition, each definition begins with a concise sentence fragment. During this first pass, note any definitions that are significantly more or less detailed than the others. These entries may require some substantive editing or a query to the author asking for a rewrite.

The second pass consists of reading down the main entries to be sure they are in alphabetical order. (For a discussion of some quirks of alphabetical order, see the next section in this chapter, "Indexes.")

The third pass of the glossary is the occasion for careful copyediting, entry by entry. Each entry consists of the term being defined and one or both of the following: a definition (or definitions) and a cross-reference to other entries in the glossary. If no definition appears, the cross-reference begins with *See;* if the term is defined, the cross-reference begins with *See also, Contrast,* or *Compare.*

At the designer's discretion, each part of the entry—term, definition, cross-reference indicator, cross-referenced term—may receive a different typographical treatment; for example:

Term	Lowercase, boldface, followed by a period.
Definition(s)	Initial capital letter and terminal period. Technical terms within the definition are italicized. Multiple definitions are numbered (1), (2), and so on; each ends with a period.
Cross-reference indicator	Italics for indicator: *See* or *See also.*
Cross-referenced term	Lowercase and set in roman type. Multiple references are separated by a semicolon. Cross-reference is followed by a period.

The resulting glossary will look like this:

negative. (1) A photographic image in which light values are reversed (i.e., black appears as white); *see also* positive. (2) Film used in photo-offset.
numerals. *See* arabic numerals; roman numerals.
nut. Printer's term for an *en. See also* em; molly.

If instructions for styling the entries do not accompany the manuscript, ask the editorial coordinator for advice.

So, on the third pass, as you read each entry

- Make sure that the terms, definitions, and cross-references are styled consistently.
- Copyedit the spelling, capitalization, hyphenation, and punctuation of the definitions.
- Query or correct definitions that are wordy, tautological, or unclear.
- Check every cross-reference to be sure the cross-referenced term appears in the glossary.

Copyeditors are usually not expected to verify that every term listed in the glossary appears in the manuscript or that every technical term in the manuscript is included in the glossary.[1] Based on your understanding of the intended audience, however, you may want to suggest terms that could be added to or deleted from the glossary.

The fourth pass is a quick read-through to catch any overlooked errors.

INDEXES

Since an index cannot be prepared until the final pagination of the publication has been determined, the index never accompanies the manuscript. Copyeditors who work solely as manuscript editors are thus spared the task of handling indexes. But someone has to read and copyedit them, and that someone needs to have a very careful eye and a good sense of the conventions for indexes.

Copyediting an index usually requires four passes. The first pass is delightfully simple: Race through the index and make sure there is a blank line before the first entry that begins with a *b*, the first entry that begins with a *c*, and so on. To save space, short indexes (a page or two) are often set without this additional linespacing.

The second pass sounds simple: Read down the main entries to check the alphabetical order and the capitalization style (either all entries begin with

---

1. *Exception:* In some manuscripts—for example, training manuals, reference books, and technical reports—technical terms are given special typographical treatment (e.g., bold or italic type), and readers are told that all such terms are defined in the glossary. In such cases, the copyeditor is expected to make sure that all specially marked terms do appear in the glossary.

an initial capital letter or only those entries that are proper nouns and proper adjectives begin with a capital letter). In practice, however, there are several tricky issues in alphabetization:

Letter-by-letter versus word-by-word. The index must be consistent in using either the letter-by-letter system or the word-by-word system of alphabetization. Under the word-by-word principle, terms are alphabetized by the first full word in the entry; thus "San Francisco" would precede "sanctuary." Under the letter-by-letter principle, wordspaces are ignored; thus "sanctuary" would precede "San Francisco." Among the style manuals, *Chicago* and *CSE* offer the best guidance on alphabetization. For the most thorough treatment of the topic, see Nancy Mulvany, *Indexing Books.*

Personal names. Surnames beginning with particles (e.g., *de, Della, La, van*) or with *Mac, Mc, St.,* or *Saint,* and foreign names present special problems in capitalization and alphabetization. For example, Ludwig van Beethoven is alphabetized under *b* (Beethoven, Ludwig van), but Willem de Kooning is alphabetized under *d* (de Kooning, Willem). The best references to consult are *Chicago, CSE,* and Mulvany's *Indexing Books.*

Numerals. Main entries that begin with numerals are alphabetized as though they were spelled out: an entry for the television program *60 Minutes* would appear after "sixpenny nails" and before "sizing."

Nonalphabetical characters. Main entries that consist of nonalphabetical characters are collected at the beginning of the index, in a group preceding the *a* words, and also listed in their spelled-out form (for the names of common nonalphabetical characters, see chapter 9). For example:

#, use of, 19, 25 [Would also appear under "pound sign" and "numeral sign."]
< >, in commands, 12 [Would also appear under "angle brackets."]
&, syntax for, 38 [Would also appear under "ampersand."]

AAs, 128
abacus, 2
abbreviations, 76–78
acronyms, 82, 87, 125

There is no consensus on how to order the list of nonalphabetical characters that precedes the *a* words. Some indexers arrange these characters by name; others place them in numerical order using their ASCII code equivalents;[2] others use the proprietary algorithms embedded in their indexing software. For a detailed discussion of sorting sequences, see Mulvany's *Indexing Books*.

The third pass is for the slow, careful reading and copyediting of the entries, entry by entry. There are eight key tasks—and one optional, time-consuming chore—at this stage:

1. Correct all typographical errors. Check any unusual spellings, capitalization, and hyphenation choices against the page proofs.
2. Make sure the wording of the main entries matches the readers' expectations. For example, in a consumers guide that covers automobiles, large appliances, and small appliances, readers interested in tips on buying a new car are likely to look under "cars, new," not under "new cars."
3. If the entry has subentries, the subentries should be parallel in form.

    > *Not parallel:* quotations 12–18; accuracy, 14; capitalizing, 15; using ellipsis points in, 16
    > *Parallel:* quotations, 12–18; accuracy of, 14; capitalization of, 15; ellipsis points within, 16
    > *Or:* quotations, 12–18; accuracy, 14; capitalization, 15; ellipsis points, 16

    A subentry may include prepositions or conjunctions that link it to the main entry and form a grammatical phrase (e.g., "accuracy of [quotations]," "ellipsis points within [quotations]"), or subentries may represent logical subdivisions of the main entry (e.g., "accuracy," "ellipsis points").

4. If the entry has subentries, check the order of the subentries. Most often, subentries are arranged in alphabetical order; but sometimes numerical order or chronological order is preferable.

---

2. Each nonalphabetical character in the basic ASCII set has a two- or three-digit number; for example, the pound sign (#) is 35 and the open angle bracket (<) is 60.

Numerical order: amended returns, filing procedures: form 1057, 285–90; form 1124, 293–300; form 1335A, 310–15; form 5252, 415–17

Chronological order: tombs, design of: in First Dynasty, 17–35; in Second Dynasty, 267–92; in Third Dynasty, 389–402

5. Check the punctuation within each entry. The conventions for a standard run-in index[3] are:

Use a comma to separate portions of an inverted main entry: diseases, tropical.

Place a comma after the main entry when the entry is immediately followed by a page number; place a colon after the main entry when the entry is immediately followed by a subentry heading.

Place a comma after a subentry heading (to separate it from the page numbers that follow).

Use a semicolon to separate successive subentries.

Place internal cross-references (i.e., cross-references that apply to only one subentry) in parentheses at the end of the subentry; lowercase and italicize the cross-reference indicator (*see* or *see also*):

magazines: binding of, 25–26; citation of (*see* articles, magazine); titles of, 121–23

Terminal cross-references (i.e., cross-references that apply to the entire entry) carry an initial capital letter and are set in italics. The text immediately preceding the cross-reference takes a terminal period. When the cross-reference is to a specific term, that term is set in roman type; when the cross-reference is to a class of terms, the entire cross-reference is set in italics.

legal citations: in bibliographies, 238–42, 251; in footnotes, 230–37. *See also* laws

legends. *See* captions and legends

planets. *See names of individual planets*

There is no punctuation at the end of an index entry.

---

3. In a run-in index, the subentries are set in the same paragraph as the main entry (as illustrated by all the examples in this chapter); the first line of each entry is set flush left, and the remaining lines are indented (this style is called "flush and hang"). Alternatively, an index may be set in indented style, in which each subentry begins on a new indented line.

6. Scrutinize the page numbers in the entry and subentries:

> A series of page numbers should be in ascending order: 16, 23, 145.
>
> Page ranges must be logical: 34–35 (*not* 34–34 *or* 35–34 *or* 34035).
>
> The treatment of page ranges should be consistent, following one of the three systems shown in "Inclusive Numerals" in chapter 7.

7. Verify that terms listed in cross-references do appear in the index. If you encounter a pair of entries like the following:

> fire safety. *See* smoke detectors
> smoke detectors, 198, 211–12

you can replace the cross-reference with the page numbers, because the page numbers take up less space than the cross-reference:

> fire safety, 198, 211–12
> smoke detectors, 198, 211–12

8. If an entry has many subentries, but few page numbers, consolidate the entry. For example,

> termites, 205–6; damp-wood, 205; dry-wood, 205; identifying, 205–6; subterranean, 206

could be shortened to

> termites, 205–6

The optional task at this stage, time permitting, is to rewrite any entries that have a long string of pages numbers but no subentries to guide the reader. *Chicago* offers a few paragraphs of helpful advice; for a comprehensive discussion, see Mulvany, *Indexing Books*. Be warned, however, that this task can be extremely time consuming.

The fourth pass should be a relatively quick scanning to make sure that you have not inadvertently inserted an error and have not overlooked anything.

EXERCISE N

Copyedit the following portion of a glossary that will appear in a book for novice computer users. The answer key is on pages 521–23.

alphanumeric sorting. Sorting that treats numbers like letters so that words with numbers and numbers of equal length can be sorted.

ASCII. Acronym for **A**merican **S**tandard **C**ode for **I**nformation **I**nterchange, one of the standard forms for representing characters so that files can be shared between programs. A DOS Text File is in ASCII format.

backspace. A key on your keyboard which deletes the character to the left of the cursor.

backup. To copy files for safe keeping.

baud rate. The rate of speed at which information is sent between two computer devices. It is used, for example, when sending files across modems.

bit. A *binary* *d*igit; the smallest storage unit for data in a computer.

boot. To start a computer by loading the operating system into the computer's memory.

byte. The amount of space needed to store a single character (number, letter or code). 1024 bytes equals one kilobyte (Kb or K).

buffer. A temporary data storage area used by computers and some printers.

❖ 13 ❖

Typecoding

Many manuscripts contain material other than sentences and paragraphs of running text. The most common of these elements are book, article, and chapter titles; heads and subheads; extracts; tables; and captions for illustrations.

Decisions about the physical appearance of these elements—e.g., typeface, type size, indention, vertical and horizontal location and spacing—are the province of the publication's designer. But it is often up to the copyeditor to identify for the designer which elements appear in the manuscript and the location of each element. The designer will then supply specifications (always called *specs*) that detail the desired treatment of those elements.

TYPECODING ON HARD COPY

Copyeditors working on hard copy are usually asked to typecode the elements with a colored pencil. As shown in figure 14, the copyeditor also marks the beginning and end of any element whose boundaries are unclear in the manuscript. Typecodes are written in the left margin—or to the left of an indented item—and circled.

Every publisher has its own set of hard-copy typecodes, and a list of these codes will be given to you. In book publishing the following mnemonic codes are typical.

Part openings

PN   part number
PT   part title
PST   part subtitle
PEP   part epigraph
PES   part epigraph
      source line

Chapter openings

CN   chapter number
CT   chapter title
CST   chapter subtitle
CEP   chapter epigraph
CES   chapter epigraph
      source line

Heads (headings)
within the document

A   first-level head[1]
B   second-level head
C   third-level head

Display text within the
body of the document

EX   extract (block quote)
PX   poetry extract
EQ   equation

Lists

UNL   unnumbered list[2]
NL   numbered list
BL   bulleted list
MCL   multicolumn list

Back matter

BMT   back matter section title
BIB   bibliography text
AN   appendix number
AT   appendix title

Documentation

FN   footnote
EN   endnote

Figures

FGC   figure caption
FGN   figure number

Copyeditors must also code the elements in each table. The coding in figure 15 is based on the following set of codes:

TN   table number
TT   table title
TST   table subtitle
TSQ   table squib
TCH   table column head

T1   table first-level head
T2   table second-level head
TB   table body
TS   table source line
TFN   table footnote

1. Alternatively, heads are coded as 1, 2, and 3; see the discussion later in this chapter.
2. The formatting of lists is discussed later in this chapter.

Figure 14. Typecoding on Hard Copy

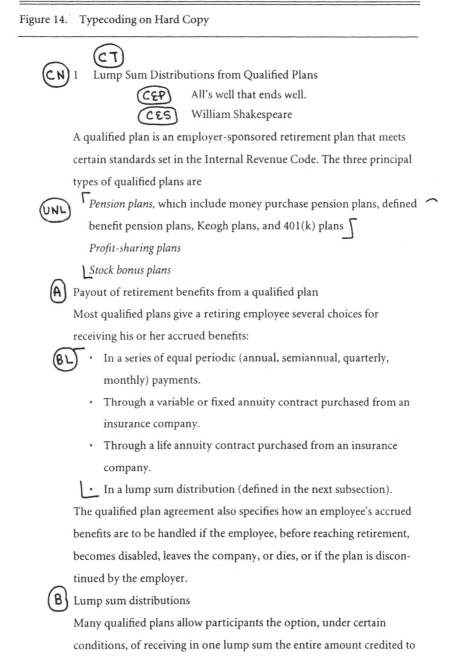

(CT)

(CN) 1 Lump Sum Distributions from Qualified Plans

(CEP)   All's well that ends well.

(CES)   William Shakespeare

A qualified plan is an employer-sponsored retirement plan that meets certain standards set in the Internal Revenue Code. The three principal types of qualified plans are

(UNL) ⌐*Pension plans,* which include money purchase pension plans, defined benefit pension plans, Keogh plans, and 401(k) plans ⌡

Profit-sharing plans

⌊*Stock bonus plans*

(A) Payout of retirement benefits from a qualified plan

Most qualified plans give a retiring employee several choices for receiving his or her accrued benefits:

(BL) • In a series of equal periodic (annual, semiannual, quarterly, monthly) payments.

• Through a variable or fixed annuity contract purchased from an insurance company.

• Through a life annuity contract purchased from an insurance company.

⌊• In a lump sum distribution (defined in the next subsection).

The qualified plan agreement also specifies how an employee's accrued benefits are to be handled if the employee, before reaching retirement, becomes disabled, leaves the company, or dies, or if the plan is discontinued by the employer.

(B) Lump sum distributions

Many qualified plans allow participants the option, under certain conditions, of receiving in one lump sum the entire amount credited to their retirement account.

Figure 15.   Typecodes for a Table

(TN/TT)(TSQ) Table 1. Virus-Neutralization Tests on Sera from Mammals and Birds (Performed under IASA standards)

(TCH) Species	Number Tested	Positive	
		N	%
(T1) Mammals			
Camel	9	7	78
Cow	36	6	17 (TB)
Donkey	15	7	47
(T1) Birds			
Chicken*	24	4	16 (TB)
Crow	18	9	50
Duck	14	$2^{\dagger}$	14

(TS) *Source:* Chris T. Author, *Book Title* (New York: Big Books, 1990), 536–37.

(TFN) * Chickens were retested by PSA-3 analysis.

† Retest results were inconclusive for 2 additional ducks.

TYPECODING ON-SCREEN

Copyeditors working on-screen may be asked either to place typecodes into the file or to verify the typecoding (also called *tagging*) that has been done by an in-house production editor. The codes and the procedures depend on the publisher's production process, and the instructions given to the copyeditor will include a list of the codes and an explanation of the procedures. The following examples illustrate the general principles and some of the conventions now in use.[3] Figure 16 shows one system for the on-screen coding of the manuscript page that is hand-coded in figure 14.

Coding text elements.   The codes for elements are short mnemonic combinations. There are various systems for formatting the codes. Some place the codes in angle brackets, others use square brackets, and still others use special characters before and after the code:

Element	Angle brackets	Square brackets	Special characters
chapter number	<CN>	[CN]	@cn:
chapter title	<CT>	[CT]	@ct:

The end of the element is indicated either by a </> or <\> code (which may be accompanied by a repeat of the opening code) or by a hard return, depending on the particular system:

```
<CN>1</><CT>Rules of the Road</>

<CN>1</CN><CT>Rules of the Road</CT>

[CN]1[\][CT]Rules of the Road[\]

@cn:1
@ct:Rules of the Road
```

Coding character attributes.   *Attributes* are features that apply to typed characters: boldface, italics, and small capitals, and subscripts and superscripts. In some systems, the copyeditor need only verify that the author's word processing codes are correct. For example, assume that house style calls for an italic comma after a word in italics. In the following sentence, you would make sure that the second comma (the one at the end of the novel's title) is an italic comma:

Author's coding: His best novel, *For Whom the Bell Tolls,* is also his most personal.

3. In recent years, some book publishers have abandoned coding in favor of templates and styles in Microsoft Word or in proprietary software. Other publishers are using XML (extensible markup language), which facilitates the publication of content in various forms (books, e-books, PDFs) without recoding. For a discussion of XML, see *Chicago* 16, appendix A.

Figure 16.   On-Screen Typecoding. In this sample the running text is the default setting and so it carries no codes. Uppercase paired codes are used for text elements, lowercase paired codes for character attributes. The line breaks are generated by the hard return codes in the word processing program.

```
<CN>1<CN><CT>Lump Sum Distributions from Qualified Plans<CT>

<CEP>All's well that ends well.<CEP>

<CES>William Shakespeare<CES>

A qualified plan is an employer-sponsored retirement plan that meets

certain standards set in the Internal Revenue Code. The three

principal types of qualified plans are

<UL><i>Pension plans,<i> which include money purchase pension plans,

defined benefit pension plans, Keogh plans, and 401(k) plans

<i>Profit-sharing plans<i>

<i>Stock bonus plans<i><UL>

<A>Payout of retirement benefits from a qualified plan<A>

Most qualified plans give a retiring employee several choices for

receiving his or her accrued benefits:

<BL>In a series of equal periodic (annual, semiannual, quarterly,

monthly) payments.

Through a variable or fixed annuity contract purchased from an

insurance company.

Through a life annuity contract purchased from an insurance company.

In a lump sum distribution (defined in the next subsection).<BL>

The qualified plan agreement also specifies how an employee's accrued

benefits are to be handled if the employee, before reaching

retirement, becomes disabled, leaves the company, or dies, or if the

plan is discontinued by the employer.

<B>Lump sum distributions<B>

Many qualified plans allow participants the option, under certain

conditions, of receiving in one lump sum the entire amount credited

to their retirement account.
```

Other systems require the copyeditor to delete the author's word processing codes and substitute special attribute codes:

> *Attribute coding:* `His best novel, <I>For Whom the Bell Tolls,<I> is also his most personal.`
>
> *Or:* `His best novel, <I>For Whom the Bell Tolls,<i> is also his most personal.`
>
> *Or:* `His best novel, <I>For Whom the Bell Tolls,</> is also his most personal.`

As these examples show, attribute codes come in pairs, one to start the feature, the other to turn off the feature. In some systems, the "turn-off" code is always </> or <\>. In other systems, the closing code is a repeat of or a variant on the opening code:

> `<BF>Amendment 1.<BF> The term of city council members shall be four years.`
>
> `H<SUB>2<sub>O<SUB>2<sub> is highly unstable.`
>
> `Who can fail to appreciate the poetry of E = mc<SUP>2<sup>?`

Coding or entering special characters.   Some manuscripts contain characters that do not appear on a standard keyboard, such as European diacritics and punctuation marks, non-Latin alphabets, mathematical expressions, and scientific symbols. Authors and copyeditors can select many of these characters from the symbols lists and tables in their word processing program. Sometimes, however, those characters do not survive the transition from one font to another or from one platform (e.g., print, website, e-reader) to another. To ensure that special characters are correctly retained, a copyeditor may be asked to use the Unicode standard, an international cross-platform system for representing over 100,000 characters in those fonts that are Unicode-compliant.

By convention, Unicode codes mentioned in running text are prefixed by "U+"; for example, U+00B1 represents the plus-or-minus sign (±). In versions of Microsoft Word that fully support Unicode, one types the alphanumeric string that follows the "U+" and then enters Alt+x. Presto: the "00B1" is replaced by the ± character. *Chicago* 16 includes several charts listing Unicode codes, and the complete set is available at the Unicode Consortium website (www.unicode.org).

Coding for paragraph indents.   In some typesetting systems, all hard returns in the running text automatically force a paragraph indent at the beginning of the next line. In these systems, then, a code must be inserted only when this default paragraph indent is not desired. In other systems, paragraph indents are signaled by two successive hard returns, or a hard return followed by a word processing tab code, or a hard return followed by a <p> code.

Procedures.   Whether the codes are inserted by a production editor or by the copyeditor, the copyeditor is expected to make sure the coding is correct. This step includes checking to see that

> there are no typographical errors within the codes
>
> there is no extra wordspacing before or after the codes
>
> there is no extra linespacing before or after displayed elements
>
> punctuation that is to be set in italic or bold is correctly coded[4]
>
> all paired codes have closing mates
>
> all codes used in the manuscript appear on the master list that will be sent to the compositor

---

4. In traditional typesetting: Periods, commas, colons, and semicolons are set in the same style as the word that immediately precedes them. Question marks and exclamation points are set in italic or bold only if they are part of the expression preceding:

The best children's book this season is Anderson's *Why Is the Sky Blue?*

How can one explain the enduring popularity of *Gone with the Wind*?

Both members of paired marks (i.e., parentheses, brackets, quotation marks) are set in the same typeface, and they are set in italics or bold only when all the text within them is italic or bold.

A newer convention calls for all punctuation to be set in the style of the running text except for a question mark or exclamation point that is part of an italicized (or bold) term.

HEADS AND SUBHEADS

In addition to typecoding the heads and subheads, a copyeditor must regularize the capitalization of these heads, using either headline style or sentence style (see "Titles of Works" in chapter 6). Both headline style and sentence style may be used in the same document as long as all heads of the same level are treated consistently. (More about levels of heads in a moment.)

As for the frequency of heads and subheads, the number that is "just right" depends on the nature of the document and the intended readership. For most nonfiction trade books, one head every four or five pages is probably sufficient; more-frequent heads may give the text a choppy feel or a textbook look. Reference books and computer manuals, in contrast, may require several heads and subheads per page. For journal articles printed in two-column formats, one head per column may be appropriate. The length of the heads is also a consideration. When the heads are long (two or three lines of type), frequent heads will disrupt the appearance of the pages. When the heads are quite short (two or three words), their presence is not as disruptive.

After checking the frequency of heads and subheads, you must look at the heads in each chapter or section to make sure they are logical. All first-level heads should be of roughly the equivalent "weight." For example, a chapter on house pets could have first-level heads like those shown on the left; the set on the right is illogical.

Logical	*Illogical*
Dogs	Dogs
Cats	Small dogs
Hamsters	Cats
Fish	Long-haired cats
	Hamsters

Because "small dogs" is a subset of "dogs," "small dogs" would have to be a second-level head, and logic suggests that if there is a second-level head for small dogs, the chapter should also have a second-level head for large dogs—and quite possibly one for medium-size dogs. Similarly, "cats" and "long-haired cats" are not logically equivalent, because the second is a subset of the first. And if there is to be a section on long-haired cats, logic requires a section on short-haired cats as well. Thus, one would expect to see

First-level head	Dogs
Second-level head	Small dogs
Second-level head	Medium-size dogs
Second-level head	Large dogs
First-level head	Cats
Second-level head	Short-haired cats
Second-level head	Long-haired cats
First-level head	Hamsters
First-level head	Fish

The small dogs and long-haired cats exemplify a second issue concerning the logic of heads. As a rule—though this rule admits some exceptions—for each level of head used, there must be at least two instances of that level. Thus when a document or chapter contains first-level heads, there must be at least two such heads in the document. And if second-level heads are used in a section that begins with a first-level head, there should be at least two second-level heads within that section; and so on. This principle, like the schoolbook principle for making outlines, is based on the premise that is it illogical to have only one subordinate item or subtopic within a category:

Logical	*Illogical*
Dogs	Dogs
Small dogs	Small dogs
Large dogs	Cats
Cats	Long-haired cats
Short-haired cats	Hamsters
Long-haired cats	
Hamsters	

Some coding systems use letters (A, B, C) to indicate heads, and other coding systems use numerals (1, 2, 3). Under both systems, the code assigns a level of importance to each head; the codes are *not* used to count up the number of heads in a section. Thus a chapter may have nine heads, all of which are coded A (or coded 1).

Two other conventions for heads are followed by some publishers:

A head cannot immediately follow a chapter opening. This prohibition largely reflects an aesthetic preference—that a page with a display head directly below the chapter opening display is unattractive—although some editors also argue that it is illogical to immediately divide the content of a chapter into subtopics before introducing the chapter's overarching main topic.

Heads cannot be stacked. Stacked heads occur when a head is immediately followed by a subordinate head, with no intervening text; for example:

Dogs

Small dogs

Small dogs have become very popular in recent years, especially among apartment dwellers. But even the smallest dogs require daily care and regular exercise.

The ban on stacked heads is based partly on aesthetics and partly on logic, the latter objection being that one should not discuss a subtopic before saying something about the topic as a whole.

LISTS

There are four basic formats for displayed lists: numbered, unnumbered, bulleted, and multicolumn. Numbered lists are best used when the items are instructions to be done in sequence, when the numbers denote some type of hierarchy (e.g., "The ten largest markets are . . ."), or when the subsequent discussion refers back to items on the list (e.g., "In the third situation . . ."). Otherwise, the numbers serve little purpose other than to clutter the text, and unnumbered or bulleted lists are preferable. Bulleted lists are extremely popular in corporate communications, less so in scholarly writing, where unnumbered lists predominate. A multicolumn list may contain unnumbered, numbered, or bulleted items.

The capitalization and punctuation of items in a displayed list depend on the nature of the items in the list:

- When at least one item is a complete sentence, all the items are punctuated as though they were complete sentences. Thus each item begins with a capital letter and ends with a period.
- When all the items are single words, phrases, or sentence fragments, each item is treated as a sentence fragment. Thus each item begins with a lowercase letter (unless the first word is a proper noun or adjective) and carries either no terminal punctuation or a comma or a semicolon. When the items carry terminal punctuation, the last item ends with a period.

In documents that contain many displayed lists, however, some publishers prefer that all lists be formatted by the first principle except when each item in a list consists of a single word, in which case the second system is used.

Regarding the punctuation of the regular text that introduces a displayed list, *Chicago* and *WIT* recommend the following:

- When the introductory text includes the phrase "as follows" or "the following," the lead-in should end with a colon.
- When the introductory text is the beginning of a sentence that is concluded by the items in the list, the lead-in should carry no terminal punctuation, unless a comma or a colon is desired after "for example" or "that is."
- In all other cases, the lead-in text may end with a colon or a period.

Here's a checklist for copyediting displayed lists:

1. Typecode the list, following the publisher's coding scheme for numbered, unnumbered, bulleted, and multicolumn lists. Mark the beginning and end of the list, and make sure that the compositor can discern the beginning and end of each item on the list.
2. Verify that all items are in their correct order (e.g., alphabetical, numerical, chronological, geographical), or determine that there is no logical ordering principle that can be imposed upon the items.
3. Make sure that the items are parallel in structure (logic, syntax, length, importance).

4. Check the logic, syntax, and length of any sub-items.
5. Enforce consistency in the capitalization of items.
6. Regularize the punctuation preceding the list, at the end of each item, and at the end of the list.
7. Enforce consistency in the choice of item markers:

Bullets

circular, closed (filled)   ● • ·

circular, open   ○ ∘ ∘

square, filled   ■ ▪ ·

square, open   ☐ ⊔ ▫

Special characters   ☞ ✓ ☆ ❑

Uppercase or lowercase letters (followed by a period).

Numerals (followed by a period).[5] In long lists, the numerals should align on the last digit, not the first:

Correct alignment	*Incorrect alignment*
1. wheat	1. wheat
2. rice	2. rice
10. textiles	10. textiles
110. paper	110. paper

In publishing jargon, the vertical alignment of numerals on the last digit is called "clearing for 10s." When copyeditors working on hard copy come upon an incorrectly aligned list, they write a circled instruction to the compositor: Clear for 10s. Copyeditors working on-screen are expected to insert the needed tabs or codes. Parentheses are best reserved for run-in lists; in display lists long columns of parentheses are unattractive.

5. An alternative style calls for extra wordspacing, rather than a period, after the numerals in a numbered list:

1   wheat

2   rice

10   textiles

8. Check for consistency in the

> leading (linespacing) above and below the list
> indents
> spacing between the item marker and the start of the item text

Of course, not every enumeration or series need be treated as a displayed list. When a list has only three or four items, each of which is short, it is often preferable to set it as a run-in list; for example:

Awkward: Our analysis is based on

> the USGS survey,
> the USFS survey, and
> field research we conducted in 1997.

Revision: Our analysis is based on the USGS survey, the USFS survey, and field research we conducted in 1997.

Or: Our analysis is based on (1) the USGS survey, (2) the USFS survey, and (3) field research we conducted in 1997.

However, sometimes even a short list containing short items may be displayed, for the reader's convenience:

> In order to complete this form, you will need
> your 1999 federal income tax return
> your 1999 state income tax return
> a stub from a recent paycheck

DESIGN SPECS

While the copyeditor is busy working on the content of a manuscript, the designer is making decisions about how the final printed product will look—decisions about the jacket design, the paper, the typefaces, and so on. At several points, the paths of the copyeditor and the designer cross. As we have seen, it is the copyeditor who informs the designer—either in a formal memo or through notes on the style sheet—that the manuscript contains unusual alphabetical or nonalphabetical characters (e.g., mathematical symbols, foreign language characters or diacritic marks, musical notation) or that the manuscript contains elements other than straight running text (e.g., heads, tables, extracts).

In large publishing outfits, the designer usually works with the editorial coordinator or a production editor rather than with the copyeditor. In smaller businesses, however, a copyeditor may be asked to implement some of the designer's intentions. But even if you are never asked to work directly with a designer, you should have at least a basic understanding of design specs.

SYSTEMS OF MEASUREMENT

Designers and compositors use three systems of linear measurement: inches, points and picas, and em and en spaces.

Inches.   Inches are used to specify the *trim size* (the size of the document's pages) and occasionally to specify the dimensions of the *type page* (the trim size minus the top, bottom, and side margins) and the margins.

Points and picas.   Points and picas are units unique to publishing. Just as there are twelve inches to a foot, there are twelve points to a pica. But when one expresses picas and points in terms of inches, the equivalences are awkward, because the pica is based on the eighteenth-century French precursor of the modern centimeter:

1 pica = 0.1656 inch   1 point = .0138 inch
6.039 picas = 1 inch   72.464 points = 1 inch

For a copyeditor's purposes, the following rules of thumb suffice:

6 picas = 1 inch   72 points = 1 inch

The metric equivalences are equally awkward; the following approximations are used:

1 pica = 4.2 millimeters   1 point = 0.35 millimeter

The varied uses of points and picas are described on the following pages.

Em and en spaces.   The size of an em space depends on the size of the type being used. If the text is set in 8-point type, an em space is 8 points wide; if the text is set in 24-point type, an em space is 24 points wide. An en space is half the width of an em space.

Em spaces and en spaces are most often used to indicate the width of paragraph indentions (e.g., "Indent 1 en") and other small amounts of lateral spacing (e.g., a thin space is usually specified as $\frac{1}{4}$ em, also written as "4-to-em," and the space between ellipsis points is $\frac{1}{3}$ em, also written "3-to-em").

SPECS FOR BOOK PAGES

The dimensions of a page of a book are expressed in inches: 6 in. × 9 in. These dimensions constitute the *trim size,* the size of the entire book page.

The dimensions of the *type page* (the trim size minus the margins on all four sides) may be expressed in inches or in picas: 25 × 43 picas.

The size of the margins is also expressed in inches or in picas. Each book page has four margins: top, bottom, inside, and outside. The inside margin (also called the *back margin* or the *gutter margin*) is the right margin of a left-hand page of a book, but the left margin of a right-hand page of a book—a necessary distinction so the pages can be properly bound.

The *text page* or *text area* (the area covered by the running text) is usually given in picas, as are the margins in between columns on a multicolumn page.

SPECS FOR RUNNING HEADS, FOOTERS, AND PAGE NUMBERS

In the specs the designer indicates the location of the running heads, footers, and page numbers: how far across the page, in relation to the margins, these elements start or end, and how far up or down the page they are to be placed.

The horizontal location of the running elements is stated with reference to the left and right margins of the text area. Three common horizontal locations are flush left (beginning at the left margin), centered (centered across the text area), and flush right (ending at the right margin). The instruction "fl. out." calls for the element to be placed flush outside: on a left-hand page the element begins at the left margin, and on a right-hand page the element ends at the right margin. Similarly, the instruction "fl. in." calls for the element to be placed flush inside: on a left-hand page the element ends at the right margin, and on a right-hand page it begins at the left margin.

Some designers indicate the vertical location of the running heads or footers by reference to the type page: "Running heads at top outside of type page." Other designers indicate how much vertical space is to fall between the running head or footer and the text area. This vertical space is specified by the number of points from the baseline of the type in the running head to the baseline of the type in the first line of text (or from the base of the last line of text to the base of the footer). For example, the instruction "16 pts b/b" calls for sixteen points of vertical space between the two baselines.

The location of page numbers (also called *folios*) is specified with reference to the inner or outer margin and to the top or bottom margin. Page numbers that appear at the bottom of the page are called *drop folios*. The spec may also call for "lining figures" (or numbers) or "old style figures" (sometimes abbreviated o.s.). Lining figures sit on the baseline. Old style figures have ascenders and descenders:

Lining figures:	123456789	123456789
Old style figures:	123456789	123456789

TYPE SPECS

In the type specs, the designer indicates the face, weight, style, and size of the type for each element in the document. Here are some examples of each of these attributes:

Face: Franklin Gothic, Times Roman, Gill Sans, Minion

Weight: light, regular, **medium**, condensed

Style: roman, *italic,* **bold**

Size: 8 point, 10 point, 12 point

The designer also specifies the amount of *leading*—that is, the amount of vertical space between lines of type. (*Leading* is pronounced "ledding," because linespaces were once created by inserting strips of lead.) The size of the type and the amount of leading are expressed in points.[6]

Notation	*Meaning*	*Amount of leading*
8/9	8-point type on a 9-point form	1 point
9/11	9-point type on an 11-point form	2 points
10/13	10-point type on a 13-point form	3 points
24/28	24-point type on a 28-point form	4 points

6. In traditional typography, type size is measured from the bottom of the descenders (the lowest point of the letters g j p y) to the top of the ascenders (the highest point of the letters b d f h). The height of lowercase letters that have neither ascenders nor descenders (a c e i m) is called the *x-height.*

The specs for running text also indicate the size of the paragraph indent (para indent), expressed in picas ("para indent 1 pica") or em spaces ("para indent 1 em #").

INTERPRETING TYPE SPECS

Here are some sample type specs and their "translations."

Running text (also called general text *or* main text). The designer writes

> Main text: Garamond roman, 10/13 x 25 picas x 42 lines, para indent
> 1 pica. No para indent following display type.

This spec means: Set the text in 10-point Garamond type, roman, with 3 points of leading. Each line of type will be 25 picas wide, and each page will run 42 lines deep. Each paragraph will be indented 1 pica, except that the first paragraph after a line of display type (e.g., chapter title, heading, subheading) will be set flush left. Since no instruction is given regarding justification, the compositor will assume that the left and right margins are to be justified. To obtain text that is justified at the left margin, but not at the right margin, the designer would write "ragged right" or "rag right."

Running heads. The designer writes

> Running heads: 6 pt. Bodoni, small caps, centered, 36 pts b/b to
> text line.

This spec means: Set the running heads in 6-point Bodoni type, all small capitals, and centered on the text page. The baseline of the running head should sit 36 points above the baseline of the first line of running text.

Prose extracts. Extracts (block quotes) are differentiated from regular text in one or more of the following ways: (1) set on a narrower line (i.e., with wider margins) than regular text, (2) set with additional leading above and below the block, (3) set in a smaller point size than regular text, (4) set in the same point size but with less internal leading. In the following spec, the designer ensures that the extracts will be centered on the page but 2 picas narrower than the regular text:

> Prose extract: Bembo ital, 9/11 x 25 picas, indent 1 pica each side,
> leading 16 pts b/b above & below.

This spec means: Set the prose extracts in 9-point Bembo italic with 2 points of leading. Each extract will run 23 picas wide (25 picas minus the 1 pica indent on each side), and there will be 16 points of linespacing base to base between the regular text and the first line of the extract, and again between the last line of the extract and the first line of the regular text.

Chapter titles. The specs for chapter titles must indicate which of the three capitalization styles is to be used:

Style	Abbreviation	Example
All uppercase (all capitals)	UC All caps	TYPE SPECS FOR FRENCH EDITORS
Capitals and lowercase (headline style)	UC/lc Clc C & lc	Type Specs for French Editors
Initial capital only (sentence style)	Init cap only Init cap	Type specs for French editors

So, the designer writes

Chapter title: 24/27 x 25 picas, Goudy bold, Clc, flush left, sink 6 picas.

This spec means: Set the chapter titles in 24-point Goudy bold type. The capitalization style is Clc. Set the chapter titles flush with the left margin and 6 picas below where a regular text page would start.

Displayed math equations. The designer writes

Displayed equations: 10/12 Baskerville, centered, runovers indented 2 ems, 18 pts b/b between successive equations; 24 pts b/b above and below.

This spec means: Displayed equations are to be set in 10-point Baskerville, with 2 points of leading, centered across the text page. Runover lines (the second and following lines of a long item, also called *turnovers*) are to be indented 2 ems. When several equations follow one another, the spec asks for 18 points base to base between them. There will be 24 points base to base above and below each set of equations.

Index. Most indexes to books and manuals are set two columns to a page, so the specs must give the width of the columns and the amount of space between them. A typical index spec might read:

> Index text (2 cols): 8/9 Times Roman x 12 picas x 40 lines; rag r;
> 1 pica between cols; runover 1.5 em indent.

This spec means: Set the index in 8-point Times Roman with 1 point of leading. Each of the two columns will be 12 picas wide and 40 lines long, and each column will have a ragged right margin. There is to be 1 pica in between the columns. Runover lines are to be indented 1.5 ems.

EXERCISE O

Compositors and printers use the term *Latin* to denote Latin-like nonsense text that is used to provide samples of typefaces. Typecode the following Latin, using this set of codes:

CN	chapter number
CT	chapter title
CST	chapter subtitle
A	first-level head
B	second-level head
UNL	unnumbered list
NL	numbered list
BL	bulleted list
MCL	multicolumn text
EX	extract
PX	poetry extract
EQ	equation

The answer key is on pages 524–25.

```
3      Quick Guide to Typecoding: It's All Greek

       to Me

Lorem ipsum dolor sit amet, con sectetuer

adipiscing elit, sed dis nonummy nibh euismod

tincidunt ut laoreet dolore magna aliquam:

    •  Lorem ipsum dolor sit amet.

    •  Con sectetuer adipiscing elit.

    •  Sed dis nonummy nibh euismod.

    Aliquam erat voluptat. Ut wisi enim ad
```

minim veniam, quis nostrud exerci tation
ullamcorper suscipit lobortis nisl ut aliquip
ea commodo consequat:

Lorem ipsum dolor   Dolore magna ut

sit amet, con sect   aliquam erat ut

etuer adipiscing   voluptat ut wisi

elit, sed dis   enim ad minim ad

nonummy nibh.   veniam.

Lorem ipsum dolor sit amet, con sectetuer
adipiscing elit.

Sed dis nonummy nibh euismod tincidunt ut
laoreet dolore magna aliquam erat voluptat.
Ut wisi enim ad minim veniam, quis nostrud:

$$\sum fx \pm 4y \geq 6$$

Lorem ipsum dolor sit amet, con sectetuer
adipiscing elit.

Sed dis nonummy nibh euismod tincidunt ut
laoreet dolore magna aliquam erat voluptat:

Lorem ipsum "dolor sit amet," con

sectetuer adipiscing elit, sed dis

nonummy nibh euismod tincidunt ut laoreet

dolore magna aliquam erat voluptat.

Lorem ipsum dolor sit amet, con sectetuer

adipiscing elit, sed dis nonummy nibh

euismod:

1. Voluptat suscipit lobortis nisl.

2. Wisi enim dolore magna aliquam erat.

3. Ad minim veniam dis nonummy nibh.

Quis Nostrud Exerci

Tation ullamcorper suscipit lobortis nisl ut

aliquip ea commodo consequat. Lorem ipsum

dolor sit amet, con sectetuer adipiscing.

PART 3

❖ Language Editing

In part 3 we move beyond mechanics to look at grammar and usage (chapter 14) and selected stylistic and substantive issues (chapter 15). Here, as in mechanical matters, copyeditors are expected to correct or query whatever is incorrect in the manuscript, but the differences between correct and incorrect are sometimes harder to discern. On many points of grammar and usage, for example, even the experts offer conflicting advice. Thus copyeditors need to be able to distinguish between inviolable rules and personal stylistic preferences, with the goal of enforcing the former and respecting the author's choices in the latter. Chapter 14 surveys the gaffes most often committed by even good writers as well as the major battles in the grammar and usage wars.

The final challenge for copyeditors is to ensure that the text is clear and unambiguous at all levels—from individual words to sentences, paragraphs, sections, and chapters. Chapter 15 examines matters pertaining to organization, expository style, and the recent controversies over bias-free language. The last section of the chapter summarizes four legal topics (libel, privacy, obscenity, and copyright) of concern to copyeditors.

❖ 14 ❖

Grammar: Principles and Pitfalls

Even if you haven't formally studied English grammar, you know countless aspects of grammar. You would never say or write "I are hungrily very," no matter how many hours had passed since your last meal. Not all questions of grammar are that simple, of course, but many tangles are easily resolved once you know the rules and conventions. In some cases, however, the rules are unclear or disputed, and the experts offer conflicting analyses. The number of these disputes—and the passion, indeed, the moral fervor they sometimes inspire—is far greater than you might imagine, until you begin to pore over the shelves of grammar and usage books in the library or in a well-stocked bookstore. For example, the editors of *DEU* describe their work as an examination of "common problems of confused or disputed English usage" (p. 4a)—and note that their volume treats some five hundred such problems.

The perplexities are compounded when an author and a copyeditor have different positions about what constitutes correct English. In *Style: Toward Clarity and Grace,* Joseph M. Williams describes the contours of this plight.

> A few especially fastidious writers and editors try to honor and enforce every rule of usage; most careful writers observe fewer; and there are a few writers and editors who know all the rules, but who also know that not all of them are worth observing and enforcing, and that they should observe other rules only on certain occasions.
>
> What do those of us do who want to be careful writers?
>
> We could adopt the worst-case policy: follow all the rules all the time because somewhere, sometime, someone might criticize us for something. . . . And so, with a stack of grammar books and usage manuals close by, we scrutinize every

sentence for all possible "errors." . . . But once we decide to follow all the rules, we deprive ourselves of stylistic flexibility. And sooner or later, we will begin to impose those rules—real or not—on others. . . .

But selective observance has its problems too, because that requires us to learn which rules to ignore, which always to observe, and which to observe in some circumstances and to ignore in others. This freedom to choose is further complicated by the fact that those who invoke every rule of grammar always seem to have the moral upper hand: they claim to be dedicated to precision, and they seem to know something about goodness that we don't. Conversely, if we know enough to dismiss some "rule" of grammar as folklore, we risk being judged permissive by those who are ignorant of the history of our language. (p. 178)

Here we hit upon an inevitable occupational hazard: Almost daily, copyeditors confront minor episodes of "damned if you revise, damned if you don't." Although some authors will eagerly respect your expertise, accept all your revisions, and thank you profusely for fixing their mistakes, others will view grammatical revisions on the copyedited manuscript as a challenge to their intellectual ability or professional identity. Among this latter group, some will defend their personal tics and preferences as representing universal grammatical norms and will reject your editing as uninformed; others will accuse you of needlessly nitpicking and tampering with wording that they find unobjectionable ("It's clear enough. Readers will know what I mean").

Moreover, on some points of grammar both authors and copyeditors can invoke the equally impressive authority of equally impressive experts who happen to disagree. For the working copyeditor, deference is the better part of valor: if the author's preference is at all acceptable, it should be respected. But when your desk is free of manuscripts and you have time to mull, you might want to think a bit about how you go about choosing your experts and the reference books you rely on. Is the newest grammar and usage book always to be trusted, or is there a value in sometimes sticking with the dog-eared classics? Is Expert A's attack on a certain expression based on a functional rationale (the expression is unclear or ambiguous) or on some airy pretension to elegance? Is Authority B honestly trying to help readers write with greater clarity and precision, or is he (for few of them are shes) promulgating pedantry for pedantry's sake or playing an erudite game of "gotcha" in which the reader is always the loser? Does Maven C have any real expertise or just the chutzpah to remake the language in his image and the arrogant self-confidence of a lone prophet on a moral crusade? Is Guru D someone who values idiomatic English or someone who would replace "put one's best foot forward" with "put one's better foot forward" on the grounds that one cannot use the superlative when only two items are being compared? (See *DEU*, s.vv. "best foot forward" and "superlative of two.")

In this chapter we'll take a peek at the main contenders in the ongoing battle over English grammar and then look at a basket of grammar problems that vex even experienced copyeditors. If you want to brush up on some of the less contentious topics, turn to one of the grammar books mentioned in chapter 3.

(If you're hoping that your word processing program's grammar checker will save you any time or spare you any errors—forget it. Even for the shortest of texts, these checkers are time consuming and frustrating. They routinely ignore simple errors, repeatedly question unmistakably correct constructions, and suggest substitutions that are flat-out wrong. Most copyeditors simply disable the grammar checker.)

WHOSE GRAMMAR?

As noted, one source of difficulty for people who care about written language is that even the experts sometimes disagree. In broadest terms, the battle is between the descriptivists, who seek to document how language is used, and the prescriptivists, who champion an edenic vision of how the language *should* be used. A principal charge against the descriptivist position, summarized by John Updike, is that it "proposes no ideal of clarity in language or, beyond that, of grace, which might serve as an instrument of discrimination."[1] Across the battlefield, however, Steven Pinker dismisses the prescriptivists' finicky discriminations and differentiations as bosh: "Most of the prescriptive rules of the language mavens make no sense on any level. They are bits of folklore that originated for screwball reasons several hundred years ago and have perpetuated themselves ever since. For as long as they have existed, speakers have flouted them, spawning identical plaints about the imminent decline of the

---

1. John Updike, "Fine Points," *The New Yorker* (December 23 and 30, 1996), p. 145. In this review of Burchfield's *New Fowler's*, Updike offers a spirited defense of Fowler's brand of prescriptivism ("a dynamic guidance that promises a brighter future, rather than a helpless wallow in the endless morass of English as it was and is").

language. . . . The rules conform neither to logic nor to tradition, and if they were ever followed they would force writers into fuzzy, clumsy, wordy, ambiguous, incomprehensible prose."[2]

Cooler commentators describe these "screwball reasons" as having to do with the desire of British elites, beginning in the late sixteenth century, to confer grandeur on the English language and the burgeoning English empire through the imitation of classical Latin and the august Roman Empire: "The best historical model of an influential empire with a language to match was Rome; and in this period, the perfection of the Latin language was still seen as closely connected to the success of Roman political expansion. So (the reasoning went), for England to achieve equivalent political success, its language had to be rendered as 'perfect' as Latin—preferably by coaxing it into the model of Latin, making it as much like Latin in form as possible."[3]

The American Revolution may have freed the colonies from British rule (and British spelling), but the legacy of post-Elizabethan social and political anxiety is still with us, in the form of, among other niceties, the taboo on ending sentences with prepositions, the turmoil over *less* and *fewer*, and the injunction against splitting infinitives. For it was Dryden who, in 1672, proclaimed that English sentences were no longer to end with prepositions because Cicero and his brethren did not do so—and, after all, to have a sentence-ending preposition was to violate the term's etymological soul, which comprises the Latin *prae-* (in front of, before) and *ponere* (to put, to place). Henceforth, only a scoundrel would place a preposition anywhere that was not pre.

Prescriptions and proscriptions of this sort multiplied over the centuries, as each new generation promulgated its view of proper, decorous usage. Since the time when Dryden is alleged to have confessed that "he sometimes had to translate an idea into Latin to find the correct way to express it in English,"[4] scores of commentators have added their own inventions, discover-

2. Steven Pinker, *The Language Instinct: How the Mind Creates Language*, p. 373. The passage appears in the chapter "The Language Mavens," a deft skewering of the contemporary state of a tradition by which "the manuals tried to outdo one another by including greater numbers of increasingly fastidious rules that no refined person could afford to ignore." Similar terrain is covered, more sedately and with an emphasis on written English, by Williams in *Style*, chapter 10.

3. Robin Tolmach Lakoff, *Talking Power: The Politics of Language* (New York: Basic Books, 1990), p. 289.

4. Robert McCrum, William Cran, and Robert MacNeil, *The Story of English* (New York: Viking, 1986), p. 129; see also *DEU*, s.v. "preposition at end."

ies, and pet peeves to the list of acts that an educated writer dare not commit. Sometime in the mid–nineteenth century, for example, the taste-masters decided that infinitives were no longer to be split in the King's and Queen's English because Latin infinitives, consisting of a single word, could not be split.

Thus as you gingerly tiptoe around the landmines that dot the prescriptive-descriptive battlefield, you will encounter dozens of "rules" that were never really rules, just the personal preferences or prejudices of someone bold enough to proclaim them to be rules. Despite what may have been drilled into you (or one of your authors) in high school, all of the following taboos are routinely broken (even scoffed at) by well-respected writers and editors and by experts in contemporary American usage:

> Never begin a sentence with *and, but, or, also,* or *however.*
> Never end a sentence with a preposition.
> Never split an infinitive.
> Never use *which* to refer to an entire preceding clause.

But maybe I don't know what I'm talking *about. Or* perhaps my sole intention is to *further* addle your brain by breaking the rules, *which* would be a despicable betrayal of your trust. *However,* even if you should happen to feel betrayed, it is now time for us to confront the vexatious creatures one by one.

SUBJECT-VERB AGREEMENT

The textbook statement of subject-verb agreement seems simple enough: A singular subject takes a singular verb, and a plural subject takes a plural verb. According to the professional grammarians, however, there are three, sometimes competing, principles of subject-verb agreement in modern English: formal agreement, notional concord, and attraction (or proximity).

Formal (or grammatical) agreement is the fancy name for the textbook rule just stated: A singular subject requires a singular verb, and a plural subject requires a plural verb. But not all subjects neatly proclaim themselves to be singular or plural, and in some situations the overt grammatical form of the subject conflicts with our sense of the intended meaning. In these cases, we tend to discard formal agreement and rely on notional concord, selecting the verb that matches the meaning, not the overt grammatical form:

> Fifty pages of manuscript are sitting on his desk.

> Fifty pages of manuscript is a day's worth of work.

Grammarians have also observed that certain constructions "sound right" to educated native speakers of English, even though the constructions defy formal or notional agreement. Such constructions exemplify the principle of attraction (or proximity), under which the verb tends to take the form of the closest subject:

> For those who attended the second day of the annual meeting, there was an early morning panel and afternoon workshops.

But as *DEU* cautions, "Proximity agreement may pass in speech and other forms of unplanned discourse; in print it will be considered an error" (s.v. "agreement, subject verb: the principle of proximity").

An elementary principle of subject-verb agreement is that it is the grammatical subject that determines the number of the verb. Nouns that appear in the predicate have no bearing on the number of the main verb—with the one disputed exception discussed at paragraph 25 below. Thus the following sentence is correct:

> The only sign of Christmas was the stockings on the mantel.

The singular verb "was" is needed because the subject of the verb—"the only sign of Christmas"—is singular; the "stockings" are irrelevant because they are in the predicate of the sentence. Note that the given sentence is not an inversion of "The stockings on the mantel were the only sign of Christmas." In that version, "the stockings" is the subject and "the only sign" is in the predicate.

The following paragraphs summarize the twenty-five most prevalent perplexities and controversies in subject-verb agreement; for a detailed discussion and more examples, see the several entries under "agreement, subject-verb" in *DEU*. One day, however, despite all your diligence, you will meet a sentence that sounds wrong no matter which verb form you use. A bit of rewriting can rescue you: Select a verb that has the same form in the singular and the plural—for example, an auxiliary verb *(can, may, might, should, will)* or a past tense verb other than *was* or *were.*

1. *And.* A pair of singular nouns joined by *and* requires a plural verb, with two exceptions:

(a) Appositive nouns joined by *and* are treated as singular.

> Such an injustice and inequity is intolerable.

(b) Nouns joined by *and* to form a collective idea or unitary whole are singular.

> Bacon and eggs is her favorite breakfast.

Notice, too, how *and* may be used in an elliptical construction:

> Consumer and business confidence remain high.

Here, "remain" is plural, even though "confidence" is singular, because the subject is "consumer [confidence] and business confidence." To use a singular verb would imply that there is an entity known as "consumer and business confidence."

2. *As well as.* Prescriptive grammar handbooks treat a pair of singular nouns joined by *as well as* as singular, but descriptive analyses show that usage is mixed. The best advice comes from *DEU* (s.v. "as well as"): When a singular verb sounds better, use commas to set off the *as well as* phrase. When the plural verb sounds better, do not set off the *as well as* phrase.

> For copyeditors, a style manual, as well as a dictionary, is useful.

> A style manual as well as a dictionary are always on his desk.

3. Collecting noun phrase. In recent years, the notionalists have gained the upperhand: Collecting noun phrases usually take a plural verb, although they may take a singular verb when the collecting noun (rather than the items being collected) imposes itself as the main idea.

> A host of competitive offers have been received.

> A fraction of the students are causing the disruptions.

> A rash of glitches has [*or* have] slowed production.

> A set of keys is on the desk.

A few staunch formalists, however, hold out for the singular in all cases.

4. Collective idea. The notionalist view is the norm: No matter the grammatical form a collective idea takes, it requires a singular verb.

> Do you think that three cars is enough for one family?

> Eight hundred words is at least a hundred words too long for this summary.

> A physician's overarching objective and mission is to do no harm.

5. Collective noun. Collective nouns (e.g., administration, class, committee, couple, jury, majority, management, population, staff, team) are singular when the members of the collectivity are deemed to be acting as a group, plural when the members are acting as individuals.

> The couple is in therapy.

> The couple disagree about money.

When the plural sounds unnatural, the sentence should be revised.

> *Awkward:* The orchestra are tuning their instruments.

> *Preferable:* The members of the orchestra are tuning their instruments.

6. *Combined with; coupled with.* Phrases headed by *combined with* or *coupled with* are set off by commas and do not affect the number of the main verb.

> The recent divestiture, combined with rising costs, is expected to affect profits.

> The recent divestiture, coupled with rising costs, is expected to affect profits.

If the singular sounds awkward, the sentence should be revised.

> The recent divestiture and rising costs are expected to affect profits.

> The recent divestiture as well as rising costs are expected to affect profits.

The recent divestiture, combined with rising costs, should affect profits.

We expect the recent divestiture, coupled with rising costs, to affect profits.

7. *Each.* The pronoun *each* takes a singular verb, even when its antecedent is plural.

    Each reflects a different view of what constitutes the good life.

    The two sides are deadlocked in negotiations, and each has offered few concessions.

    When the adjective *each* follows a plural noun, the verb is plural.

    We each are entitled to our own opinions.

8. *Each of* is usually followed by a singular verb, although the plural is sometimes used.

    Each of these arguments is well reasoned.

    Each of these principles have stood the test of time.

9. Fractions. In such constructions as "two-thirds of x," the verb agrees with x.

    Two-thirds of the work is done.

    Two-thirds of the guests are here.

10. Inverted word order. Although the verb precedes the subject, the subject determines the number of the verb.

    In the employee handbook is a sample expense voucher.

    Also in the handbook are procedures for submitting expense vouchers.

11. Money. Amounts of money are singular when a specific sum is named, plural when the sum is vague.

    Eighty-five dollars is too high. Seventy-five dollars is a fair price.

    Billions of dollars were wasted, and millions are unaccounted for.

12. *Neither . . . nor.* Formalists insist that a pair of singular nouns joined by *neither . . . nor* is singular.

> Neither the president nor the secretary was at the meeting.

But notionalists allow the pair to be treated as singular or plural, depending on the emphasis desired.

> Neither the president nor the secretary were at the meeting.

13. *None of.* When the noun following *none of* is singular, the verb is singular. When the noun following *none of* is plural, either a singular or a plural verb is acceptable.

> None of the work was finished.

> None of the workers are here.

> None of these books seems [*or* seem] appropriate for this course.

14. Nouns ending in *-ics. Acoustics, economics, mathematics, physics, politics,* and *statistics* are singular when referring to a subject or field of study; otherwise, they are plural.

> Economics is a dismal science, politics a dismal craft.

> These statistics look incorrect. His politics are distasteful. The acoustics are excellent.

15. *Number.* "The number of *x*" takes a singular verb; "a number of *x*," a plural verb.

> The number of magazines devoted to technology is increasing.

> A number of magazines devoted to technology are available.

16. *One in* x. Formalists recommend a singular verb, arguing that "one" is the subject.

> One in two marriages ends in divorce.

Notionalists allow for a singular or a plural verb.

> One in nine Americans lives in California.

> One in five children are not covered by health insurance.

17. *One of those* x *who.* Formalists insist on a plural verb, arguing that "those *x*"—not "one"—is the subject of the verb.

> Mlynar, one of the few non-Russians who know Grachev well, denies the report.

Notionalists hold out for a singular verb.

> Mlynar, one of the few non-Russians who knows Grachev well, denies the report.

This controversy rages on, leaving authors and copyeditors free to use either verb—and sure to be condemned by someone no matter which verb they use.[5]

18. *One or more* x. The expression *one or more* always takes a plural verb.

> One or more files are missing.

> One or more of these reports are out of sequence.

19. *Or.* A pair of singular nouns joined by *or* almost always takes a singular verb.

> Heavy editing or rewriting is not needed.

On rare occasions, however, the intended meaning requires a plural verb.

> His presence or absence are irrelevant to the proceedings.

20. Percentages. After the construction "*x* percent of *y*," the verb is singular if *y* is a singular noun or a collective noun, and the verb is plural if *y* is a plural noun.

---

5. William Safire ("On Language," *New York Times Magazine,* July 6, 1997, p. 12) reports having received a one-word note ("Ouch!") from William F. Buckley in response to a column he wrote that began " 'Conduct unbecoming an officer and a gentleman' is one of those phrases that sounds as if it comes out of Kipling." Safire spots the problem: "The ouchifying word was the verb *sounds.*" Soon, a second message arrived, this one from Alistair Cooke, who homed in on "as if it comes out of Kipling." In Cooke's view, Safire's sentence should read " 'Conduct unbecoming an officer and a gentleman' is one of those phrases that sound as [it would sound] if it came out of Kipling." Safire apologizes at length for both of his offenses, but he does not question the nature of this game of "Gotcha!" To wit, if Safire, who has for decades written a weekly column on language, did not catch himself in the act of breaching subject-verb agreement, and if his copyeditor at the *New York Times* didn't spot the "error" either, then perhaps the Rule is not inviolable, but just a matter of preference.

Thirty percent of her practice is devoted to tenant law.

Forty percent of the town's population is illiterate.

Eighty percent of older voters are undecided.

After the phrase "a large percentage of *z*," the verb is singular when *z* is a singular or a collective noun, plural when *z* is plural.

Because of faulty handling, a large percentage of food is wasted.

A large percentage of the electorate has registered absentee.

A large percentage of voters have registered absentee.

21. *There is, there are.* In the constructions *there is* and *there are,* the verb agrees with the anticipated subject.

There is nothing we can do.

There are many ways to approach the problem.

22. Time. The singular verb is used when referring to a period of time.

Thirty minutes is too long a commute.

Five years is now the average "time to degree" for under-graduate students.

The 1950s is often regarded as a golden age for television.

23. Titles of works. Titles of works always take a singular verb.

Dickinson's *Selected Poems* is a fine introduction to her work.

24. *Variety. Variety* is singular when preceded by the definite article, plural when preceded by the indefinite article.

The variety of magazines is astonishing.

A variety of magazines are available.

25. *What.* The misconception is that *what* always requires a singular verb, but this is not the case. When *what* is the subject of the main verb, the copulative verb immediately after *what* is singu-

lar, but the main verb in the sentence agrees with the predicate noun.

> What is needed is a simpler way to estimate production costs.
>
> What impresses our clients is innovation and cost-effectiveness.
> [Here, "innovation and cost-effectiveness" is a collective idea; see paragraph 4.]
>
> What troubles us are the frequent cost overruns.

When *what* is the object of the main verb, problems arise only when the predicate noun is plural.

> What the company has done is laudable.
>
> What the directors are asking for is [*or* are] new policies on overtime.

In this last example, usage is divided, and some writers and copyeditors prefer to finesse the issue by revising the sentence.

TROUBLESOME VERBS

Table 24 lists common irregular verbs that sometimes cause trouble. Of the irregular verbs, perhaps *lay* (the transitive verb meaning "to place something down") and *lie* (the intransitive verb meaning "to recline") cause the most difficulties. A useful mnemonic is to hear the long "a" sound in *lay* and *place* and the long "i" sound in *lie* and *recline:*

> Lay (place) the book on the table.
>
> If you're tired, lie (recline) down for a while.

Notice that even though "Now I lay me down to sleep" is referring to the act of reclining, the verb in this sentence is transitive—the direct object of "lay" is "me."

Once you've sorted out the transitive and intransitive verbs, be sure to use the correct past tense:

> He laid the book on the table before he lay down.
>
> I had lain in bed for an hour before falling asleep.

TABLE 24. Principal Parts of Common Irregular Verbs

Base Form	Past Tense	Past Participle
bear	bore	borne
begin	began	begun
bid (to command)	bade, bid	bidden, bid
dive	dived, dove*	dived
drink	drank	drunk
fit	fitted, fit	fitted, fit
forbid	forbade, forbad	forbidden
forgo	forwent	forgone
get	got	got, gotten
hang (a picture)	hung	hung
hang (a person)	hanged	hanged
lay (to place)	laid	laid
lead	led	led
lie (to recline)	lay	lain
lie (to falsify)	lied	lied
prove	proved	proved, proven
rise	rose	risen
shine (to emit light)	shone	shone
shine (to polish)	shined	shined
sink	sank	sunk
sneak	sneaked, snuck†	sneaked, snuck
spring	sprang, sprung	sprung
strive	strove, strived	striven, strived
swim	swam	swum
weave	wove, weaved	woven, weaved

*DEU: "Dive is a weak verb with the past tense dived. In the 19th century it developed a past tense dove—probably by analogy with drive, drove. . . . Although dived is somewhat more common in writing in the U.S. and is unusual in British English, dove is an acceptable variant." The past tense of nose-dive, however, is always nose-dived.

†In a usage note (s.v. "sneak"), M-W Collegiate observes that "snuck has risen to the status of standard and to approximate equality with sneaked."

The verbs *may* and *might* also cause some confusion because they crisscross in several situations.

Might is the past tense of *may*.

We feared that we might have to postpone the project.

Might is a polite alternative to *may* in the present tense.

Might I be of some assistance?

Both *might* and *may* are used to describe unlikely future events, with *might* denoting less certainty.

Due to bad weather, the flight to Toronto may be delayed, and it might be canceled.

Might have is used to denote a counterfactual past event (that is, an event that did not take place).

He might have won the election, had he been a better debater.

The company might have shown a profit last quarter, had the price of oil remained low.

May have is used to denote a speculation about a past event.

He may have won the election; the absentee votes are still being counted.

The company may have shown a profit last quarter; we are awaiting the earnings report.

A handful of other verbs sometimes cause trouble, not because they are irregular but because they have cousins. About some look-alike pairs, there are no usage disputes: No one has proposed that *precede* may be used to mean *proceed,* or that *absorb* and *adsorb* are synonymous. But the use and misuse of the following verbs are hotly contended.

Assure/ensure/insure. Copyeditors, especially in the business and financial services sectors, are usually expected to enforce the traditional distinctions among these words. To *assure* is to "alleviate doubt"; to *ensure* is to "make certain that"; and to *insure* is to "cover by insurance." Thus:

Your broker will review your portfolio quarterly to ensure that it continues to meet your investment goals. However, we can offer no assurances about the short-term performance of your portfolio. If you are concerned about market volatility, you may wish to consider investing in an FDIC-insured savings account.

Nonetheless, it is worth noting the following comment in *M-W Collegiate* (s.v. "ensure"):

> ENSURE, INSURE, ASSURE, SECURE mean to make a thing or person sure. ENSURE, INSURE, and ASSURE are interchangeable in many contexts where they indicate the making certain or inevitable of an outcome, but INSURE sometimes stresses the taking of necessary measures beforehand, and ASSURE distinctively implies the removal of doubt and suspense from a person's mind.

Compose/comprise. Wilson Follett's summary (*MAU,* s.v. "compose, comprise") neatly illustrates the distinction at issue:

> The whole comprises the parts;
> The parts are comprised in the whole;
> The whole is composed of its parts;
> The parts compose the whole.

In this schema, *compose* is a synonym for "constitute," and *comprise* a synonym for "include," "embrace," or "take in." According to *DEU,* however, *comprise* has been used since the late eighteenth century to mean "constitute," and this denotation did not come under attack until the early twentieth century. Yet *M-W Collegiate* rightly cautions those who would use *comprise* to mean "constitute" and suggests that they "choose a safer synonym such as *compose* or *make up*" (s.v. "comprise"). Burchfield predicts that the frequency with which *comprise* is used as a synonym for *compose* "seems likely to take it out of the disputed area before long" (*New Fowler's,* s.v. "comprise").

Flaunt/flout. To *flaunt* is to display ostentatiously; to *flout* is to show contempt and disregard for. Thus one flaunts one's wealth and flouts another's rules. However, according to a usage note in *M-W Collegiate* (s.v. "flaunt"), *flaunt* has acquired a second meaning—"to treat contemptuously"—which "undoubtedly arose from confusion with *flout* [and yet] the contexts in which it appears cannot be called substandard." Muddying the waters a bit is the following observation in *DEU* (s.v. "flaunt, flout"):

> All [usage commentators] regard the use of *flaunt* to mean "flout" as nothing less than an ignorant mistake. Many of them also note with dismay or astonishment that . . . it occurs even among the well-educated. . . . Nowhere is there the least suggestion, however, that its common occurrence among the highly educated makes it at all defensible. Even those commentators who are relatively liberal in other matters take a hard line when it comes to *flaunt* and *flout.* . . .

It is an oversimplification, however, to say that the use of *flaunt* to mean "to treat with contemptuous disregard" is merely the result of confusion. Certainly this sense originated from confusion of *flaunt* with *flout*, but those who now use it do so not because they are confused—they do so because they have heard and seen it so often that its use seems natural and idiomatic. . . .

Nevertheless, the notoriety of *flaunt* used for *flout* is so great, and the belief that it is simply an error is so deep-seated and persistent, that we think you well-advised to avoid it, at least when writing for publication.

And avoid it copyeditors do.

Lend/loan. In figurative expressions, only *lend* will do: "Lend me your ears" or "Lend me a hand." In literal expressions, both verbs are acceptable, although *lend* tends to be the choice in more formal writing, probably because *lend* is the inevitable choice in contemporary British English. (See *DEU,* s.v. "loan, lend," on how *loan* fell out of use in England after the seventeenth century and is now regarded by the British as an Americanism, and by some misinformed Americans as nonstandard.)

SPLIT INFINITIVES

Most language experts label the prohibition against splitting an infinitive (that is, allowing a word to come in between the *to* and the verb) a bugaboo, but they advise writers and editors to continue to enforce the ban because readers expect them to do so. As noted earlier in this chapter, the fetish seems to have sprung from the desire that English emulate Latin, and Latin's one-word infinitives are, by nature, unsplittable.

Copyeditors may choose one of two paths. The safer is to ascertain whether the author is a pro-splitter or an anti-splitter and to respect the author's preference. The riskier path is to try to educate the anti-splitter in those cases when the refusal to split an infinitive produces an unclear or ungainly sentence. For this purpose, citing the following authorities may prove useful. First, you could show your author a page or two from Theodore Bernstein's *The Careful Writer.* Bernstein offers several instances in which splitting is preferable, even if one is an anti-splitter by nature:

1. When avoiding the split infinitive produces ambiguity. "The Thanksgiving Day setback was sure to defer further American hopes of keeping pace

with the Soviet Union in lunar exploration." Does "further" modify "defer" or "hopes"? All would be clear if it read "to further defer." . . .

2. When avoiding the split infinitive is almost impossible. "Rumania's Communist rulers expect the nation's industrial output to more than double in the next five years"; "The Governor has decided to all but give up on his minimum wage bill"; "He refused to so much as listen to the prisoner's appeal."

3. When avoiding the split infinitive produces clumsiness or artificiality. . . . "The Premier proceeded to admonish sharply the ten die-hard Opposition speakers." A reader can only wonder why "sharply" is in that position. Another unnatural placement: "The objective is apparently almost to double coffee consumption in the Soviet Union in the next three years." Only fear of the taboo prevented these writers from saying the natural things: "to sharply admonish" and "to almost double."

. . . When an infinitive contains an auxiliary—a part of the verb *to be* or *to have*—even the most hair-splitting anti-infinitive-splitter does not contend that an adverb cannot stand before the main verb. Complete sanction is given to such a construction as "His aim in life was to be constantly improving." (pp. 426–27)

The second authority you could bring to bear is Wilson Follett, long regarded as among the most conservative of modern authorities. Invoking Henry Fowler, who is even more revered by the prescriptive set, Follett goes several steps beyond Bernstein:

Long before Fowler's defense of splitting, [George Bernard] Shaw had delivered the controlling opinion: "Every good literary craftsman splits his infinitives when the sense demands it. I call for the immediate dismissal of the pedant on your staff (who chases split infinitives). It is of no consequence whether he decides to go quickly or to quickly go." (*MAU*, s.v. "split infinitive")

SUBJUNCTIVE MOOD

Obituaries for the subjunctive date from the late eighteenth century, according to *DEU* (s.v. "subjunctive"), and at least one linguist has concluded that "English has no subjunctive," only special uses of the base forms of verbs ("Heaven help us" and "I demand this be discussed") and special uses of *was* and *were* ("If I were king").[6] Be that as it may, most usage and grammar handbooks recommend that careful writers be attentive to the subjunctive mood,

---

6. Frank Palmer, *Grammar* (Middlesex, England: Penguin, 1971), pp. 195–96.

and these manuals use "subjunctive mood" to describe the *be* in "be that as it may" and in "recommend that careful writers be attentive."

FORMS OF THE SUBJUNCTIVE

The feeling that the subjunctive has all but disappeared in modern English (or that it does not exist at all) in part reflects the fact that the subjunctive forms are hard to spot. For all verbs except *be*, the subjunctive forms differ from the indicative forms only in the third-person singular:

Present indicative	*Present subjunctive*
I go	I go
you go	you go
he goes, she goes	he go, she go
we go	we go
they go	they go

Thus the subjunctive is noticeable in "We recommend that he go alone" but invisible in "We recommend that they go with him."

For the verb *be*, the situation is more complicated. First, the present subjunctive differs from the present indicative in all persons. Second, *be* is the only verb to retain what most grammarians call a subjunctive past tense (though, as we will see, the uses of this tense have everything to do with uncertainty and counterfactuality and nothing to do with the past). The forms are

Present tense		*Past tense*	
INDICATIVE	SUBJUNCTIVE	INDICATIVE	SUBJUNCTIVE
I am	I be	I was	I were
you are	you be	you were	you were
he is, she is	he be, she be	he was, she was	he were, she were
we are	we be	we were	we were
they are	they be	they were	they were

Some grammar books also use the term *subjunctive* to describe the appearance of *should* (the past tense of *shall*) and *would* (the past tense of *will*) in dependent clauses that state future or hypothetical events:

They doubt he would ever go alone.

They wondered if he should go alone.

But other grammarians categorize such *should*s and *would*s as past-tense indicative forms that are enlisted as auxiliary verbs in expressions of future conditional events.

USES OF THE SUBJUNCTIVE

The subjunctive appears in various set phrases, phrases so formulaic that their subjunctiveness usually passes unnoticed:

The public be damned	Far be it from me	Lest it be thought
Heaven forbid	Come what may	Be that as it may
The devil take him	Heaven help him	If need be

These phrases are so fixed (some say "fossilized") that they do not cause native speakers any problem.

A second use of the subjunctive also causes few problems. The subjunctive is required in *that* clauses following verbs of command, demand, suggestion, recommendation, wish, request, or necessity.

The director insisted that he audition for the role.

The senator urged that the vote on the amendment be postponed.

The defense asked that the witness be excused.

I wish [that] I were on vacation now.

This committee recommends that the board adopt the plan before the end of the year.

It is imperative that the meeting begin at once.

Third, the subjunctive form *were* (the so-called past tense of the subjunctive) may be used in dependent clauses expressing a condition of uncertainty in the future. Here, matters of nuance and tone come into play:

Subjunctive: If he were to take this case, how many hours would it require?

Indicative: If he takes this case, how many hours will it require?

The subjunctive emphasizes the uncertainty of the condition, because readers will silently add the implicit qualification: We read "If he were to take this case" and supply the tacit "which is not to say that he will, but *if* he were." The subjunctive *were* also conveys a more formal tone than does the unadorned indicative.

The final use of the subjunctive is the one that causes careful writers and copyeditors the most grief. The principle is, Use the subjunctive form *were* to emphasize that a condition is contrary to fact or hypothetical.

> She speaks as though he were out of the room.

> If Mexico were not just across the border from the United States, its domestic economy would be even more troubled.

> Many small businesses would face bankruptcy if Congress were to revise the tax laws.

When no special emphasis on the counterfactual or hypothetical quality of the statement is desired, the indicative is often used.

> The debate over the land permit could be resolved if there was a consensus about the value of mixed-use zoning.

> Many small businesses will face bankruptcy if Congress revises the tax laws.

Much of the confusion concerning this last use of the subjunctive results from the mistaken assumption that most clauses introduced by *if* are contrary to fact and therefore might benefit from a subjunctive. This is not at all the case. For example, when an *if* clause introduces a condition that has not yet come to pass, an indicative verb is mandatory:

> If each employee is informed of company policy on e-mail, there are likely to be few complaints.

> If her calculations are correct, the project will come in under budget.

An *if* clause may also express a condition whose truth or falsity is unknown, and in this case, too, the indicative is called for:

> She did not answer when asked if she was in favor of the restrictions.

> But if he is not responsible for the error, who is?

> We wondered if she was aware of the deadline.

And when an *if* clause refers to a condition in the past whose truth or falsity is unknown (in the grammarians' jargon, "a real past possibility"), the indicative is used:

> If he was aware of her plans, he knew nothing of the details.

Nor do *as if* and *as though* always transport us to the realm of the counterfactual:

> Doug looks as though he is ill. *Or:* Doug looks as if he is ill.
>
> Wendy looks as though she were ill. *Or:* Wendy looks as if she were ill.

The indicative form *is* in the sentences about Doug convey the writer's belief that Doug is ill, but the subjunctive form *were* in the sentences about Wendy express the writer's observation that Wendy looks sickly even though she is not ill.

DANGLING PARTICIPLES

There is no dispute about the impropriety of dangling one's participles, yet some days you will find dangling participles everywhere you turn, even in manuscripts by able writers. Because this class of errors is so prevalent, every copyeditor needs to develop a special alertness. The problem arises when a sentence begins with a clause that contains a participle—with the exception of the absolute participles discussed below—and the subsequent independent clause does not begin with the subject that is doing the action denoted by the participle. For example:

> ✗ While writing the memo, the phone rang and interrupted me.

Here, the phone is doing the writing as well as the ringing. One remedy is to provide the correct subject for "writing" in the opening clause:

> While I was writing the memo, the phone rang and interrupted me.

A second remedy is to begin the independent clause with a subject capable of performing the writing:

> While writing the memo, I was interrupted by the phone ringing.

[On "the phone ringing" versus "the phone's ringing," see the final paragraphs of "Case of Nouns and Pronouns" later in this chapter.]

Similarly,

✗   Although watched by 25.8 million viewers, the program's ratings disappointed the advertisers.

Because it was the program, not the program's ratings, that was watched by millions of viewers, the sentence should read:

Although the program was watched by 25.8 million viewers, the ratings disappointed the advertisers.

Dangling is inevitable when the independent clause begins with "there is [are]" or "it is":

✗   Relieved of responsibility for the Woodrow project, there is no reason for us to delay the end-of-quarter review.

Again, one solution is to introduce the correct subject in the first clause:

Now that we have been relieved of responsibility for the Woodrow project, there is no reason for us to delay the end-of-quarter review.

Another solution is to rewrite the independent clause:

Relieved of responsibility for the Woodrow project, we have no reason to delay the end-of-quarter review.

Dangling is also inevitable when the independent clause is headed by a verb:

✗   Having been reprimanded for tardiness, buying a clock was her first priority.

One solution is to add a subject that will serve as the subject for both verbs in the sentence:

Having been reprimanded for tardiness, she made buying a clock her first priority.

Another solution is to place the subject in the first clause:

> Because she had been reprimanded for tardiness, buying a clock was her first priority.

And dangling is almost inevitable when the independent clause is in the passive voice:

> ✗   Driving down the street, the Empire State Building was seen.

The solution is to change the passive construction into an active one and supply an appropriate subject:

> Driving down the street, we saw the Empire State Building.

The absolute participles pose an exception to the anti-dangling rule. Because absolute participles function as prepositions or adverbs, they do not have a grammatical subject.

> *Regular participle:* Given a block of wood and a knife, he carved a small deer.

> *Absolute participle:* Given the limits of this plan, the alternative proposal seems more practical.

> *Regular participle:* Based in Boston, CanDo Corporation is poised to expand throughout New England.

> *Absolute participle:* Based on her report, the panel approved the director's request.

The most common absolute participles are:

according	based [on]	excepting	granting
acknowledging	beginning	excluding	including
admitting	conceding	failing	judging
allowing	concerning	following	leaving
assuming	considering	given	looking
barring	depending	granted	owing

| provided | reading* | regarding | taking‡ |
| providing | recognizing | speaking† | viewing |

* In expressions such as "reading from left to right."
† In expressions such as "broadly speaking."
‡ In expressions such as "taking into account."

DANGLING AND MISPLACED MODIFIERS

A similar stricture against dangling applies to sentences that begin with modifying phrases. The noun that heads the second clause must be the element that is being modified by the phrase in the first clause. For example:

✗   Unlike meat or poultry, the federal government does not inspect fish.

True, the federal government is unlike meat or poultry, but this should read "Unlike meat or poultry, fish is not inspected by the federal government" or "Fish, unlike meat or poultry, is not inspected by the federal government." Similarly:

✗   With one hundred years of experience, you can count on Sears.

On hearing this advertisement, "you" (or I) can only say, "Sorry, Sears, I don't have one hundred years of experience."
Four more out-of-joint sentences, for good measure:

✗   As a scientist, his laboratory is his home away from home.

✗   Fresh out of law school, finding a job was difficult for Kim.

✗   With the broadest range of cellular calling plans, no one serves you better than PhoneCo.

✗   A former general who revels in the image of blunt-spoken maverick, the latest criticism was especially stringent, even for Mr. Clippard.

Misplaced modifiers are not always located at the head of a sentence, however:

✗   This novel is a haunting tale of deception, sexual domination, and betrayal by one of South America's most important writers.

✗   Neonatologists seldom see healthy babies once they begin their subspecialty training.

✗   The Century Building has been reincarnated after years of disuse as a beautiful bookstore.

✗   Both prosecutors and defense attorneys will present jurors with evidence.

✗   They are editing a national newsletter for parents of teenagers based in Seattle.

The common modifier that causes the most trouble is *only*. The general rule is to place the *only* directly before the noun, adjective, or verb it is to modify. Each of the following sentences, for example, has quite a different meaning:

Only CanDo Company works to serve the interests of its client.

CanDo Company works only to serve the interests of its client.

CanDo Company works to serve the interests of its only client.

Language experts agree, however, that this general rule must yield to idiomatic expression:

I can only try to explain the problem.

She only thought she was being helpful.

Their newest offer can only be called an insult.

Also, the meaning of a sentence changes when *only* comes in the final position. Compare:

The experiment was conducted only yesterday.

The experiment was conducted yesterday only.

A final example of a pitfall in the placement of modifiers:

The copyeditor who can do this well deserves praise.

Did you read this sentence as "who can do this well" or as "well deserves praise"? A copyeditor's job is to make sure that readers don't have to face such choices.

PRONOUN-ANTECEDENT AGREEMENT

Like subject-verb agreement, pronoun-antecedent agreement relies on what appears to be a straightforward principle: Every pronoun must have a clear, unambiguous antecedent and must agree with that antecedent in gender and in number.

During the 1990s, however, a revolution occurred in the treatment of pronouns whose antecedents are indefinite pronouns, such as *everyone* and *anyone*. Through the 1980s most grammar and usage books insisted on "Everyone took his seat." The rationale was that *every*one and *any*one were incontrovertibly singular, that therefore the subsequent pronoun must be singular, and that the correct singular pronoun was the third-person male pronoun (the so-called generic *he*). A few well-respected voices pointed to the illogicality of the singular,[7] and gradually more voices objected on the grounds of gender bias. ("Everyone registered for the postpartum self-care course should bring his partner to the first class"?)

The tide has now turned, and the newer grammar books recommend using the plural pronoun after an indefinite subject: "Everyone took their seat." "Everyone should bring their partner to the first class." To assuage those who denounce this construction as a new barbarism, *DEU* (s.v. "everybody, everyone") notes that the use of plural pronouns in reference to indefinite subjects has a four-hundred-year history in English literature and that the pluralizers are in the majority in Merriam-Webster's files of twentieth-century citations. *Chicago* 14 recommended "the 'revival' of the singular use of *they* and *their*," citing "its venerable use by such writers as Addison, Austen, Chesterfield, Fielding, Ruskin, Scott, and Shakespeare" (pp. 76–77, note 9). *Chicago* 15 and 16 half-reversed course, repudiating the singular *they* but allowing an indefinite pronoun that "carries a plural sense" to serve as a plural antecedent: "nobody could describe the music; they hadn't been listening to it" (section 5.64 in both editions).

A final twist on the topic is provided by Steven Pinker, who in effect makes the problem vanish by explaining that

---

7. Jacques Barzun, never accused of being permissive, argued the point as early as 1946: "It seems clear that good sense requires us to say 'Everybody took their hats and filed out.' . . . If *everybody* aren't plural now, it's high time they were"; in "Mencken's America Speaking" [1946], reprinted in *A Word or Two Before You Go . . .* (Middletown, Conn.: Wesleyan University Press, 1986), p. 162. (We'll look at "their hats" versus "their hat" in a moment.)

everyone and *they* are not an "antecedent" and a "pronoun" referring to the same person in the world, which would force them to agree in number. They are a "quantifier" and a "bound variable," a different logical relationship. *Everyone returned to their seats* means "For all X, X returned to X's seat." The "X" does not refer to any particular person or group of people; it is simply a placeholder that keeps track of the roles that players play across different relationships. . . . The *their* there does not, in fact, have plural number, because it refers neither to one thing nor to many things; it does not refer at all. (*The Language Instinct*, pp. 378–79)

For copyeditors, however, "everyone . . . they" is sure to remain a sticky wicket. Some authors will denounce the construction as barbaric, and a copyeditor has little to gain (and much to lose) by attempting to impose the newest old fashion on a reluctant author. Conversely, those copyeditors who are discomfited by the construction—the authorities' blessing notwithstanding—are advised to keep their preferences to themselves when they encounter an author who embraces the construction. Copyeditors who find this use of *they* distasteful need not use it in any documents they write, but it's not cricket to impose this preference on authors who view linguistic change as a virtue, not a vice.

Among the other pronoun-antecedent pitfalls that await the unwary, the most obvious is a pronoun whose intended antecedent is absent:

> *AWOL antecedent:* The governor described his health-care proposal to an enthusiastic crowd of banner-waving supporters. It was one of the best-attended campaign rallies of the year.

Readers will intuit that the "it" at the start of the second sentence is supposed to refer to the rally. But looking backward from "it," the closest singular noun is the "enthusiastic crowd," and the desired antecedent, "rally," is nowhere to be found.

> *Revision:* The governor described his health-care proposal to an enthusiastic crowd of banner-waving supporters at one of the best-attended campaign rallies of the year.

> *Or:* The governor described his health-care proposal to an enthusiastic crowd of banner-waving supporters. This campaign rally was one of the best attended of the year.

An unanchored *this* at the start of a sentence often invites confusion:

Unanchored pronoun: During June consumer prices rose sharply, unemployment declined, but wages remained flat. This has perplexed some economists.

The reader is left to wonder how broadly to interpret this sentence-opening "this." Are the economists perplexed only by the last item in the list (flat wages) or by the simultaneous occurrence of flat wages, lower unemployment, and rising consumer prices? To avoid such ambiguities, careful writers and copyeditors add a noun after a leading *this* to name the desired referent:

Revision: This trio of indicators has perplexed some economists.

Or: This unexpected combination has perplexed some economists.

When the subject is a corporation or other group, writers sometimes shift between treating the organization as a singular and treating it as a plural:

Shifting pronouns: Today IBM announced that it would be ready to ship its new line of computers by February 1. Citing pent-up demand, weak competition, and a falling dollar, they are predicting strong sales in the European market.

It is usually best to treat a corporation as a singular subject and to reword clauses in which "it" cannot serve as the subject:

Revision: Today IBM announced that it would be ready to ship its new line of computers by February 1. Citing pent-up demand, weak competition, and a falling dollar, company executives are predicting strong sales in the European market.

Many writers avoid *one,* feeling it is overly formal. When *one* does appear, British grammarians insist that the subject *one* always be followed by the pronoun *one:*

British style: One is entitled to do as one likes as long as one does not betray one's promises.

But American grammarians advise us to avoid an endless train of *ones* and either turn to *he* or recast the sentence:

> *American style:* One is entitled to do as he likes as long as he does not betray his promises.

> *Or:* We are entitled to do as we like as long as we do not betray our promises.

> *Or:* People are entitled to do as they like as long as they do not betray their promises.

A final logical conundrum is related to pronoun-antecedent agreement and remains insolvable:

> It was a horrible dream. I saw a roomful of people, each of whom was picking their nose and shouting at their spouse.

Some grammarians follow Follett (*MAU*, p. 235) and reject "their nose" and "their spouse" because, they explain, not everyone in the room shares the same nose and spouse. But, the counterargument runs, the plural "their noses" and "their spouses" would suggest that some or all of these people have more than one nose and one spouse apiece: "To avoid ambiguity a singular noun is often used with a plural possessive when only one of the things possessed could belong to each individual" (*WIT*, 3d ed., p. 357).

CASE OF NOUNS AND PRONOUNS

Case refers to the form of a noun or pronoun that indicates its function in a sentence:

> The nominative case is used for the subject of a verb and for a predicate noun.
> The objective case is used for the object of a verb and for the object of a preposition.
> The possessive (or genitive) case indicates ownership (my hat), origin (my offer), or purpose (girls' shoes).

The case forms of nouns present few problems (see "Possessives" in chapter 5).

Singular

NOMINATIVE	OBJECTIVE	POSSESSIVE
boy	boy	boy's
girl	girl	girl's
child	child	child's

Plural

NOMINATIVE	OBJECTIVE	POSSESSIVE
boys	boys	boys'
girls	girls	girls'
children	children	children's

The pronouns, however, sometimes cause difficulties.

	Nominative	*Objective*	*Possessive*
Personal	I	me	my, mine
	you	you	your, yours
	he	him	his
	she	her	her, hers
	it	it	its
	one	one	one's
	we	us	our, ours
	they	them	their, theirs
Indefinite	everyone	everyone	everyone's
	somebody	somebody	somebody's
Relative	who	whom	whose
	whoever	whomever	whosever
	which	which	whose, of which[8]
	that	that	—

8. Theodore Bernstein, *The Careful Writer*, p. 479: "Since *which* has no genitive of its own, it is only fair to let it borrow *whose* when the loan is useful to avoid clumsiness. It is nonsense to compel one to write, 'The car, the carburetor, brakes, and steering wheel of which need overhauling, is to be sold at auction.' . . . And never forget that banner 'whose broad stripes and bright stars' have inspired us all these many generations."

Here are the headaches. First, a pair of sentences that are correct, however awkward they may sound:

This experiment will put your and my hypotheses to the test.
[Correct, although "your hypotheses and mine"—or "your hypothesis and mine" if each person has only one hypothesis—would sound more natural to most readers.]

A group of us taxpayers protested.
[The objective case is needed because the pronoun is the object of the preposition "of."]

Since being correct is only half the goal, it is perhaps best to revise.

Revision: Our taxpayers' group protested.

Or: Our taxpayers group protested.
[This second revision treats "taxpayers" as an attributive noun rather than as a possessive; see "Possessives" in chapter 5.]

The appearance of *who* and *whom* at the head of a subordinate clause often sends writers into a tizzy. The rule is straightforward: When *who* introduces a subordinate clause, the correct case of *who* depends on its function in that subordinate clause.

Smith is the candidate who we think will win.
[We think *he* will win (nominative case) → the candidate *who* we think will win.]

Jones is the candidate whom we hope to elect.
[We hope to elect *him* (objective case) → the candidate *whom* we hope to elect.]

This book offers sound advice to whoever will accept it.
[In the subordinate clause "whoever" functions as the subject of "will accept." The object of the preposition *to* is the entire clause "whoever will accept."]

Take a moment to make sure the antecedent of the *who* or *whom* is secure:

A leading American scholar on the Pilgrims, who lived in the Dutch town of Leiden before setting out for America in 1620, has been ordered to leave the Netherlands.

[The "American scholar" competes with "the Pilgrims" as the antecedent of "who."]

Now for two disputed usages, the first relatively minor. Grammarians disagree about which case should follow the expression "everyone but." As Bernstein points out, the *but* in "everyone but" may be regarded as a conjunction (and therefore followed by a pronoun in the nominative case) or as a preposition (and therefore followed by a pronoun in the objective case). Bernstein's advice neatly splits the difference:

> 1. If the pronoun is at the end of the sentence, regard *but* as a preposition and put the pronoun in the objective case ("Everyone laughed at the quip but him"). Not only is this grammatically acceptable, but in addition it sounds inoffensive since normally a [pro]noun at the end of a sentence is in the objective case. 2. If the pronoun appears elsewhere in the sentence, put the pronoun in the same case as the noun to which it is linked by the *but* ("Everyone but he laughed at the quip"; "The quip, directed at no one but him, fell flat"). (*Miss Thistlebottom's Hobgoblins,* p. 93)

The second disputed usage arises from the fact that a gerund is usually preceded by a possessive noun or pronoun.

May's singing is atrocious.

The staff objected to his having made a change in the agenda.

This rule is not invariable, however; witness the following examples: "without a shot being fired," "long odds against that happening," and "Imagine children as young as twelve years old being haled into court!"[9] And there's a further wrinkle: Although the *-ing* forms that function as gerunds are preceded by possessive pronouns, the *-ing* forms that function as verbal participles are preceded by objective pronouns. Fortunately, Strunk and White come to the rescue with a pair of sentences that elucidate this mystery:

> Do you mind me asking a question?
> Do you mind my asking a question?

9. Bernstein, *Miss Thistlebottom's Hobgoblins,* p. 104. Rebutting Fowler's insistence that the genitive always precedes the gerund, Bernstein writes: "In the clause 'Which will result in many having to go into lodgings,' [Fowler] suggested making it *many's,* and in the sentence 'It is no longer thought to be the proper scientific attitude to deny the possibility of anything happening,' he favored altering it to *anything's.* The suggested changes can hardly be called English."

In the first sentence, the queried objection is to *me,* as opposed to other members of the group, putting one of the questions. In the second example, the issue is whether a question may be asked at all. (*Elements of Style,* p. 13)

Fowler labeled the "me asking" construction a *fused participle,* and abhorred it. Follett devoted two double-column pages to the topic and issued what remains the definitive opinion: "Whenever the idea that governs the verbal noun (participle) is one that clearly calls for stress on the person, the fused participle may be used; whenever the stress falls equally well, or better, on the action expressed by the participle, the possessive case must be used" (*MAU,* p. 158).

PARALLEL FORM

The terms in a series are said to be parallel when they all belong to the same part of speech; that is, each member in the series is a noun, a verb, an adjective, or an adverb:

✗   She likes swimming, playing tennis, and to run marathons.

She likes to swim, play tennis, and run marathons.

Or: She likes swimming, playing tennis, and running marathons.

✗   The passive voice may be used either for variety or to emphasize the activity accomplished, rather than the agent who accomplished it.

The passive voice may be used either to achieve variety or to emphasize the activity, rather than the agent who accomplished it.

Parallelism, however, does not require that all the items in the series be identical in length or structure. In the following examples, the items are parallel (they are all nouns), even though some are one-word nouns and others are noun phrases:

She spent her vacation reading, writing letters in French, and lying on the beach.

The documents must be checked for spelling, punctuation, and the correct use of abbreviations.

When *or* enters the picture, parallel structure alone may not ensure clarity:

> Critics of Internet filtering devices question whether they are appropriate shields against offensive material or high-tech censorship.
> [The writer wants to oppose "appropriate shields" and "high-tech censorship," but the syntax suggests "shields against offensive material" as opposed to "shields against high-tech censorship."]

In complex sentences, the preference for parallelism is sometimes relaxed. *DEU* (p. 434) offers the following example, from an essay by E. B. White, a well-respected English prose writer and co-author of *The Elements of Style:* "I have written this account in penitence and in grief, as a man who failed to raise his pig, and to explain my deviation from the classic course of so many raised pigs. The grave in the woods is unmarked, but Fred can direct the mourner to it unerringly and with immense good will." To insist on schoolbook parallelism here—to have Fred directing mourners "without error and with immense good will" or "unerringly and cheerfully" or some such—would be to distort the meaning and mar the dignity of the moment. Nor is there any way to force "and to explain" into line with what precedes it.

ADJECTIVES AND ADVERBS

We are usually taught that *adjectives* are words that modify a noun or pronoun, and *adverbs* are words that modify an adjective, verb, or another adverb. The circularity of the latter point aside (an adverb is a word that modifies an adverb?), these schoolroom definitions ignore the so-called copulative verbs— verbs that express a state of being, rather than an action; for example: *be, become, feel, seem, smell, sound, taste.* Although an adverb is used to modify a verb expressing an action, a copulative verb is followed by an adjective:

> I am fine; he became sad; she feels bad; they felt ill; you seem happy.

> This fish smells bad; the band's new song sounds good; the soufflé tastes delicious.

> Identical twins may look different, sound different, and walk differently.
> [*Walk* is not a copulative verb, so an adverb is required. For euphony, change the final item to "have different ways of walking."]

Some verbs may be used in both a copulative and a noncopulative sense:

Copulative: She looked happy.

Noncopulative: She looked happily at the page proofs of her first novel.

Copulative: He felt hesitant.

Noncopulative: He felt hesitantly for his keys.

The copulative-noncopulative distinction is one of the issues in the multiple controversies concerning the pairs "feel good" and "feel well," "look good" and "look well," and "feel bad" and "feel badly." These disputations are too tortuous to even summarize here; excellent guidance is provided by the lengthy entries in *DEU* (s.vv. "feel bad, feel badly" and "good").

The adjectives and adverbs whose comparative and superlative forms are irregular (e.g., bad, worse, worst; little, less, least) cause few problems. Rather, difficulties tend to arise with some of the regularly formed comparatives and superlatives. When in doubt, consult your dictionary. The typical forms are:

Base form has one syllable
   large, larger, largest
   soon, sooner, soonest
   Exception: Base is a participle:
     lost, more lost, most lost
     told, better told, best told

Base has two syllables ending in an unstressed *-y* or *-ow*
   early, earlier, earliest
   narrow, narrower, narrowest
   Also: Un- forms of these bases
     unhappy, unhappier, unhappiest

Other base forms
   difficult, more difficult, most difficult
   efficiently, more efficiently, most efficiently

There are also disputes about whether certain adjectives and adverbs are absolute (that is, they cannot be used in the comparative or the superlative and cannot be modified by the intensifier *very*). As *DEU* points out (s.v. "absolute adjectives"), most adjectives and adverbs do not lend themselves to comparison or intensification, and each generation of usage experts proposes its list based on its notions of semantics and logic. Today, the most controversial of the adjectives are *perfect* (at which point someone always cites the "more perfect union" promised by the U.S. Constitution) and *unique*. As to the former, *DEU* (s.v. "perfect") cites many examples of "more perfect" and "most perfect" and notes that it has been "in respectable use from the 14th century to the present." As to the latter, *DEU* (s.v. "unique") notes that the meaning "one of a kind," which invites the label of absolute adjective, is not the sole meaning of the term. *Unique* also means "distinctive" or "unusual," and these meanings certainly admit comparison and intensification.

A final problem related to adjectives and adverbs arises from the fact that neither "adjectiveness" nor "adverbiality" is a quality inherent to a word. *Home*, for example, may function as a noun ("This is our home"), as an adjective ("Taste our home cooking"), or as an adverb ("We went home"). Because nouns may function as adjectives (the technical term for a noun that modifies a subsequent noun is *attributive noun*), "government offices" is as correct as— and many would say preferable to—"governmental offices."

FEWER AND LESS

The schoolbook rule is: Use *fewer* for number and countable nouns; use *less* for quantity, measure, degree, and noncountable nouns. Thus, fewer apples, fewer books, and fewer cats, but less advice, less beef, and less comity.

DEU, however (s.v. "less, fewer"), notes that this "rule" was invented by Robert Baker, the author of *Reflections on the English Language* (1770): "Almost every usage writer since Baker has followed Baker's lead, and generations of English teachers have swelled the chorus. The result seems to be a fairly large number of people who now believe *less* used of countables to be wrong, though its standardness is easily demonstrated." The examples in *DEU* include "less than" preceding amounts (e.g., distances, sums of money, and units of time) and the constructions "no less than," "*x* objects or less," and "one less *x*." Here are a few other examples.

> Seasonal workers are usually employed less [*or* fewer] than 150 days a year.

[Either *less* or *fewer* is acceptable here, according to Follett (*MAU*, p. 151), because in this sentence "the ideas of quantity and number are hardly distinguishable. . . . Here *150 days* can be felt as either a specified number of days or a unitary measure of time (as *five months* or *less than half a year* would be).”]

Less than 75 percent of the electorate voted.
[The "75 percent of the electorate" functions as a noncountable noun.]

Fewer [*or* Less] than one in four voters requested absentee ballots.
[Here, "one in four voters" may be construed as either a countable number or a unitary amount.]

Your troubles are less [*or* fewer] than mine.
[Both locutions are acceptable, though not identical in meaning. "Your troubles are less than mine" means "Your troubles are not as great as mine," and "Your troubles are fewer than mine" means "Your troubles are not as numerous as mine.”]

PREPOSITIONS

The most memorable dismissal of the hobgoblin about never ending a sentence with a preposition is attributed to Winston Churchill: "This is the sort of English up with which I will not put." Although the superstition is still afoot in some quarters (see *DEU*, s.v. "preposition at end”), the more pressing issue for copyeditors is to ensure that the author has selected the correct preposition. In addition to consulting your dictionary, you might want to review the fourteen-page list "The Right Preposition" in *WIT* (3d ed.), which runs from "abashed: at, before, in" to "zeal: for, in."

Into and *in to.*   The preposition *into* is used with a verb of motion to indicate entry, insertion, or inclusion (movement toward the inside of a place). Thus one goes into a building, jumps into a lake, drives into a garage, and enters into a pact. *Into* is also used to indicate

involvement: check into the facts; take into account
occupation: go into teaching
condition: get into trouble, get into a fight
extent: far into the night

direction: look into the sky
contact: run into a wall
transformation: turn into a frog

In contrast, *in to* is the adverb *in* (an adverb because it "completes" the meaning of a verb, e.g., hand something in) followed by the preposition *to*, which links the verb to an indirect object:

They turned themselves in to the police.

He handed the memo in to his supervisor.

We refused to give in to his demands.

Onto and *on to.*   *Onto* is used to indicate movement to a position on or atop something: They ran onto the field; he wandered onto the grounds; the cat jumped onto the desk. *Onto* is also used to indicate attachment: Hook this wire onto the nail. And *onto* is used colloquially to mean "aware of": She's onto his methods; they're onto us. In contrast, *on to* is the adverb *on* followed by the preposition *to:* Please hold on to this; pass the news on to her; they flew on to London.

On line and *in line.*   All across the country people stand *in* line; but in the greater metropolitan New York area, people stand *on* line. Both expressions are acceptable. Manufactured items, however, are produced *on* an assembly line—never *in* one.

Due to.   Some traditionalists still parse *due to* as the adjective *due* followed by the preposition *to,* rather than treating *due to* as a compound preposition like *because of* or *owing to.* In the traditionalists' view, the adjective *due* must have a noun to modify, and thus *due to* is correct only as a substitute for *attributable to:*

The delays at the Denver airport were due to bad weather
in Chicago.

But this preference is largely ignored, and all but the most fastidious purists allow *due to* as a substitute for *because of* or *owing to:*

Planes were delayed at the Denver airport due to bad weather
in Chicago.

MISCELLANEOUS BUGABOOS

While. All dictionaries acknowledge that *while* has a temporal meaning ("during the time that" or "at the same time that"), a concessive meaning ("although"), and a contrastive meaning ("whereas"). *DEU* (s.v. "while") notes that although the earliest meanings of *while* are temporal, "senses unrelated to time have been established in English since Shakespeare's time." Nonetheless, some prescriptivists reject the use of *while* as a synonym for *although* or *whereas.* Follett's judgment is among the more vitriolic: "To tolerate *while* as a link between events patently not simultaneous is to misapply tolerance. . . . The mind accustomed to ignoring what *while* means will soon not respond to its true meaning in *One idles while the other works*" (*MAU,* p. 358).

But all the other experts agree with Burchfield (*New Fowler's,* s.v. "while") that the different uses of *while* "pose no threat to one another and are all part of the normal apparatus of the language." For copyeditors, then, the task is not to eradicate the concessive or contrastive *while* but to make sure that no ambiguity follows in its wake. Also, as Bernstein (*Miss Thistlebottom's Hobgoblins,* p. 85) points out, careful writers and editors reject the use of *while* to mean "and":

✗ The older computers have been moved to the basement, while the new ones are in the main office.

Since. English is also blessed with the temporal *since* and the causal *since:*

Temporal: Since 1990 the state has constructed twelve new prisons.

Causal: Since new prisons provide jobs, town officials courted the state prison commissioners.

Because *since* has these two meanings, some prescriptivists urge writers to shun the causal *since,* lest readers mistake a causal *since* for a temporal one. But banning the causal *since* deprives writers of a much-needed tool: a causal conjunction that is weaker than *because* and stronger than *as.* The sensible course is to avoid using *since* in sentences in which the temporal and causal meanings contend:

Ambiguous: Since the state has spent so much money on prisons, the education budget has suffered.

Ambiguous: Since the female prison population has doubled, the number of children in foster care has increased by 35 percent.

As.   Just as English has a bivalent *since,* so it has a bivalent *as,* and again some would banish the causal conjunction for the sake of the temporal one. Instead, writers should confine the weak-kneed causal *as* to sentences in which there is no possibility that readers will mistake it for the temporal *as:*

Temporal: As the overnight temperatures dropped, the road became icy and slick.

Causal: As Lila had no need for another hammer, she walked past the display without stopping.

Ambiguous: As the rain continued into the evening, Pat felt morose.

And because *as* is so weak an indicator of causality, it seems too lightweight when the cause-and-effect relation concerns a matter of any import:

Inappropriate: As the parts are no longer available, the entire unit has to be replaced.

Inappropriate: As the earthquake caused the double-decked freeway to collapse, new seismic-safety regulations are under discussion.

As and *like.*   In the 1950s a bit of a brouhaha erupted when a cigarette maker claimed that its product tasted "good, like a cigarette should" rather than "as a cigarette should." In the parsers' analysis, a conjunction must be used to link the clauses "Winston tastes good" and "a cigarette should," and the most punctilious parsers insisted that *like* was a preposition, not a conjunction. *DEU* (s.v. "like, as, as if"), however, notes that *like* has been used as a conjunction "for more than 600 years. . . . A noticeable increase in use during the 19th century provoked the censure we are so familiar with. . . . [Since then] the belief that *like* is a preposition but not a conjunction has entered the folklore of usage. . . . Be prepared."

If you don't want to make waves, you can apply the following conventions:

Use *as, as if,* or *as though* to express similarities or comparisons that involve a verb.

Mark the proofs as shown in the example.

We are pledged to upholding democracy, as were our forebears.

They sing as if they were angels.

He played the concerto as though possessed by the spirit of Stravinsky.

Use *like* to express similarities or comparisons that involve a noun.

This example is like the previous one.

They sing like angels.

His music is like Stravinsky's later work.

Cannot help but.   Follett approves of three idioms for expressing inevitability— "I cannot help doing it," "I cannot but do it," and "I can but do it"—but excoriates a fourth, "I cannot help but do it," as a "grammarless mixture" (*MAU,* s.v. "help"). Both grammar and logic, however, yield to idiom, as illustrated by the citations in *DEU,* which labels all four constructions standard (s.v. "cannot but, cannot help, cannot help but").

❖ 15 ❖

Beyond Grammar

There is no easy way to catalog all the types of structural, conceptual, and stylistic problems a copyeditor encounters. In this chapter, we'll look at how copyeditors handle common problems in four broad areas: organization, expository style, bias-free language, and publishing law.

ORGANIZATION

The overall structure of a piece (whether a report, an article, or a book) is dictated by its central purpose. As you read a manuscript, be sure you can discern the structure of the entire piece and each major section of the text. Look at the table of contents and the opening and closing paragraphs of each chapter (for a book), the headings and subheadings (for an article), or the opening sentences of each paragraph (for a short essay). Copyeditors are usually instructed not to fix large-scale structural deviations—doubling back, omissions—but are expected to bring them to the author's attention. Easily repaired minor structural errors should be corrected and flagged for the author's attention.

FORMS OF ORGANIZATION

Alphabetical order is useful for directories, inventories, glossaries, and catalogs. Note, however, that if the work is to be translated into another language, the alphabetized elements—with the exception of personal names—will have to be reordered. For example, the alphabetical sequence "England, France,

Germany, Spain" would have to be reordered as "Alemania, España, Francia, Inglaterra" when the document is translated into Spanish.

Chronological order is useful for historical studies, biographies, memoirs, and step-by-step how-to manuals. Within a broadly chronological framework, some biographers, historians, and memoirists incorporate flashbacks or flash-forwards. When used effectively, these out-of-sequence episodes can emphasize key points or create tension, drama, or suspense. The pitfalls, however, are that poorly handled flashbacks and flash-forwards may confuse the reader, deflate the narrative tension, or require the author to spend too much time backtracking or repeating information.

Numerical order can be used to organize analyses of alternative proposals or choices: from smallest to largest, from least expensive to most expensive (or vice versa).

Spatial order can be used to organize geographical surveys (from northeast to southwest), fashion books (from head to toe), and auto repair manuals (from front fender to back bumper).

Degree of difficulty is a principle used in many instructional books: the easiest topics are presented first, and succeeding sections build on those basic topics.

A *system-by-system* approach is often used for studies of complex physical organisms, social systems, or manufacturing processes and procedures. For example, a medical book might describe the circulatory system, the nervous system, the digestive system, and so on. A book on the federal government's role in ensuring free speech might have three principal parts: the executive branch, the legislative branch, and the judicial branch.

Short documents may follow the contours of the author's method of inquiry:

> *Compare and contrast.* After an overview of the subject or theme, the author points out the similarities and differences between A and B. The author then analyzes how or why A and B differ and explains the significance of those differentiating factors.
>
> *Observations and predictions.* The author describes the investigative methods (e.g., lab experiments, fieldwork, library research), presents the pattern of observations, offers an explanation for that pattern of findings, and explains the significance of that pattern or makes predictions based on that pattern.

Problem and solution. The author defines a problem, explains how the quantitative or qualitative dimensions of the problem were measured, describes a solution to the problem, and discusses how the solution resolved (or can be expected to resolve) all or part of the problem.

Argument. The author proposes a thesis and presents the data or reasons (usually from most important to least important) that support his or her point of view. Counterarguments may also be presented and disposed of.

Other arrangements are possible. For example, recipes in a cookbook can be arranged

in alphabetical order (from abalone to zucchini)
in diurnal order (from breakfast to after-dinner snacks)
in seasonal order (from springtime meals to wintertime meals)
course by course (appetizers, main dishes, salads, desserts)
by difficulty of preparation (from hard-boiled eggs to Beef
   Wellington)
by geographical provenance (from northern Europe to southern
   Europe and northern Africa)
by cooking technique (boiling, broiling, sautéing, pan frying)
by food groups (breads, meats, fruits, vegetables)

Sometimes an author's ordering principle is not transparent. For example, a discussion of the planets in our solar system may treat the planets in any of the following sequences:

A	B	C
Earth	Mercury	Jupiter
Jupiter	Venus	Saturn
Mars	Earth	Neptune
Mercury	Mars	Uranus
Neptune	Jupiter	Earth
Pluto	Saturn	Mars
Saturn	Uranus	Pluto
Uranus	Neptune	Mercury
Venus	Pluto	Venus

Obviously, sequence A relies on alphabetization. But only copyeditors who are astronomy buffs will immediately detect that sequence B presents the planets in order of their mean distance from the sun, from the closest to the furthest; and even most of that select editorial group is likely to be stumped by sequence C, which presents the planets in order of their period of rotation, from the shortest to the longest. The best editorial response to a set of items whose order appears random is to query the author ("What is the ordering principle here? Are these items in order?") rather than to assume that reordering is needed.

Items presented in lists, tables, and other arrays should also be in order, whether alphabetical, chronological, numerical, spatial, or according to some other scheme. For example, each of the following lists needs to be reordered.

Electoral votes (1996)		*Atlantic coastline (miles)*	
Alabama	9	Maine	228
Alaska	3	New Hampshire	13
Arkansas	6	Massachusetts	192
Arizona	8	Rhode Island	40
Colorado	8	New Jersey	130
California	54	New York	127

Since the list of states by electoral strength is alphabetical, Arizona must precede Arkansas, and California must precede Colorado. The list of North Atlantic coast states, however, does not appear to be intended as an alphabetical list. Rather, it seems that the author is following the coastline from north to south. Thus the copyeditor would request an entry for Connecticut (after Rhode Island) and move the entry for New Jersey down, after the entry for New York.

EMPHASIS

The major points in a piece should be emphasized by their prominent location and the length of their treatment. Relatively minor points should receive minor attention. Detours from the main points, dead ends, straw-man arguments (that is, weak points raised solely to be refuted), and irrelevant details should be severely restricted or eliminated.

Copyeditors should query minor infractions of these principles: "Paragraphs on semiconductors seem off the point here—consider moving (perhaps to p. 12), trimming, or deleting." If you encounter serious problems, consult your editorial coordinator before you spend time suggesting major structural changes.

In some types of texts, the issue of placement is more than a matter of logic or aesthetics. For example, in training or instructional materials that describe hazardous procedures, any warnings or precautions should precede— not follow—the description of the step to be taken.

> *Original:* Insert the probe into slot A (see diagram 2). Make sure the unit is unplugged before you insert the probe.

> *Revision:* Unplug the unit. Insert the probe into slot A (see diagram 2).

> *Or:* WARNING: Unplug the unit before you begin the following procedure.
> Insert the probe into slot A (see diagram 2).

CROSS-REFERENCES

Some kinds of documents require or benefit from cross-references that lead readers to look at (or recall) another part of the text. As noted in chapter 10, each table and figure in a document is given a number, and a cross-reference is placed in the text to direct the reader's attention to the item. Similarly, appendixes to a document are labeled (Appendix A, Appendix B, etc.) and introduced in the main body of the text by means of cross-references.

Cross-references may also be used to refer readers to chapters in a book or to numbered sections in a document. When copyeditors encounter such cross-references, they are expected to verify that each cross-reference is correct and to revise the cross-references if sections of text are relocated or cut during the editing.

Because cross-references by page entail extra work on the page proofs, some publishers strongly discourage, or even prohibit, authors from using such cross-references. The issue, of course, is that the correct page numbers cannot be inserted until the document is in final page form. At that time, the proofreader must locate all the placeholders for page-number cross-references (e.g., "see pages 00–00" or "see pages **II–II**"), replace the placeholders with the correct page numbers, and hope that no further repagination of the document will be made. So that the replacement of the placeholders will not require adding or subtracting characters from a line of text (and possibly producing bad line breaks, widows, or orphans), the thoughtful copyeditor tries to estimate the correct number of digits for each page-number placeholder. Thus if the cross-referenced page falls toward the end of a book-length manuscript, the placeholder should have three digits ("see page 000"), not one or two.

In some documents, cross-references by chapter may not be that helpful to the reader. If the chapters are long, for example, or if the cross-reference is only to a small portion of a chapter, a cross-reference by chapter number alone will not help readers locate the relevant section of text (especially if the document does not have an index). One way to provide for closer cross-references without using page-number references is to direct readers to a major heading within a chapter:

> The technical specifications are given in chapter 5, under "CPU Specs."

> For more information, see "Crossing the Frontier" in chapter 12.

Another way to provide for close cross-referencing without resorting to page-number references is to insert section numbers, or even paragraph numbers, in the document. For example, most cross-references in *Chicago* are of the form "see 6.24–27," where "6" is the chapter number and "24–27" are the section numbers. This system obviates the need for page-number placeholders but does require the rechecking of all cross-references if sections are cut or moved during copyediting or cleanup.

SIGNPOSTING

Good writers avoid too much signposting, phrases that refer backward or forward to other parts of the text. Although an occasional cross-reference can help the reader follow the thread of a complex argument or a long document, the use of unduly frequent or long signposts is dizzying, and copyeditors should help writers eliminate these cross-references.

> *Disorienting:* As we have seen in chapter 1 and will examine in more detail in chapters 4 and 6 . . .

> *Disorienting:* But this point is getting ahead of the argument, and we will return to it after we have laid the proper groundwork.

> *Disorienting:* Now that we have seen the three major causes of the citizens' discontent—high property taxes, poor municipal services, and unresponsive local officials—and the role of the two major grass-roots groups, the Community Action Caucus and the Citizens

Taskforce, we need to consider the relationship between local politics and regional issues.

Frequent thickets of signposts may also indicate faulty overall organization. In such cases, the solution is to recommend that the author consider reordering the pieces of the document to better serve the reader.

EXPOSITORY STYLE

As noted in chapter 3, there are several useful books on expository style, but most of them are, quite naturally, addressed to writers. For copyeditors, however, the task is not to develop one's own style nor to revise a manuscript to meet one's own taste. Rather, the task is to decide which kinks or knots in someone else's writing seem likely to disrupt communication with the intended readers and then to revise those patches as unobtrusively as possible.

These judgments are among the most difficult a copyeditor makes, and they require a careful assessment of both the author's purpose and intended audience. As long as a sentence is grammatically correct, for example, minor stylistic infelicities will not trouble or perplex most readers of a technical report or a business document, although a series of off-kilter sentences may confuse or distract all but the very determined. Readers of scholarly books and serious trade books, however, are likely to have higher standards and may dismiss the work of an author who disappoints their expectations.

Judgments about issues of style also require copyeditors to undertake a bit of self-examination. Before making discretionary changes to a manuscript, you might pause a moment to make sure that your proposed revisions are motivated by an effort to help the author improve the manuscript for the sake of the readers—not by a desire to prove that you are a better writer than the author is, not by the need to make every document conform to your tastes, and not by the fear that any sentence left unmarked will leave you open to criticism for not having high-enough standards.

For copyeditors, the perils of doing too much rewording often outweigh the hazards of doing too little: Every time you make a change, you run the risk of misinterpreting the author's meaning, introducing an inadvertent error, frustrating the author's goodwill, and overshooting your editorial schedule or budget.

The amount of time a copyeditor spends unkinking and unknotting sentences and paragraphs thus depends on the nature of the project and the level-of-edit instructions that accompany it. Here, we focus on common problems that can be corrected with minimal intervention.

DICTION

The standard advice on word choice is the Fowler brothers' five-part dictum: "Prefer the familiar word to the far-fetched, prefer the concrete to the abstract, prefer the single word to the circumlocution, prefer the short word to the long, and prefer the Saxon word to the Romance."[1] Many high school and college students encounter these preferences, converted into commandments, in Strunk and White's *The Elements of Style* ("Avoid fancy words"; "Use definite, specific, concrete language"; "Omit needless words"; "Use figures of speech sparingly"; "Prefer the standard to the offbeat") or in George Orwell's essay "Politics and the English Language."[2]

Unfortunately, some copyeditors take these proposals too seriously and enforce them with a self-defeating rigor. "Self-defeating" because the author who uses the occasional far-fetched word, abstraction, circumlocution, or polysyllabic Latinate term will question the judgment of a copyeditor who appears to be "dumbing down" the text. The goal for the copyeditor is not to eradicate every unusual or unnecessary word and thereby turn every sentence into a predictable procession of neat monosyllables. Rather, the goal is to identify those patches of text in which so many far-fetched, abstract, or polysyllabic words cluster that the reader either loses the thread of the discussion or questions the expertise, skill, or judgment of the writer.

Level of diction. A writer's word choices set the tone for a piece (formal, informal, colloquial). In general, slang and colloquialisms are suitable only in highly informal pieces, while sesquipedalian Latinisms are rarely appropriate out-

---

1. H. W. Fowler and F. G. Fowler, *The King's English,* 3d ed. (1931; reprint, London: Oxford University Press, 1973), p. 11.

2. Working from the premise that ridding ourselves of bad linguistic habits is the first step toward clear thinking and "political regeneration," Orwell proposes six rules:

  (i)   Never use a metaphor, simile or other figure of speech which you are used to seeing in print.
  (ii) Never use a long word where a short one will do.
  (iii) If it is possible to cut a word out, always cut it out.
  (iv) Never use the passive where you can use the active.

side of academic journals. However, a well-chosen word from a level that is noticeably higher or lower than the rest of the piece can add a touch of emphasis, realism, or humor. When an unimportant word calls too much attention to itself, however, a copyeditor may replace it or ask the author to select a substitute from a short list of synonyms.

Under the guise of making life easier for readers, some copyeditors change a word merely because they are unfamiliar with the word and had to look it up in the dictionary. This impulse seems misguided. Obviously, unusual words have no place in instructions for handling a toxic spill; emergency crews do not carry dictionaries to disaster sites. But for articles and books addressed to educated adults, there is no reason to restrict the author to some hypothetical list of five or ten thousand common words. As long as the word appears in the dictionary (abridged or unabridged) and the author has used it correctly, there's no reason for you to replace it. When copyediting books designed for young readers, however, you may be asked to restrict the vocabulary to a "grade-appropriate" list or to those words that appear in a particular abridged dictionary.

Jargon. Word choice also gives cues to the readers about the author's conception of them. Shop talk, jargon, and lingo should be reserved for publications aimed at a specialized audience that is familiar with the argot. When such terms are used in documents intended for a general readership—perhaps to give readers the flavor of conversation in the field—translations should be appended, either in parentheses or introduced by a "that is" or a "which means." At times, you will need to ask the author to supply a sentence or two that explains to lay readers the significance of the jargon. For example, the manuscript reads

> Some economists have revised their estimate of the NAIRU from 6 percent to as low as 5.3 percent.

If the piece is for a specialized audience, you might assume that readers will recognize NAIRU or you might ask the author to supply the spelled-out form

---

(v) Never use a foreign phrase, a scientific word or a jargon word if you can think of an everyday English equivalent.

(vi) Break any of these rules sooner than say anything outright barbarous.

"Politics and the English Language" (1946), in *A Collection of Essays by George Orwell* (New York: Doubleday Anchor, 1954), p. 176.

of NAIRU. But if the piece is for a general readership, you would ask the author both to spell out NAIRU and to add an explanation of what NAIRU is. In response, the author might offer the following:

> According to basic economic theory, low rates of unemployment put upward pressures on wages, and higher wages translate into higher rates of inflation. The healthiest economy, therefore, is one which has the lowest rate of unemployment that does not cause inflation to accelerate. Some economists have revised their estimate of this magic number, known as NAIRU (nonaccelerating inflation rate of unemployment), from 6 percent to as low as 5.3 percent.

Deadwood.   Some words and phrases add bulk, but nothing of substance, to the text. The occasional redundancy or circumlocution is fine and may even be commendable if it emphasizes a key point or provides a bit of relief in a patch of extremely dense text. But copyeditors should help authors prune brambles that obscure the meaning or force the reader to work too hard for too little gain.

Redundancies

adequate enough	major breakthrough
big in size	paramount importance
bisect in two	past history
close proximity	persist still
descend down	plan in advance
eliminate altogether	prejudge in advance
few in number	serious danger
final outcome	sufficient enough
follow after	total annihilation
habitual custom	trained professional
important essentials	violent explosion
joint cooperation	warn in advance

Circumlocutions

a large proportion of (= many)
are in possession of (= have)
at this point in time (= now)

in spite of the fact that (= although)
in the not too distant future (= soon)
in the vicinity of (= near)
in this day and age (= today)
made a statement saying (= stated, said)
put in an appearance (= appear)
take into consideration (= consider)
was of the opinion that (= believed, thought, said)
was witness to (= saw)

Notice, for example, what pruning can do for this brier:

> In spite of the fact that a large proportion of parents are at this point in time of the opinion that schools need trained professional nurses, there is a serious danger that funding for these jobs will be eliminated altogether in the not too distant future. [Forty-six words.]

> Although many parents believe that schools need nurses, funding for these jobs may soon be eliminated. [Sixteen words.]

The effort to prune deadwood, however, should never dissolve into knee-jerk deletion. Surely "methods that are new at this point in time" sounds better than "methods that are new now" or (gasp!) "the now new methods." Nor should a copyeditor insist that authors always avoid the copyeditor's pet-peeve phrases. Some copyeditors, for example, routinely strike the first two words of almost every "in order to" and delete any "that" that they believe is not absolutely required. While such practices are useful when space is at a premium, in most cases these deletions do not substantially improve the author's sentence. Worse still, although such tinkering may save a few millimeters of space, the resulting text can be confusing or ambiguous. For example, the following sentence is clear and correct:

> Congress modified the administration's proposal in order to exempt small businesses.

If a parsimonious copyeditor deletes the "in order," the meaning is ambiguous:

> Congress modified the administration's proposal to exempt small businesses.

In sum, you must continuously weigh the value of brevity against the value of clarity:

> The thoughtful writer strives not for mere conciseness, but also for ease of communication. Many of the little phrases that brevity buffs think unnecessary are the lubrication that helps to smooth the way for your message to get across. (*DEU*, s.v. "in order to")

Clichés.   Writers and copyeditors are always told to shun clichés, but this maxim is overly broad and unenforceable. The occasional cliché is almost unavoidable and does little harm; after all, set phrases become set because they are useful. (Why reinvent the wheel?) Moreover, a phrase that is a cliché to one clique of readers may seem fresh and vivid to another, if the expression has not yet migrated beyond the in-group into general circulation. Then, too, given the pace at which phrases become shopworn, even the diligent cliché stomper can barely keep up. The honest answer to the question "What is a cliché?" is either the tried-and-true "I know it when I see it" or the equally hackneyed "If it looks like a duck and quacks like a duck . . ."

Thus copyeditors should aspire not to eradicate every cliché but to curb the following common abuses of clichés. First, you should propose new wording to authors who too often turn to canned phrases or who try to put an awkward twist on a cliché: "one cannot see the proverbial forest for the trees" or "an exercise in pedagogical futility" or "a cog in an unforgiving machine."

Second, you should ensure that the author has chosen the correct cliché and has not inadvertently mangled the commonplace expression. "To go back to square one" (to start at the beginning) is not the same as "to stand at ground zero" (the target of a nuclear attack). And one does not "lift an eye" but rather "bat an eye" or "lift [or raise] an eyebrow." In the universe of clichés, the only place lines are drawn is in the sand; all opinions are considered or humble, and all plans are best laid; each swoop is fell, every end is bitter, and every peeve is pet.

Third, you should test to see if the sentence would be improved by the deletion of the deadwood part of the set phrase. For example, would the sentence seem more vivid if "vanish into thin air" were reduced to "vanish," "bewildering variety" to "variety," "built-in safeguards" to "safeguards," or "at first blush" to "at first"?

Fourth, because clichés are, by definition, ready-made, they are inappropriate in describing events of magnitude or gravity. The use of a commonplace at such a moment suggests that the author is an insensitive wretch, incapable of sincere emotion:

> Adding insult to injury, the first jolt of electricity to reach the condemned man was not strong enough to be fatal.

> Words fail to express the sights that greeted the soldiers as they entered the death camps.

Even in circumstances that are not matters of life and death, the predictability of a cliché undermines the authenticity of the idea being expressed.

> It goes without saying that our company will spare no effort to iron out the difficulties in our distribution procedures.

You should also be on the alert for incongruous clichés, which will elicit groans or chuckles from careful readers:

> The highway bill is water over the dam now, unless we can light a fire under Senator Snowe.

> In the rapid-fire debate, Jones's arguments in favor of gun control were right on target.

> In order for them to mend fences, they will have to escape the quicksand of inertia.

> If Jefferson were alive, he would be rolling over in his grave at this revisionist interpretation.
> [This formula has become popular, but if Jefferson were alive, why would he be in his grave?]

> This legislation is intended to level the playing field without leading us down the slippery slope of reverse discrimination.

Euphemisms.   Another class of words that writers and copyeditors have long been advised to avoid is euphemisms. Like the ban on clichés, the ban on euphemisms has merit, but applying it requires judgment and care, not ruthless slashing. Euphemism is an essential rhetorical tool that writers use to exert some form of "spin control." The Reagan White House floated "revenue enhancements" (for "taxes"), and the best-known euphemism of the 1970s, also from Washington, was the comment by Ron Ziegler, then President Nixon's press secretary, that certain earlier statements from his office were "inoperative" (that is, "lies"). One of the longest chains of euphemisms comes from corporate America, where employees have been terminated, laid off, riffed (from "reduction in force"), and downsized—but never fired—as a result of restructuring, re-engineering, or right-sizing.

It is easy to poke fun at political and bureaucratic euphemisms, but harder to answer the questions, Why all the fuss about euphemisms? What harm is done by a bit of sugarcoating? What difference does it make whether the trash is picked up by garbage collectors, refuse haulers, sanitation crews, or waste management engineers? What's wrong with an expression intended to spare us from offensive or unpleasant utterances? The issue for copyeditors thus becomes retaining those of the author's euphemisms that contribute to the author's purpose and deleting those that detract from it. The former category includes euphemisms sincerely intended to spare readers' feelings; the latter category includes euphemisms that readers will perceive as silly or deceptive and that will undermine their faith in the author's credibility.

Because framing the terms of an argument is crucial to making an argument, the line between euphemism and persuasive rhetoric is a fuzzy one. Compare the following two paragraphs, both of which discuss how the trade treaties NAFTA and GATT have affected employment, wages, and prices in the United States:

> The free-trade opportunities offered by NAFTA and GATT have enabled manufacturers to maximize productivity by relocating employment. This redeployment has, in turn, created redundancies in the more industrialized nations, which will provide substantial insurance against wage-driven inflationary spirals. Thus inflation should remain below 3% a year.

> In the wake of NAFTA and GATT, U.S. manufacturers have closed factories in the United States and moved their operations to low-wage enclaves in Mexico and Southeast Asia. The resulting high level of unemployment in the United States leaves American workers with no leverage in requesting cost-of-living increases. Thus the purchasing power of the average worker's wages will remain stagnant or will continue to decline.

Clearly, the first author wants readers to view NAFTA and GATT as wholly positive: The treaties provide opportunities, enable companies to maximize productivity, and offer substantial insurance against inflation. For the second author, NAFTA and GATT have been a disaster: Jobs have vanished; higher unemployment means that companies do not have to raise wages to attract workers, and those workers who have jobs feel insecure and are reluctant to demand higher wages; in the end, working people's wages barely keep up—or fail to keep up—with price increases.

As you might imagine, the first author will ignore a copyeditor who suggests replacing any of the pleasant terms with unpleasant ones ("layoffs," "unemployment," "wage stagnation"), just as the second author will ignore any suggestions to add a cheering sentence about the upside of flat wages, such as the prospects for low rates of inflation. To earn and maintain the goodwill of authors, you must respect the author's right to frame opinions and arguments in charged terms.

How euphemistic or how charged a statement should be, of course, depends on the purpose of the document and the intended readership.[3] Here a copyeditor may do the author a great service in pointing out wording that seems too euphemistic or too emotional or language that seems evasive rather than persuasive. Spin control and damage control may belong in the advertising, marketing, and public relations toolbox, but outside those domains most readers will resent feeling manipulated rather than informed.

Connotation.   Many words and phrases have shadings that are not precisely conveyed by their dictionary definitions. For example, although "thanks to" is a close cousin of "owing to," "due to," and "because of," any note of thank-

---

3. An example from politics. In 1997 residents of Houston who wanted the city to discontinue its affirmative action policy proposed the following ballot measure:

> The City of Houston shall not discriminate against or grant preferential treatment to any individual or group on the basis of race, sex, ethnicity or national origin in the operation of public employment and public contracting.

The mayor of Houston, who favored continuing the city's affirmative action policy, proposed a rewriting of the measure:

> Shall the Charter of the City of Houston be amended to end the use of preferential treatment (affirmative action) in the operation of the City of Houston employment and contracting?

In preelection polling, 68.1 percent of the respondents said they were for the first measure, but only 47.5 percent said they favored the second measure; Sam Howe Verhovek, "Houston to Vote on Affirmative Action," *New York Times,* November 2, 1997, p. 16, national edition. The proposition that appeared on the ballot was quite similar to the second version and was defeated (the yes vote was 45 percent).

fulness is inappropriate in a sentence about disaster: "Thanks to winter storms, the wheat harvest was ruined." Similarly, "eligible for" is a poor choice in "Though only sixteen, he is eligible for the death penalty"; rather, "he is subject to the death penalty."

Denotation.   Obviously, communication between a writer and a reader collapses when a writer uses a word that does not mean what the writer seems to think it means.[4] Common misuses that arise from homonyms are discussed in chapter 5. Other problems arise from incorrect assumptions about parts of words:

> *disinterested* does not mean "uninterested"
> *enervate* does not mean "stimulate the nerves"
> *fitful* does not mean "fit"
> *fortuitous* does not mean "fortunate"
> *fulsome* does not mean "full"
> *impracticable* does not mean "impractical"
> *inflammable* does not mean "not flammable"
> *noisome* does not mean "noisy"
> *sensuous* does not mean "sensory"
> *sinuous* does not mean "sinewy"
> *tortuous* does not mean "torturous"

Other problems arise from carelessness:

> *legacy* does not mean "inheritance"
> *aggravate* does not mean "annoy"
> *elicit* does not mean "evoke"

---

4. Remember Humpty Dumpty in chapter 6 of *Through the Looking-Glass:*

> [Humpty Dumpty] "There's glory for you!"
> "I don't know what you mean by 'glory,' " Alice said.
> Humpty Dumpty smiled contemptuously. "Of course you don't—till I tell you. I meant 'there's a nice knock-down argument for you!' "
> "But 'glory' doesn't mean a 'nice knock-down argument,' " Alice objected.
> "When *I* use a word," Humpty Dumpty said, in rather a scornful tone, "it means just what I choose it to mean—neither more nor less."
> "The question is," said Alice, "whether you *can* make words mean so many different things."
> "The question is," said Humpty Dumpty, "which is to be master—that's all."

"uncharted waters" are those that have not been mapped;
    they are not *unchartered*
"heartrending tales" *rend* (break) the heart; they do not *render*
    (extract fats and oils from) the heart
parameters does not mean "perimeters"
regretfully does not mean "regrettably"
respectively does not mean "respectfully"
temblors (not the nonword *tremblors*) cause the earth to tremble

And some arise from an oversimplified sense of a complex denotation:

anxious does not mean "eager" (any more than *anxiety* means
    "eagerness")
ironic does not mean "coincidental"

The list of malapropisms is endless. The sole recourse for a copyeditor is to be aware of the most commonly misused words and to double-check at every turn.

Rollercoastering.   Some writers have little sense of the physicality of words. Because they do not hear or feel the "under" in "underlie" or the "over" in "overcome," they do not perceive the rollercoaster movement in a phrase like "the underlying problem in overcoming poverty" or "this overemphasis on internal structure underlines fundamental problems," and they see nothing amiss in "over the long run, these short-term problems can be solved." Copyeditors should suggest revisions that are less disorienting.

Pet peeves.   Every copyeditor has at least a short list of words he or she simply detests. Among the words that raise the most hackles are the noun or verb *impact* when used to describe anything other than a car crash, the verbs *enthuse, liaise,* and *interface,* and nonce modifiers ending in *-wise* (*business-wise, spacewise*). The charges against these words range from "ugly and unnecessary—we already have a word for it" to "dreadful back-formation" and "corruption of the language by illiterate bureaucrats."

    When pressed, however, these rationales wobble and collapse. Why is a particular combination of letters or sounds any uglier than some other combination of letters or sounds? Since some of the beauty and utility of English derive from its wealth of synonyms and near synonyms, what's wrong with having a few more? And aren't back-formations also part of the richness of the language?

For authors, the matter is a simple one: Authors may freely exert their prerogative to banish whatever words they dislike. For copyeditors, however, the decision to banish an unlikable word should be based on something other than the copyeditor's own prejudices. Before you outlaw a word because *you* don't like it, do a bit of research in *DEU* or a trusted usage guide. You may find a sound argument for replacing a controversial word, or you might be persuaded to reconsider your bias against the word.

VERBS

Verbs are the muscle of a sentence. Strong writers let finite verbs—rather than participles and verbal phrases or adjectives and adverbs—do the work of the sentence. As the following examples show, when verbs convey the action, sentences become a bit crisper. By pointing an author to the correct verb, copyeditors can also rescue text that suffers from an overabundance of "is" and "are" or "was" and "were."

> *Weak:* The primary focus of this workshop is recent developments in computer scanning.
>
> *Better:* This workshop focuses on recent developments in computer scanning.

> *Weak:* This is a difficult problem that is going to require months of research.
>
> *Better:* This difficult problem will require months of research.

> *Weak:* This house is old and is in danger of collapsing during an earthquake.
>
> *Better:* This old house could collapse during an earthquake.

> *Weak:* Smith's report is a most valuable contribution to our understanding of hypoxemia.
>
> *Better:* Smith's report contributes greatly to our understanding of hypoxemia.

> *Weak:* The results of our field testing are that the new manufacturing process is more cost-effective than current procedures.

Better: Our field testing shows the new manufacturing process to be more cost-effective than current procedures.

Weak: There was a strong disagreement between the two sides over the estimate of damages.

Better: The two sides strongly disagreed on the estimate of damages.

Weak: Before the commencement of the program, there was a brunch served for the guests.

Better: Before the program began, the guests were served brunch.

Weak: After completing an inspection of the factory, the engineers still could not provide an explanation for the malfunction.

Better: After inspecting the factory, the engineers still could not explain the malfunction.

PASSIVE VOICE

Some well-meaning people have truncated Orwell's rule "Never use the passive where you can use the active" to "Never use the passive." But the passive voice has its place. The passive is the correct choice when the doer of the action is indefinite, unimportant, or unknown:

Fax machines are no longer considered a luxury in home offices.

Each panelist was identified by institutional affiliation and field of expertise.

No other problems were reported.

The passive is also preferable when the result of the activity is more important than the performer:

These statistics are drawn from thirty field tests.

Temperature and humidity readings were made at 9 A.M., noon, and 3 P.M.

Hundreds of dead seabirds were sighted near the oil spill.

Unpleasant messages are often framed in the passive:

Three hundred workers were let go, and dividend payments were cut.

However, the passive voice is wordy, and its use can create intentional or unintentional mysteries:

It has been determined that . . . [Who determined it?]

It has been alleged that . . . [Who made the allegation?]

Mistakes were made . . . [Who made the mistakes?]

For clarity and brevity, then, strong writers tend to prefer the active voice and reserve the passive voice for one of the purposes mentioned above or for the sake of cadence or variety. In turn, copyeditors are expected to help authors avoid the overuse or awkward use of the passive, but this effort should be tempered. For readers, the judiciously placed passive construction can provide welcome relief from an onslaught of sentences in the active voice.

SUBORDINATION

Copyeditors should query or revise strings of short sentences that sound like a grade-school primer:

Choppy: To initiate an action from a dialog box, click on a command button. The three command buttons are OK, Cancel, and Help. These command buttons are most often located at the bottom of the dialog box. Sometimes, though, they are located at the right border of the dialog box.

Decide which points are most important and subordinate the incidental details:

Revision: To initiate an action from a dialog box, click on a command button. The three command buttons—OK, Cancel, and Help—are located at the bottom of the dialog box or at the box's right border.

Here's a more complicated example of a string of sentences, each competing for the reader's attention because the writer has not subordinated any of the details:

Unfocused: The most recent study of local air pollution was performed by the Metropolitan Air Quality District (MAQD). The study was released on November 15, 1997. (A limited number of copies are available to professional researchers from local MAQD offices.) The MAQD documents provide detailed measures of the level of five airborne pollutants during the past ten years. The level of each of these pollutants has increased dramatically since 1987. In 1997 the daytime level of carbon monoxide in the downtown area exceeded federal standards on 165 days. (Daytime levels are taken at 1 P.M.)

How best to revise this passage depends on the paragraph's function in the document. The author must decide which point is most important: that the MAQD recently released a report on air pollution? that levels of five airborne pollutants have increased dramatically since 1987? that in 1997 the daytime level of carbon monoxide in the downtown area exceeded federal standards on 165 days? The choice of the key point will dictate the order of the sentences and the relocation, subordination, or elimination of minor points. The following revision focuses on the findings rather than on the administrative details:

> *Possible revision:* During the last ten years, the levels of five airborne pollutants increased dramatically in Metro City, according to a study released by the Metropolitan Air Quality District (MAQD) on November 15, 1997. In 1997 the midday level of carbon monoxide in the downtown area exceeded federal standards on 165 days.

UNTANGLING NEGATIVES

In general, positively worded statements are easier for readers to understand correctly than are negatively worded statements.[5] The interpretive difficulties caused by the use of *no* or *not* are compounded when a sentence includes negative verbs *(fail, disappear, decrease)*, negative modifiers *(poorly, inappropriate, ill-considered)*, or negative qualifiers *(unless, without, absent)*, and copyeditors should untangle these pretzels. For example:

> *Tangled:* Not all the students, but a majority, failed to turn in the assignment before the deadline.

> *Direct:* Less than half the students turned in the assignment before the deadline.

5. See E. D. Hirsch Jr., *The Philosophy of Composition,* pp. 93 and 150.

Or: More than half the students turned in the assignment after the deadline.

Tangled: Crime rates will not decline without a citywide effort to reduce poorly lit downtown streets.

Direct: To reduce crime, the city should increase lighting on downtown streets.

Tangled: You will not be charged your first monthly fee unless you don't cancel within the first 30 days.[6]

Direct: To avoid being charged a fee, cancel your service within 30 days.

But accentuating the positive doesn't require eliminating all clusters of negatives. For example, if an author labels an issue "not unimportant," a copyeditor should not substitute "important." There is more than a shade of difference between the two expressions.

VARIETY

Word choice.   Copyeditors should intervene when the quest for variety has led an author to create a passage that sounds like a transcription from a thesaurus.

> *Overwritten:* Students were asked to sketch a picture of their home. The subjects were given 3 minutes to complete these drawings of their residences. The test compositions were later analyzed independently by four professionally trained scorers. Subsequently, the four evaluators convened to reach a consensus assessment of each subject. [Only the fear of repeating "home" can explain the choice of "residences." More importantly, renaming the "trained scorers" as "evaluators" doubles the cast, although these refer to the same four people.]
>
> *Clearer:* Students were given 3 minutes to draw their home. The drawings were independently scored by four trained evaluators.

---

6. This statement appeared in an offer for a free thirty-day trial subscription to America Online; see *New York Times,* December 7, 1997, business section, p. 9.

After discussing the drawings, the evaluators provided a consensus assessment of each student.

Copyeditors should also intervene when the author's repetition of a key word becomes monotonous. In the following passage, the author packed seven *beginning*s and five *new*s into eighty-three words:

> *Monotonous:* We have just celebrated the Lunar New Year and the beginning of the Year of the Rat. It represents the beginning of a new year, but also the beginning of a new cycle, as the Rat leads the twelve-animal Chinese zodiac. This new beginning in Asia is symbolic perhaps of other noteworthy Asian beginnings. For example, the beginning of a new economic and interest rate cycle in Japan. Also the beginning of a mighty transition for China, involving Hong Kong and Taiwan.

An edited version features four *beginning*s and three *new*s; the word count is sixty-four.

> *Revision:* We have just celebrated the Lunar New Year and the beginning of the Year of the Rat, which also represents the start of a new twelve-year cycle in the Chinese calendar. Two other Asian beginnings are noteworthy: the beginning of a new economic and interest rate cycle in Japan, and the beginning of a mighty transition for China, involving Hong Kong and Taiwan.

Of course, the passage could be rewritten with only one *beginning* and one *new*, but the result sounds quite strained.

> *Overwritten:* We have just celebrated the Lunar New Year and the beginning of the Year of the Rat, which inaugurates the twelve-year cycle on which the Chinese calendar is based. Two other Asian commencements are noteworthy: the onset of another economic and interest rate cycle in Japan, and the start of a mighty transition for China, involving Hong Kong and Taiwan.

Sentence structure.   Good writers also try to provide some variety in the structure of their sentences. A copyeditor can offer suggestions to authors who go to one extreme (every sentence always begins with the subject) or the other (no sentence ever begins with the subject).

You must also be on the alert when the quest for variety leads an author to write a sentence that cannot be correctly deciphered on first reading:

> *Confusing:* Despite our relatively small sample, extensive observer evaluations, measures of self-perceptions, and the length of the study permitted us to obtain information that cannot be provided by epidemiological investigations.

Only when the reader reaches "permitted" is it clear that "Despite" governs only "our relatively small sample" and that "extensive observer evaluations, measures of self-perceptions, and the length of the study" are the factors that enabled the researchers to obtain valuable information. You might propose:

> *Revision:* Although our sample was relatively small, our use of extensive observer evaluations, measures of self-perceptions, and the length of the study permitted us to obtain information that cannot be provided by epidemiological investigations.

Sentence length.   A mistake many beginning copyeditors make is to use a word-count approach to sentence length, assuming that any noticeably short sentence is "too short" and that any noticeably long one is "too long." But word count alone is only one measure of the readers' perception of length. A sentence may have many words, but if these are arranged in well-structured phrases and clauses, readers will not complain that the length of the sentence interferes with their understanding of its meaning. Conversely, a short sentence whose meaning is opaque, its structure twisted, may leave readers at sea.

Copyeditors who take the cookie-cutter approach are thus robbing their authors of a valuable tool: the ability to control the readers' attention (even their breathing) by varying the lengths of their sentences to suit the task at hand. For many purposes, indeed, shorter is better. Each period gives the reader a split second to consolidate all the information in one sentence and prepare for the next. But this is not to say that shorter is always better. For when there are too many start-and-stop sentences in a row, some readers will feel that the author is blurting out tidbits of information rather than conveying well-shaped thoughts. Indeed, complicated concepts often require long sentences; to cut a complex idea into two short sentences is to leave the reader with two useless stubs, rather than a valid ticket.

Often the disagreeable aspect of a long sentence is less a matter of its length than of its overstuffed shape. In explaining this problem to an author, you can appropriate John Gardner's advice to fiction writers:

> As a rule, if a sentence has three syntactic slots [subject, verb, object], as in
>
>   1   2   3
>   The man walked down the road
>
> —a writer may load one or two of the slots with modifiers, but if the sentence is to have focus—that is, if the reader is to be able to make out some clear image, not just a jumble—the writer cannot cram all three syntactic slots with details. (*The Art of Fiction* [New York: Knopf, 1984], p. 105)

This notion of slots can also be used to explain a guideline for constructing long sentences: Although the most important information in a sentence usually belongs in the first slot, when that piece of information is very long, move it to the last slot.

> *Unbalanced:* The effectiveness of administering a ten-day regimen of penicillin for the treatment of complications arising from periodontal surgery is their current research topic.
>
> *Balanced:* Their current research topic is the effectiveness of administering a ten-day regimen of penicillin for the treatment of complications arising from periodontal surgery.

In sum, the interweaving of shorter and longer sentences is not a matter of mathematics nor of injecting variety for variety's sake. The subject matter, the intended readership, the rhythm and tone of the entire piece, the architecture of individual sentences and paragraphs, and the ebb and flow of emphasis—all these enter into decisions about sentence length.

TRANSITIONS

Traditionally, the sentence is described as the core unit of expository prose. The disadvantage of this concept is that a writer may construct lovely individual sentences, but the relationship of one sentence to the next may be unclear. A more useful approach is to view the core unit of composition as the chunk of text running from the last words of one sentence to the beginning of the next:

Lorem ipsum dolor sit amet. Consecteteur elit, sedianonummy nibh euismod dolor. Ut wisi ad minim ven iam, quis nostrud exerci. Duis autem vel eum iriure dolor.

This scheme reinforces the importance of making clear connections between one point and the next.

One way to specify the relationship between two consecutive sentences is to use a transitional expression:

further, in addition, also, moreover
first, second, third, last, finally
next, later, meanwhile, subsequently
similarly, in the same way, likewise
in contrast, yet, even so, alternatively
but, however, nevertheless, nonetheless, on the contrary
although, while
above all, in particular, indeed
accordingly, so
for example, for instance, in other words, that is
for this reason, for this purpose
as a result, in consequence, therefore, thus
in short, once again, to repeat
of course, surely, certainly, after all
in sum, as we have seen, on the whole, all in all

A second type of transitional device is repetition. The following sentences are held together by the repetition of key words and synonyms as well as by transitional phrases:

Inconsistencies can damage a writer's credibility. For example, readers are often confused by inconsistencies in hyphenation, such as "drop-down menu" versus "dropdown menu." When hyphenation is inconsistent or haphazard, readers will start to wonder whether the writer's inattentiveness extends to issues of content and accuracy.

Similarly, the repetition of pronouns can provide continuity.

Of course, all copyeditors like to read; no one who finds reading a tiresome chore would take up editorial work. Most copyeditors are also fascinated by language. They are intrigued by new words and unusual expressions. They enjoy debates about grammar and are as interested in an opponent's reasoning as in his or her solution to the problem at hand. Even in their spare time, they are often found playing word games.

PARAGRAPHING

Expository writers usually rely on medium-length paragraphs (say, 75 to 150 words), broken up by the occasional short paragraph. But conventions about the length of paragraphs vary from field to field, as well as among different types of publications. In newsletters or documents printed in two-column formats, short paragraphs predominate; in scholarly studies long paragraphs are quite common.

A very short paragraph here or there usually requires no editorial intervention. Nor does the occasional very long paragraph—unless the paragraph will seem truly monolithic when poured into a narrow-column format. More important than the mere length of a paragraph is whether the paragraphing facilitates or hinders comprehension. Sometimes the meaning will be clearer if short points are separated into brief paragraphs, and sometimes the meaning will be clearer if a long, complex point is not broken across two paragraphs. When clarity, rather than simple length, is at issue, copyeditors routinely reparagraph.

However, if a manuscript is plagued by paragraphs so brief as to suggest breathless thoughtlessness or if the text is beset by clumps of page-long paragraphs, reparagraphing every page may be quite time consuming, as well as a waste of your efforts. Ask your editorial coordinator for advice. The usual course in these cases is for the copyeditor to remind the author that paragraphs serve as useful guideposts for readers, to point out several spots that could benefit from either fewer or more paragraph breaks, and to ask the author to reconsider his or her original paragraphing while reviewing the editing.

CADENCE

For many expository writers and their copyeditors, cadence—the rhythm of sentences and paragraphs—is not of great concern. Novelists and essayists, of course, do care about the sound of their prose, as do some literary critics and historians, but technical writers, business writers, researchers, engineers, and the rest of the nonliterary workaday crowd do not. Nonetheless, copyeditors working on nonliterary materials should be alert enough to the sound of the text to catch the following types of infelicities: unintended rhymes, tongue-twisting consonant clusters, heavy alliteration, and overly dramatic rhythms.

TYPOGRAPHICAL DEVICES

Strong writers rely on diction, syntax, and content to convey the desired tone or emphasis in their sentences. Less confident writers, however, sometimes rely on typographical devices (italic or bold type, exclamation points, and quotation marks). Copyeditors are expected to reduce the visual clutter.

Italics and bold.   In running text, italics and boldface should be used sparingly to set off specific terms and phrases. Most publishers discourage the use of italics or boldface for entire sentences and paragraphs: Long passages of wavy italic type are often difficult to read, and large patches of boldface (or frequent small patches of bold type) look unattractive. In addition, when italics and bold are used in the running text as well as in headings, captions, and other display elements, the various typographical treatments compete for the reader's attention.

Exclamation points.   Only rarely are exclamation points needed in expository writing. (Novelists, letter writers, and playwrights, of course, are free to revel in them.) And no amount of emphasis or irony in expository prose calls for more than one exclamation point nor for an exclamation point preceded or followed by a question mark.

Quotation marks.   Quotation marks may be used for emphasis or irony, but copyeditors should curb authors who overuse this device.

All caps.   In running text, there is no call for individual words or phrases to be printed in all caps.

BIAS-FREE LANGUAGE

Copyeditors are expected to query or revise any material—text, diagrams, or photographs—that promotes stereotyping (based on sex, ethnicity, religion, age, or other group designation), that needlessly excludes groups of people, or that is insensitive to cultural differences. The principle here is not to censor authors who wish to enunciate "politically incorrect" views but rather to prevent authors from unwittingly offending, marginalizing, or excluding groups of people. For example:

> The pioneers crossed the mountains with their women, children, and possessions.

This sentence implies that only men are pioneers and that women and children are of a status roughly equivalent to possessions.

> *Revision:* The pioneers and their children crossed the mountains with their possessions.

> *Or:* The pioneer families crossed the mountains with their possessions.

In the following sentence, in contrast, a possession is accorded the status of a person (Deep Blue is a computer that plays grand master–level chess):

> Deep Blue sacrificed his bishop, but three moves later he could not avoid losing his rook to Kasparov's pawn.

For a computer, surely the pronoun "it" is preferable. Also, using "he" only reinforces the stereotype that competitive chess is a "man's world."

> *Revision:* Deep Blue sacrificed its bishop, but three moves later it could not avoid losing its rook to Kasparov's pawn.

A different kind of occupational stereotype is implied by

> The lives of rock musicians seem to involve a passion for money, women, and fame.

—which assumes that all rock musicians are either heterosexual men or gay women.

> *Revision:* The lives of rock musicians seem to involve a passion for money, sex, and fame.

Sports metaphors can add energy and color, but they may also make some women feel that they are not part of the intended audience:

> As an investor, you need to know your tolerance for risk. On fourth down and two, would you punt or pass?

> Every team leader dreams of making the Hail Mary pass or the three-point shot at the buzzer.

> An attorney must be able to read opposing counsel's strategy: Is the other side likely to call for a hit-and-run play or a suicide bunt?

Similarly, certain kinds of domestic imagery signal that women, and only women, are the intended audience:

> Beyond an understanding of anatomy and physiology, visiting nurses must have good interpersonal skills and not be afraid to let their maternal instincts show.

Some sentences, of course, concern subjects who are all of one sex:

> A mother-to-be is encouraged to bring her spouse to the lecture on prenatal genetic testing.

"Her" is the correct pronoun, but "spouse" implies that the only concerned partner a pregnant woman may have is a husband or wife. But some pregnant women are not in intimate relationships, others are in nonmarital relationships (with men or with women), and some married women—for various reasons—rely primarily on a family member or friend for support during their pregnancy.

> *Revision:* A mother-to-be is encouraged to bring a spouse, partner, family member, or close friend to the lecture.

In a lighthearted or personal essay, the following hyperbole would be unobjectionable.

> Like all the great ideas of our time, this one appeared unbidden one morning, in the bathroom, during the Zen-like satori brought about by the daily ritual of shaving.

Indeed, to raise any objection is to risk being labeled as humorless—the insult most often hurled at people who pose questions about biased language. But notice that this sentence attributes all the great ideas of our time to beardless men. In addition, satori (the state of intuitive enlightenment brought about through the practice of Zen Buddhism) is demoted to a "Zen-like" experience. (For comparison's sake, would one ever refer to immaculate conception as a "Catholic-like concept"?) If one wants to be precise, the "like" should modify "satori," not "Zen": "during the satori-like experience." And will those readers who have never experienced the daily ritual of shaving understand what aspect of this experience is satori-like? Is it the scraping of one's cheeks, chin, and throat with a sharp razor blade, the white-noise whirring of an electric razor, or the mindful mindlessness induced by a daily routine?

> *Possible revision:* Like all the great ideas of our time, this one
> appeared unbidden one morning, in the bathroom, during a
> moment of intuitive clarity brought about by the daily rituals
> that entail staring at your face in the mirror.

In medical manuals and reference books, in contrast, biased language can have serious consequences:

> Jaundice is fairly common in newborns and usually clears up within
> a week. After that, if your infant's skin looks yellow or greenish, call
> your doctor.

The question here is whether this skin-tone indicator is reliable for infants of all ethnicities, or whether the author has unintentionally excluded infants of color. A copyeditor should query: "Is 'yellow or greenish' a good indicator for nonwhite infants? If it is not, please supply another indicator."

At other times, biased language introduces illogicalities:

> The high school lunchroom is wholly segregated: No one ever shares
> a lunch table with any of the Vietnamese students.

What this author seems to want to say is that one never sees Vietnamese students and non-Vietnamese students at the same lunch table. Yet surely some of the Vietnamese students eat together, and so it is not true that "no one" shares a table with "any of the Vietnamese students." Inadvertently, the author has turned those Vietnamese students into "no one."

Revision: The high school lunchroom is wholly segregated: Students of different nationalities never share a lunch table.

Or: The high school lunchroom is wholly segregated: The Vietnamese students always eat at their own lunch tables.

In the following sentence, changing the Eurocentric "Oriental" (Asia is "the East" only if one is standing in Europe) to "Asian" marks a start:

Ms. Lin's Oriental background makes her an asset to our company.

Initial revision: Ms. Lin's Asian background makes her an asset to our company.

But Asia is a vast continent that includes many distinct cultures, and the sentence would also be more informative if it stated the specific skills or attributes that are valuable to the company—for example, Ms. Lin's fluency in Mandarin, her knowledge of Japanese history, her fieldwork in Indonesia, or her personal contacts in the Pakistani business community.

Despite the success of basketball and other competitive events for wheelchair athletes, one still encounters

Though confined to a wheelchair, Granger nonetheless writes at least five articles a year.

The first problem here is that wheelchairs are mobility aids, not prisons; users of wheelchairs are no more "confined" to their chairs than bicyclists are "confined" to their bikes, or motorists "confined" to their cars. Indeed, people who use wheelchairs say that it is when they are without their chairs—not when they are in them—that they feel confined. Second, the "nonetheless" implies that using a wheelchair is an obstacle to being a prolific writer—as though Granger's disability was located in his brain, not his body. Depending on the context, a copyeditor could propose relocating the mention of Granger's disability or, if Granger's health is irrelevant to the theme, deleting the wheelchair entirely.

DEFAULT ASSUMPTION

A second issue of concern is avoiding what has come to be called the "default assumption." Here, the writer identifies only those people who belong to some special category; people in the so-called majority pass unmarked. For example:

The jury includes five men and two African American women.

If the sex and race or ethnicity of the jurors are important, then the author should state both factors for each of the jurors; if race or ethnicity is not relevant, then the author should not identify any of the jurors by race. Then, too, unless this jury has only seven members, some of the jurors (the non–African American women) are unaccounted for.

The following sentence presents the careful reader with a conundrum:

The panel includes three professionals, two blue-collar workers, and two women.

Does this panel have five members (three professionals and two blue-collar workers, among whom are three men and two women) or seven members? By identifying some of the panelists by an occupational category and some by sex, the author bungles the count.

The next sentence may seem unremarkable:

The conference was chaired by a female aerospace engineer.

—until one considers that one would never see its counterpart ("The conference was chaired by a male aerospace engineer") in print.

Out of context, this next sentence also appears to demonstrate the default assumption (no mention is made of the physical health or abilities of the other team members).

The winning design was submitted by a team that includes an architect who is physically disabled.

But one cannot be sure until one has read the full account. If the design is for a new bridge across the Hudson River, then the team members' level of physical ability or disability is irrelevant, and this one architect has been singled out for mention solely because of his or her membership in a minority group. But if the design is for a plan to improve access to a library and the architect uses a wheelchair, cane, or braces, the architect's familiarity with the problems faced by people who use mobility aids (rather than his or her disability in general) may well be relevant.[7]

BIASED TERMINOLOGY

Copyeditors almost never encounter overt ethnic or racial slurs in manuscripts, but some authors will use derivative terms that may strike some readers as insensitive. Controversies abound: Are colloquial verbs like *gyp* and *welsh* (or *welch*) offensive? Do expressions such as *dutch treat, French letter,* and *Siamese twins* (scientists now use *conjoined twins*) promote stereotyping? Or are phrases objectionable only when they attribute negative characteristics to the named group: *Indian giver, French leave, Dutch uncle?* Should writers avoid metaphors in which the adjective *black* is used to connote discredit (*black sheep*), illegality (*black market*), or exclusion (*blackball, blacklist*)? What about the metaphoric use of the astronomer's *black hole* to refer to a project that consumes endless financial resources? Or what about the metaphoric *white knight,* which confers goodness on whiteness?

Proponents and opponents of these kinds of phrases are quick to marshal their arguments. The pro faction appeals to etymology ("*Blackball* refers to the color of the token used to veto a person's entry into an organization, not to the skin color of a person") and utility ("There is no good equivalent expression for *Indian giver*") or accuses opponents of hypersensitivity ("Who really hears *gypsies* in *gyp?*"), overly literal readings ("Using the phrase *black sheep* or *call the kettle black* doesn't mean one is a racist"), and self-righteous humorlessness ("Must every single syllable be ever so politically correct?"). The anti faction notes that some of the phrases are insulting ("If anyone is a so-called Indian giver, it was the European colonists and their descendants, who stole the country from its native peoples"), that the cumulative effect of such "colorful" language is denigrating, and that perhaps it is better to err on the side of caution than to run roughshod over entire nationalities, cultures, and social groups.

---

7. The difficulties entailed in judging the relevance of a person's physical disability and the prominence to accord it in a piece are illustrated by a review in the *New York Times* of a recital by Evelyn Glennie, a percussionist and composer. The review, extremely enthusiastic about her performance and range, consists of nine long paragraphs. The eighth paragraph reads: "One would be remiss not to mention that Ms. Glennie has been deaf since her teenage years, a point that is not noted in her program biography. In a way, it is beside the point: there is no question of making allowances here, Ms. Glennie's musicianship is extraordinary by any measure";

A more frequent problem—and a less controversial one—is gender-biased language. Many publishers have explicit guidelines on avoiding gender bias and expect their copyeditors to replace gendered terms:

Instead of	Use
chairman	presiding officer, convener, coordinator, chair, president
congressman	member of Congress, congressional representative
fathers (figurative use)	pioneers, founders, innovators, trailblazers
fireman	firefighter
housewife	homemaker, householder, woman
mailman	mail carrier, postal worker
man (noun)	people, human beings, individuals
man (verb)	work, staff, operate, serve
man-hour	operator-hour, work-hour, staff-hour
mankind	humanity, humankind, human beings
manmade	manufactured, artificial, synthetic, fabricated
manpower	staff, workforce, workers, personnel
newsman	reporter, journalist, newscaster
spokesman	representative, spokesperson, press agent, public relations agent
statesman	elected official, appointed official, legislator, leader
watchman	guard, security guard
weatherman	weather reporter, weathercaster
workmanlike	skillful, expert

For more examples and substitutes, see the books mentioned in the resources subsection on page 416. No matter what your ideology, some examples in each of those books are bound to strike you as hypersensitive, overly fussy, or wrongheaded. But you will also find valuable pointers and provocative ideas about the power (or tyranny) of language.

Allan Kozinn, "Clay Pots and Bells with a Different Drummer," *New York Times,* February 2, 1998, p. B1, national edition. (The comma after "making allowances here" may have been an oversight, but some writers defend this comma as preferable to a semicolon to emphasize a contrast; see Edward D. Johnson, *The Handbook of Good English,* pp. 122–23.)

THE GENERIC *HE*

The use of *he* as a generic singular pronoun has long been considered standard in formal writing.

> *Generic* he: A senator should meet with his staff at least once a day.

> *Generic* he: An astronaut must prepare himself, physically and mentally, to endure the isolation he will feel as he sees Earth recede in the distance.

> [In both sentences, "he" is supposed to be understood as referring to both men and women; thus the term "generic *he.*"]

The practice still has its adherents, but today this group is declining in number and is clearly on the defensive. For the copyeditor, the generic *he* presents two problems. The first is one of policy: When should a copyeditor intervene to eliminate the generic *he?* The second concerns the selection of techniques.

Policy.   Decisions about removing the generic *he* are relatively easy when a copyeditor is working for a publisher that supplies its authors and editors with written guidelines on bias-free language. The copyeditor can apply the policy to the manuscript, quote the policy in a cover note to the author, and feel confident that the editorial coordinator will support the emendations should the author question them.

When the publisher does not have a formal policy on bias-free language, however, the copyeditor is in a more difficult position. Some copyeditors always eliminate the generic *he* from every manuscript that crosses their desk, trusting that their authors will not raise a fuss. Other copyeditors recast the occasional generic *he,* but consult with their editorial coordinator before revising a long manuscript that is replete with generic *he*s and *his*es and *him*s. In these cases, the editorial coordinator will provide on-the-spot suggestions or propose a pre-edit conversation with the author or ask the copyeditor to submit a short sample edit for the author's approval.

Techniques.   Although a writer or a copyeditor can always toss in an "or she," there are many ways to avoid the generic *he* without introducing awkward strings of "he or she" or "his and her." For example:

> Everyone has his problems.

> *Delete the masculine pronoun:* Everyone has problems.

Change to the first-person plural: We all have our problems.

Use the plural pronoun "their" after an indefinite pronoun: Everyone has their problems.
[If your authors scowl at this "betrayal" of pronoun-antecedent agreement, you might show them the discussion under "Pronoun-Antecedent Agreement" in chapter 14.]

Every student must pay his tuition in full by October 1.

Change to the third-person plural: Students must pay their tuition in full by October 1.

Substitute for the masculine pronoun: Every student must pay this semester's tuition in full by October 1.

Change to the second person: You must pay your tuition in full by October 1.

Make no reference to people: October 1 is the deadline for the full payment of tuition.

Use the passive voice: Tuition must be paid in full by October 1.
Or: All tuition payments must be made by October 1.

Ibenz argues that an alcoholic cannot be cured of his disease, that he cannot become a social drinker.

Change to the third-person plural: Ibenz argues that alcoholics cannot be cured of their disease and cannot become social drinkers.

Use an article and repeat a noun: Ibenz argues that an alcoholic cannot be cured of the disease, that an alcoholic cannot become a social drinker.

Delete a phrase: Ibenz argues that an alcoholic cannot be cured and cannot become a social drinker.

Revise the sentence: Ibenz argues that alcoholism cannot be cured, that no form of treatment will enable an alcoholic to become a social drinker.

Three methods of avoiding the generic *he* should themselves be avoided:

- Slashed constructions (*he/she* or *s/he*) are too stenographic and casual for formal writing. They are also unpronounceable, and seem to suggest a cavalier attitude toward writing. ("Oh, just slash in some *she*s, would you?")

- Alternating *he* and *she* from paragraph to paragraph, or chapter to chapter, may confuse readers, and the effect may be missed by readers who skim the book or see only an excerpted chapter.
- A note at the beginning of the text stating that "all uses of the generic *he* are intended to be read as 'he or she'" is tokenism at its worst. Despite the note, pages and pages of *he*s and *him*s will leave readers with the impression that men are the true subject of the book and that women are only incidental to the main themes.

An author's use of a nongeneric *he* in an example is perfectly fine unless all the examples in the document use *he* and women are invisible. But a copy-editor should query or revise when an author repeatedly casts women in the subordinate role (female patients and male doctors; female clerks and male managers) or uses personal pronouns in stereotypical ways (female nurses and kindergarten teachers; male physicists and pilots).

NAMES FOR GROUPS OF PEOPLE

Civility and courtesy suggest that groups, like individuals, be called by the name they prefer. ("My name is William, but please call me Bill.") Like individuals, groups may change their preferences over time. As Henry Louis Gates Jr. wrote in 1969: "My grandfather was colored, my father was a Negro, and I am black";[8] today Gates chairs the Department of African American Studies at Harvard University. In addition, at any given time, members of a group may express different preferences. In recent years, *blacks, Blacks, African Americans, African-Americans,* and *people of color* each have their partisans.

Undoubtedly, the most difficult debates in the United States today concern terms for racial and ethnic groups. Scientists now agree that the concept of race has no scientific validity, that it is a carryover from nineteenth-century pseudo-anthropology. But even though *race* has no meaning as a biological term, it has become a convenient shorthand term for denoting the role of skin color, ethnicity, and class in society. Whether the topic is foreign pol-

8. Quoted by Justin Kaplan and Anne Bernays, *The Language of Names* (New York: Simon & Schuster, 1997), p. 70.

icy, law enforcement, reapportionment, or employment policies, writers need terms to describe groups of people.

For copyeditors, the best course is to read widely enough to know about historical usage and current conventions, preferences, and controversies. As noted earlier, a copyeditor's job is not to censor authors but to help authors avoid inadvertently antagonizing or stereotyping people. If you come upon questionable language in a manuscript, discuss it with your editorial coordinator. If your coordinator agrees that the wording or content is troublesome, present these concerns to the author, propose substitute language, and ask the author to consider revising the manuscript.

Writers and copyeditors should also be wary of euphemisms that may offend some of the people they are meant to show empathy for. For example, some older people sneer at *senior citizen,* noting that it has no younger counterpart (there are no *junior citizens*) and that the term oddly emphasizes citizenship. (What, they ask, shall we call older people who are not citizens of the country in which they reside?) Similarly, many people who have physical, mental, or sensory disabilities resent such euphemisms as *the physically challenged* or *the differently abled,* and they prefer terms that emphasize the person (*persons who are disabled, people with physical disabilities,* or *disabled persons*) to terms that emphasize the disability *(the disabled, the deaf).* [9]

A final example: Some people object to phrases like *cancer victim* or *afflicted with AIDS,* arguing that these terms turn people into passive objects lacking agency; but others feel that *victim* and *afflict* are accurate in connoting that these illnesses randomly attack people. To those who propose *cancer patients* or *AIDS patients,* the counterargument is that these terms—compared to *people with cancer* or *people with AIDS*—emphasize the illness, not the person who has the illness, and that people's medical status as patients or nonpatients is often irrelevant.

For those of us not now suffering from any infirmity, some of the debates over terminology may seem to be quibbling word games. More than name-calling is at stake, however, for stigmatizing language "leads not only to per-

---

9. Working along similar lines, some have proposed that "enslaved person" be substituted for "slave" since "slavery was a temporary condition imposed upon people, not part of their essence as human beings." But, the opposition counters, "'slave' is a far more stark and powerful word, expressing more accurately the horror of the owning, buying, and selling of human beings. The term 'enslaved person' sounds like a bureaucratic euphemism"; see Alexander Stille, "The Betrayal of History," *New York Review of Books,* June 11, 1998, p. 15.

sonal pain, but contributes both directly and indirectly to discrimination in jobs, insurance, and society at large."[10]

Resources.   For detailed advice on bias-free writing, including issues of gender, race, nationality, religion, disability, sexual orientation, and age, see Marilyn Schwartz and others, *Guidelines for Bias-Free Writing* (Bloomington: Indiana University Press, 1995); Rosalie Maggio, *Talking about People: A Guide to Fair and Accurate Language* (Phoenix: Oryx Press, 1997); and *APA* (6th ed., pp. 71–77). You may not agree with the analyses and recommendations presented in these books, but they will help you become aware of the kinds of controversies that swirl around various terms—controversies that almost every copyeditor confronts at one time or another.

PUBLISHING LAW

In book publishing, the copyeditor is often the only person in the publishing house who reads the entire manuscript word by word. For this reason, it falls upon the book copyeditor to alert the editorial coordinator to any material in the manuscript that might prompt a lawsuit. (The four areas of concern—libel, privacy, obscenity, and copyright—are discussed below.) Copyeditors are not expected to become experts on legal issues nor to determine definitively if there is a problem, but you should know enough about publishing law to flag material that might present a problem. Your editorial coordinator will review your concerns and forward any troublesome passages to the author, the author's attorney, or the publisher's attorney.

Notice that the preceding paragraph emphasizes book publishing. In magazine publishing and corporate publications departments, several veteran editors and administrators usually read every item that is in production. Many magazines and corporate publishers also routinely send the final drafts of

---

10. Kay Redfield Jamison, *An Unquiet Mind: A Memoir of Moods and Madness* (New York: Knopf, 1995), p. 180. Jamison is no Pollyanna: In the next paragraph, she acknowledges that "rigidly rejecting words and phrases that have existed for centuries" is unlikely to transform public attitudes. She also explains that as a clinician and researcher, she values medical terminology but that "as a person and patient, . . . I find the word 'bipolar' strangely and powerfully offensive: it seems to me to obscure and minimize the illness it is supposed to represent. The description 'manic-depressive,' on the other hand, seems to capture both the nature and the seriousness of the disease I have, rather than attempting to paper over the reality of the condition" (pp. 181–82).

upcoming publications to their in-house legal staff for review. But in book publishing, often only those manuscripts known to be controversial receive a full-dress legal review. If you are in doubt about the legal review procedures for a project, consult with your editorial coordinator.

LIBEL

Libel is the publication of a defamatory false statement about an identifiable living person. Packed into this short definition are four criteria, and a statement is libelous only if it meets *all four:*

1. The statement must be false. A true statement is not libelous.
2. The false statement must be presented as a statement of fact, not as an opinion. An author's expression of a personal opinion, no matter how pejorative, does not constitute libel.
3. The false statement must be defamatory; that is, it must cause—or be reasonably likely to cause—the individual to suffer shame, ridicule, or contempt; a damaged reputation; or loss of employment. Thus all of the following kinds of statements *if untrue* are defamatory:
   Accusations that an individual has committed a criminal act.
   Declarations that an individual has a serious illness or disease.
   Imputations that the individual is dishonest or incompetent at work.
   Mention of an individual's membership in a group held in disrepute.
   Mention of an individual's sexual activities.
4. The person must be alive and identifiable. Disguising a person's name and changing various details are not always sufficient to make the individual unidentifiable. (Oddly enough, a few novelists have found themselves in court because they invented characters and details that resembled real people, who then sued.) However, if the author has obtained an individual's signed consent to publish material (for example, a series of family letters), the individual cannot later sue for libel.

Defamatory statements about public officials and public figures are subject to a different standard. (The definition of *public figures* is somewhat vague. The class includes people who wield "pervasive power," who voluntarily enter public controversies, and who have regular and continuing access to the media.) One can print defamatory statements about public officials and public figures as long as one is acting in good faith and not out of malice; that is, the author must have a legitimate purpose for having published the statement (e.g., the purpose cannot be solely to injure an individual's reputation); the author must not publish a statement he or she knows to be false; and the author must have made a good-faith effort to verify the veracity of the statement.

If you find any statements in a manuscript that might constitute libel, be sure to note those passages for your editorial coordinator and the author.

INVASION OF PRIVACY

Privacy is an individual's right to not be subjected to undeserved publicity, regardless of whether the published material is true. Thus the issue here is *not* the truth or falsity of the published material, but whether an individual's right to be left alone was intruded upon by a writer or a photographer.

In general, the personal affairs of private individuals who have done nothing newsworthy are protected. Public figures are not accorded the same level of protection, but it is recognized that certain aspects of their personal lives are not newsworthy.

To avoid lawsuits charging invasion of privacy, the careful writer or photographer always obtains a signed consent form (also called a release) from the subject of an interview or any identifiable person in a photograph.

Examples of invasion of privacy:

- Publishing non-newsworthy facts about a nonpublic figure's personal life without that person's permission.
- Publishing an embarrassing photograph simply because it is embarrassing (that is, the photograph has no news value) without the subject's permission.
- Using a text or photograph for commercial publicity purposes without the subject's permission (commercial misappropriation).

If you spot anything in a manuscript (text or photographs) that raises a privacy issue, bring your concerns to the attention of your editorial coordinator and the author.

OBSCENITY

Obscenity refers to published materials (text or illustrations) that offend current community standards and have no redeeming literary, artistic, political, or scientific value. "Community standards" vary, of course. If you encounter borderline materials or profane or off-color language in a manuscript, ask your editorial coordinator for advice.

COPYRIGHT INFRINGEMENT

The author of a work is responsible for obtaining written permission to reprint copyrighted material. In general, works published before 1978 remain under copyright for ninety-five years after the date of publication; works published after 1978, when U.S. copyright law was revised, remain under copyright for seventy years after the death of the author; special rules apply to works created before 1978 but not published until after 1978. (For a detailed laypersons' discussion of copyright, see *Chicago* or one of the books mentioned in the last paragraph of this chapter.)

Since many authors are not experienced in the ways of copyright, the copyeditor is expected to call to the author's attention any quotations and artwork that may require permission to reprint. The copyeditor also advises the author about the form of credit lines for artwork and source lines for tables.

On the style sheet, in the "Permissions/Credits needed" box (see figure 6 in chapter 2), the copyeditor indicates by manuscript page number the following types of materials:

- Lengthy quotations from published nonfiction works that exceed *fair use*. There are no hard-and-fast rules about what constitutes fair use. Most publishers use the following rule of thumb: Fair use allows an author to quote up to about fifty words from a short nonfiction article and about four hundred words from a nonfiction book. The copyeditor should count up the total number of words quoted from each source throughout the entire manuscript and flag any cases that exceed fair use.[11]
- Any quotation from a poem, novel, short story, play, or song that is still under copyright—Shakespeare's works are not under copyright, Bob Dylan's are. Reprinting even one or two lines from a creative work usually requires permission.

11. Extensive paraphrasing and quotations for purposes other than the presentation of evidence or examples for analysis, commentary, review, or evaluation may not be considered fair use. For this reason, some publishers ask copyeditors to note lengthy passages of paraphrase, and some publishers may require an author to obtain permission for epigraphs and other quotations that are not discussed by the author if the original work is still under copyright.

- Any quotation from unpublished materials (e.g., correspondence, archives, private manuscripts). Quotations from unpublished materials are not covered by fair use, and the author or owner of the unpublished materials retains full rights in perpetuity.
- Any table, graph, chart, photograph, or illustration that is not the author's own work and is not from a U.S. government publication. (All federal government publications are in the public domain and may be freely used.)

As noted earlier, copyeditors are not asked to render judgments or opinions on matters of law, only to flag material that may merit further review.

Resources.   For a detailed discussion of legal issues of concern to editors, writers, and publishers, see the latest edition of Leonard D. DuBoff, *The Law (in Plain English) for Writers*; Tad Crawford, *The Writer's Legal Guide*; Jonathan Kirsch, *Kirsch's Handbook of Publishing Law*; or Brad Bunnin and Peter Beren, *The Writer's Legal Companion*. William Strong's *The Copyright Book*, 5th ed. (MIT Press, 1999), is authoritative and quite readable (even for nonlawyers) if you have the need or desire to plumb the topic.

Checklist of Editorial Preferences

The checklist on the following pages presents a range of common variants in editorial style in three categories:

1. Mechanics
2. Formatting
3. Documentation

The checklist can be used both as a training tool and as an adjunct to the copyeditor's style sheet. A copyeditor who is about to begin a project for a new publisher can ask the editorial coordinator to complete the checklist according to house style. Freelance copyeditors who work for several publishers can maintain a checklist for each—a convenient way to keep track of variations in house style. The checklist can also be used by an editorial coordinator in preparing a list of do's and don'ts or an informal tipsheet for in-house and freelance copyeditors.

Publisher's name _____

Preferred dictionary _____ , _____ edition

Style manual_____ , _____ edition,
    with these exceptions:

1. MECHANICS

Abbreviations and acronyms

- ☐ Replace all common Latin abbreviations (etc., i.e., e.g.) with English equivalents.
- ☐ Common Latin abbreviations may be used in parenthetical expressions and in notes.

- ☐ Delete periods in acronyms and abbreviations for organizations except U.S. and U.N.
- ☐ Delete periods in acronyms and abbreviations for organizations including US and UN.
- ☐ Use periods in acronyms or abbreviations for organizations.
- ☐ Follow the author's preference.

- ☐ Use full capitals for all acronyms: HMO, NAFTA, NAACP.
- ☐ Use an initial capital for an acronym five letters or longer that is pronounced as a word (Nafta, Erisa, Basic); use full capitals for all other acronyms.

- ☐ On first mention of a term, introduce its acronym in parentheses: Health maintenance organizations (HMOs) are preparing . . .
- ☐ When the acronym is better known than the spelled-out version, introduce the spelled-out version in parentheses on first mention: Under ERISA (Employee Retirement Income Security Act of 1974) employers cannot . . .
- ☐ Spell out in parentheses only those acronyms likely to be unfamiliar to readers.
- ☐ Do not introduce acronyms or their spelled-out versions in parentheses; if readers cannot deduce the meaning of the acronym from the context, spell out the term on each mention.

- ☐ Do not abbreviate state names in running text.
- ☐ Use traditional abbreviations (Calif., N.Y., N.J.) in bibliography, notes, and tables.

☐ Use two-letter postal abbreviations (CA, NY, NJ) in bibliography, notes, and tables.

☐ Use two-letter postal abbreviations only in addresses.

☐ Use small caps for A.M., P.M., A.D., and B.C.

☐ Use small caps, no periods, for AM, PM, AD, and BC.

☐ Use regular caps for A.M., P.M., A.D., and B.C.

☐ Lowercase a.m. and p.m.; uppercase A.D. and B.C.

Capitalization of titles, subtitles, and heads

☐ Capitalize prepositions of four or more letters; prepositions that are the first or last word of the item; and prepositions that are an inseparable part of the verb (e.g., *Growing Up Absurd*).

☐ Capitalize prepositions of five or more letters; prepositions that are the first or last word of the item; and prepositions that are an inseparable part of the verb.

☐ Capitalize only prepositions that are the first or last word of the item or that are an inseparable part of the verb.

Contractions

☐ Spell out all contractions except for the expressions "do's and don'ts" and "aren't I?"

☐ Follow the author's preference.

Foreign terms, names, quotes

☐ Use English-style plurals, not the Latin- or Greek-influenced forms: curriculums (*not* curricula), syllabuses (*not* syllabi), memorandums (*not* memoranda).

☐ For French and Spanish words, delete accent marks on capital letters.

☐ For French and Spanish words, keep or add accent marks on capital letters.

☐ For the transliteration of foreign names, use _____ as a reference book.

☐ Do not italicize a quotation in a foreign language; place it in quotation marks.

☐ Mark quotations in foreign languages for special typographic treatment.

Hyphenation
- [ ] Follow _____ [style manual/dictionary] for hyphenation.
- [ ] Hyphenate compounds in which the last letter of a prefix ending in a vowel is the same as first letter of the root: intra-arterial, re-elect, anti-intellectual, micro-organism.
- [ ] Hyphenate compounds in which the last letter of a prefix ending in a vowel is the same as first letter of the root, *except* if the vowel is an *e:* intra-arterial, anti-intellectual, micro-organism, *but* reelect.
- [ ] Hyphenate when a closed compound would produce a misleading diphthong or syllable: pre-image, co-op, co-worker.

Numbers and numerals
- [ ] For dates, use January 1, 1990.
- [ ] For dates, use 1 January 1990.
- [ ] Follow the author's preference.

- [ ] For decades, use 1990s.
- [ ] For decades, use 1990's.

- [ ] Treat *mid* as a prefix: in the mid–twentieth century; in the mid-'60s.
- [ ] Treat *mid* as an adjective: in the mid twentieth century; in the mid '60s.

- [ ] For plurals of numerals, add *'s:* F-111's, AK-47's.
- [ ] For plurals of numerals, add *s:* F-111s, AK-47s.

- [ ] Spell out numbers under 101.
- [ ] Spell out numbers under 10.
- [ ] Spell out numbers under _____.
- [ ] Always use numerals with units of measurement: 3 inches, 6 miles.
- [ ] Follow the author's preference.

- [ ] Use American measurements only (inches, feet, miles, ounces).
- [ ] Use SI (metric) measurements only (meters, liters, grams).
- [ ] Use American measurements and the SI equivalent in parentheses: 100 yards (91.4 m).
- [ ] Use SI measurements and the American equivalent in parentheses: 100 kilometers (62 mi).
- [ ] Follow the author's preference.

☐ Use a comma in four-digit numbers (except dates, addresses, serial numbers, page numbers).

☐ Use a comma only for five-digit and larger numbers (including dates and page numbers).

☐ Follow the author's preference.

☐ Spell out large sums of money: fifty-five million dollars.

☐ For large sums of money, use numerals and a dollar sign: $55 million.

☐ Follow the author's preference.

☐ Always spell out *percent*.

☐ Spell out *percent* in running text; OK to use % in parenthetical comments.

☐ Follow the author's preference.

☐ For page ranges, use all digits: pp. 102–105, pp. 215–217.

☐ For page ranges, use two digits after the en dash: pp. 102–05, pp. 215–17.

☐ For page ranges, show only the digits that change: pp. 102–5, pp. 215–7.

☐ For page ranges, follow the elision system described in *Chicago*.

☐ Italicize N (= the size of the data base, e.g., number of subjects in an experiment).

☐ Mark N for roman small caps.

☐ Mark N as an uppercase roman letter.

Possessives

☐ For proper names ending in -*s*, add '*s* for the possessive: Jones's.

☐ For proper names ending in -*s*, add only an apostrophe for the possessive: Jones'.

☐ Follow the author's preference.

Punctuation

☐ Use the serial comma.

☐ Do not use the serial comma.

☐ Follow the author's preference.

Spelling
- ☐ For words with variant spellings, always use the first entry in the dictionary that is named at the beginning of this checklist.
- ☐ Change British spellings such as *theatre, colour, organise* to preferred American spellings.
- ☐ For words that have variant spellings, follow the author's preference.

2. FORMATTING

Cross-references
- ☐ In cross-references, lowercase *chapter:* see chapter 1.
- ☐ Uppercase *chapter:* see Chapter 1.
- ☐ Uppercase *chapter* and spell out the number: Chapter One.
- ☐ Eliminate cross-references to pages or change them to cross-references to chapters.
- ☐ Instruct the typesetter to set page cross-refs as 00 or 000.
- ☐ Instruct the typesetter to set page cross-refs as solid quads (▮▮▮).

Extracts
- ☐ Run in prose quotes of fewer than ＿＿ words or ＿＿ lines.
- ☐ Run in poetry quotes of fewer than ＿＿ lines.
- ☐ Set as extracts quotes longer than ＿＿ words or ＿＿ lines.

Heads
- ☐ Do not open a chapter with a 1-level head.
- ☐ OK to have chapter begin with a 1-level head.

- ☐ Do not stack a 2-level head directly under a 1-level head.
- ☐ OK to stack a 2-level head directly under a 1-level head.

- ☐ For each level of head used in a chapter or section, there must be at least two instances in that chapter or section. A chapter may not have only one 1-level head; a section may not have only one 2-level or 3-level head.

Lists
- ☐ Do not use bulleted lists.
- ☐ Use numbered lists only when there is need for numbering the items.
- ☐ When all items in a list consist of a single word, lowercase the items (except for proper nouns and proper adjectives). In all other cases, capitalize the first word of each item.

3. DOCUMENTATION

Bibliography ⸱

- ☐ Alphabetize names beginning with *Mc* as though spelled *Mac:* MacDonald, McKillan, McStuart, MacWilson, Mayfield.
- ☐ Alphabetize names beginning with *Mc* as *Mc:* MacDonald, MacWilson, Mayfield, McKillan, McStuart.

- ☐ If a work has many authors, list the first three and then "and others."
- ☐ List the first three and then "et al."
- ☐ List all authors.
- ☐ Follow the author's preference.

- ☐ If there is more than one entry by a given author, list the entries in alphabetic order, disregarding any initial *the, a,* or *an.*
- ☐ List the entries in chronological order.
- ☐ Follow the author's preference; query any inconsistencies.

- ☐ Use traditional abbreviations (Calif., N.Y., Mich., Ill.) for state names in bibliography entries.
- ☐ Use the two-letter postal abbreviations (CA, NY, MI, IL) for state names in bibliography entries.

- ☐ Follow the bibliographical format in _____.
- ☐ Follow the author's preference, as long as it is consistent.

- ☐ To indicate second and third editions: 2d ed., 3d ed.
- ☐ To indicate second and third editions: 2nd ed., 3rd ed.

- ☐ To indicate page numbers in a book: p. 1, pp. 1–3.
- ☐ Use *p.* and *pp.* only if there might be some confusion that the numbers are page numbers.
- ☐ Follow the author's preference.

In-text citations

- ☐ For joint authors, use "and": Smith and Wilson.
- ☐ For joint authors, use &: Smith & Wilson.
- ☐ Follow the author's preference.

- ☐ If there are many authors, list the first two, followed by "et al."
- ☐ If there are many authors, list the first two, followed by "and others."
- ☐ Follow the author's preference.

☐ Arrange multiple in-text citations alphabetically: see Doe, 1978; Jones, 1990; Smith, 1977.

☐ Ask author to arrange multiple citations in order of importance or value to the reader.

☐ Follow the author's preference.

Footnotes or endnotes

☐ To indicate page numbers in a book: See p. 1, pp. 1–3.

☐ Use *p.* and *pp.* only if there might be some confusion.

☐ Follow the author's preference.

☐ Use traditional abbreviations for state names (Calif., Wash., Ore., N.Y.) in notes.

☐ Use the two-letter postal abbreviations (CA, WA, OR, NY) in notes.

Glossary of Copyediting Terms

AA.   Short for *author's alteration;* used to indicate changes made by an author on a set of proofs. *Compare* **PE.**

acute accent.   Diacritic mark: ´ [á, é, í, ó, ú].

A-head.   First-level heading within a chapter (or comparable section of a document); also called *1-head.*

all cap.   Text printed in FULL CAPITALS.

ampersand.   Name of the & character.

angle brackets.   Name of the < and > characters.

AP style.   Editorial preferences specified in *The Associated Press Stylebook and Libel Manual.*

APA style.   Editorial preferences specified in the *Publication Manual of the American Psychological Association.*

apos.   Short for *apostrophe.*

art.   Illustration (e.g., drawing, photograph, map, graph); also used as a collective singular noun, to refer to all illustrations in a work. *See also* **line art.**

art log.   Chart used to inventory and track all art in a manuscript.

ASCII.   [American Standard Code for Information Interchange; pronounced "ASS-key."] Set of 128 alphanumeric and nonprinting characters (e.g., wordspace, tab, hard return) used in converting word processing files from one format to another. When files are converted into ASCII, all typeface formatting (e.g., italics, bold), diacritics, and other non-ASCII characters are lost.

asterisk-dagger sequence.   Sequence of symbols used for nonnumbered reference notes: asterisk (*), dagger (†), double-dagger (‡), section mark (§), parallels (||), number sign (#).

at sign.   Name of the @ character.

AU.   Short for *author;* used in queries ("AU: Revision OK?").

author-date.   System for providing references for works quoted, paraphrased, or cited as evidence in a document. The surname of the author and the year of publication of the cited work are given in the text, and full bibliographical information is supplied in an alphabetized reference list at the end of the document. Also called *name-year.*

back matter.   General term for material that comes at the end of a book or book-length document: appendixes, endnotes, glossary, bibliography, index.

backnote.   *See* **endnote.**

bad break.   Incorrect division of a word that falls across two lines of type (*bad word break*). Unpleasing division of a paragraph that falls across two pages (*bad page break*). *See also* **orphan; widow.**

baseline.   Imaginary line on which printed characters sit. For example:

........The dotted line is the baseline for this text...

b/b.   Short for *from baseline to baseline.* The notation *16 pts. b/b* asks for 16 points (of vertical space) between the baselines of two successive lines of text.

B-head.   Second-level heading within a chapter (or comparable section of a document); also called *2-head.*

blind proofing.   Proofreading pass in which the proofreader is not supplied with an earlier version of the text against which to compare the current version. Also called *cold proofing.*

block quote.   *See* **extract.**

boilerplate.   Block of text that is reused, without change, in various documents.

bold.   Short for *boldface.* **These words are boldface.**

braces.   Name of the { and } characters; also called *curly brackets.*

brackets.   Name of the [and] characters; also called *square brackets.*

broadside.   Printed page whose top is at the left-hand side of a regular page; readers must turn the document 90 degrees clockwise to read the text. Used to accommodate wide tables and maps. In word processing programs, called *landscape orientation.*

bubble.   Penciled-in circle or box in which an editor writes a query, comment, or instruction on hard copy.

built-up fraction.   Printed fraction in the form 1/2, 3/4, 7/8. *Compare* **case fraction.**

bullet.   Heavy centered dot used as an ornament or as a marker in a vertical list. Bullets are solid (• ●; also called *closed* or *filled*) or open (○ ○); square bullets are also solid (▪ ■) or open (□ □).

bulleted list.   Vertical list (also called *set-off list*) in which each item is introduced by a bullet or other graphic character (☞ ✓ ❑).

callout.   (1) Boxed notation on hard copy (usually in the left margin) to indicate the placement of art or a table or to signal a cross-reference. (2) Label identifying an item in an illustration.

camera-ready copy.   Text and art positioned in their final printed format, ready to be shot (filmed) by the printer; the printing plates are made from this film. Also called *CRC.*

caps.   Short for *capital letters.*

caption.   Heading or title of an illustration—as distinct from the **legend;** but *caption* is often used to refer to all explanatory text that accompanies a piece of art.

case fraction.   Printed fraction in the form $\frac{1}{3}, \frac{2}{3}, \frac{7}{8}$; also called a *piece fraction. Compare* **built-up fraction.**

castoff.   Estimate of the typeset or printed length of a manuscript.

cedilla.   Diacritic mark: ₵ [Ç ç].

cell.   Single entry or location in the body of a table. *See* **table.**

change bar.   Very thick vertical rule, as shown here, placed in the outer margin of a technical manual to indicate a paragraph that has been revised since the previous edition. *See also* **redline.**

Chicago style.   Editorial preferences specified in *The Chicago Manual of Style.*

CIP data.   [Cataloging-in-publication.] Block of publishing information about a book supplied to the publisher, upon request, by the Library of Congress. The CIP block is printed on the copyright page.

circumflex accent.   Diacritic mark: ˆ [â, ê, î, ô, û].

citation-sequence.   System for providing references for works quoted, paraphrased, or cited as evidence in a document. On first mention, each cited work is assigned a number, in sequence, which is used in all subsequent references to that cited work. The citation numbers appear in the text, usually as superscripts, and complete bibliographical information is supplied in a numbered list at the end of the document.

clean up.   To incorporate an author's responses to the copyediting into the final hard copy or computer files.

clear for 10s.   To align numerals on the last digit (rather than the first digit) in a numbered vertical list. For example:

Cleared for 10s	Not cleared for 10s
1.	1.
2.	2.
10.	10.
100.	100.

close paren.   Name of the) character.

close up.   To delete unwanted horizontal or vertical space.

CN.   Standard coding for a chapter number. *See* **typecoding.**

CO.   Standard coding for a chapter opening. *See* **typecoding.**

coding.   *See* **typecoding.**

compositor.   Person who "sets" the type, either by hand or by computer; also called *comp* or *typesetter.*

compound.   Adjective, adverb, conjunction, noun, or preposition composed of two or more words.

continued line.   Line of text, usually set in italics [*Continued on next page; Table 14—Continued*], placed at the foot or top of a page when an element such as a table extends over two or more pages.

CRC.   *See* **camera-ready copy.**

credit line.   Brief statement of the source of an illustration, often placed at the end of the legend.

cross-reference.   Phrase that mentions another part of the document or text ("in chapter 5 we discussed," "as table 6 shows"). Also called *x-ref* or *in-text ref. See also* **signposting.**

CSE style.   Editorial preferences specified in *Scientific Style and Format: The CSE Manual for Authors, Editors, and Publishers.* (The CSE is the Council of Science Editors.)

CT.   Standard coding for a chapter title. *See* **typecoding.**

curly quotes. Name of the " and " characters (as compared to the " character); also called *smart quotes.*

cut-in head. Head that cuts across the columns of a table. *See* **table.**

dagger. Name for the † character.

dead copy. Manuscript that has been typeset and proofread.

decked heads. Pair of heads in a table consisting of a **spanner** atop two or more single-column heads. *See* **table.**

designer. Person responsible for the physical appearance of a book or document, including the typography (typeface, type size, etc.), layout (margins, leading, location of running heads, etc.), and style of the art (drawings, maps, charts).

diacritic. Mark that changes the phonetic value of an alphabetical character. Common diacritic marks include the acute accent (á, é), cedilla (ç), circumflex (â, ô), grave accent (è, ì), tilde (ñ, õ), and umlaut or diaeresis (ö, ü).

dingbat. Ornamental character: ✌ 📖 🗁 ☺ ✂ ◆.

display equation. Mathematical expression set on its own line. *Compare* **run-in text.**

display type. Large type, used for part titles, chapter titles, headings, and the like.

DOI. Permanent, unique alphanumeric string assigned to an online document by the International DOI [Digital Object Identifier] Foundation and the document's publisher.

dot leaders. Row of periods between horizontal entries in a table or list; for example: Annual turnover. 93.4%

double dagger. Name of the ‡ character.

double numeration. Use of two numerals (separated by a period, hyphen, or other character) in the numbering of pages, figures, tables, or other materials. For example, the pages in chapter 1 are numbered 1.1, 1.2, 1.3, 1.4, etc.; the pages in chapter 2 are 2.1, 2.2, 2.3, 2.4, etc.; in chapter 3, the pages are 3.1, 3.2, 3.3, 3.4, etc.

ellipsis. Name of the . . . character.

em. Typesetting measurement whose value depends on the size of the type: In 10-point type, an em space is 10 points wide; in 18-point type, an em space is 18 points wide.

em dash. Name of the — character. In manuscripts the em dash is often typed as --.

en. Half an em.

en dash.   Name of the – character. An en dash is longer than a hyphen (-) but shorter than an em dash (—). In manuscripts the en dash is often typed as a hyphen.

end-line hyphen.   Hyphen that falls at the end of a line of text. A *soft hyphen* is dropped in the final copy if the hyphenated word falls on one line; a *hard hyphen* is always retained no matter how the word falls.

endnote.   Reference or explanatory note that appears at the end of a book or document, in a section titled "Notes"; also called *backnote. Chapter endnotes* appear at the end of each chapter of a book (or comparable section of a document).

EX.   Standard coding for an extract. *See* **typecoding.**

extract.   Quoted passage set off from the running text. Extracts are often set in a smaller type size and on a shorter measure than the running text. Also called *block quote.*

figure.   Illustration printed as part of the running text. *Compare* **plate.**

first ref.   First appearance of a proper name ("Identify all characters on first ref") or of a source in reference notes ("Give a full citation on first ref").

flag.   (1) To call to someone's attention ("Flag all math symbols"). (2) Gummed slip of paper, attached to hard copy, on which a copyeditor writes a query.

flopped.   Transposed; used to describe an illustration that is mispositioned or misprinted as a mirror image of the desired image.

flush.   Positioned at the margin of the text page, either *flush left* or *flush right.*

flush and hang.   Style of setting indexes and lists. The first line of each entry or paragraph is set flush left, and the remaining lines of the entry are indented.

FN.   Standard coding for a footnote. *See* **typecoding.**

folio.   Page number in typeset text. A *drop folio* is a page number placed at the bottom of a page. A *blind folio* (also called a *suppressed folio*) is not printed, although the page is counted in the numbering of the pages; an *expressed folio* is one that is printed.

font.   Characters in a given size and style of a typeface (10-point Courier roman; 12-point Helvetica italics; 14-point Baskerville roman small caps).

footer.   One or two lines of copy, such as a chapter title or section title, set at the bottom of each page of a document or book; also called *running foot. Compare* **running head.**

front matter.   General term for material that comes at the front of a book, before the first chapter: half-title page, title page, copyright page, dedication, table of contents, list of illustrations or tables, foreword, preface, acknowledgments, introduction.

full caps.   Text to be set in ALL CAPITALS.

full measure.   Width of a **text page** (i.e., the width of a page from margin to margin).

galley.   First printed version (*proof*) of a document; so called because these proofs were once printed on long sheets of paper (rather than in page form). *Compare* **page proof.**

global search.   Search of one or more computer files to locate all instances of a word or words, either to double-check their styling (capitalization, hyphenation, etc.) or to replace them with a specified substitute (*global search and replace* or *global change*).

GPO style.   Editorial preferences specified in the *United States Government Printing Office Style Manual.*

grave accent.   Diacritic mark: ` [à, è, ù].

hairline rule.   Lightest (or thinnest) horizontal line available. *See also* **rule.**

hard copy.   Printout of a computer file; by extension, any text that appears on paper.

hard hyphen.   *See* **end-line hyphen.**

hard space.   Special word processing character that produces a wordspace but does not permit a line to break at that space.

head.   Title that indicates the start of a section or subsection of a document or book chapter. Heads are given distinctive typographic treatment (type size, weight; capitalization; set off or run in). *See also* **running head.**

headline style.   Capitalization style for heads, display lines, or titles of works in which all words are capitalized except articles (*a, an, the*), coordinating conjunctions, and prepositions. Alternatively, prepositions shorter than four or five letters are lowercased, and longer prepositions are capitalized. Also called *UC/lc. Compare* **sentence style.**

headnote.   Brief introductory or explanatory material that follows a part, chapter, or section title and precedes the running text.

horizontal rule.   Thin horizontal line. *See also* **rule.**

house style.   Editorial style preferences expressed by a publisher.

hyphen.   *See* **end-line hyphen.**

initial cap only. *See* **sentence style.**

intercap. Capital letter that appears in the middle of a company or product name (BankAmerica, WordPerfect, MasterCard); also called *midcap.*

in-text ref. *See* **cross-reference.**

ISBN. [International Standard Book Number.] Thirteen-digit number assigned by a publisher to uniquely identify a book. Before January 2007, ten-digit ISBNs were used.

ital. Short for *italics. These words are in italics.*

jacket copy. Text that appears on the protective paper wrapper of a clothbound book or on the cover and inward folding flaps of a paperback book.

justify. To set type so that the margin is aligned. Most book pages are justified left and right; but some documents are justified only at the left margin (also called *ragged right*).

kerning. Tightening of the spacing between the letters of a word. *See* **letterspacing.**

kill. To order the deletion of text or an illustration.

landscape orientation. *See* **broadside.**

leaders. *See* **dot leaders.**

leading. [Pronounced "ledding."] Linespacing in a printed text, measured in points.

leading zero. Zero placed before a decimal point to improve comprehension: 0.25 acre.

legend. One or more sentences of explanation that accompany an illustration; **caption** is often used to refer to the legend as well.

letterspacing. Space between the letters of a word. Tight and loose letterspacing are used to enhance the appearance of letters set in display type.

WALLPAPER	normal letterspacing
WALLPAPER	tight (kerned) letterspacing
WALLPAPER	loose letterspacing

ligature. Compound typographic character: æ, œ, ff, ffi, fi.

line art. Illustration that contains only blacks and whites, no gray tones.

linespacing. "White space" between successive lines of text; usually called **leading.**

lining figures. Typographical style of numerals in which all digits sit on the baseline: 1 2 3 4 5 6 7 8 9 0. *Compare* **old style figures.**

macro.   Series of computer keystrokes, commands, and operations that are stored as a unit so that the entire routine plays out when the user invokes the macro.

measure.   Width of a line of printed text. Running text is set *full measure* (from margin to margin); extracts and lists may be set on a narrower measure.

midcap.   *See* **intercap.**

monospace type.   Printed lettering in which characters are of equal width. `This type is monospace.` Also called *nonproportional type. Compare* **proportional type.**

MS.   Short for *manuscript.*

mult.   Short for *multiplication sign* ($\times$), as distinct from a lowercase "x."

N.   Short for *number;* used in statistical tables to indicate the size of the sample; often set as a small cap.

name-year.   *See* **author-date.**

nonbreaking space.   *See* **hard space.**

nonproportional type.   *See* **monospace type.**

numbered list.   Vertical list in which each item is introduced by a numeral.

old style figures.   Typographical style in which some numerals have ascenders and descenders: 1 2 3 4 5 6 7 8 9 0. *Compare* **lining figures.**

on-screen editing.   Editing that is performed on a document's computer files rather than on hard copy; also called *on-line editing* or *electronic manuscript (EMS) editing.*

open paren.   Name of the (character.

orphan.   First line of a paragraph that is stranded at the bottom of a printed page, separated from the remainder of the paragraph by a page break. *Compare* **widow.**

page proof.   Printed version *(proof)* of a document in page form; also called *pages. Compare* **galley.**

para-indent.   Width of the indention of the first line of a paragraph, usually specified in picas or em spaces.

pass.   Read-through of a manuscript by a copyeditor.

PDF.   Electronic file format (Portable Document Format) that preserves the font, page layout, and images of the original file independent of a computer's operating system or software.

PE.   Short for *printer's error;* used to indicate an error made by the typesetter on a set of proofs. *Compare* **AA.**

penalty copy.   Hard-copy manuscript that is difficult to typeset (heavily corrected, replete with math symbols or foreign language text) for which a typesetter charges a premium.

pica.   Linear measurement: 1 pica = 12 points. *See* **point.**

pick up.   To reuse previously printed text or illustrations.

plate.   Page of illustrations, usually printed on special paper, that is printed separately from the regular text and is inserted between text pages during production.

PO.   Standard coding for a part opening. *See* **typecoding.**

point.   Linear measurement:

> 1 point = 0.0138 inch
> 12 points = 1 pica = 0.1656 inch (rule of thumb, 6 picas = 1 inch)
> 72.464 points = 1 inch (rule of thumb, 72 points = 1 inch)

proportional type.   Printed lettering in which characters are of unequal width. *Compare* **monospace type.**

query.   Publishing jargon for "question"; used as a verb or a noun.

QY.   Short for *query;* used in queries ("QY: where is table 3?").

ragged right.   Text aligned at the left margin but not at the right margin. *See also* **justify.**

recto.   Right-hand page of a book, magazine, or brochure. *Compare* **verso.**

redline.   On-screen or hard-copy version of a manuscript that indicates which text has been added or deleted since the previous version. In the redline version, the added text is also called *redline,* and the deleted text is called *strikeout.* Here, the redline text is enclosed in braces, and the strikeout text is slashed: I pledge ~~thy~~ allegiance to {the} flag.

roman.   Type style used most often in printed materials—as distinct from *italic,* GOTHIC, or *script.*

rule.   Horizontal or vertical line. The thickness (or *weight*) of a rule is measured in points or in inches.

hairline	1 point	4 point

run-in text.   Text that is not set off on its own line. For example:

> *Run-in heads.* Run-in heads are often preceded by a para-indent, set in italics, and followed by a period. The regular text continues on the same line, just as this example shows. (*Run-in* is also used to describe lists and quotations that are not displayed.)

running foot.   *See* **footer.**

running head.   One or two lines of copy, such as a book title or chapter title, set at the top of each page of a document or book; also called *header. Compare* **footer.**

running text.   Portion of a document consisting of sentences and paragraphs, rather than set-off display lines, tables, and other elements; also called *general text* or *regular running text.*

runover.   Continuation of a lengthy head, displayed equation, line of poetry, and the like onto a second line; also called *turnover.*

sans serif.   Printed letters that do not have short cross lines (*serifs*) projecting from the main strokes. This sentence is printed in a sans serif typeface.

sentence style.   Capitalization style for heads, display lines, and titles of works in which all words are lowercased except those that would be capitalized in a sentence (i.e., the first word, proper nouns, proper adjectives, and the word *I*). Also called *initial cap only. Compare* **headline style.**

serial comma.   Comma preceding *and* or *or* in a list of items (a, b, and c; d, e, f, or g).

serif.   Short cross line that projects from the main stroke of a printed letter. For example:

| These letters have serifs | A C E F M N T W |
| These letters do not | A C E F M N T W |

short title.   Abbreviated title of a book or article used in a note or in-text citation after the full title has been cited on its first occurrence in the chapter or document.

SI.   [*Système international d'unités.*] System of measurement based on the metric system and used by scientists around the world. SI has seven base units: meter (length), kilogram (mass), second (time), ampere (electric current), kelvin (temperature), mole (amount of substance), and candela (luminosity).

signposting.   Excessive cross-references to topics previously discussed and to be discussed ("The court's decision, as we saw in chapters 2 and 3, was controversial but firmly grounded in precedent. We will examine the legacy of this controversy in chapter 5 after we have reviewed the major precedents for the decision").

sink.   Distance from the top of a printed page to the baseline of a particular element on that page (e.g., a chapter title).

slash.   *See* **solidus.**

small caps.   Capital letters slightly shorter and squatter than regular caps: B.C., A.D., A.M., P.M.

soft hyphen.   *See* **end-line hyphen.**

solidus.   Name of the / character; also called *slash, slant,* or *virgule.*

spanner.   Head that extends across two or more columns in a table. *See* **table.**

specs.   Type specifications created by a designer to indicate typeface, point size, vertical and horizontal spacing, margins, and the like.

spine.   Backbone of a book that connects the front and back covers. Spine copy usually includes the book title, the author's surname, the publisher's name, and the publisher's logo.

stacked heads.   Two or more heads with no text intervening. For example:

Unpacking the Wondermatic

Identifying the Parts

After you remove the packing straps, slide each component out of its fiberboard sleeve, and write down the serial number of each component. Begin assembling the base . . .

stet.   [Latin for "let it stand."] Used to reinstate text that had been marked for deletion.

strikeout.   *See* **redline.**

stub.   Leftmost column of a table, which lists the categories or variables.

style sheet.   Form filled in by the copyeditor as a record of editorial choices he or she made.

subscript.   Numeral or character set below the baseline: H_2O.

superscript.   Numeral or character set above the baseline: mc^2.

suspended compound.   Set of compound adjectives or nouns in which an element common to all members is not repeated. For example: the fourth-, fifth-, and sixth-graders; steel-plated or -cased equipment; the pre- and posttest scores.

T of C.   Short for *table of contents.*

table.   Arrangement of words or numbers in columns and rows. For example:

	Alpine County [1]		Bemine County [2]	
	1810	1820	1810 [2]	1820 [2]
Domesticated Animals [3]				
Mammals [4]				
Dogs	5,212 [5]	7,022	3,272	6,265
Cats	4,242	6,888	2,212	8,122
Birds				
Canaries	822	933	544	755
Parrots	912	723	454	267
Wild Animals				
Mammals				
Lions	153	162	83	64
Tigers	101	135	27	18
Birds				
Condors	98	90	33	38
Eagles	125	143	88	86

[1] A *spanner head* ("Alpine County," "Bemine County") applies to two or more columns.

[2] *Decked heads* (name of county atop years) sit one atop another.

[3] A *cut-in head* ("Domesticated Animals," "Wild Animals") cuts across the columns.

[4] A *stub head* ("Mammals," "Birds") divides the stub into categories.

[5] A *cell* is an entry in the body of a table. (Here, each of the thirty-two cells contains a numeral.)

tagging. *See* **typecoding.**

tearsheet. Pages "torn" from a printed document for reuse in a new document.

text page. Area on a printed page in which the body of the text appears. *Compare* **type page.**

thin space. Space that is narrower than a regular wordspace, approximately 1/4 to 1/6 of an em. Sometimes used between personal initials: A. B. Jones.

tilde. Diacritic mark: ˜ [ñ, õ].

TK. Short for *to come;* used to refer to material not yet in place.

trade books. Books intended for general readers, as distinguished from books intended for professionals, scholars, or students.

trim size.   Dimensions of a page of a book.

turnover.   *See* **runover.**

typecoding.   Marking of a manuscript (hard copy or computer files) to indicate all design elements (i.e., any copy that is not running text: extracts, display equations, part and chapter titles, footnotes, captions, etc.). Typical codes for books include PO (part opening), CO (chapter opening), CT (chapter title), CN (chapter number), FN (footnote), EX (extract). Also called *tagging.*

type page.   Area on a printed page defined by the top, bottom, left, and right margins. The type page includes the running heads and footers, folios, and sidebars.

typo.   Short for *typographical error;* a misprint.

UC.   Short for *uppercase* (capital letters).

UC/lc.   Short for *uppercase and lowercase;* used to indicate that display text is to be capitalized according to **headline style**—as distinct from text to be set **sentence style.**

umlaut.   Diacritic mark: ¨ [ü, ö]; also called *diaeresis.*

Unicode.   International coding system that enables keyboarders to produce over 100,000 linguistic, mathematical, and scientific characters.

unnumbered list.   Vertical list in which items carry neither numbering nor bullets. *Compare* **bulleted list, numbered list.**

verso.   Left-hand page of a book, magazine, or brochure. *Compare* **recto.**

vertical rule.   Thin vertical line. *See also* **rule.**

vetting.   Substantive review of a manuscript by an expert in the subject matter; similarly, the checking of a translation by someone who is proficient in both languages.

widow.   Short line (i.e., the last few words of a paragraph) stranded at the top of a printed page, separated from the remainder of the paragraph by a page break. Used, more generally, for an *orphan* as well as for a line that contains only part of a word or a word of three or four characters.

wordspacing.   Amount of space between printed words. For example:

Tight wordspacing:
   The very big dog and the very fat cat sat on the mat.
Normal wordspacing:
   The very big dog and the very fat cat sat on the mat.
Loose wordspacing:
   The very big dog and the very fat cat sat on the mat.

XML. System for coding elements in a digital document that reduces or eliminates the need for reformatting when the document is produced on new platforms (e.g., print, Web, e-readers, computer tablets). Short for *extensible markup language*.

x-ref. Short for **cross-reference.**

Glossary of Grammar Terms

absolute participle.   Present or past participle that functions as a preposition or an adverb and therefore does not have a grammatical subject. Examples: <u>Barring</u> an unanticipated delay, the library will reopen in September. <u>Depending</u> on the price, we might increase our order. <u>Granted</u> these exceptions, the new policy takes effect immediately. *Compare* **dangling modifier.**

active voice.   Grammatical form in which the doer of the verb is stated. Examples: She fired two shots. He authorized the break-in. TopCo laid off fifty workers. In contrast, in the *passive voice* the recipient of the action conveyed by the verb is stated. Examples: Shots were fired. A break-in was authorized. Fifty workers were laid off.

adjective.   Word that modifies (i.e., describes, limits, or qualifies) a noun by stating a characteristic or a quantity. Examples: a <u>green</u> pencil; a <u>fair-weather</u> friend; <u>Canadian</u> cheese; <u>three</u> books; a <u>few</u> pointers. *See also* **attributive adjective; compound adjective; coordinate adjective; noncoordinate adjective; predicate adjective; proper adjective.**

adverb.   Word that modifies (i.e., describes, limits, or qualifies) an adjective, verb, or another adverb. Adverbs indicate "time, place, manner, or degree"—that is, when, where, or how an action is performed—or specify the extent or degree of an adjective. Examples: She is <u>very</u> smart. We cut the tubes <u>precisely.</u> That is a <u>rather</u> strange view. I am leaving <u>now.</u> Put your books <u>here.</u> *See also* **sentence adverb.**

adverbial clause.   Dependent clause that functions like an adverb; it may modify a verb, adjective, or adverb. Examples: He is slower <u>than she is.</u> I'll come over <u>when I finish my work.</u>

adverbial phrase.   Phrase that functions like an adverb; it may modify a verb, adjective, or adverb. Examples: He stood <u>at the corner.</u> I've lived here <u>for fifteen years.</u>

agreement.   *See* **pronoun-antecedent agreement; subject-verb agreement.**

antecedent.   Noun or pronoun to which a pronoun refers; also called *referent.* Examples: <u>Jane</u> lost her jacket. <u>Tom, Dick, and Harry</u> had their hands full. <u>We</u> cannot find our books.

appositive.   Substantive placed after another substantive to name or identify it. Examples: My hometown, <u>New York,</u> is a fine place to visit. His youngest brother, <u>Max,</u> is a plumber. Appositives are usually **nonrestrictive,** but they may be **restrictive:** Their son <u>Joe</u> lives in Fresno, but their son <u>Jim</u> lives at home. *See also* **nonrestrictive modifier; restrictive modifier.**

article.   Part of speech comprising the words *a, an,* and *the. The* is the *definite article; a* and *an* are *indefinite articles.*

attributive adjective.   Adjective that precedes the noun it modifies. Examples: a <u>tall</u> tree, an <u>over-the counter</u> medication. *Compare* **predicate adjective.**

attributive noun.   Noun that modifies the noun immediately following it. Examples: <u>college</u> textbooks, <u>desk</u> lamp, <u>awards</u> banquet, <u>Veterans</u> Administration.

case.   Form of a noun or pronoun that indicates its grammatical relation to other words in the sentence. *See also* **nominative case; objective case; possessive case.**

clause.   Group of words that includes a subject and a finite verb. *See also* **dependent clause; independent clause.**

collecting noun phrase.   Expression of the form "a(n) *x* of *y*," where *x* is a singular noun and *y* is a plural noun. Examples: a bunch of bananas, a set of papers, a flock of geese.

collective noun.   Noun that denotes two or more people or items. Examples: class, couple, crowd, pair, staff, team.

compound adjective.   Adjective that consists of two or more words. Examples: <u>hand-lettered</u> sign, <u>matter-of-fact</u> approach, refunds <u>smaller than expected.</u>

compound predicate.   Predicate containing two or more finite verbs governed by the same grammatical subject. Examples: Yesterday I <u>went to the store and then drove home.</u> He says he <u>will look for a job but hasn't yet sent out any résumés.</u> *Compare* **compound sentence.**

compound sentence.   Sentence containing two independent clauses joined by a conjunction. Examples: I went to the store, but he went home. We are pleased, and they are too.

conjunction.   Part of speech comprising the so-called linking words. *Coordinate conjunctions* join words, phrases, or clauses of equal rank: and, but, for, or, nor, yet. *Subordinate conjunctions* join dependent clauses to independent clauses: although, as, because, if, since, so that, unless, while. *Correlative conjunctions* come in pairs: both/and; either/or; neither/nor; not only/but also.

coordinate adjective.   Adjective that is "of the same rank" as an adjacent adjective; that is, both adjectives apply equally and independently to the noun. Coordinate adjectives are separated by "and" or by a comma. Examples: This is a <u>funny and wise</u> book. She solved a <u>complex, intricate</u> problem. His <u>wise, witty, authoritative</u> speech was well received. *Compare* **noncoordinate adjective.**

coordinate conjunction.   *See* **conjunction.**

copula.   Verb that expresses a state of being (rather than an action). Copulative verbs link the subject to another noun, pronoun, or adjective. Examples: We <u>are</u> a party of five. The enemy <u>is</u> us. The ride <u>seems</u> long. The oil <u>smells</u> rancid. It <u>remains</u> true. His opinion <u>has become</u> ours as well.

correlative conjunction.   *See* **conjunction.**

countable noun.   Noun whose singular form may be preceded by a definite or an indefinite article (*a* or *an*); its plural form may be preceded by a number or by *some*. Examples: apple, book, cat, desk. *Compare* **noncountable noun.**

dangling modifier.   Grammatically incorrect construction in which a modifying phrase or clause is not directly followed by its grammatical subject. Examples: <u>Driving down the street,</u> the campanile rang. [Driving down the street, we heard the campanile ring.] <u>Offered the job,</u> it's hard for her to say no. [Offered the job, she found it hard to say no.] <u>To write well,</u> a dictionary is necessary. [To write well, one needs a dictionary.] *Compare* **absolute participle.**

dependent clause.   Clause that cannot stand alone as a complete sentence; also called *subordinate clause. Compare* **independent clause.**

direct address.   Speech or dialogue that names the person being spoken to. The name or noun is set off from the rest of the speech by commas. Examples: "Let's eat, grandma" [Compare: "Let's eat grandma"]; "Mom, don't bug me!"; "Can we try, sweetheart, to settle this out of court?"

direct object.   Noun, pronoun, noun phrase, or noun clause that directly follows a verb and directly "receives" the action conveyed by the verb. In contrast, an *indirect object* follows a preposition or an implied preposition. Examples: He gave the book [direct object] to me [indirect object]. He gave me [indirect object, "to" implied] the book [direct object]. We wrote them [indirect object, "to" implied] a letter [direct object].

direct question.   Speech or dialogue that asks a question. Examples: "Why did you do that?" I asked her. "Who are you?" she asked me. In contrast, an *indirect question* rephrases the question. Examples: I asked her why she had done it. She asked me who I was.

direct quotation.   Speech or dialogue directly reproduced and placed in quotation marks. Examples: "I can't wait for summer," I said. She said, "I don't trust you." In contrast, an *indirect quotation* rephrases the words that were spoken. Examples: I said that I couldn't wait for summer. She said she didn't trust him.

ellipsis (elliptical clause).   Omission of a word or phrase implied by the syntax or context. Examples: He was the nominee of the Democrats, she of the Republicans. The new machine has eight speeds, the old only three.

finite verb.   Verb showing tense (e.g., present, past, future), person (first, second, or third), and number (singular or plural). *Compare* **nonfinite verb.**

fragment.   *See* **sentence fragment.**

fused participle.   Gerund preceded by a noun or pronoun in the objective case. Examples: We see no likelihood of DotCom accepting the proposed merger. The thought of him receiving a promotion is laughable.

genitive case.   *See* **possessive case.**

gerund.   Present participle that functions as a noun. Examples: Writing neatly is important. His acting as though he were innocent fooled no one.

historical present tense.   Use of the present tense to convey actions that occurred in the past.

hypercorrection.   Grammatical error committed in the attempt to avoid a grammatical error. Examples: "Whom shall I say is calling?" He felt badly about the accident. Just between you and I . . .

impersonal construction.   Sentence in which "there is," "there are," or "it is" (with the "it" lacking any referent) serves as the subject and main verb. Examples: There is little we can do. There are ten apples on the tree. It is safe to cross now.

independent clause.   Clause that can stand as a complete sentence. *Compare* **dependent clause.**

indirect object.   *See* **direct object.**

indirect question.   *See* **direct question.**

indirect quotation.   *See* **direct quotation.**

infinitive.   Form of a verb that is always introduced by *to.* Examples: I like to sing. To be here is always a pleasure. To be invited to present this award is an honor. *See also* **verbal.**

intransitive verb.   Verb that does not require a direct object. Examples: He will go. They have come. I am done. You seem tired. She is lying down. *Compare* **reflexive verb; transitive verb.**

modifier.   Word or phrase that describes, defines, or qualifies another word or phrase. *See also* **adjective; adverb; adverbial clause; adverbial phrase; dangling modifier; nonrestrictive modifier; restrictive modifier.**

nominative case.   Form of a noun or pronoun used to indicate that it is the subject of the verb.

noncoordinate adjective.   Adjective in a series of attributive adjectives that modifies the unit formed by a succeeding adjective and the noun. Examples: She solved a complex calculus problem ["complex" modifies "calculus problem"]. This is a large green clothbound book ["large" modifies "green clothbound book"; "green" modifies "clothbound book"]. Noncoordinate adjectives are not separated by commas. *Compare* **coordinate adjective.**

noncountable noun.   Noun whose singular form may be preceded by a definite article or by *some,* but not by an indefinite article (*a* or *an*). Examples: advice, furniture, mail, music, sand, training. The singular of a noncountable noun may also stand alone. Example: Music soothes the soul. Sand is gritty.

nonfinite verb.   Infinitive (to be, to do, to go), present participle (being, doing, going), or past participle (been, done, gone). *Compare* **finite verb.**

nonrestrictive modifier.   Clause or phrase that describes its subject but is not essential to the meaning of the sentence. Nonrestrictive modifiers are set off by commas. Examples: Dogs, <u>which are members of the canine family,</u> make good pets. I want to thank my mother, <u>who always encouraged me to write.</u> In contrast, a **restrictive modifier** is essential to the meaning of the sentence and is not set off by commas. Examples: Dogs <u>that have shiny black coats</u> are my favorites. I want to thank those teachers <u>who encouraged me</u>—and "So there!" to those <u>who did not.</u>

object.   Noun, pronoun, or noun clause that follows a transitive verb or a preposition and is the "recipient" of the action. *See also* **direct object.**

objective case.   Form of a noun or pronoun used to indicate that it is the object of a verb. We told <u>her</u> the rules. They gave <u>us</u> instructions.

parallel construction.   Principle requiring items in a pair or series to have the same grammatical form. Examples: Our goals are to <u>expand</u> customer services and <u>improve</u> employee morale. The skills needed for this position include <u>proofreading, copyediting,</u> and <u>indexing.</u>

participial phrase.   Phrase introduced by a present participle (being, going, doing) or a perfect participle (having been, having gone, having done). *See also* **dangling modifier.**

participle.   *See* **past participle; perfect participle; present participle.**

parts of speech.   Categorization of words into classes that reflect their function: adjectives, adverbs, articles, conjunctions, interjections, nouns, prepositions, pronouns, and verbs. Many words function as members of more than one class.

passive voice.   *See* **active voice.**

past participle.   Verb form that usually ends in *-ed* (wanted, noticed), although some verbs have irregular forms (been, gone, said). Past participles are used to form the perfect tenses (I have been, I had been, I will have been) and passive constructions (it was said that; there are thought to be).

perfect participle.   Verb form consisting of *having* or *having been* followed by a past participle. Examples: having gone, having been gone.

phrase.   Group of related words that functions as one part of speech (e.g., adverbial phrase, noun phrase, verb phrase).

possessive case.   Form of a noun or pronoun used to indicate that it "possesses" an object. Examples: <u>my</u> house, <u>Chris's</u> book, <u>children's</u> toys, art for <u>art's</u> sake. Also used in expressions of temporal duration: a <u>week's</u> worth of errands; six <u>months'</u> vacation.

predicate.   Portion of a sentence that makes a statement about the grammatical subject of the sentence. The predicate includes the verb and all its modifiers, objects, and complements. Examples: His four older brothers and their wives <u>are coming tomorrow.</u> We <u>can't think about that nor do anything about it right now.</u> June 21, summer solstice, <u>is the longest day of the year in the northern hemisphere.</u>

predicate adjective.   Adjective that follows the noun it modifies, coming in the predicate of the sentence. Examples: Iced tea is <u>thirst quenching.</u> He received a bill that was <u>larger than usual.</u> *Compare* **attributive adjective.**

predicate nominative.   Noun in the nominative case that is in the predicate of a sentence. Examples: She is the <u>president</u> of the club. He hopes to become an <u>expert</u> in his field. They are a happy <u>couple.</u>

preposition.   Word that expresses the physical or temporal relation between a noun or pronoun and other elements in a phrase, clause, or sentence. Examples: above, after, at, before, by, during, for, from, in, of, on, over, to, up, with. *Compound prepositions* consist of two or more words: according to, in place of, instead of, out of, together with, up to, with regard to.

prepositional phrase.   Phrase consisting of a preposition and the noun or pronoun that it pertains to. Examples: <u>Before sunrise</u> is the best time to view the skyline. They are requesting a refund <u>instead of a replacement copy.</u> <u>On Friday</u> he appealed <u>to his supervisor</u> for assistance.

present participle.   Verb form ending in *-ing* (being, doing) that is used to form the progressive tenses: I am singing, I was singing, I have been singing, I had been singing. The present participle may also be used as a noun (I like her <u>singing</u>) and as a modifier (<u>Standing</u> on an empty stage, he looked lost). *See also* **dangling modifier; gerund; verbal.**

pronoun-antecedent agreement.   Principle by which the form of a pronoun is determined by the number and gender of its antecedent.

proper adjective.   Adjectival form of a proper noun. Examples: We purchase only <u>American</u> products. She studied <u>Euclidean</u> geometry.

proper noun.   Name of a specific person, group, place, or thing. Examples: Jane Doe, Europeans, Latin America, the Great Wall of China.

referent.   *See* **antecedent.**

reflexive verb.   Verb whose subject and direct object are the same. Examples: I hurt myself. The dog scratched itself. She washed herself. *Compare* **intransitive verb; transitive verb.**

relative clause.   Dependent clause introduced by a relative pronoun, adjective, or adverb (e.g., that, what, when, where, which, who, whom, whose, why). Examples: This is the office <u>that she used.</u> Give this report to the journalist <u>who asked for it.</u>

restrictive modifier.   Clause or phrase that limits its subject and therefore is essential to the meaning of the sentence. Examples: Editors <u>who have at least five years' seniority</u> will receive a bonus ["who have" limits the set of editors]. Buildings <u>that are scheduled for renovation</u> will close early on Thursday ["that are" limits the set of buildings]. We must vigorously protest <u>when our civil rights are threatened</u> ["when" limits when we must protest]. *Compare* **nonrestrictive modifier.**

run-on sentence.   Grammatically incorrect construction consisting of two independent clauses joined by a comma (rather than by a coordinate conjunction or a semicolon). Example: The multinational peace force is patrolling the streets, the international food agencies are providing food and medicine.

sentence adverb.   Adverb that modifies an entire independent clause. Examples: <u>Surprisingly,</u> inflation has remained flat. No tickets are available, <u>unfortunately.</u>

sentence fragment.   Expression punctuated as though it were a complete sentence, even though it lacks either a subject or a finite verb. Fragments are acceptable when used for special effect.

split infinitive.   Construction in which one or more words separate *to* from the verb form. Examples: to boldly go, to more than double, to further insist.

subject.   Person, place, or thing that performs the action expressed by a finite verb.

subject-verb agreement.   Principle by which the form of a finite verb is determined by its subject: I am, she is, you are.

subjunctive.   Set of verb forms used in dependent clauses to express wishes, requests, commands, necessity, uncertainty, and contrary-to-fact or hypothetical conditions. Examples: They asked that the program <u>be</u> canceled. We insist that he <u>be</u> excused. If the commission <u>were</u> to agree to hear the case, the merger might be delayed. It is imperative that construction <u>be</u> halted.

subordinate conjunction.   *See* **conjunction.**

substantive.   Word, phrase, or clause that functions as a noun.

transitive verb.   Verb that has a direct object. Examples: I trust you. I wrote a letter. She is laying the tile. *Compare* **intransitive verb; reflexive verb.**

verb.   Word or group of words that expresses an action or a state of being. *See also* **copula; finite verb; infinitive; intransitive verb; nonfinite verb; reflexive verb; transitive verb.**

verbal.   Infinitive or participle of a verb that functions as a noun, adjective, or adverb. Examples: <u>To accept</u> this award gives me great pleasure. There is work <u>to be done.</u> They play <u>to win.</u> <u>Seeing</u> is <u>believing.</u> The <u>opening</u> bars imitate the rhythms of a <u>speeding</u> train. Her long-<u>awaited</u> novel has been published.

❖ Answer Keys

EXERCISE A

```
1. The man wearing the long-sleeved red

gingham shirt told amusing tall tales ⊙
                                       ∧
```

No commas in **long-sleeved red gingham shirt** because the adjectives are not coordinate. (Test for coordination: One would not write "the long-sleeved and red shirt" or "the red and gingham shirt"). No commas in **amusing tall tales** either, because these adjectives are not coordinate: **amusing** modifies the unit **tall tales**. In contrast, a comma is required in "This is a healthy, tall tree" or "This is an amusing, sad tale."

```
2. The accountant asked whether the receipts

   were in order ⊙
                 ∧
```

This sentence ends with a period, not a question mark, because the question is an indirect one.

```
3. The accountant asked ˌ "Are the receipts in
        ?
   order ˌ "
         ∧
```

Mandatory comma after **asked** to separate the speaker's tag from the direct quotation. The sentence ends with a question mark because the speaker's statement is a direct question. And since the question mark belongs to the dialogue being quoted, the question mark goes inside the closing quotation marks. In contrast, the question mark goes outside the closing quotation marks when the act of asking a question is not part of the quotation:

Who said, "Beware of all enterprises that require new clothes"?

Do you have a copy of the poem "Sunday Morning"?

```
4. School curriculums have traditionally been

the domain of politicians and educators, not
                                         ͻ
judges ⊙
       ʌ
```

Mandatory comma to set off the antithetical **not judges**. Note that a midsentence antithetical phrase is both preceded and followed by commas: Politicians and educators, not judges, have traditionally set school curriculums.

```
5. The promoter said that if no more ticket

requests came in the concert would be
                   ͻ
canceled ⊙
         ʌ
```

Mandatory comma after a dependent clause that precedes an independent clause. In this sentence the comma also prevents the reader from construing **came in the concert** as a unit of thought. Notice that if we reverse the order of the clauses, the new sentence has no comma because the independent clause is followed by a restrictive dependent clause: The promoter said that the concert would be canceled if no more ticket requests came in. No comma before or after *that* in a phrase of the form "he said that *x*" or "she wrote that *y*."

```
6. Harvard freshmen who have reading scores

below the national average performed better

than expected on the math aptitude test ⊙
                                         ʌ
```

No commas here. The context signals that the *who* clause is restrictive (that is, the subject is *only* those Harvard freshmen who have below-average reading scores). If one inserts commas to set off this *who* clause, it becomes nonrestrictive, which would mean that *all* Harvard freshmen have below-average reading scores. If you cannot determine from the context whether a clause is restrictive or nonrestrictive, query the author (see sentence 10 below). Also, note that **better than expected** functions here as an adverb and therefore carries no hyphens; in "the better-than-expected results," in contrast, the attributive adjective is hyphenated.

7. You can teach yourself basic computer

skills using a how-to book‿but a better

choice is to ask a knowledgeable‿sympathetic

friend for tutoring ⊙

Mandatory comma before **but** because it links two independent clauses. (To use a semicolon here would be incorrect; semicolons are used to join two independent clauses when there is no intervening conjunction.) Comma between the coordinate adjectives **knowledgeable** and **sympathetic**. (Test for coordination: One could say "a sympathetic and knowledgeable friend" and "my friend is knowledgeable and sympathetic.")

8. Each hospital has a service office whose

staff members will answer your questions

about hospital policies ⊙

Initially, the *whose* clause appears nonrestrictive: it does not limit or restrict the meaning or extent of **service office**. But the meaning of the sentence (that the service office's staff members will answer questions) requires us to treat the *whose* clause as restrictive. If you are under the misimpression that *whose* should not be used to refer to inanimate objects, see *DEU* (s.v. "whose"), which forcefully puts this bugaboo to rest.

9. From June 1 through June 3‿1998‿the

Chamber of Commerce of Oakland‿California‿

hosted its third annual conference for small

businesses ⊙

Mandatory commas before and after the year in a month-day-year construction. Mandatory commas before and after the name of the state.

```
10. All part-time employees who are not        (?)

covered by the new contract will be laid off
```

Taken out of context, the *who* clause could be restrictive (the layoff affects *only those* part-time employees who are not covered by the contract) or non-restrictive (the layoff affects *all* the part-time employees, none of whom are covered by the contract). You should query the author and perhaps propose a revision that will be clearer to readers:

> *Query:* Does the layoff affect *only those* part-time employees who are not covered by the contract *or* does it affect *all* the part-time employees (none of whom are covered by the contract)? If the former, the sentence could read

>> Those part-time employees who are not covered by the new contract will be laid off.

> If the latter, the sentence could read

>> None of the part-time employees are covered by the new contract, and all will be laid off.

EXERCISE B

When comparing your version with this key, read slowly to make sure you
spot each correction. A detailed commentary follows the marked-up manuscript. The advice in this exercise is based on two paragraphs from Arthur
Plotnik, *The Elements of Editing: A Modern Guide for Editors and Journalists*
(New York: Macmillan, 1982; reissued by Macmillan General Reference,
1997), pp. 2–4, but much of the language has been changed and all the errors
were introduced for the purpose of this exercise.

                                              pore

    Some overly zealous copyeditors will ~~pour~~

over a manuscript ⸜ and change every "till"

to "until" or vice versa, depending on their

training, their grammatical ear, and their

5   ideas about prose style. Although editors

must try to forestall the deprecation of

English into colloquial swill, they should

never adopt a self-styled purism that does ⓠ1

not allow for some variety of expression.

10   When a tyrannical editorial coordinator waves

Fowler, Wilson Follett, and other venerable ⓠ2

guardians, ~~his~~ *the* staff should wave back ⓠ3

Theodore Bernstein's *Miss Thistlebottom's*

Hobgoblins, a thoughtful debunking of

15   scared cows in usage, or William Morris and

Mary Morris's *Harper Dictionary of*

Contemporary Usage, which explores the ⟮*italic* comma⟯

differences of opinion among the so-called ⸂experts.⸃

20   A second danger: Some novice copyeditors misinterpret the recommendations in *The Elements ⸠of Style* as a mandate to change such sentences as "the outcry was heard round the

25   world" to "every⸍one in the world heard the outcry." True, the active voice is more forceful, and a procession of passive constructions is a sure cure for insomnia. (Q4)

30   But the passive voice is preferable when the writer's goal is variety or emphasi~~zing an~~ So⊙ ~~important word in a sentence.⸃ (Q5)

DID YOU CATCH MOST OF THE ERRORS?

There were ten typographical errors (typos) in this exercise:

Line	Error
1	**pour** for **pore**
2–3	double quotation marks on **till**, single quote marks on **until**
6	**deprecation** = disapproval; **depreciation** = decline in value
9	**vareity** for **variety**
10	**tyrranical** for **tyrannical**
14	**Hobogoblins** for **Hobgoblins**
14	**thoughtfull** for **thoughtful**
15	**scared** for **sacred**
16	**Morrris** for **Morris**
25	**every-one** for **everyone**

If you missed more than two of these typos, you should try to read more slowly: Force yourself to read letter by letter, not word by word.

Many of the other errors in this manuscript concern issues discussed in chapters 5 through 8, so don't worry if you missed them now. But here's a taste of the kind of reasoning and reliance on convention that copyeditors develop. Queries to the author are labeled Q1, Q2, and so on.

Line	Comment
2	Comma after **manuscript** is incorrect because it interrupts the compound predicate **copyeditors will pore . . . and change.**
Q1	OK or revise to avoid the sequence of negatives "they should never" and "that does not allow"?
Q2	Please supply Fowler's first name (for consistency with other authorities in this paragraph).
Q3	Word(s) missing? Guardians of what?
12	Change **his** to **the** to avoid the implication that all editorial coordinators are male. (See the discussion of the generic *he* under "Bias-Free Language" in chapter 15.)
15–16	**William Morris and Mary Morris's** is correct. In cases of joint ownership, only the last owner's name takes the possessive *'s*. On the differing views about the possessive form for a proper name that ends in *s*, see "Possessives" in chapter 5.
17	Comma needed to set off the nonrestrictive clause introduced by *which*. (See *nonrestrictive modifier* in the Glossary of Grammar Terms.)
19	By convention, no quotation marks around a word or phrase introduced by *so-called*.
20	Some editors are uncomfortable about the colon here, believing that only an independent clause may precede a colon. But that isn't the case: "The colon is used after a word, phrase, or sentence to introduce something that follows, such as a formal question or quotation, an amplification, or an example" (*WIT,* p. 180). Here, "A second danger" functions as an introductory label; cf. "Warning: Do not leave the hot stove unattended" or "First order of business: Review last quarter's report." One could expand "A second danger" into an independent clause "There is a second danger" or "Here is a second danger," but these additions are not required and do not significantly improve the text.

22   Lowercase a preposition in the title of a book. (See "Titles of
        Works" in chapter 6.)

24–25   Preferable to capitalize the first word of each quoted example be-
        cause each is a complete sentence.

Q4   Rhyme ("sure cure") OK?

31   Parallel structure requires either "variety or emphasis" (with *or*
        linking two nouns) or "to achieve variety or to emphasize a key
        word" (with *or* linking two verbs).

Q5   Revision for parallel structure OK?

DID YOU OVEREDIT?

If you made a number of other changes, they may have been for the better—
in the sense of clarifying or tightening the prose—but they were probably
unnecessary. And every time you make a change, you run two risks: that of
introducing new errors and that of frustrating the author. Whenever you
copyedit, consider the following:

- Almost any sentence can be improved, but a copyeditor has to be
  able to leave well enough alone.
- The text is the author's text, not the copyeditor's.
- If the assignment is a light copyedit, copyeditors are not expected
  to spend their time working on a sentence that is already "good
  enough."
- If a copyeditor misses scattered mistakes in the text, he or she will
  be forgiven—after all, no one is perfect. But when a copyeditor
  introduces a mistake or changes something correct into something
  incorrect, those acts of commission are much harder to forgive.

EXERCISE C

The hyphenation choices shown here follow the rules in *Chicago*; other style manuals prefer other conventions. Copyeditors enter their hyphenation decisions in the alpha section of the style sheet (see pages 50–51).

> 1. There was an above‗average turnout by
> middle‗aged working‗class voters in the south‿
> eastern states.

above-average turnout: Attributive compound adjectives of the form "adverb (non -*ly*) + adjective" may be left open, or a hyphen may be added for clarity. They are open when they follow the noun: the turnout was above average.

middle-aged [voters]: Hyphenate an attributive compound adjective whose first element is *high, low, upper,* or *middle* (for an exception, see sentence 3 below). Compounds of this form are open when they follow the noun: These voters are middle aged. Notice that there is no comma after **middle-aged** because **middle-aged** and **working-class** are not coordinate adjectives.

working-class voters: Hyphenate an attributive compound adjective of the form "adjective or participle + noun." Compounds of this form are open when they follow the noun: Most of the voters in this district are working class.

southeastern: Terms that denote points of the compass are solid.

> 2. He submitted a hastily written report that
> documented his half‗baked effort to revise his
> predecessor's ill‗conceived cost‗cutting plan.

hastily written report: Compound adjectives of the form "-*ly* adverb + participle or adjective" are open in both the attributive and predicate position.

half-baked effort: Compound adjectives whose first element is *half* are hyphenated unless the word is shown closed in the dictionary—for example, *halfhearted, halfway.*

ill-conceived [plan]: Compound adjectives of the form "*well, ill, better, best, little, lesser,* or *least* + adjective or participle" are hyphenated in the attributive position. There is no comma after **ill-conceived** because **ill-conceived** and **cost-cutting** are not coordinate adjectives. (Test for coordination: One could not write "his ill-conceived and cost-cutting plan" or "his cost-cutting and ill-conceived plan" because "ill-conceived" modifies the unit "cost-cutting plan.")

cost-cutting plan: Compound adjectives of the form "noun + participle" are hyphenated in the attributive position.

```
 3. To replicate this early nineteenth century

    experiment, the high school students needed

(?) two gallon test bottles, a four inch long

    tube, a six or seven foot plank, and two to

    three teaspoons of salt.
```

early-nineteenth-century experiment: Compound adjectives that include *century* are hyphenated. The modifier *early* may take a hyphen or be left open. The noun forms are open: in the early nineteenth century.

high school students: *High school* is a permanent open compound noun and adjective, as shown in the dictionary.

two gallon test bottles: If the students need two test bottles, each of which is a one-gallon bottle, no hyphens are needed, but the text would be clearer if it read "two one-gallon test bottles." If the students need several two-gallon test bottles, the text should read "two-gallon test bottles." When you cannot determine from the context which meaning is intended, you must query the author.

four-inch-long tube: Compound adjectives of the form "number + unit of measure" are hyphenated in the attributive position. Compare: The tube is four inches long.

six- or seven-foot plank: This expression is a shortened form of "six-foot or seven-foot plank." A hyphen and a wordspace follow the first element of a suspended compound.

two to three teaspoons of salt: No hyphens are needed because **two to three teaspoons** is *not* a compound adjective. Compare: A two- to three-teaspoon dose is recommended.

4. The ideal candidate will have strong

skills in problem solving, decision making,

film making, book keeping, and proof reading.

problem solving, decision making: Compound nouns of the form "noun + gerund" are open unless they are shown in the dictionary as closed or hyphenated. But compound adjectives of the form "noun + gerund" are hyphenated when they precede the noun: problem-solving and decision-making skills.

filmmaking, bookkeeping, proofreading: The dictionary shows these words as closed.

5. He is self conscious about his 45 percent

productivity decline and five fold increase

in tardiness.

self-conscious: Compound adjectives whose first element is *self* are hyphenated in both the attributive and predicate positions. (*M-W Collegiate* retains the hyphen in *unself-conscious*, but *Chicago* recommends the more appealing *unselfconscious*.)

45 percent decline: Compound adjectives of the form "numeral + *percent*" are not hyphenated.

fivefold: Adjectives formed with the suffix *-fold* are solid unless the first element is a numeral—for example, a 125-fold increase.

6. As a comparison of the pre and post test

scores for the fourth, fifth, and sixth grade

students showed, highly motivated young

students can learn the most basic aspects of

socio economic theory.

pre- and posttest scores: This expression is a shortened form of "pretest and posttest scores." When a prefix stands as the first element in a suspended compound, the prefix is followed by a hyphen and a wordspace. Like most words that begin with a common prefix, *posttest* is solid; for exceptions to this rule, see "One Word or Two?" in chapter 5.

fourth-, fifth-, and sixth-grade students: Compound adjectives of the form "ordinal number + noun" are hyphenated in the attributive position, as are all attributive adjectives of the form "adjective or participle + noun." When a comma follows an element in a suspended compound, there is no word-space between the hyphen and the comma.

most basic aspects: Compound adjectives of the form "adverb (non -*ly*) + adjective" may be left open unless the open form would be ambiguous. In this sentence, the only possible interpretation is that **most** modifies **basic** (i.e., students are learning those aspects of theory that are the most basic); an alternative reading—"students are learning the most [the maximum number of] basic principles" makes no sense. In comparison, consider "much heralded music" and "much-heralded music." In the former, "much" denotes a quantity; in the latter, it modifies "heralded."

socioeconomic: Words that begin with the prefix *socio-* are solid.

```
7. He sat cross‿legged at the cross‿roads

cross‿questioning the pollster about the

cross‿over vote and the cross fire over the

nomination.
```

cross-legged, crossroads, cross-questioning, crossover, cross fire: There are no simple rules for compound adjectives, nouns, or verbs beginning with *cross*. You should always consult the dictionary to see which forms are conventional.

```
8. The state‿of‿the‿art amplifier is over

there with the other out‿of‿order equipment

that the under‿appreciated copy‿editors and
```

their anti⁼intellectual co⁼workers left
        ᴧ   ᴧ

behind.

state-of-the-art amplifier and **out-of-order equipment:** Phrases that function as compound adjectives and that precede the noun are hyphenated. These phrases are usually not hyphenated in the predicate position: This equipment is out of order.

underappreciated: Words that begin with the prefix *under-* are solid.

copyeditors: See chapter 1, note 5.

anti-intellectual: *Chicago* style calls for closing up words beginning with the prefix *anti-* (anticlimax, antiauthoritarian, antitrust) unless the second element begins with *i* (anti-intellectual, anti-incumbent, anti-imperialism) or the closed form is misleading or hard to read (anti-union). Because strict adherence to *Chicago* yields *anticonsumerism, antifamily, antilabor,* and so on, some publishers prefer to hyphenate all *anti-* compounds that do not have specific, well-established meanings: antibiotic, antifreeze, antitrust *but* anti-consumerism, anti-family, anti-labor.

co-workers or **coworkers:** On the dispute over *co-* compounds, see the section on prefixes and suffixes under "One Word or Two?" in chapter 5.

EXERCISE D

This exercise is based on blurbs that appeared in the winter 1995 catalog published by Daedalus Books, PO Box 9132, Hyattsville, Md. 20181-0932, and is used with permission of the publisher. For the purpose of this exercise, errors were introduced and other changes were made to the published text.

A FROLIC OF HIS OWN. William Gaddis. Poseidon.

$25.00

A *Frolic of His Own,* William Gaddis'/ long= ^

anticipated fourth novel, is a funny,

5   accurate tale of lives caught up in the toils
     the
     of ^ law. Oscar Crease, middle-aged college

     instructor, savant, and playwright, is suing a

     Hollywood producer for pirating his play *Once*

     at Antietam, based on his grandfather's

10   experiences in the Civil War, and turning it

     in to a gory block|buster called *The Blood in*

     the Red White and Blue. Oscar's suit/ and a   (Q1)

     host of other lawsuits--which involve a dog

     trapped in an outdoor sculpture, wrongful

15   death during a river baptism, a church versus
               =
     a soft ^ drink company, and even Oscar himself

     after he is run over by his own car--engulf

     all who surround him, from his free|wheeling

     girlfriend to his draconian/ nonagenarian

20   father, Federal Judge Thomas Creese. Down   (Q2)

this tortuous path of depositions and

decrees, suits and countersuits, the ~~most~~

loft*iest* ideas of our culture are *w* rung dry in

the often surreal logic and language of the

25   law.

THE BIRD ARTIST. Howard Norman. FSG. $20⊙00

Howard Norman's spellbinding novel is set in

Newfoundland in 1911. The novel *shares* not only

~~shares~~ its place, but also its tone and

30   passion, with *The Shipping News.* Fabian Vas's   (Q3)

story, told with simplicity and grace, takes

place against a spare, beautiful landscape. At

(sp)   age (20, Fabian is working at the boatyard,

taking a correspondence course in bird

35   painting, and sleeping with Maraget Handle, a   (Q4)

woman of great beauty, intelligence, and

waywardness. When his father leaves on a long

hunting expedition and his mother takes up

with the lighthouse keeper, Fabian loⱷses his

40   bearings. The author's intense observation of

people and nature make*s* for a remarkably good

novel.

(Q5)

A PERSONAL MATTER. Kenzaburo Oë. $7.95

45 *A Personal Matter,* here translated by John
Nathan, is probably Oë's best known novel. It
is the story of a man's relationship with his
severely brain-damaged child. As he plots the
child's murder, he finally realizes that he
must take responsibility for his son. The

50 novel, written out of Oé's profound despair (Q6)
after the birth of his own disabled child
(now a ~~31~~ thirty-one-year-old successful composer) is
original, different, tough in its candor, and
beautiful in its faithfulness to both

55 intellectual precision and human tenderness.

ARE THE ENTRIES CONSISTENT IN FORMAT?

When copyediting catalogs and similar types of documents, you should make a special pass to double-check that the entries are consistent in format. For example, in the headings for each of the three entries (lines 1–2, 26, and 43), the writer has consistently used all-capital boldface for the book titles (followed by a period); the remaining elements (author's name, publisher's name, price) are in regular type, separated by periods. The two inconsistencies are discussed below, in the comment on line 26 and in Q5.

Line	Comment
3	There is no need to insert a paragraph sign at the start of this paragraph (nor at the start of the paragraphs that begin on lines 27 and 44). The decision about how to style the first paragraph following a line of display type (that is, large type, used for chapter

titles and heads) is up to the publication's designer. Most often, the first paragraph after a line of display type is set flush left (that is, with no paragraph indent). In books and magazine articles, each subsequent paragraph is indented; in corporate documents, paragraphs may be indicated by the indention of the first line or by extra linespacing between paragraphs.

3 The writer has correctly used italics for the title of a book.

3–4 Hyphenate the two-word attributive adjective **long-anticipated.**

4 Keep the comma after **funny** because **funny** and **accurate** are coordinate adjectives. (This pair of adjectives passes the test for coordination: One could write "a funny and accurate tale," "an accurate and funny tale," or "an accurate, funny tale.")

7 Add a comma at the end of the tucked-in "middle-aged college instructor, savant, and playwright" description that intervenes between **Oscar Crease** and the verb **is suing.**

8–9 By convention, italics are used for the title of a play.

11–12 Italics are correct for the title of a film.

Q1 No serial commas in title OK? Or *the Red, White, and Blue?*

12 Delete the comma, since **Oscar's suit and a host of other lawsuits** is the compound subject of the verb **engulf** (in line 17).

16 Some copyeditors will view **soft drink** as a fixed open compound noun and will not add a hyphen to the adjective form here (cf. post office hours). Other copyeditors will insert a hyphen to prevent a momentary misreading.

19 No comma between noncoordinate adjectives **draconian** and **nonagenarian.** (This pair of adjectives does not pass the test for coordination: One would not write "a draconian and nonagenarian father" nor "a nonagenarian and draconian father.")

20 **Federal Judge** capitalized because it is a civil title preceding a proper name.

Q2 Please reconcile: Creese here, but Crease above.

23 For most two-syllable adjectives that end in *y,* the superlative form ends in *-iest,* and, indeed, *loftiest* is the form shown in the dictionary; cf. happy, happiest; funny, funniest.

26 Notice that in the two other entries, the price of the book is given in dollars and cents.

28–29 Revise for parallel structure: "shares not only its place but also its tone." Preferable not to have a comma interrupt a "not only ... but also" chain.

Q3   Supply name of author for *The Shipping News*. [Note: Readers unfamiliar with *The Shipping News* may assume that it is an earlier novel by Howard Norman. Not so: *The Shipping News* was written by E. Annie Proulx and was awarded the Pulitzer Prize for fiction in 1994.]

32   Add a comma between the coordinate adjectives **spare** and **beautiful.** (This pair of adjectives passes the test for coordination: One could write "spare and beautiful landscape," "beautiful and spare landscape," or "beautiful, spare landscape.")

33   In nontechnical text, spell out numbers under 101; see "Words or Numerals?" in chapter 7.

33   Because *boatyard* does not appear as a permanent closed compound in desktop dictionaries, some copyeditors may prefer to treat it as a temporary compound and add a hyphen: boat-yard. On the other hand, since many *boat-* compounds are closed (*M-W Collegiate* shows *boathouse, boatload,* and *boatman*), and *-yard* compounds are closed (*backyard, schoolyard*), the closed form seems unobjectionable.

Q4   Maraget OK? or Margaret?

40–41 Subject-verb agreement requires either **observation . . . makes** or **observations . . . make.**

Q5   Supply publisher's name, for consistency with the other entries.

45   Hyphenate the two-word adjective **best-known.**

47   In the complex attributive adjective **severely brain-damaged,** no hyphen after **severely** (an adverb ending in *-ly*); keep the hyphen in **brain-damaged** (a two-word attributive adjective).

Q6   Reconcile: Oé here, but Oë (twice) above.

52   Add a comma to indicate the end of the long interrupter that comes between the subject **The novel** and the verb **is** [**original, different, tough**].

53   Add a serial comma before **and.**

STYLE SHEET ENTRIES

Numbers
Spell out numbers under 101

Punctuation
Serial comma
Possessives of names ending in *s:* Gaddis's, Vas's

Miscellaneous

Listing line for each book is: **TITLE ALL CAPS.** Author's Name.
   Publisher. $xx.xx

Titles: In the body of the review, book titles are italic, upper- and
   lowercase

Alpha list

best-known (adj.)	girlfriend
blockbuster (n.)	long-anticipated (adj.)
boatyard	middle-aged (adj.)
brain-damaged (adj.)	soft-drink company
countersuits	spellbinding
freewheeling	

Note: Some copyeditors choose not to provide style sheet entries for words
that have no recognized variants (e.g., blockbuster, countersuits). Entries for
these items, however, may be helpful to the author, and they serve as an aide-
mémoire for the copyeditor. Similarly, some copyeditors choose not to enter
hyphenation choices that follow the house style manual. But an author who
does not have a copy of the style manual will appreciate seeing the entries on
the style sheet.

EXERCISE E

This exercise is based on an excerpt from Samuel Kernell and Samuel Pop-
kin, editors, *Chief of Staff: Twenty-five Years of Managing the Presidency* (University of California Press, 1986), pp. 13–15, and is used with permission of
the publisher. For the purpose of this exercise, errors were introduced and
other changes were made to the published text.

After serving for five years as President

Eisenhower's ¢taff ¢ecretary, General Andrew

J. Goodpaster assumed many of the duties of

¢hief of ¢taff in 1958. During Eisenhower's

5   administration, General Goodpaster supervised

the National Security Council ¢taff, briefed

the ₱resident on intelligence matters, and

was White House Ḷiaison for defense and

national security.

10   Before being appointed special assistant

and counsel to President Johnson in 1965,

Harry McPherson had served as counsel to the

Democratic policy committee in the Senate,

Ḍeputy Ụndersecretary of the Ạrmy, and

15   assistant ¢ecretary of ¢tate. He is now an

attorney in Washington, D.C., and vice=⌐

chairman of and general counsel to the John

F. Kennedy Center for the performing arts.

General Alexander Haig was deputy to

20   national security adviser Henry Kissinger

during the early days of President Nixon's

administration. He became Nixon's chief of

staff in 1973. In 1974 he was named supreme

commander of NATO, a post he held until 1979,

25   when he retired to enter private industry. He

returned to government service as secretary

of state during the first eighteen months of

President Reagan's first term.

Line	Comment
2	Lowercase **staff secretary**; this title is not part of the general's name in this sentence but is in apposition to his name.
4	Lowercase **chief of staff**; this title is not followed by a personal name.
5	Author's lowercasing of **administration** follows the down-style convention.
6	Lowercase **staff**; this common noun is not part of a proper name of an organization.
7	Lowercase **president**; this title is not followed by a personal name.
8	Lowercase **liaison**; this common noun is not part of a proper name or title.
13	The author's treatment of **Democratic policy committee** denotes that "policy committee" is a common noun (a generic term for a

committee that debates policy) rather than a proper name. A copy-editor should either let this stand or query (Should this be a proper name?) but should not independently make it uppercase (thereby creating a committee out of thin air).

14–15   Lowercase both offices, since neither is followed by a proper name.

16   There is no uniformity in the treatment of *vice* compounds in dictionaries and editorial style manuals; for example, *M-W Collegiate* shows *vice admiral, vice-chancellor, vice-consul,* and *vice president* as the preferred forms. To maintain consistency throughout a document, always enter your choices about the hyphenation of *vice* compounds on your style sheet.

17–18   Uppercase the full name of this institution.

20   Uppercase this title preceding a proper name.

23–24   Lowercase this title because no proper name follows.

24   Comma after 1979 to set off the nonrestrictive *when* clause.

26–27   Lowercase the common adjective **government** and the common noun **secretary of state.**

EXERCISE F

If you want to break into publishing, you

probably know that the center of book

publishing in the United States is New York

City. But you don't have to move to New York

5 to work in book publishing. Go to the public

Library and look at the most recent edition

of *Literary Market Place* (*LMP,* published

annually by R.R. Bowker, New York). Use the

geographical index to locate book publishers

10 in your town. Then turn to the full entries

for each publisher and take note of how many

titles the company publishes. A company that

produces fewer than eight or ten titles a

year is most likely a two-or-three-person

15 operation, staffed by it's owners. But the

names of any larger publishers should go on

your job hunting list.

While you have *LMP* in hand, turn to the

subject index and notice how many different

20 kinds of book publishers there are, not just

fiction and nonfiction but el-hi (elementary

and high school) and college textbook

publishers, legal and medical publishers,

science and math publishers, foreign language

25   publishers, and publishers of children's

books, art books, scholarly books, wilderness

books, computer books, gardening books, cook

books, and every stripe of how-to books.

While you're at the library, you might also

30   ~~also~~ look at the current edition of *Magazine*

Industry Market Place (R. R. Bowker) or   (Q1)

Writer's Market (Writer's Digest Books).

You'll be surprised to see how large the

universe of magazine publishers is. There are

35   hundreds of small trade magazines, and

hundreds of local and regional magazines.

Check the directories to see which magazines

have editorial offices in your town.

As you're compiling your list, don't forget

40   the corporate sector. The obvious employers

in the corporate sector are direct-mail and

catalogue companies, but many firms whose

primary business lies elsewhere do an

enormous amount of publishing: banks, law

45   firms, phone companies, hospitals,

universities, museums, manufactures of high=

tech equipment, and consulting firms in all

fields. Any business that provides client

manuals, documents, or reports, or that

50   produces a newsletter for employees or for

clients needs editors. Some companies do not

advertise, but post their openings at the

company's personnel office. Call that office

and ask how openings are publicized.

55   Finally, there's the government sector.

Hordes of editors are employed in almost   (Q2)

every department of municipal, county, state,

and federal goverments. Some of these

positions require subject-matter expertise,

60   but others do not. Check with nearby

government offices to find out whether you

need to take a civil service exam and how

openings are posted.

(¶)In all four sectors, there is stiff

65   competition for entry-level jobs. To improve

your chances of landing a job:

1. Make sure your résumé and cover letter

are easy to read, error free, and ~~have a~~

consistent in editorial style (punctuation,

70   treatment of dates, use of abbreviations,

etc) . Don't just list your previous job

titles; take a sentence or two to describe

what you did in those positions. Be sure to

include any relevant subject-matter expertise

75   and auxiliary skills (pasteup, graphic

design, typesetting) .

2. Don't dwell on your writing skills   (Q3)

(unless the job calls for writing); most

managing editors believe there is little or

80   no correlation between writing skills and

editing skills. And don't dwell on your

academic credentials unless you're applying

to a scholarly press or journal.

3. If you have work samples, bring them to

note

85   an interview. Attach a Post-It to each sample

describing the work you did on the project.   (Q4)

4. Be prepared to take proofreading and

copyediting tests. Some employers will also

test your word processing skills.

Line	Comment

4   You may have been taught that it is incorrect to begin a sentence with *but*. But that so-called rule is no rule at all; see *DEU*, s.v. "but." Writers should not overuse this device, of course, but the ban on initial *but*s and *and*s is baseless.

4   Contractions fit the conversational tone of this piece, and a newsletter is likely to allow contractions. But some publishers ban contractions as too informal. Copyeditors should always inquire about house policy.

4   Do not add "City" after **move to New York,** since the full name of the city has just been mentioned.

6   Do not add a comma after **library.** Although this sentence consists of two independent clauses joined by *and,* no comma is needed since both imperatives are short, there is no change of person, and there is no danger of ambiguity or misreading.

7   Notice that *LMP* is (correctly) in italics. Both the full title and the shortened title of a book are italicized. Also, although the common noun *marketplace* is one word, the name of this publication is *Literary Market Place.* [The author recommends going to the library because a copy of *LMP* costs about $200.]

8   Space between personal initials. Notice that two paragraphs down, in line 31, the initials are spaced: **R. R. Bowker.** Some publishers prefer a thin space to a wordspace; to request a thin space, write "th #."

14   The author's **most likely** is correct. There are two common functions for *most:* (1) It is used to form the superlative of an adjective or an adverb (likely, more likely, most likely), and (2) it is used before an adjective or an adverb as an intensifier (she is a most effective speaker). Here, **most** serves the second function.

14–15 A suspended compound: "two- or three-person operation." Make sure the hyphens and wordspaces are indicated correctly. Similarly:

       The fourteen- and fifteen-year-old students attended.

       Steel-plated or -cased vaults were used.

15   Here, **staffed by its owners** could be deemed restrictive or nonrestrictive; follow the author's lead.

17   Hyphenate a compound adjective of the form "noun plus participle" when it precedes a noun: **job-hunting list**. In contrast, the noun *job hunting* is not hyphenated: "I detest job hunting."

18–28   This is indeed a long sentence, and a one-sentence paragraph at that. Nonetheless, the sentence is clear and coherent; the punctuation is correct; and the very length of the sentence seems designed to convey the breadth and diversity of the industry. Thus a copyeditor need not intervene. If you are tempted to intervene nonetheless, it would be better to query (Consider splitting this long sentence in two?) than to take up arms and rewrite. Resist the temptation to delete some of the instances of **publishers;** they serve a useful function in signaling the end of the individual items in this long list.

20   The author's comma after **there are** is correct. A colon would be incorrect here because **not just fiction** is not the first item in a list but rather an antithetical phrase. Compare: There are many kinds, not just two or three. In the following example, in contrast, a colon is required because "there are" introduces a list:

Notice how many different kinds of book publishers there are: fiction and nonfiction, legal and medical . . .

20–21   No commas needed between coordinate clauses such as "not just" and "but." Some people insist that the pairs must be "not just . . . but also" and "not only . . . but also," but this is a personal preference, not a requirement (see *DEU*, s.v. "not only . . . but also").

21   *M-W Collegiate* shows "elhi," but most people in publishing use "el-hi." If you have a question about a piece of jargon, query the author.

24–25   No hyphen needed in **foreign language publishers** because "foreign language" is a permanent open compound noun being used as an attributive adjective and there is no possibility of misreading. For other compounds in the *foreign* family, a hyphen is needed if the hyphenless compound is ambiguous: foreign-currency restrictions *and* foreign-service officers *but* foreign aid bill *and* foreign policy staff.

28   **stripe** is unobjectionable; see *M-W Collegiate,* s.v. "stripe," definition 3: "a distinct variety or sort: TYPE <persons of the same political stripe>." When "stripe of" precedes a noun, the noun is singular (every stripe of person). Or you could change this to read "and how-to books of every stripe."

28   Dictionaries show a hyphen in the adjective **how-to,** but there's no hyphen between the adjective **how-to** and the noun **book.**

Q1   For consistency, either supply the place of publication for these two directories or drop "New York" in the first paragraph for *LMP.* (*Note:* Since this piece was written, Bowker has suspended the annual publication of *Magazine Industry Market Place.*)

35   **small trade magazines** is correct. *Trade magazine* is a standard term in publishing, used to describe a magazine written for readers in a particular industry (as opposed to general-interest magazines like *Time, Newsweek,* or *Reader's Digest*). To write "small, trade magazines" is to convert **small** and **trade** into coordinate adjectives, which they are not. (Test: It is nonsense to say "The magazines are small and trade.") To write "small-trade" is to create an entity known as a "small trade" (as opposed to a "big trade" or a "large trade"). Although we do have "small business," there is no set phrase "small trade."

35   The comma after **magazines** isn't needed, but it isn't incorrect. Your choice to delete or keep it.

35–36   A copyeditor should resist the temptation to save a word or two by changing this to "There are hundreds of small trade, local, and regional magazines." That revision is inaccurate: The author uses "small" to modify only "trade magazines," not the local and regional magazines.

41   Keep the hyphen in the attributive adjective (**direct-mail** modifies **companies**), though the noun *direct mail* is not hyphenated. Compare:

>   We are a direct-mail company.

>   The new advertising campaign relies on direct mail.

42   The entry in *M-W Collegiate* reads "catalog *or* catalogue," which means that the two spellings are equal variants. Some copyeditors always respect the author's choice among equal variants; other copyeditors tend to impose the first spelling, even when the variants are equal. Whichever form you choose, be sure to enter it on your style sheet.

42–43   The author has correctly punctuated the *whose* clause as restrictive; the sentence is not about "many firms" but about "many firms whose primary business lies elsewhere."

49   Keep the comma after **reports,** even though the syntactical skele-

ton ("that provides *x* ... or that produces *y*") does not require one. The comma alerts the reader that **or that produces** is not an add-on to the series **client manuals, documents, or reports.**

52   The comma after **advertise** is not needed, because one usually does not have a comma between the parts of a compound predicate. But the comma is not incorrect either; it emphasizes the contrast between the two methods of publicizing openings.

Q2   Horde = swarm, teeming crowd, throng. Tone OK or revise?

62   Lowercase because **civil service exam** is a generic term, not a specific test. That's why the author used the indefinite article *a.* Compare:

> Applicants must take the Calculus Achievement Test.

> Applicants must take a calculus achievement test.

62   Do not add a hyphen to **civil service exam;** *civil service* is a permanent open compound, and the hyphenless term poses no danger of misreading.

65   Keep the hyphen in the attributive adjective **entry-level.**

67ff.   The author has chosen to treat these items as a set of numbered paragraphs, with the numerals serving to emphasize the items on the list. This technique is fine. One could also convert the numbered paragraphs into a set-off list, as shown below. (The formatting and typecoding of numbered lists are discussed in "Lists" in chapter 13.)

(ꟼ) In all four sectors, there is stiff

     competition for entry-level jobs. To improve

     your chances of landing a job:

    ⌐⊏1. Make sure your résumé and cover letter

(NL) are easy to read, error free, and ~~have a~~
                                       in
     consistent ˄editorial style (punctuation,

     treatment of dates, use of abbreviations,
          ͻ
     etc) . . . .
     ˄

```
⌐2. Don't dwell on your writing skills
                       ⌒                  ;
(unless the job call⌿s for writing)⋀most
                   ⌣
managing editors believe . . . .
      ∅
⌐3⋀If you have work samples, bring
    ⋀
them . . . .

⌐4. Be prepared to take proofreading and

⌞copyediting tests . . . .
```

68   No hyphens in the predicate adjectives **easy to read** and **error free**. In the attributive position, these adjectives are hyphenated: She has an easy-to-read résumé. She has an error-free résumé.

68–69   Author's construction is not parallel. Fix by changing the last item into an adjective ("consistent in editorial style") or break the sentence in two: "Make sure your résumé and cover letter are easy to read and error free. They should also have a consistent editorial style . . . " The least appealing way to mend a faulty parallel is to insert a "with" (easy to read and error free, with a consistent editorial style). Follett, in particular, lambastes the use of *with* to loosely link items: "The writer addicted to the facile but evasive *with* is shirking the rigors of thought about what he means and how to say it" (*MAU*, s.v. "with").

71   Some publishers consider the abbreviations *e.g., i.e.,* and *etc.* too informal to appear in print. Other publishers allow these abbreviations only in parenthetical comments and in footnotes. Always follow house policy. Here, **etc.** could be changed to "and the like."

72   The dash seems overly informal. The choices are:

> Don't just list your previous job titles. Take a sentence . . .
> Don't just list your previous job titles; take a sentence . . .
> Don't just list your previous job titles: Take a sentence . . .

But one cannot replace the dash with a comma, because a comma is not sufficient to join two independent clauses.

75–76   **pasteup** and **typesetting** are solid in the dictionary.

Q3   Both sentences in this item contain "don't dwell." OK or reword?

78   Parentheses are fine here, to de-emphasize the comment.

78   This dash is not incorrect, but it seems a bit lazy and informal. A semicolon is preferable.

81   It's OK to begin a sentence with "And," as long as this device is not overused.

82   No comma before **unless** because the clause is restrictive.

85   Author capitalized **Post-It** because it is a trademark. But the actual trademark is "Post-it," and the convention is to affix a noun to a trademark (Post-it note) because a trademark is, strictly speaking, not a noun. No need to insert the symbol ™ after the trademark (see "Company Names, Trademarks, and Brand Names" in chapter 6). You could also substitute a generic term: a self-adhering note, a sticker, a note.

Q4   More graceful to say "To each sample attach a note that describes the work you did"?

89   The author hyphenated **word-processing,** treating it as a compound adjective of the form "noun plus participle" preceding a noun. More often, however, both the noun and the adjective are treated as permanent open compounds: *word processing, word processing skills.* Some high-tech publications close all forms of the term: *wordprocessing, wordprocessing skills,* and *wordprocessor.* Whichever form you pick, make an entry on your style sheet.

STYLE SHEET ENTRIES

Numbers and Dates
Spell out numbers under 101

Punctuation
Serial comma
Contractions OK
Suspended compound: two- or three-person (adj.)

Abbreviations
LMP (italic)
R. R. Bowker (space between personal initials)
etc. is OK in parenthetical expressions only

Miscellaneous
Author to decide whether to include place of publication for directories
in paragraphs 1 and 3

Alpha list

catalogue	job-hunting (adj.)
civil service exam	pasteup
cookbook	personnel office
copyediting	Post-it note
direct-mail (adj.)	public library
el-hi (adj.)	résumé
entry-level (adj.)	subject-matter expertise
error free (predicate adj.)	two-person (adj.)
high-tech (adj.)	typesetting
how-to book	word processing skills

EXERCISE G

```
   1. The mortgage loans in default range from
         ⌄ 000
   $35 to $500,000.      ⟨OK?⟩
       ^
```

The context suggests that **$35 to $500,000** is shorthand for "$35,000 to $500,000"—no mortgage loan is for a mere $35. Circled OK? asks the writer to confirm the change.

```
   2. For more information, see Degas's article
                    42
   in volume xlii of the Journal of Higher
              ^
   Studies.
```

In regular text, arabic numerals are used for volume numbers, even if the publication uses roman numerals on its cover and title page. Write in the arabic numeral; do not circle a roman numeral and expect the typesetter to "translate" it. The last clause could also read: see Degas's article in the *Journal of Higher Studies,* volume 42.

```
                     to
   3. From 1991∧1994, the town's population
                    10
    .increased by ten percent.
                  ^
```

By convention, an en dash is not allowed in a "from 19xx to 19xx" or "between 20xx and 20xx" construction. Percentages are always expressed in numerals; in nontechnical text, *percent*—not %—is correct.

```
                            $250  m
   4. The new fighter planes cost $.25 billion
                                ^   ^
   each.
```

It is awkward to have a decimal less than 1.0 in this construction, unless this sentence appears in a paragraph in which other sums of money are expressed in billions. Since 1 billion = 1,000,000,000 = 1,000 million, then 0.25 billion = 250 million.

> 5. The insurance surcharge is $.75 for ~~coverage up to $25;~~ ~~twenty-five-dollars' coverage,~~ $1.40 for ~~coverage up to $50;~~ ~~$25-50,~~ and $1.80 for ~~$50-100.~~ coverage up to $100. ⓘ

(handwritten: coverage up to $25; ... coverage up to $50; coverage up to $100; query mark ⓘ)

If you feel that 75¢ is clearer than $.75, change it. Or keep $.75 for consistency with the $1.40 and $1.80 later in the sentence. Either choice is acceptable. Revise to avoid the awkward possessive **dollars'** and to clarify the indecipherable cluster of numbers. Query the overlapping inclusive ranges (Does a package to be insured for exactly $50 cost $1.40 or $1.80?).

> 6. The atmosphere weighs 5,700~~,000,000,~~ trillion ~~000,000~~ tons.

A sixteen-digit number is hard to comprehend and can produce awkward line breaks. (When a line break comes midnumeral, a hyphen is inserted after one of the commas in the numeral.) One could also change this to read "5.7 quadrillion tons."

> 7. The sales data for the ~~3d~~ third quarter of 19/94 are presented on pages 113-5, 300-8, and 201-09. ⓘ

(handwritten annotations: third; 19; 1; 30; 9)

In running text, one would spell out **3d,** and one would not abbreviate 1994; use these shortcuts only in tables when space is at a premium. You should also regularize the treatment of the inclusive numbers using one of the three systems discussed under "Inclusive Numerals" in chapter 7. The choices are:

pages 113–115, 300–308, 201–209

pages 113–5, 300–8, 201–9

pages 113–15, 300–308, 201–9

Ask the author whether these page numbers should be placed in numerical order.

> 8. ~~The first ten~~ Amendments ~~1 through 10 of~~ to the
>
> Constitution are known as the Bill of Rights.

By convention, amendments to the U.S. Constitution are referred to by spelled-out ordinal numbers. Here, "The first ten amendments" seems less clumsy than "The First through the Tenth Amendments."

> 9. In 1876 the vote in the Electoral College was 185
>
> to 184 ~~in 1876~~.

The sentence reads better when the year is moved. The use of "to" in the tally is fine; only sports scores take an en dash (The Giants beat the Dodgers, 8–2). The *U.S. Government Printing Office Manual* shows "electoral college," but *Chicago* and the *AP Stylebook* uppercase the term.

> 10. The year 1492 is the one year most American
>
> schoolchildren can identify correctly.

A sentence cannot begin with a numeral. There are many ways to revise this sentence, including spelling out the year (Fourteen ninety-two is . . .).

> 11. Using carbon-14 dating, scientists have
>
> determined that the Hopewell earthworks first
>
> appeared in southern Ohio in about 100 B.C.
>
> and that the last elaborate valley earthwork
>
> was constructed in about 550 A.D.

Traditionally, B.C. follows the year, but A.D. precedes the year. Some publishers set these abbreviations in small capitals.

```
12. The burial mounds on the Hopewell farm

range from 160 to 470 feet (48 to 141 km/)  in   (OK?)

length and from 20 to 32 feet (6 to 10 m) in

height.
```

SI, or metric, abbreviations do not take periods. Even if you're not a metric expert, you should have noticed the discrepancy between the two sets of equivalences: If 160 feet = 48 kilometers, then 20 feet ≠ 6 meters. Use a conversion table or a rule of thumb (a meter is roughly a yard) to detect the error and ask the author to verify the change.

EXERCISE H

Bobonia's economy contracted sharply in the

2d quarter. Exports declined by 14.5%, the

worst monthly performance in 12 ~~and a half~~ (½) [Q1]

years. Electronic manufacturers were [s inserted]

5   particularly hard hit. Imports, however,

continued to rise, which ~~plunged~~ [caused / to soar] the trade

deficit to $1.25 billion. This deficit is

likely to worsen before it improves, and the

revised government forecast ~~calls for it to~~ [predicts that the deficit will]

10   reach $1.75 billion by late fall.

~~Domestically~~ inflation remains almost

invisible [~~nonexistent~~], at an annual rate of only 1%.

The Unemployment rate [fell to] 6.5% in June, ~~compared to~~ [from]

6.8% in March ~~also continued to move lower.~~

15   On the good news, consumer confidence, as

measured by the University of Bobonia

National Feelgood Scale, rose from 105.5 in

March to 109 in June. [Q2]

Short-term interest rates were unchanged:

20   the overnight rate is 5.25%, and the average

yield on 30-year government notes is 5.35%. [Q3]

The currency has strengthened since mid=

March when the Bobonian ₿obble traded at

5.4550 to the U.S. dollar. On June 30 the

25   ₿obble closed at 5.580 to the dollar on the   (Q4)

London Worthless Currency exchange.

If you were working for a company, you would, of course, have a copy of the in-house style guide, which would detail preferences for the treatment of numbers. Absent such guidelines, editorial instinct suggests that the density of numerical data in this summary calls for using the percentage sign, rather than spelling out *percent,* and using numerals for all sums of money and other quantities.

Line	Comment
2	In corporate publishing, there are four common conventions for treating the quarters of the year:

first quarter, second quarter, third quarter, fourth quarter

1st quarter, 2d quarter, 3d quarter, 4th quarter (or 2nd *and* 3rd)

Q1, Q2, Q3, Q4

1Q98, 2Q98, 3Q98, 4Q98 (where the last two digits represent the year)

Q1	Supply name of month (previous sentence places us in the second quarter but not in any particular month) or should this read "worst quarterly performance"?
4	The industry is "the electronics industry"; thus, **Electronics manufacturers** (compare: an electronic device).
5	No hyphen in the predicate adjective **hard hit.** The attributive adjective is hyphenated: the hard-hit electronics industry.
6	The context makes it clear that the trade deficit is increasing. (Exports fell and imports continued to rise.) An increasing deficit does not plunge—it soars, balloons, or swells.
8	Mandatory comma before a coordinating conjunction that joins two independent clauses.

9–10   **calls for it to reach** suggests that a higher deficit is a sought-after goal.

10   Names of seasons are capitalized only when an author is employing personification.

11   **Domestically** is awkward (not every adverb can be called into service as a sentence adverb) and contributes nothing to the meaning. (By definition, inflation is a domestic economic indicator.)

11–12   Whether anything can **remain nonexistent,** much less **remain almost nonexistent,** is a question best left for philosophers.

13–14   There are many ways to revise this awkwardly constructed sentence. In the revision shown here, the comma marks **from 6.8% in March** as a nonrestrictive phrase. Note that **also continued to move lower** is illogical, since nothing else in this paragraph has moved lower.

15–16   Clearer to treat **consumer confidence** as the subject, add "as," and insert a pair of commas to set off the long nonrestrictive descriptor (**measured . . . Scale**).

Q2   Reconcile treatment of confidence survey scores; both to one decimal place?

Q3   Can't have the rate for 30-year notes in a sentence that discusses short-term rates. Do you mean 30-day rate? Or else start a new sentence for 30-year rate.

23   Comma needed to set off the nonrestrictive clause; here, **when** is in apposition to **mid-March.**

23   Lowercase the name of the currency.

Q4   Give both rates to the same number of decimal places. Also, move from 5.4550 to 5.580 is a weakening, not a strengthening. Please recheck numbers. [*Note:* A copyeditor should not lop off a digit or add a zero here to regularize the decimal. As for the exchange rate: The more bobbles per dollar—5.580 compared to 5.4550—the less each bobble is worth, and so these numbers show a weakening bobble.]

24   No comma after this short introductory adverbial phrase.

EXERCISE I

Every month the It's Our Money Institute

in New York city publishes a list of
              ≡

particularly outrageous, ironic⌃or ridiculous
                                  ⌄
                        money⊙
wastes of tax� payers ~~taxes~~. Here are some of
                       ⌃
5   last year⌄s winners:
                 ⌃

(Q1)   The Economic Develop⌃ment gave Bedord, (Q2)
                            ⌄
            $700,000
Indiana⌄, ~~$.7 million dollars~~ to build a model
        ⌃
                                      n   oot
of the pyramid of Cheops and a⌃800-f~~eet~~
                               ⌃   ⌃

repli͟c͟a of t͟he Great Wall of China to

10   ℯ⌃attract tourists and "demonstrate the value

of limestone in the building industry⌃.)
                                       ⌃
                                      t
The National Science Foundation spen⌃ds
                                     ⌃
              ℯ
(Q3)$14,4012 to test the ℯffects of inflation on

the behavior of rats and pigeons. The

15 (Q4) studies' conclusion⌃s: when given a choice⌃,
                           ⌄   ≡   ⌃
animal "consumers" opt for cheaper goods,

just as people do.

The Federal Highway Administration broke
                                 ⌃
the record for cost over⌃runs on a civilian
                        ⌄
                                              has
20   project. ⌃ r he Inte͟state Highway System⌃now
              ⌃ ⌃   ⌃
                     ⌃g b   percent
cost $⌃100⊙3⌀0 ⌃million⌄, or 267⌃ of what
                       ⌃   ⌃
congress originally approved⊙ ~~due to~~
                            ⊙
                                         ℯ
D͟u͟e͟ t͟o inflation, delay, and mismanag⌃ment⌄,
                                       ⌃   ⌃

                                                    $40,000
        The Department of Agriculture spent ~~fourty-~~

25   ~~thousand dollars~~ on a year͡long study of food

     preferences and popular stereotypes. Results ?

     The public sees fast-food͡addicts as

                                              ingo
     patriotic, conservative, and hard working͡s,
              viewed as
     Vegetarians are intellectual and creative,
     and   are thought to
30   gourmets like small families, mixed doubles

     in tennis, and "live in the fast lane" (OK?)

   ⒬ The National Endowment for the Arts granted

     $7,000 for a sound and light show to make

     Wisconsin's state capital building in

35   Milwaukee "send forth human and planetary (Q5)

     energies in a message of world peace." The (OK?)

     one performance was marred when half the

     lights failed to work and the recorded
                              unintelligible
     broadcast from the dome was ~~illegible~~

40   The U. S. Army's Materiel Development and
             i
     Readyness Command (DARCON) spent $38 million (Q6)

   (SP) and (13) years to develop a new gas mask, the
              which
     XM30, ~~that~~ usually malfunctions within (48) (SP)

     hours. The Army's training and Doctrine
                                                   (Q7)
45   Command found the XM-30$ generally inferior

   (SP) to the (17)-year old M17AL mask it was designed

     to replace.

The Defense Department paid $13,000 to

test the possible side effects of extremely-^

50   low-frequency radio waves on a hereford bull

named Sylvester. After 6 years, Sylvestre was Q8

autopsied and judged "essentially a normal

bull though somewhat obese." A Navy Vice

Admiral admitted that the experiment has no

55   value due to "the limited size of the sample

data base."

Line	Comment
5	Either a colon or a period may be used to introduce a multiparagraph list.
Q1	Supply full name of agency (e.g., Office of Economic Development?).
Q2	Bedord or Bedford?
7	Commas are needed both before and after the state's name.
7	Avoid decimal numeral. Cannot have both $ and **dollars;** use the dollar sign with numerals.
8	Lowercase or uppercase for **pyramid** is OK, since the word may be construed as either a generic descriptor or a part of a proper name; indicate your choice on your style sheet.
8	"An," not "a," before **800-foot** (read aloud to hear the numeral).
10–11	There are two sets of opening quote marks but only one closing set. Since this is not a formal research paper with citations from published articles, you can simply delete the extra set of opening quote marks (rather than ask the author to supply a second set of closing quote marks).
12	Past tense—**spent**—to match other paragraphs.
Q3	Please fix $14,4012. Is it $144,012 or $14,xxx?
Q4	"Studies'"or "study's"?
15	"conclusion," since only one is given here.

21   Comma needed to set off appositive introduced by "or."

23   Move the **due to** clause to prevent the misreading that it modifies **what Congress originally approved.**

26   A nitpicky point: An analysis of survey data yields "findings," not "results." In either case, there should be no space between the word and the question mark.

28   "hardworking" (one word) for parallel structure.

29–30   Revise to clarify that these descriptions are the stereotypes people hold.

32   Capitalization of the names of organizations follows the rules for titles (see "Titles of Works" in chapter 6).

34   The building in a state capital (= a city) is a "capitol."

Q5   Milwaukee or Madison (the current capital)?

Q6   DARCON or DARCOM (for *Com*mand)?

43   The restrictive **that usually malfunctions** makes it sound as though the goal was to develop a mask that would malfunction. Change "that" to "which" to make the clause nonrestrictive.

Q7   XM30 or XM-30? (Compare lines 43 and 45.)

45–47   Plural **XM-30s** cannot be the antecedent of **it.**

49–50   Compound adjectives of the form "adverb ending in -*ly* plus adjective" are not hyphenated: extremely low scores. But here "extremely low frequency" is a phrase (see *M-W Collegiate,* s.v. "extremely low frequency"), and phrases are hyphenated when they serve as attributive adjectives.

Q8   Sylvester *or* Sylvestre?

53–54   Lowercase the title since no proper name follows. *M-W Collegiate* shows "vice admiral" as preferred, but see the discussion of line 16 in the key for Exercise E.

55   Awkward to have the opening quotation mark interrupt the phrase **due to.**

56   **Data base** is conventional in this context. (Computer programs create databases, but in social science research the number of subjects is often called the "data base.")

STYLE SHEET ENTRIES

Punctuation
Serial comma
Commas before & after geographical units

Numbers and Dates
Spell out numbers under 101, except percentages
seventeen-year-old (adj.)

Abbreviations
U.S. (no internal space)
DARCON (? DARCOM)

Miscellaneous
XM30 or XM-30?

Alpha list

Congress	National Endowment for the Arts
data base	overruns (n.)
extremely-low-frequency waves	pyramid of Cheops
fast-food addict	side effects
the Great Wall	sound-and-light show
hardworking	taxpayers
Hereford bull	vice admiral
Interstate Highway System	yearlong

EXERCISE J

This exercise is based on an excerpt from Diane Johnson, "Doctor Talk," in *The State of the Language*, edited by Leonard Michaels and Christopher Ricks (University of California Press, 1980), pp. 396–98, and is used with permission of the publisher. For the purpose of this exercise, errors were introduced and other changes were made to the published text.

Until recent times, doctors spoke a magic

language, usually Latin, and mystery was part

of your cure. But modᴀⁿ doctors are rather

in the situation of modern priests; having

5   lost their magic language, they run the risk

of losing the‸ir magic powers too.

For us, this means that ~~the~~ doctorˢ‸ may lose

~~his~~ their ability to heal us by our faith; and   (Q1)

doctors, sensing powerlessness, have been

10   casting about for new languages in which to

conceal the nature of our afflictions and the

ingredients of their cures. They have devised

two dialects, but neither seems qui/et/ to   (Q2)

serve for every purpose. For this is a time

15   of transᵢtion and trial for them, marked by

various strategies, of which the well‗known

illegible handwriting on your prescription is

but one. For doctors themselves seem to have

20   lost faith too, in themselves and in the old   (Q3)

mysteries and arts. They have been taught to

think of themselves as scientists, and so it

is first of all to the language of science

          at
they they turn, to control and confuse us.

Most of the time scientific language can do

25   this perfectly. We are terrified, of course,

to learn that we have "prolapse of the mitral

valve"--we promise to take our medicine and

stay on our diet, even though these words
                              u
describe a usually innocuous finding in the
                                    ^
30   investigation of an innocent heart murmur. Or

we can be lulled into a false sense of

security when the doctor avoids a scientific

term: "You have a little spot on your lung"--

even when what he puts on the chart is

35   "probable bronchogenic carcinoma."

With patients, doctors can use either

scientific or vernacular speech, but with

each other they speak Science, a strange

argot of Latin terms, new words, and

40   acronyms that yearly becomes farther removed

from everyday speech and is sometimes

comprised almost entirely of numbers and

letter: "His pO₂ is 45; pCO₂, 40; and pH 7.4."

Sometimes it is made up of peculiar verbs

45   originating from the apparatus with which

they treat people: "well, we've bronched him,

tubed him, bagged him, cathed him, and PEEPed

him" the intern tells the attending

physician. ("We've explored his airways with

50   a bronchoscope, inserted an endotrachial

tube, positioned a cathater in his bladder to

monitor his urinary output, provided assisted

ventilation with a resuscitation bag, and

used positive end-expiratory pressure to

55   improve oxygenation.") Even when discussing

things that can be expressed in ordinary

words, doctors will prefer to say "he had a

pneumonectomy" to saying "he had a lung

removed."

60   One physician remembers being systematically

instructed, during the fifties, in scientific-

sounding euphemisms to be used in the

presence of patients. If a party of interns

were examining an alcoholic patient, the

65   wondering victim might hear them say he was

      "suffering from hyperingest/a/tion of ethanol."

      In front of a cancer patient they would

      discuss his "mitosis." But in recent years

      such discussions are not conducted in front

70   of the patient at all, because, since

      Sputnik, lay~~men's~~ understanding of scientific

      language has increased so greatly/ that

      widespread ignorance cannot be assumed.

                              also
          Space exploration has had its influence/ (Q4)
                                ∧
75   ~~especially~~/ on the *sound* of medical language.
                ⊕   axial
      A CAT/scanner (computerized ~~automated~~
                                                (rom)
      tomography), (*de rigueur*) in an up-to-date
                                      used
      diagnostic unit, might be something to look (Q5)
                                        ∧
                            ○
      at the surface of Mars ~~with~~ The resonance of
                          ∧
80   physical, rather than biological, science has
              ;   ;
      doubtless been fostered by doctors

      themselves, who, mindful of the extent to

      which their science is really luck and art,

      would like to sound microscopically precise,
                                          be so○
85   calculable and exact, even if they cannot
                                              ∧
   ⊕ Acronyms and abbreviations play the same part
              ine
      in medical ~~language~~ that they do in other

walks of modern life. We might be irritated

to read on our chart that this SOB patient

90   complained of DOE five days PTA." (It means

"this short of breath patient complained of

dyspnea on exertion five days prior to

admisssion.") To translate certain syllables,

the doctor must have yet more esoteric

95   information. Doctor A, reading Doctor B's

note that a patient has TTP, must know

whether Dr B is a hematologist or a chest

specialist in order to know whether the

patient has thrombotic thrombocytopenic

100   purpura or traumatic tension pneumothorax.

That pert little ID means identification to

us, but intradermal to the dermatologist,

inside diameter to the physiologist, and

infective dose to the bacteriologist.

105   But sometimes doctors must speak vernacular

English, but this is apparently difficult for

them. People are always being told to discuss

their problem with their doctor, which,

considering the general inability of doctors

110   to reply except in a given number of reliable

phrases, must be some of the wors*t* advice (Q6)

ever given. Most people/ trying to talk to

the doctor--trying to pry or to wrest meaning

from ~~his~~ evasive remarks ("I'd say you're

115   coming along just fine ")--have been maddened

by the vague and slightly inconsequential

nature of statements ~~which,~~ *that* meaning

everything to you, ought in themselves to

have meaning but do not, are noncommittal/ or

120   unengaged, *or* have a slightly rote or rehearsed (Q7)

quality, sometimes a slight inappropriateness

in the context ("it's nothing to worry about

really"). This is the doctor's alternative

dialect, phrases so general and bland as to

125   communicate virtually nothing.

(Q8)

This dialect originates from the emotional

situation of the doctor. In the way passers

by avert their eyes from the drunk in the

gutter or *from* the village idiot, so ~~the~~ doctor*s*

130   must avoid the personality, the individ-

or uality, (any involvement with) the destiny/

Doctors   *themselves*

of ~~his~~ patients. He must not let ~~himself~~

patientso
think and feel with ~~them.~~ In order to retain

objective professional judgment, ~~the~~ doctor^s

135   ha~~s~~^{ve} long since learned to withdraw ^{their} ~~his~~

emotions from the plight of the patient.

LEVEL OF EDIT

The instructions called for a light copyedit that respected the author's idio-syncratic style. If your version was considerably more heavily marked than this key, go back and review your editing: Did you make revisions that weren't necessary? Did you change sentences that were not incorrect simply because they were not the sentences you would have written? If so, you are running the risk of frustrating the author and wasting your time and the author's time. Remember, the author must read through every syllable of your editing, taking the time to accept, reject, or reword each of your suggestions. And then, either you or a cleanup editor will have to read through the author's review of the copyediting.

Line	Comment
Q1	Three of the first four sentences in this paragraph begin with "For." OK or revise?
7	Plural "doctors" avoids the generic *he* and matches the second half of the sentence.
Q2	Name the two dialects here?
Q3	Three "themselves" here OK or revise?
23	Stet comma after **turn** (to avoid misreading of "turn to" and to set off the qualifying **to control and confuse**). Delete comma after **control**—syntactical framework is simply an *a* or *b* choice.
34	OK to have a male pronoun here, to refer to one doctor, as long as not every doctor in the piece is male.
38	Stet **Science**—uppercase indicates that it is being treated as a language, just like English, French, Italian, or Spanish.
40	Delete comma after **acronyms**—to avoid breaking the phrase **a strange argot . . . that becomes**. Remember, no comma after the last item in a series: *A, b,* and *c* are my goals. If *x, y,* or *z* cannot be calculated, we must revise our procedure.
40	Nowadays *farther* and *further* are wholly interchangeable; see *DEU* s.v. "farther, further."
41–42	**is comprised** is incorrect here. As Follett puts it (*MAU*, s.v. "com-

pose, comprise"): "The whole comprises the parts; the parts are comprised in the whole; the whole is composed of its parts; the parts compose the whole."

43 Comma after pH to indicate an elliptical expression. If pO₂, pCO₂, or pH looks odd to you, ask the author to confirm; never change technical notations on your own. Here, all the notations are correct: pO₂ and pCO₂ are measures of oxygen and carbon dioxide in the blood, and pH is a measure of acidity or alkalinity.

45 **apparatus** is fine. Do not change to "apparatuses" because *apparatus* is both a collective singular noun and one of the equal variants for the plural noun.

46 **they** lacks an adequate referent.

47 **PEEPed** is an acronym for "positive end-expiratory pressure" transmuted into a verb, and the unusual capitalization distinguishes it from "peeped." If you think there's a problem, query the author. Don't just charge ahead and change the capitalization of a technical term.

51–53 Reorder the "translation" to match the order of the acronyms: **positioned a catheter** ("cathed") should follow **provided assisted ventilation** ("bagged").

54 The term refers to positive pressure (= pressure that exceeds atmospheric pressure) applied at the end of the patient's exhalation. It is styled with a hyphen: positive end-expiratory pressure.

57–58 **to say . . . to saying** is not a parallel construction. No commas after either **saying** because the quotations function as direct objects of the verb.

61 Hard end-of-line hyphen for **scientific-sounding**, an attributive compound adjective of the form "noun plus participle."

63–64 **a party of interns were** is OK ("party of" construed as a modifier of the plural subject "interns"); also OK to change to "a party of interns was."

71 *M-W Collegiate* shows "Sputnik" uppercase, as the generic term for the satellites the USSR launched in the 1950s. The wording here, however—**since Sputnik**—indicates that the author is referring to the launch of the first satellite (named Sputnik I) in 1957. *Chicago* calls for names of spacecraft to be set in italic (*Sputnik I*). The marking here follows the convention that a comma following an italicized word is also italicized (see page 114).

71   To avoid gender bias: lay, laypersons', *or* laypeople's.

72   Delete the comma after **greatly** (to avoid breaking the "so + adverb + that" phrase).

Q4   Revision OK to clarify transition here?

76   The hyphenation and correct spelled-out form of "CAT scanner" are in the dictionary.

77   **de rigueur** should not be italicized, since it has been naturalized into English. (Test: If a foreign-sounding term appears in the main section of your dictionary, it is a bona fide English word and should not be italicized.)

Q5   Unclear how this example relates to the "sound of medical language." Revise?

80   Commas to set off the antithetical **rather than biological.**

82   Stet commas before and after **who.** First comma marks the *who* clause as nonrestrictive; second sets off **mindful . . . luck and art.**

84–85   **precise, calculable and exact**—no serial comma because this phrase is not a list of three. Here, **calculable and exact** is meant as a pair in apposition to **precise.**

85   **even if they cannot** stops midphrase. Fix or query the author.

87   **medical language** is not "a walk of life" and thus cannot be compared to **other walks.**

91–93   Lowercase spelled-out expressions; caps used only for acronyms.

99–100 All these terms are in a desktop dictionary.

101   Two choices here for treating **ID** (a word used as a word): italicize it or place quotation marks around it. All the spelled-out versions should be lowercased.

105–6   Fix (or query the author on) two **buts** in one sentence.

Q6   Two "givens" in one sentence OK?

112   Delete comma after **people;** the subject of the sentence is **Most people trying to talk to the doctor** (not just "Most people").

Q7   Repetition of "slightly inconsequential," "slightly rote," and "slight inappropriateness" OK or revise?

Q8   "emotional situation of the doctor"—too clinical, abstract?

126   *WIT* provides three examples of prepositions with *originate:* "Baseball originated *from* the old game of rounders. The idea originated *in* his own mind. This plan originated *with* the board"(3d ed., p. 442).

129   Add a "from" to prevent misreading.

131   Move **any involvement with** for clarity and cadence.

132–36 To avoid the generic *he:* "Doctors must not let themselves think and feel with patients. In order to retain objective professional judgment, doctors have long since learned to withdraw their emotions from the plight of the patient." Other changes you could suggest: (1) for **think and feel,** substitute "empathize"; (2) change **have long since learned** [since when?] to "learn" or "are taught to."

STYLE SHEET ENTRIES

Numbers and dates
Spell out numbers under 101 except for medical test values

Punctuation
Serial comma

Abbreviations
SOB   DOE (no internal periods)
pO_2 pCO_2 pH
Doctor A, Doctor B

Miscellaneous
Italics for word used as word

Alpha list

CAT scanner	positive end-expiratory pressure
computerized axial tomography	Science (as language)
de rigueur (roman)	*Sputnik* (italics)
hyperingestion	up-to-date (adj.)
passersby	well-known (adj.)
PEEPed	

EXERCISE K

TABLE 20. Present Value of One Dollar

Year	5%	6%	8%	9% *(9% is missing – pls fix.)*
1	0.952	0.943	1.0926	0.917 ← (OK?)
2	0.907	0.890	0.857	0.842
3	0.864	0.840	0.794	0.772
(OK?) ǂ4	0.823	0.592	0.735	0.708 *(Supply final digit)*
5	0.784	0.747	0.681	0.65

(Pls recheck value)

The trouble spots are:

- The column heads jump from 6% to 8%. Query the author about the missing column for 7%.
- The rightmost column head lacks a percentage sign. Add it.
- The stub contains two lines labeled 3. Logic strongly suggests that the second 3 should be a 4; change it and ask author to reconfirm.
- When you look at the numbers as a set, you should suspect that the first entry under 8% has its decimal point in the wrong place: 0.926 would be far more likely than .0926 in this context. Correct it and ask author to reconfirm. (If .0926 were correct, you would need to add a zero before the decimal point and round off to three decimal places: 0.093.)
- The last entry in the last column is missing its final digit.
- Notice that the numbers decrease by a small fraction in each row as one reads across from left to right and the numbers also decrease as one reads down each column. According to this pattern, the entry 0.592 for 4 years at 6% looks incorrect; query the author.

When checking tables, you should also make sure that the entries in a given column are shown to the same number of decimal places, that commas (not periods) are used in large numbers, and that periods (not commas) appear in decimals.

EXERCISE L

TABLE A. Degree Recipients, Departments of History,
English, and Psychology, 1993–1995

Department	1993	1994	1995
History			
Bachelor's	456	778	892
Master's	87	95	106
Doctoral	5	8	12
English			
Bachelor's*	745	798	695
Master's	47	52	65
Doctoral	9	11	9
Psychology			
Bachelor's	275	298	302
Master's	32	29	30
Doctoral	4	7	9

Source: Office of the President, *Utopia University Data
Profile, 1995,* pp. 13, 15, and 18.

*Does not include students in the dual-major program.

You may have thought of an alternate way to arrange this table; for example, your solution might look like table B. The advantage of table B is that it takes up fewer lines than table A, but the drawbacks of table B are several: (1) table B is harder to use, because the reader cannot easily pick out trends by department; (2) table B looks crowded and unappealing; (3) the ten-column layout may present problems in page design. Thus unless vertical space is at an absolute premium, table B is not a good solution.

Note also that a copyeditor who proposes table B must query the author about whether the column for master's degrees should read "MA" or "MA/MS" because students in the psychology department (although not those in English or history) may have earned a Master of Science rather than a Master of Arts degree.

TABLE B.   Degree Recipients, Departments of History, English, and Psychology, 1993–1995

Department	1993			1994			1995		
	BA	MA/MS	PhD	BA	MA/MS	PhD	BA	MA/MS	PhD
History	456	87	5	778	95	8	892	106	12
English*	745	47	9	798	52	11	695	65	9
Psychology	275	32	4	298	29	7	302	30	9

Source: Office of the President, *Utopia University Data Profile, 1995*, pp. 13, 15, and 18.

*Data for English bachelor's degree recipients do not include students in the dual-major program.

EXERCISE M

Abben, Pilar. 1985. "A Modern Approach to
Algebra." *Mathematical Monthly* 17: 55–68.

Adder, William, and Mary. 1980. *Statistics*   (Q1)
in the Social Sciences. Evanston, Illinois.
Schoolbooks Press. 1980

Adder, William, and Mary. 1982. *How To Write*   (Q2)
Social Science Papers. New York: Wise Owl.

Akmore, G. 1983. "A Study of the Effects of   (Q3)
Peer Teaching in College Remedial Mathematics
Courses." *American Mathematical Monthly* 18:   (Q4)
149–67.

Aiken, Lydia, ed. *Problems in English*   (Q5)
Grammar. Boston: Tiara Books.

Allen, Pattrick. 1993. *Composition for*   (Q6)
Beginning ESL Students. New York: Language
Laboratory.

Allen, P.ˌand Anita Zamorraˌ 1994. "Error (Q7)

Analysis in Quasi-Experimental Designs."

Analytic Quarterly 9:63̲–53.   (Q8)

N

Ammonds, Carolyn. 1794. *A Short Course in*   (Q9)
Califo:
Speedwriting. Santa Barbara, ˌSanta Luisa

Community College.

Anderson, Vito. 1991. "A Response to   (Q10)

President Clinton's Proposal for Head

Start." *Preschool Reporter* 15:1.

Queries

Q1   Supply Mary's last name.
Q2   Supply Mary's last name. If this book and the preceding entry are by the same pair of authors, we'll replace their names with a 3-em dash in the second entry.
Q3   Supply Akmore's full first name.
Q4   If Akmore article is from the same journal as Abben article, reconcile the title (*Mathematical Monthly* or *American Mathematical Monthly*) and the volume numbers. (We have Akmore's 1983 article in vol. 18, and Abben's 1985 article in vol. 17.)
Q5   Please supply year of publication.
Q6   Double t in Pattrick OK?
Q7   For Allen, P., supply full first name.
Q8   Recheck page range, can't be 63–53.
Q9   Recheck year: 1974 or 1994?
Q10   Recheck 1991 as date of publication (Clinton was inaugurated in January 1993).

A FEW POINTERS ABOUT REFERENCE LISTS

Take extra care in hunting for typographical errors in reference lists. Few authors are diligent enough to proofread this section, and many do not bother spellchecking the reference list because it is so time consuming. (The spell-checker stops and questions almost every proper name.)

Remember the rules for capitalizing titles (see "Titles of Works" in chapter 6). Thus the **to** in the second Adder entry should be lowercased.

Don't make assumptions about names; for example, don't assume that the Mary in both the Adder entries is "Mary Adder."Always ask the author to supply the facts. If her surname is Adder, it is preferable for the entry to read "Adder, William, and Mary Adder." (One surname is sufficient on a social invitation to a married couple, but a reference list is not a casual document, and William and Mary may well be father and daughter, brother and sister, son and mother, or first cousins.)

When two or more works are written by the same author or authors, some publishers use a 3 em dash in the author slot for the second and subsequent listings:

Frank, F. 1990. *Short History of Uruguay.* New York: International Press.

———. 1993. *Short History of Argentina.* New York: Overseas Press.

———. 1996. *Short History of Chile.* Los Angeles: Small World Press.

If you are observing this convention, you would want to make a note to yourself to use a 3-em dash in the second Adder entry if indeed both books are written by the same pair of authors:

Adder, William, and Mary Adder. 1980. *Statistics in the Social Sciences.* Evanston, Ill.: Schoolbooks Press.

———. 1982. *How to Write Social Science Papers.* New York: Wise Owl.

However, even if "Allen, P." turns out to be "Allen, Pattrick [sic]," one would repeat his name (and not use a 3-em dash) because a second author appears in the second entry.

Always query illogical numbers (e.g., 63–53 in the Allen and Zamorra entry; 1794 as the date for the Ammonds entry); don't guess.

Try to catch possible inconsistencies in the titles of journals (e.g., in the Abben and Akmore entries) and in the context of the entry (e.g., the Anderson entry predating Clinton's election).

If you know the name of the state (e.g., in the Ammonds entry), add it; otherwise, query the author.

EXERCISE N

alphanumeric sorting. Sorting that treats
numbers like letters so that words with   (Q1)
numbers and numbers of equal length can be
sorted.

ASCII. Acronym for (American (Standard (Code for
(Information (Interchange, one of the standard
forms for representing characters so that
files can be shared between programs. A DOS
Text File is in ASCII format.   (Q2)

backspace. A key on ~~your~~ the keyboard ~~which~~ that
deletes the character to the left of the
cursor.

backup. To copy files for safe keeping.   (Q3)

baud rate. The ~~rate of~~ speed at which
information is sent between two computer
devices, ~~It is used~~ for example, ~~when~~ between
~~sending files across~~ modems.

bit. A (binary (digit; the smallest storage

unit for data in a computer.

boot. To start a computer by loading the

operating system into the computer's memory.

byte. The amount of space needed to store a

single character (number, letter, or code);

1,024 bytes equals ~~one~~ 1 kilobyte (Kb or K).

internal

buffer. A temporary data storage area used by   (Q4)

computers and some printers.

Queries

Q1   Please revise to avoid defining alphanumeric sorting as "Sorting . . .
      can be sorted."
Q2   DOS Text File—caps OK?
Q3   *Wired Style,* p. 38, shows "back up" (verb) and "backup" (noun,
      adjective); change here? Also, add where or how files are copied?
      (Since this glossary is for beginners, you wouldn't want naive read-
      ers to look for a file-copying machine.)
Q4   Addition of "internal" OK? (Again, to prevent novice readers from
      looking for a piece of equipment called a buffer.)

Of course, if you know something about computer jargon and if your schedule and editing budget allow, you could help this author by rewriting some
of the definitions. If you don't know much about computers or don't have
the time to rewrite the weaker definitions, you should draw the author's atten-

tion to the definitions that need work and supply a quick comment about the problems.

A FEW POINTERS ABOUT GLOSSARIES

When copyediting glossaries, always be on the lookout for

> Circular definitions. It is circular to define **alphanumeric sorting** as a type of "sorting" that allows words and numbers to be "sorted." To define **baud rate** as a "rate of speed" is both circular and redundant, since *speed* means "the rate at which something happens."
>
> Inconsistency in point of view. The definition of **backspace** uses the second person (**your keyboard**), while the definition of **boot** is impersonal (**To start a computer**).
>
> Inconsistent treatment of the spelled-out versions of acronyms. The author uses bold for the initials in the spelling out of **ASCII**, but italics in the spelling out of **bit** (and the italics are misplaced: *binary digit* yields "bid"), and regular roman type for the spelling out of **Kb**.
>
> Mysteries lurking in the corners of the definitions. Here, both **backup** and **buffer** are likely to remain rather mysterious to the novice user. Adding "internal" to the latter definition will at least prevent readers from wondering where their buffer is.
>
> Faulty classification. A definition must indicate whether the term is a verb, a noun, or an adjective. Thus the definition of a verb always contains an infinitive; the definition of a noun is headed by an article *(a, an, the)* or by a noun; and the definition of an adjective begins with an adjective or a phrase such as "used to describe." Here, the author consistently includes articles in the definitions of common nouns. Alternatively, one could delete these articles:
>
> > **backspace.** Key on the keyboard that . . .
> >
> > **baud rate.** Speed at which . . .
> >
> > **bit.** Binary digit; smallest storage unit . . .
> >
> > **buffer.** Temporary internal storage area . . .
> >
> > **byte.** Amount of space . . .

EXERCISE O

Of course, when you are working on a real document, the content will affect your decisions about typecoding, especially decisions about the levels of heads. But as this exercise shows, typecoding is primarily a matter of identifying and labeling visually distinctive elements.

(CN)   (CT)   (CST)

3   Quick Guide to Typecoding: It's All Greek

      to Me

Lorem ipsum dolor sit amet, con sectetuer

adipiscing elit, sed dis nonummy nibh euismod

5   tincidunt ut laoreet dolore magna aliquam:

     ⌐
(BL)   ⌐• Lorem ipsum dolor sit amet.

        • Con sectetuer adipiscing elit.

      ∟• Sed dis nonummy nibh euismod.

        Aliquam erat voluptat. Ut wisi enim ad

10   minim veniam, quis nostrud exerci tation

      ullamcorper suscipit lobortis nisl ut aliquip

      ea commodo consequat:

              ⌐
(MCL)   Lorem ipsum dolor   Dolore magna ut

          sit amet, con sect   aliquam erat ut

15   etuer adipiscing   voluptat ut wisi

          elit, sed dis   enim ad minim ad

        ∟nonummy nibh.   veniam.

      Lorem ipsum dolor sit amet, con sectetuer

      adipiscing elit.

20   Sed dis nonummy nibh euismod tincidunt ut

laoreet dolore magna aliquam erat voluptat.

Ut wisi enim ad minim veniam, quis nostrud:

(EQ) $\sum fx \pm 4y \geq 6$

Lorem ipsum dolor sit amet, con sectetuer

25   adipiscing elit.

Sed dis nonummy nibh euismod tincidunt ut

laoreet dolore magna aliquam erat voluptat:

(EX)   ⌐ Lorem ipsum "dolor sit amet," con

sectetuer adipiscing elit, sed dis

30   nonummy nibh euismod tincidunt ut laoreet

∟ dolore magna aliquam erat voluptat.

Lorem ipsum dolor sit amet, con sectetuer

adipiscing elit, sed dis nonummy nibh

euismod:

35 (NL)   1. Voluptat suscipit lobortis nisl.

2. Wisi enim dolore magna aliquam erat.

3. Ad minim veniam dis nonummy nibh.

(A) Quis Nostrud Exerci

Tation ullamcorper suscipit lobortis nisl ut

40   aliquip ea commodo consequat. Lorem ipsum

dolor sit amet, con sectetuer adipiscing.

Selected Bibliography

The ACS Style Guide: Effective Communication of Scientific Information. 3d ed. Edited by Anne M. Coghill and Lorrin R. Garson. Washington, D.C.: American Chemical Society, 2006.

AIP Style Manual. 4th ed. New York: American Institute of Physics, 1990.

American Heritage College Dictionary. 4th ed. Boston: Houghton Mifflin, 2007.

American Heritage Dictionary of the English Language. 4th ed. Boston: Houghton Mifflin, 2000.

American Medical Association Manual of Style. 10th ed. New York: Oxford University Press, 2007.

The Associated Press Stylebook. New York: Associated Press, 2010.

Barzun, Jacques. "Behind the Blue Pencil: Censorship or Creeping Creativity?" In *On Writing, Editing, and Publishing.* Chicago: University of Chicago Press, 1986.

Bernstein, Theodore. *The Careful Writer: A Modern Guide to English Usage.* New York: Atheneum, 1965.

———. *Miss Thistlebottom's Hobgoblins: The Careful Writer's Guide to the Taboos, Bugbears, and Outmoded Rules of English Usage.* New York: Farrar, Straus & Giroux, 1971.

Blake, Gary, and Robert W. Bly. *The Elements of Business Writing.* New York: Macmillan, 1992.

———. *The Elements of Technical Writing.* New York: Macmillan, 1993.

Bringhurst, Robert. *The Elements of Typographic Style.* Version 3.1. Point Roberts, Wash.: Hartley & Marks, 2005.

Burchfield, R. W. *Fowler's Modern English Usage.* 3d ed. Oxford: Clarendon Press, 2004.

Burchfield, R. W. *The New Fowler's Modern English Usage.* Revised ed. Oxford: Clarendon Press, 2000.

The Chicago Manual of Style. 16th ed. Chicago: University of Chicago Press, 2010.

Cook, Claire Kehrwald. *Line by Line: How to Improve Your Own Writing.* Boston: Houghton Mifflin, 1985.

Diagnostic and Statistical Manual of Mental Disorders: DSM-IV TR. Washington, D.C.: American Psychiatric Association, 2000.

Dickson, Paul. *Labels for Locals: What to Call People from Abilene to Zimbabwe.* Springfield, Mass.: Merriam-Webster, 1997.

Dorland's Pocket Medical Dictionary. 28th ed. Philadelphia: W. B. Saunders, 2008.

Follett, Wilson. *Modern American Usage: A Guide.* New York: Hill & Wang, 1966. Revised ed., edited by Erik Wensberg. New York: Hill & Wang, 1998.

Fowler, Henry. *A Dictionary of Modern English Usage.* 2d ed., revised by Ernest Gowers. Oxford: Clarendon Press, 1965.

Garner, Bryan A. *Garner's Modern American Usage.* 3d ed. New York: Oxford University Press, 2009.

Greenbaum, Sidney, and Randolph Quirk. *A Student's Grammar of the English Language.* London: Longman, 1990.

The Gregg Reference Manual. 11th ed. Edited by William A. Sabin. Boston: McGraw-Hill, 2010.

Higham, Nicholas J. *Handbook of Writing for the Mathematical Sciences.* 2d ed. Philadelphia: Society for Industrial and Applied Mathematics, 1998.

Hirsch, E. D., Jr. *The Philosophy of Composition.* Chicago: University of Chicago Press, 1977.

Huddleston, Rodney, and Geoffrey K. Pullum. *A Student's Introduction to English Grammar.* Cambridge: Cambridge University Press, 2005.

Johnson, Edward D. *The Handbook of Good English.* New York: Washington Square Press, 1991.

Lee, Marshall. *Bookmaking: Editing, Design, Production.* 3d ed. New York: Norton, 2004.

Lyon, Jack M. *Microsoft Word for Publishing Professionals.* N.p.: The Editorium, 2008.

Merriam-Webster's Collegiate Dictionary. 11th ed. Springfield, Mass.: Merriam-Webster, 2003.

Merriam-Webster's Dictionary of English Usage. Springfield, Mass.: Merriam-Webster, 1989.

MLA Style Manual and Guide to Scholarly Publishing. 3d ed. New York: Modern Language Association, 2008.

Mulvany, Nancy. *Indexing Books.* 2d ed. Chicago: University of Chicago Press, 2005.

The New Shorter Oxford English Dictionary. Oxford: Oxford University Press, 1993.

The New Webster's Grammar Guide. Edited by Madeline Semmelmeyer and Donald O. Bolander. New York: Berkley Books, 1991.

The New York Public Library Writer's Guide to Style and Usage. Edited by Andrea Sutcliffe. New York: HarperCollins, 1994.

Norton, Scott. *Developmental Editing: A Handbook for Freelancers, Authors, and Publishers*. Chicago: University of Chicago Press, 2009.

One Book/Five Ways: The Publishing Procedures of Five University Presses. Reprint ed. Chicago: University of Chicago Press, 1996.

Oxford English Dictionary. 2d ed. 20 vols. Oxford: Oxford University Press, 1989.

Pinker, Steven. *The Language Instinct: How the Mind Creates Language*. New York: HarperPerennial, 1995.

———. *Words and Rules: The Ingredients of Language*. New York: Basic Books, 1999.

Publication Manual of the American Psychological Association. 6th ed. Washington, D.C.: American Psychological Association, 2009.

Random House Webster's College Dictionary. 3d ed. New York: Random House, 1999.

Random House Webster's College Thesaurus. New York: Random House, 1997.

Random House Webster's Unabridged Dictionary. New York: Random House, 2005.

Rodale, J. I. *The Synonym Finder*. Revised ed. New York: Warner Books, 1986.

Roget's International Thesaurus. New York: HarperCollins, 2001.

Saller, Carol Fisher. *The Subversive Copy Editor: Advice from Chicago*. Chicago: University of Chicago Press, 2009.

Scientific Style and Format: The CSE Manual for Authors, Editors, and Publishers. 7th ed. Reston, Va.: Council of Science Editors, 2006.

Shertzer, Margaret D. *The Elements of Grammar*. New York: Macmillan, 1996.

Stedman's Medical Dictionary. 28th ed. Philadelphia: Lippincott, 2005.

Strunk, William, Jr., and E. B. White. *The Elements of Style*. 4th ed. Boston: Allyn & Bacon, 1999.

Swanson, Ellen. *Mathematics into Type*. Updated ed. Providence, R.I.: American Mathematics Society, 1999.

Tarutz, Judith A. *Technical Editing: The Practical Guide for Editors and Writers*. Reading, Mass.: Addison-Wesley, 1992.

Tufte, Edward R. *The Visual Display of Quantitative Information*. 2d ed. Cheshire, Conn.: Graphics Press, 2001.

United States Government Printing Office Style Manual. Washington, D.C.: U.S. Government Printing Office, 2008.

Webster's New World College Dictionary. 4th ed. New York: Macmillan, 1999.

Webster's Third New International Dictionary. Springfield, Mass.: Merriam-Webster, 1993.

Williams, Joseph M. *Style: Toward Clarity and Grace*. Chicago: University of Chicago Press, 1990.

Words into Type. 3d ed. Englewood Cliffs, N.J.: Prentice-Hall, 1974.

WEBSITES

Acronym Finder: www.acronymfinder.com

alt.usage.english newsgroup: www.alt-usage-english.org

American Association of University Presses: aaupnet.org

American Institute of Physics, style manual: www.aip.org/pubservs/style/4thed
    /toc.html
American Psychological Association: www.apastyle.org
Associated Press: www.ap.org
Bay Area Editors' Forum: www.editorsforum.org
Bill Walsh's *The Slot:* www.theslot.com
The Chicago Manual of Style Online: www.chicagomanualofstyle.org
CIA World Factbook: https://www.cia.gov/library/publications/the-world-factbook
Copyediting (McMurry): www.copyediting.com
Copyediting-L: www.copyediting-l/info
Council of Science Editors: www.councilscienceeditors.org
Editorial Freelancers Association (EFA): www.the-efa.org
Editorium: www.editorium.com
Editors' Association of Canada: www.editors.ca
International DOI Foundation: www.doi.org
International Trademark Association, list of trademarks: www.inta.org/Media
    /Pages/TrademarkChecklist.aspx
Language Log: languagelog.ldc.upenn.edu/nll
Legal Information Institute: www.law.cornell.edu
Library of Congress catalog: catalog.loc.gov
Merriam-Webster: www.m-w.com
Modern Language Association: www.mla.org
National Geospatial-Intelligence Agency, GEOnet Names Server: earth-info.nga
    .mil/gns/html
Society for Editors and Proofreaders (U.K.): www.sfep.org.uk
Unicode Consortium: www.unicode.org
U.S. Geological Survey, gazetteer: geonames.usgs.gov/domestic
U.S. government agencies, portal: www.usa.gov
U.S. Government Printing Office, style manual: www.gpoaccess.gov/stylemanual
    /browse.html

Index

Signs and symbols are indexed under their common names; for a list of these names, see pages 232–33. Definitions of terms may be found in the glossaries, which are not indexed here.

Copyeditor:	Suzanne Knott
Proofreaders:	Anne Canright and Desne Border
Designer:	Barbara Jellow
Compositor:	Integrated Composition Systems, Inc.
Text:	10/13.5 Minion
Display:	Minion Display
Printer and Binder:	The Maple-Vail Book Manufacturing Group